T0166882

Langenscheidt
Universal Dictionary

Chinese

Chinese — English
English — Chinese

Langenscheidt

Compiled by LEXUS with 吴乐军 (Emma Lejun Wu),
张晨阳 (Lulu Langtree), Jim Weldon, Gaius Moore

Contents

1. Auflage 2011 (1,02 - 2021)
© PONS GmbH, Stöckachstraße 11, 70190 Stuttgart 2011
All Rights Reserved.

www.langenscheidt.com

Print: Druckerei C. H. Beck, Nördlingen
Printed in Germany

ISBN 978-3-12-514032-5

Preface

This Chinese Dictionary focuses on modern usage in English and Chinese.

The Chinese is Mainland Chinese, written in simplified characters, with pinyin pronunciation.

The two sides of the book, the Chinese-English dictionary and the English-Chinese dictionary, are different in structure and purpose. The Chinese-English is a decoding dictionary, designed to enable the native speaker of English to understand Chinese. The English-Chinese is designed for productive usage, for self-expression in Chinese.

A system of signposting helps the user find the correct translation.

Grammar labels (n, adj, v/t) are given when it is necessary to identify which use or uses of an English word are being translated.

Indicators in italics (typical objects of verbs, synonyms of nouns etc) and subject area labels are given to clarify which sense or area of usage of a headword is being translated.

In the Chinese-English dictionary the Chinese headwords are alphabetically ordered according to their pinyin pronunciation. When the pinyin spelling of different words is the same, the words are then ordered by their tone and in the sequence: first, second, third, fourth tone.

White lozenges (◊) are used in the Chinese-English to separate out different English grammatical categories, when all of these correspond to one single Chinese word.

The pronunciation of Chinese

All Chinese characters in this dictionary are accompanied by a romanized script known as pinyin. Not all pinyin letters, or groups of letters, are pronounced as you would normally expect them to be in English. The following is a guide to the pronunciation of pinyin.

Initial consonants

b	more abrupt than English, like p in s*p*are
c	like ts in be*ts*
ch	like ch in *ch*urch, pronounced with the tip of the tongue curled back
d	more abrupt than English, like t in s*t*are
g	more abrupt than English, like c in s*c*are; always hard as in *g*o or *g*irl
h	like the Scottish pronunciation of lo*ch*, with a little friction in the throat
j	like j in *j*eep, pronounced with the lips spread as in a smile
k	pronounced with a slight puff of air as in *c*op
p	pronounced with a slight puff of air as in *p*op
q	like ch in *ch*eap, pronounced with the lips spread as in a smile
r	like r in *r*ung, pronounced with the tip of the tongue curled back
sh	like sh in *sh*irt, pronounced with the tip of the tongue curled back
t	pronounced with a slight puff of air as in *t*op
x	like sh in *sh*eep, pronounced with the lips spread as in a smile
z	like ds in be*ds*

zh like j in *judge*, pronounced with the tip of the tongue curled back

Finals

a as in f*a*ther
ai as in *ai*sle
an as in r*an* (with the *a* slightly longer as in *ah*); but: yan as in *yen*
ang as in r*ang* (with the *a* slightly longer as in *ah*)
ao like *ow* in h*ow*
e as in h*er*
ei as in *ei*ght
en as in op*en*
eng like *en* in op*en* and g
er like *err* – but with the tongue curled back and the sound coming from the back of the throat
i (1) as in magaz*i*ne
 (2) after c, ch, r, s, sh, z and zh like the i in b*i*rd
ia like ya in *ya*rd
ian similar to *yen*
iang *i* (as in magaz*i*ne) merged with *ang* (above) – but without lengthening the *a*
iao as in *yow*l
ie like ye in *ye*s
in as in th*in*
ing as in th*ing*
iong *i* (as in magaz*i*ne) merged with *ong* (below)
iu like yo in *yo*ga
o as in m*o*re
ou as in d*ou*gh
ong *oong* with *oo* as in s*oo*n

u	(1) as in r*u*le
	(2) after j, q and x like the 'u' sound in French t*u* or German *über*
ua	w followed by *a* (above)
uai	similar to *why*
uan	w followed by *an* (above)
uang	w followed by *ang* (above)
ue	u (above) followed by e as in *let*
ui	similar to *way*
un	like uan in tr*ua*nt
uo	similar to *war*
ü	as in French t*u* or German *über*
üe	ü followed by e as in *get*

Tones

First tone, as in 科 **kē** (department): a high, level tone with the volume held constant.

Second tone, as in 壳 **ké** (shell): rises sharply from middle register and increasing in volume, shorter than the first tone; like a surprised 'what?'

Third tone, as in 渴 **kě** (thirst ◊ thirsty): starts low, then falls lower before rising again to a point slightly higher than the starting point; louder at the beginning and end than in the middle; slightly longer than the first tone.

Fourth tone, as in 客 **kè** (guest): starts high then drops sharply in pitch and volume; like saying 'right' when agreeing to an instruction.

Abbreviations

adj	adjective	MUS	music
adv	adverb	NAUT	nautical
ANAT	anatomy	*pej*	pejorative
BIO	biology	PHOT	photography
BOT	botany	PHYS	physics
Br	British English	POL	politics
CHEM	chemistry	*prep*	preposition
COM	commerce, business	*pron*	pronoun
		PSYCH	psychology
COMPUT	computers, IT term	RAD	radio
		RAIL	railroad
conj	conjunction	REL	religion
EDU	education	s.o.	someone
ELEC	electricity, electronics	SP	sports
		sth	something
F	familiar, colloquial	TECH	technology
		TELEC	telecommunications
fig	figurative	THEA	theater
FIN	financial	TV	television
GRAM	grammar	*v/i*	intransitive verb
interj	interjection	*v/t*	transitive verb
LAW	law	→	see
MATH	mathematics	®	registered trademark
MED	medicine		
MIL	military		
MOT	motoring		

A

阿富汗 Āfùhàn Afghanistan
◊ Afghan
哀 āi sorrow; mourning
挨 āi be next to
唉 āi alas
癌 āi cancer
挨 ái undergo
矮 ǎi short *person*; low
爱 ài love
碍 ài block; hinder; obstruct
爱称 àichēng diminutive
挨打 áidǎ get a beating
挨饿 ái'è starve
爱管事 ài guǎnshì bossy
爱国 àiguó patriotic
爱国者 àiguózhě patriot
爱好 àihào hobby
爱护 àihù take care of
挨近 āijìn approach
爱情 àiqíng love
哀求 āiqiú implore
爱人 àirén husband; wife
哀伤 āishāng grieved
爱上 àishàng fall in love
with

唉声叹气 āishēng-tànqì
sigh
哀乐 āiyuè lament (*music*)
癌症 áizhèng cancer
矮子 ǎizi dwarf
艾滋病 àizībìng Aids
鞍 ān saddle
按 àn press ◊ according to
岸 àn shore
案 àn (legal) case; file
暗 àn dark; secret
案板 ànbǎn chopping board
暗淡 àndàn gloomy
安定 āndìng settle down
◊ calm
昂贵 ángguì expensive
肮脏 āngzāng dirty
安家 ānjiā set up home
暗礁 ànjiāo reef; (*fig*)
hidden danger
按揭贷款 ànjiē dàikuǎn
mortgage
安静 ānjìng calm ◊ quiet;
peaceful ◊ calm down
按扣 ànkòu snap fastener

按喇叭 **àn lǎba** honk the horn

按铃 **ànlíng** ring the bell

安眠药 **ānmiányào** sleeping pill

按摩 **ànmó** massage

按钮 **ànniǔ** button (*on machine*)

安排 **ānpái** arrange ◊ arrangement

安全 **ānquán** safe ◊ safely ◊ safety; security

安全带 **ānquándài** seat belt

暗杀 **ànshā** assassinate ◊ assassination

按时 **ànshí** on time

暗示 **ànshì** hint ◊ imply

安慰 **ānwèi** comfort

安心 **ānxīn** reassured

安葬 **ānzàng** bury *the dead*

按照 **ànzhào** according to

安装 **ānzhuāng** install ◊ installation

熬 **áo** endure; boil

傲 **ào** arrogant

澳大利亚 **Àodàlìyà** Australia ◊ Australian

懊悔 **àohuǐ** regret

奥林匹克运动会 **Àolínpǐkè Yùndònghuì** Olympic Games

傲慢 **àomàn** arrogance ◊ arrogant

澳门 **Àomén** Macao ◊ Macanese

奥秘 **àomì** profound mystery

懊丧 **àosàng** morose

熬夜 **áoyè** stay up late

奥运会 **Àoyùnhuì** Olympics

阿姨 **āyí** aunt

B

八 **bā** eight

疤 **bā** scar

拔 **bá** pull out

靶 **bǎ** target

把 **bǎ** measure word for knives, umbrellas, things with handles

爸 **bà** dad

坝 **bà** dam

把 **bà** handle

罢 **bà** stop, cease

吧 **ba** used to make

suggestions

爸爸 **bàba** dad

拔出 ◊ **báchū** extract, pull out ◊ extraction

霸道 **bàdào** domineering

罢工 **bàgōng** strike (*of workers*)

白 **bái** white

百 **bǎi** hundred

摆 **bǎi** put

败 **bài** defeat; fail

拜 **bài** congratulate

拜拜 **bāibāi** bye-bye

百倍 **bǎibèi** hundredfold

白菜 **báicài** Chinese cabbage

白痴 **báichī** idiot

白饭 **báifàn** boiled rice

摆放 **bǎifàng** set out *goods*

拜访 **bàifǎng** visit

百分比 **bǎifēnbǐ** percentage

百分之百 **bǎifēn zhī bǎi** one hundred percent

白宫 **Báigōng** White House

白喉 **báihóu** diphtheria

败坏 **bàihuài** spoil

百货商店 **bǎihuò shāng-diàn** department store

摆架子 **bǎi jiàzi** put on airs

白酒 **báijiǔ** clear grain spirit

白开水 **báikāishuǐ** boiled water

百科全书 **bǎikē quánshū** encyclopedia

白兰地 **báilándì** brandy

白领工人 **báilǐng gōngrén** white-collar worker

败露 **bàilù** emerge

拜年 **bàinián** pay New Year visit; wish happy New Year

百日咳 **bǎirìké** whooping cough

白日梦 **báirì mèng** daydream

白肉 **báiròu** white meat; boiled pork fat

白色 **báisè** white

白糖 **báitáng** white sugar

白天 **báitiān** in the daytime

摆脱 **bǎituō** get rid of

拜托 **bàituō** request

百万 **bǎiwàn** million

百万富翁 **bǎiwànfùwēng** millionaire

摆碗筷 **bǎi wǎnkuài** lay the table

白银 **báiyín** silver

柏油 **bǎiyóu** asphalt

柏油马路 **bǎiyóu mǎlù** bitumen road

拔尖儿 **bájiānr** excellent

八角 **bājiǎo** star anise

巴基斯坦 **Bājīsītǎn**

Pakistan ◊ Pakistani
芭蕾舞 **bāléiwǔ** ballet
班 **bān** class; shift (*at work*)
搬 **bān** move
斑 **bān** stain
扳 **bān** pull
板 **bǎn** board
版 **bǎn** edition
瓣 **bàn** segment; petal
半 **bàn** half
拌 **bàn** mix
绊 **bàn** trip up
扮 **bàn** play the role of
办 **bàn** do; deal with
版本 **bǎnběn** edition; version
搬出 **bānchū** move out
班船 **bānchuán** liner (*ship*)
半岛 **bàndǎo** peninsula
办到 **bàndào** manage to do sth
板凳 **bǎndèng** stool
斑点 **bāndiǎn** spot
办法 **bànfǎ** method; means
帮 **bāng** help ◊ gang
绑 **bǎng** bind
榜 **bǎng** official announcement
磅 **bàng** pound (*weight*)
棒 **bàng** stick ◊ excellent
半个小时 **bànge xiǎoshí** half an hour

绑架 **bǎngjià** kidnap
邦交 **bāngjiāo** diplomatic relations
帮忙 **bāngmáng** help
办公楼 **bàn'gōnglóu** office (*building*)
办公室 **bàn'gōngshì** office
办公时间 **bàn'gōng shíjiān** office hours
棒球 **bàngqiú** baseball
帮手 **bāngshǒu** helper
傍晚 **bàngwǎn** dusk
帮凶 **bāngxiōng** accomplice
榜样 **bǎngyàng** role model
棒子 **bàngzi** stick; pole
版画 **bǎnhuà** engraving; print
班级 **bānjí** class; grade
搬家 **bānjiā** move
绊脚石 **bànjiǎoshí** obstacle
搬进 **bānjìn** move in
半径 **bànjìng** radius
半决赛 **bànjuésài** semifinal
板栗 **bǎnlì** Chinese chestnut
办理 **bànlǐ** deal with
斑马 **bānmǎ** zebra
般配 **bānpèi** complement
半票 **bànpiào** half-price ticket
办签证 **bàn qiānzhèng**

版权 **bǎnquán** copyright

拌色拉 **bàn sèlā** dress a salad

办事处 **bànshìchù** office, bureau

扳手 **bānshǒu** wrench (*tool*)

伴随 **bànsuí** pursue; accompany; follow

半天 **bàntiān** half a day; a long time

版图 **bǎntú** territory

扮演 **bànyǎn** portray ◊ portrayal

半夜 **bànyè** midnight

板子 **bǎnzi** board; plate

搬走 **bānzǒu** move away

包 **bāo** pack

剥 **bāo** peel

雹 **báo** hail

薄 **báo** thin

宝 **bǎo** treasure

保 **bǎo** protect; keep; guarantee

饱 **bǎo** full

堡 **bǎo** castle

包 **bāo** packet; *measure word for packages etc*

报纸 **bàozhǐ** newspaper

豹 **bào** leopard

抱 **bào** hug

刨 **bào** plane (*tool*)

保安 **bǎo'ān** ensure public safety

报案 **bào'àn** report a case to the police

宝贝 **bǎobèi** treasure; darling

保持 **bǎochí** keep; maintain

报仇 **bàochóu** take revenge

报酬 **bàochóu** reward; remuneration

保存 **bǎocún** preserve

报道 **bàodào** report

暴发户 **bàofāhù** nouveau riche

报废 **bàofèi** scrap

暴风雨 **bàofēngyǔ** rainstorm

报复 **bàofù** pay back (*fig*); retaliate ◊ revenge

报告 **bàogào** break *news*; report ◊ presentation

饱嗝儿 **bǎogér** belch

报关 **bàoguān** customs declaration

宝贵 **bǎoguì** precious; valuable

包裹 **bāoguǒ** parcel

包含 **bāohán** comprise

饱和 **bǎohé** saturation

保护 **bǎohù** protect ◊

protection

包机 bāojī charter flight

保健 bǎojiàn health care

报价 bàojià quotation ◊ quote *price*

报警 bàojǐng raise the alarm

暴君 bàojūn despot; tyrant

包括 bāokuò include

暴力 bàolì violence ◊ violent

爆裂 bàoliè burst

保龄 bǎolíng bowling; bowl

保留 bǎoliú keep; hold; reserve ◊ reservation

暴露 bàolù reveal

保密 bǎomì keep secret

爆米花 bàomǐhuā puffed rice; popcorn

报名 bàomíng register

保姆 bǎomǔ nanny

报幕 bàomù announce a program

爆破 bàopò blow up

抱歉 bàoqiàn be sorry

宝石 bǎoshí precious stone

报失 bàoshī report a loss

保释金 bǎoshì jīn bail

保守 bǎoshǒu conservative

报税 bàoshuì declare tax

宝塔 bǎotǎ pagoda

包围 bāowéi encircle

保卫 bǎowèi defend ◊

defense

保险 bǎoxiǎn safe ◊ insurance

保险柜 bǎoxiǎnguì safe (*for valuables*)

保养 bǎoyǎng maintain ◊ maintenance

保佑 bǎoyòu bless

暴雨 bàoyǔ torrential rain

抱怨 bàoyuàn grumble

暴躁 bàozào hot-headed

爆炸 bàozhà explosion ◊ explode

保障 bǎozhàng guarantee

保证 bǎozhèng pledge; promise; guarantee

报纸 bàozhǐ newspaper

保重 bǎozhòng look after oneself ◊ take care!

包装 bāozhuāng pack ◊ packaging

刨子 bàozi plane (*tool*)

拔起 báqǐ pull up

八十 bāshí eighty

巴士 bāshì bus

把手 bǎshǒu handle

把握 bǎwò grasp; seize ◊ certainty

八月 bāyuè August

巴掌 bāzhang palm of the hand

杯 bēi cup; glass; *measure word for drinks*

背 bēi carry on one's back

碑 bēi monument; gravestone

北 běi north

倍 bèi -fold

辈 bèi generation; lifetime

背 bèi back

被 bèi quilt ◊ *passive indicator*

悲哀 bēi'āi sad

背包 bēibāo backpack

卑鄙 bēibǐ nasty; sordid

被捕 bèibǔ be under arrest

悲惨 bēicǎn tragic

北朝鲜 Běi Cháoxiǎn North Korea ◊ North Korean

被单 bèidān sheet

被动 bèidòng passive

北方 běifāng the North

被告 bèigào defendant; defense

悲观 bēiguān pessimistic; dim ◊ pessimism

背后 bèihòu behind ◊ behind one's back

北极 Běijí Arctic; North Pole

卑贱 bēijiàn humble

备件 bèijiàn spare part

北京 Běijīng Beijing

背景 bèijǐng background

北京烤鸭 Běijīng kǎoyā Peking duck

悲剧 bēijù tragedy

贝壳 bèiké shell (of shellfish)

蓓蕾 bèilěi bud

背面 bèimiàn back

背叛 bèipàn betray ◊ betrayal

被褥 bèirù quilt

悲伤 bēishāng sad ◊ grief

背书 bèishū endorse

被套 bèitào quilt cover

悲痛 bēitòng grief

碑文 bēiwén inscription

背心 bèixīn undershirt; vest; T-shirt

备用 bèiyòng spare

北约 Běiyuē NATO

倍增 bèizēng double

备注 bèizhù remarks; notes

杯子 bēizi cup; glass

被子 bèizi quilt

奔 bēn run fast

本 běn *measure word for books*

笨 bèn stupid

奔驰 bēnchí dash

笨蛋 **bèndàn** idiot
本地 **běndì** local; native
本地人 **běndìrén** local (*person*)
绷 **bēng** tighten
泵 **bèng** pump
蹦 **bèng** jump
绷带 **bēngdài** bandage
崩溃 **bēngkuì** collapse
崩塌 **bēngtā** collapse
本来 **běnlái** actually; originally
本领 **běnlǐng** ability
本能 **běnnéng** instinct ◊ instinctive
奔跑 **bēnpǎo** sprint
本钱 **běnqián** capital
本人 **běnrén** oneself; personally
本身 **běnshēn** itself; in itself
本性 **běnxìng** nature, character
本质 **běnzhì** nature ◊ fundamental
笨重 **bènzhòng** cumbersome
笨拙 **bènzhuō** clumsy
逼 **bī** force
鼻 **bí** nose
比 **bǐ** compare
笔 **bǐ** pen

闭 **bì** shut
毕 **bì** finish
币 **bì** currency
避 **bì** avoid
壁 **bì** wall
臂 **bì** arm
边 **biān** side
扁 **biān** flat
贬 **biǎn** devalue
辩 **biàn** discuss
变 **biàn** change
辨别 **biànbié** distinguish
辩驳 **biànbó** dispute; refute
变成 **biànchéng** become
便当 **biàndāng** lunch box
变得 **biànde** become, go
贬低 **biǎndī** belittle
变动 **biàndòng** change; upheaval
扁豆 **biǎndòu** green bean
蝙蝠 **biānfú** bat
编号 **biānhào** number ◊ serial number
辩护 **biànhù** plead; defend
变化 **biànhuà** change
辩护人 **biànhùrén** defense lawyer
编辑 **biānjí** edit ◊ editor ◊ editorial
编辑部 **biānjíbù** editorial department

边界 **biānjiè** border

边境 **biānjìng** frontier

便利 **biànlì** convenient

辩论 **biànlùn** debate

便秘 **biànmì** constipation

鞭炮 **biānpào** firework

便盆 **biànpén** chamber pot

变迁 **biànqiān** change

辨认 **biànrèn** identify

变态 **biàntài** abnormal; kinky ◊ metamorphosis

扁桃腺 **biǎntáoxiàn** tonsil

便条 **biàntiáo** note; compliments slip

变通 **biàntōng** flexible

便鞋 **biànxié** slippers

编织 **biānzhī** knit; weave ◊ knitting; weaving

贬值 **biǎnzhí** devalue ◊ devaluation

变质 **biànzhì** spoil; deteriorate

便装 **biànzhuāng** civilian dress

鞭子 **biānzi** whip

辫子 **biànzi** braid

表 **biǎo** table; form; meter; watch

表达 **biǎodá** express

表带 **biǎodài** watch strap

表弟 **biǎodì** cousin

标点 **biāodiǎn** punctuation

表哥 **biǎogē** cousin

表格 **biǎogé** form; table

标记 **biāojì** sign; symbol

表姐 **biǎojiě** cousin

表决 **biǎojué** decide by vote

表妹 **biǎomèi** cousin

表面 **biǎomiàn** surface

表明 **biǎomíng** indicate

标签 **biāoqiān** label

标枪 **biāoqiāng** javelin

表情 **biǎoqíng** expression (facial)

标题 **biāotí** heading

表演 **biǎoyǎn** act; perform ◊ acting; performance

表扬 **biǎoyáng** praise

标语 **biāoyǔ** slogan

标准 **biāozhǔn** standard

臂膀 **bìbǎng** arm

弊病 **bìbìng** disadvantage

壁橱 **bìchú** cabinet

彼此 **bǐcǐ** each other

必定 **bìdìng** must; definitely

弊端 **bìduān** corrupt practices

别 **bié** other ◊ don't ◊ leave; part

瘪 **biě** shriveled; flat tire

别离 **biélí** leave; part from

别人 **biérén** someone else;

other people

别墅 **biéshù** villa

别针 **biézhēn** safety pin

庇护 **bìhù** asylum; refuge; shelter

笔画 **bǐhuà** stroke (in writing)

壁画 **bìhuà** fresco

笔迹 **bǐjì** handwriting

笔记 **bǐjì** write down ◊ notes

比价 **bǐjià** price ratio

比较 **bǐjiào** compare ◊ comparison ◊ comparative

笔记本 **bǐjìběn** notebook

毕竟 **bìjìng** after all

鼻孔 **bíkǒng** nostril

壁炉 **bìlú** fireplace; hearth

比率 **bǐlǜ** rate

闭路电视 **bìlù diànshì** closed-circuit television

避免 **bìmiǎn** avoid

闭幕式 **bìmùshì** closing ceremony

宾 **bīn** guest

冰 **bīng** ice

兵 **bīng** soldier

饼 **bǐng** pancake

病 **bìng** illness ◊ sick

并 **bìng** combine ◊ negative intensifier ◊ and

冰雹 **bīngbáo** hail

冰川 **bīngchuān** glacier

冰冻 **bīngdòng** freeze

病毒 **bìngdú** virus ◊ viral

病房 **bìngfáng** room (in hospital)

饼干 **bǐnggān** cookie; cracker

冰棍儿 **bīnggùnr** Popsicle®

病假 **bìngjià** sick leave

并肩 **bìngjiān** side by side

冰冷 **bīnglěng** ice-cold

兵力 **bīnglì** troops

兵马俑 **bīngmǎyǒng** terracotta warriors

并且 **bìngqiě** and; besides

冰淇淋 **bīngqílín** ice cream

病人 **bìngrén** patient (sick person)

冰糖 **bīngtáng** candy sugar

宾馆 **bīnguǎn** hotel

冰箱 **bīngxiāng** refrigerator; freezer

冰鞋 **bīngxié** ice-skates

兵役义务 **bīngyì yìwù** military service

冰镇 **bīngzhèn** chilled

逼迫 **bīpò** force

壁球 **bìqiú** squash (game)

必然 **bìrán** inevitable ◊ inevitably

比如 **bǐrú** for example

比赛 bǐsài competition; match

毕生 bìshēng whole life

鄙视 bǐshì despise

壁毯 bìtǎn tapestry

鼻涕 bítì snot

笔芯 bǐxīn pencil lead; pen refill

必修 bìxiū compulsory *course*

必须 bìxū must ◊ *obligatory*

必需 bìxū necessary

必要 bìyào necessary

必要性 bìyàoxìng necessity

毕业 bìyè graduate ◊ *graduation*

笔友 bǐyǒu penpal

避孕 bìyùn birth control; contraception

避孕套 bìyùn tào condom

避孕药 bìyùn yào *contraceptive (pill)*, the pill

比喻 ◊bǐyù analogy ◊ *figurative*

逼真 bīzhēn true to life

笔直 bǐzhí straight; upright

币值 bìzhí currency value

壁纸 bìzhǐ (wall)paper

币制 bìzhì monetary system

鼻子 bízi nose

闭嘴 bìzuǐ be quiet

拨 bō dial *number*

播 bō sow *seed*; broadcast

波 bō wave

伯 bó uncle

博 bó broad

博爱 bó'ài universal love; fraternity

伯伯 bóbo uncle; *used to address a man older than one's father*

菠菜 bōcài spinach

驳斥 bóchì refute; disprove

驳船 bóchuán barge

波动 bōdòng fluctuate ◊ *fluctuation*

搏斗 bódòu battle

波段 bōduàn frequency *(radio)*

伯父 bófù uncle

脖颈儿 bógěngr (nape *of)* neck

薄荷 bòhe peppermint

簸箕 bòji dustpan

波浪 bōlàng wave

博览会 bólǎnhuì trade fair

玻璃 bōli glass

玻璃杯 bōlibēi glass *(for drinking)*

菠萝 bōluó pineapple

博士 bóshì doctor *(PhD)*

波涛 bōtāo wave

博物馆 bówùguǎn museum

跛行 bǒxíng limp

剥削 bōxuē exploit ◊ exploitation

博学 bóxué well-read

播音 bōyīn broadcast

播音员 bōyīnyuán radio announcer

脖子 bózi neck

捕 bǔ catch

不 bù no ◊ not

步 bù step

布 bù cloth

簿 bù book

不安 bù'ān uneasy

不必 búbì unnecessary

不便 búbiàn inconvenient

不变 búbiàn always, invariably ◊ unswerving

补偿 bǔcháng make up for

补车票 bǔchēpiào buy ticket after boarding

补充 bǔchōng add to ◊ additional

不错 búcuò not bad; excellent

不大 búdà small

不大可能 bú dà kěnéng improbable, unlikely

不到 bú dào under, less than

不得不 bùdébù have to, be compelled to

布丁 bùdīng pudding

不动产 búdòngchǎn real estate

不断 búduàn constant

部队 bùduì army

步伐 bùfá step

部分 bùfen part

补付 bǔfù pay extra; pay later

不符 bùfú not be in accord with

布告 bùgào announcement

不公正 bù gōngzhèng unjust

捕获 bǔhuò capture

簿记 bùjì bookkeeping

不仅 bùjǐn not only

不景气 bù jǐngqì depression

不久 bùjiǔ soon

不可口 bù kěkǒu tasteless

不可能 bù kěnéng impossible

不客气[1] bú kèqi impolite

不客气[2] bú kèqi you're welcome

不可思议 bùkě sīyì unthinkable

不利 búlì unfavorable

不满 **bùmǎn** dissatisfied

部门 **bùmén** department

不明智 **bù míngzhì** unwise

不能 **bùnéng** not be able to

不平 **bùpíng** uneven

不平常 **bù píngcháng** unusual

不清楚 **bù qīngchu** unclear

不忍 **bùrěn** cannot bear to

哺乳 **bǔrǔ** breastfeed

不如 **bùrú** not as good as

部首 **bùshǒu** radicals (of Chinese characters)

补贴 **bǔtiē** grant

不同 **bùtóng** different ◊ difference

部位 **bùwèi** position

不小心 **bù xiǎoxīn** careless

不幸 **búxìng** unlucky

不行 **bùxíng** no can do ◊ impossible

步行 **bùxíng** walk

补牙 **bǔyá** filling (in tooth)

捕鱼 **bǔyú** catch fish ◊ fishing

哺育 **bǔyù** feed; bring up

部长 **bùzhǎng** minister POL ◊ ministerial

不只 **bùzhǐ** not only

布置 **bùzhì** fit out

不重要 **bú zhòngyào** unimportant

不中意 **bú zhòngyì** unattractive

不准 **bùzhǔn** forbid

捕捉 **bǔzhuō** catch

簿子 **bùzi** notebook

不足 **bùzú** inadequate

C

擦 **cā** wipe

擦掉 **cādiào** wipe away

猜 **cāi** guess

才 **cái** talent ◊ only

裁 **cái** cut

财 **cái** assets; wealth

采 **cǎi** pick

踩 **cǎi** step on

菜 **cài** dish; vegetable

猜测 **cāicè** guess ◊ speculation

财产 **cáichǎn** property

菜单 **càidān** menu

菜刀 **càidāo** kitchen knife

彩电 **cǎidiàn** color TV

采访 **cǎifǎng** interview

裁缝 cáifeng tailor
财富 cáifù treasure; wealth
采购 cǎigòu buy
彩虹 cǎihóng rainbow
菜花 càihuā cauliflower
采集 cǎijí collect
裁减 cáijiǎn reduce
裁军 cáijūn disarm ◊ disarmament
采矿 cǎikuàng mining
材料 cáiliào materials
才能 cáinéng ability
裁判员 cáipànyuán umpire
彩票 cǎipiào lottery ticket; raffle ticket
菜谱 càipǔ recipe
彩色 cǎisè color
彩色胶卷 cǎisè jiāojuǎn color film
踩刹车 cǎi shāchē put on the brake(s)
财务 cáiwù finance ◊ financial
财务处 cáiwùchù accounts (department)
采用 cǎiyòng use
菜油 càiyóu vegetable oil
菜园 càiyuán vegetable garden
裁员 cáiyuán cut back; downsize ◊ layoff

财政 cáizhèng finance
才智 cáizhì wisdom
餐 cān meal
蚕 cán silkworm
惨 cǎn tragic; brutal
惨案 cǎn'àn massacre
残暴 cánbào cruel
餐车 cānchē restaurant car
蚕豆 cándòu broad bean
残废 cánfèi disabled
舱 cāng cabin
藏 cáng hide
苍白 cāngbái pale
仓促 cāngcù hasty
仓库 cāngkù warehouse
藏匿 cángnì hide
仓鼠 cāngshǔ hamster
参观 cānguān tour
餐馆 cānguǎn restaurant
参观者 cānguānzhě visitor
苍蝇 cāngying fly (insect)
残骸 cánhái remains
参加 cānjiā attend
蚕茧 cánjiǎn silk cocoon
餐巾 cānjīn napkin
残疾人 cánjírén disabled person
餐具 cānjù tableware
参考 cānkǎo refer to ◊ reference
残酷 cánkù cruel

惭愧 **cánkuì** ashamed

灿烂 **cànlàn** bright; brilliant

残缺 **cánquē** incomplete

参赛 **cānsài** play SP; take part (*in match, contest*)

餐厅 **cāntīng** dining hall; restaurant

惨痛 **cǎntòng** painful

参与 **cānyù** take part in, participate in

残余 **cányú** remainder

槽 **cáo** trough; groove

草 **cǎo** grass; straw

草地 **cǎodì** lawn

操劳 **cāoláo** work hard; struggle

操练 **cāoliàn** drill MIL

草帽 **cǎomào** straw hat

草莓 **cǎoméi** strawberry

草坪 **cǎopíng** lawn; meadow; green space

草图 **cǎotú** draft

操心 **cāoxīn** worry

槽牙 **cáoyá** molar

草药 **cǎoyào** herbal medicine

草原 **cǎoyuán** grasslands

嘈杂 **cáozá** noisy

操纵 **cāozòng** operate; control

操作 **cāozuò** operate ◊ operation

擦油 **cāyóu** apply cream

测 **cè** measure

侧 **cè** side

册 **cè** (exercise) book

测量 **cèliáng** measure ◊ measurement

策略 **cèlüè** tactics

侧面 **cèmiàn** side; profile

层 **céng** layer; story (*of building*); tier

曾经 **céngjīng** ever; once, formerly

厕所 **cèsuǒ** toilet

测验 **cèyàn** test

插 **chā** insert

叉 **chā** fork

茶 **chá** tea

搽 **chá** rub in

查 **chá** check; test

差 **chà** bad; poor (*in quality*); inferior ◊ badly ◊ lack; be short of

茶杯 **chábēi** teacup

差别 **chābié** difference

差错 **chācuò** mistake

茶点 **chádiǎn** refreshments; tea and snacks

查地图 **chá dìtú** consult a map

搽粉 **cháfěn** powder

茶馆 **cháguǎn** tea house

查号台 **cháhàotái** information TEL

茶壶 **cháhú** teapot

拆 **chāi** dismantle; demolish

柴 **chái** firewood

拆除 **chāichú** demolish

拆开 **chāikāi** take to pieces; unravel

拆卸 **chāixiè** dismantle

柴油 **cháiyóu** diesel

差劲 **chàjìn** disappointing

差距 **chàjù** gap; difference; distance

茶具 **chájù** tea service

察觉 **chájué** detect

缠 **chán** bind; wrap

蝉 **chán** cicada

铲 **chǎn** shovel

颤 **chàn** tremble

颤抖 **chàndǒu** shake

长 **cháng** long

尝 **cháng** taste

常 **cháng** frequent

肠 **cháng** intestines

厂 **chǎng** plant

场 **chǎng** place

唱 **chàng** sing

畅 **chàng** smooth; unimpeded

常常 **chángcháng** often

长城 **chángchéng** the Great Wall

长处 **chángchu** advantage; strength

长笛 **chángdí** flute

长度 **chángdù** length

长短 **chángduǎn** length

长方形 **chángfāng xíng** rectangle ◊ rectangular

唱歌 **chànggē** sing

常规 **chángguī** customary ◊ custom; routine

偿还 **chánghuán** pay back

唱机 **chàngjī** record player

长江 **Chángjiāng** Yangtze River

长颈鹿 **chángjǐnglù** giraffe

敞开 **chǎngkāi** open

厂矿企业 **chǎngkuàng-qǐyè** industrial enterprises

场面 **chǎngmiàn** scene

长跑 **chángpǎo** long-distance running

唱片 **chàngpiàn** record (LP)

长期 **chángqī** long-term

厂商 **chǎngshāng** commercial and industrial enterprises

昌盛 **chāngshèng** flourishing

常识 **chángshí** general

knowledge

尝试 **chángshì** try; taste

长寿 **chángshòu** long life

场所 **chǎngsuǒ** place

畅通 **chàngtōng** unobstructed

长统袜 **chángtǒngwà** stocking

长途电话 **chángtú diànhuà** long-distance call

畅销 **chàngxiāo** in demand; selling well

肠炎 **chángyán** enteritis

长椅 **chángyǐ** bench

常用 **chángyòng** in daily use

厂长 **chǎngzhǎng** factory director

忏悔 **chànhuǐ** repent; confess

搀假 **chānjiǎ** adulterate

产量 **chǎnliàng** production; capacity; output; yield; turnover ◊ turn over

阐明 **chǎnmíng** explain; interpret

产品 **chǎnpǐn** produce; product

产生 **chǎnshēng** produce; emerge

阐述 **chǎnshù** explain

铲子 **chǎnzi** shovel

抄 **chāo** transcribe; plagiarize

巢 **cháo** nest

朝 **cháo** toward

潮 **cháo** tide ◊ damp

炒 **chǎo** cook; stir fry

吵 **chǎo** argue

炒菜 **chǎo cài** cook ◊ stir-fried dish

炒菜锅 **chǎocàiguō** wok

超车 **chāochē** overtake

朝代 **cháodài** dynasty

炒饭 **chǎofàn** fried rice ◊ fry rice

超过 **chāoguò** exceed ◊ over

吵架 **chǎojià** argue ◊ argument

炒面 **chǎomiàn** fried noodles ◊ fry noodles

钞票 **chāopiào** bank note

潮湿 **cháoshī** damp

潮水 **cháoshuǐ** tide

朝鲜 **Cháoxiān** Korea ◊ Korean

嘲笑 **cháoxiào** laugh at

巢穴 **cháoxué** den

超重 **chāozhòng** overload; overweight

插头 **chātóu** plug ELEC

插图 **chātú** illustration

查询 **cháxún** enquire

茶叶 **cháyè** tea (leaves)

诧异 **chàyì** amazed

查阅 **cháyuè** look up

插座 **chāzuò** outlet ELEC

车 **chē** vehicle

扯 **chě** pull; bear; tell lies; talk nonsense

撤 **chè** withdraw

车次 **chēcì** train/bus number

彻底 **chèdǐ** thorough ◊ completely

撤回 **chèhuí** withdraw

车祸 **chēhuò** traffic accident

车间 **chējiān** workshop

车库 **chēkù** garage

车辆 **chēliàng** vehicle

车轮 **chēlún** wheel

沉 **chén** sink

晨 **chén** morning

衬垫 **chèndiàn** lining

撑 **chēng** support; hold up

乘 **chéng** by ◊ multiply

橙 **chéng** orange

诚 **chéng** honest

城 **chéng** city; wall

秤 **chèng** scales

城堡 **chéngbǎo** castle

惩处 **chéngchǔ** punish; penalize

承担 **chéngdān** undertake

呈递 **chéngdì** submit; hand

over

程度 **chéngdù** degree; measure

成堆 **chéngduī** in piles; loads of

承兑 **chéngduì** cash; accept *check*

惩罚 **chéngfá** punish ◊ punishment

成分 **chéngfèn** component

成功 **chénggōng** succeed ◊ success ◊ successful ◊ successfully

成果 **chéngguǒ** achievement; success

称号 **chēnghào** title; designation

称呼 **chēnghu** form of address

成绩 **chéngjī** achievement; results

成见 **chéngjiàn** prejudice

成交！ **chéngjiāo!** it's a deal!

成就 **chéngjiù** achievement

撑开 **chēngkāi** open *umbrella*

乘客 **chéngkè** passenger

诚恳 **chéngkěn** sincere

成立 **chénglì** establish ◊ foundation

成年 **chéngnián** come of age

承诺 **chéngnuò** promise;
commit; pledge

澄清 **chéngqīng** clarify

成人 **chéngrén** adult

诚实 **chéngshí** honest ◊
honesty

城市 **chéngshì** city

成熟 **chéngshú** mature

成套 **chéngtào** complete set

成为 **chéngwéi** become

乘务员 **chéngwùyuán**
conductor; ticket collector

成效 **chéngxiào** effect

程序 **chéngxù** procedure;
program

诚意 **chéngyì** honesty;
sincerity

成员 **chéngyuán** member

称赞 **chēngzàn** praise

成长 **chéngzhǎng** grow ◊
growth

橙汁 **chéngzhī** orange juice

诚挚 **chéngzhì** sincere ◊
sincerely

称重量 **chēng zhòngliàng**
weigh

橙子 **chéngzi** orange (*fruit*)

陈旧 **chénjiù** outmoded

陈列 **chénliè** display ◊ be
on display

沉闷 **chénmèn** close
weather; dejected; reserved
character

沉默 **chénmò** silent ◊ silence

沉默寡言 **chénmò guǎyán**
silent; taciturn

衬衫 **chènshān** shirt; blouse

沉思 **chénsī** thoughtful
◊ muse

沉痛 **chéntòng** deeply
distressed

晨曦 **chénxī** daybreak

称心 **chènxīn** be satisfied

沉重 **chénzhòng** heavy *loss*;
oppressive *weather*

沉着 **chénzhuó** level-headed

车皮 **chēpí** freight car

车票 **chēpiào** ticket

车胎 **chētāi** tire

车厢 **chēxiāng** car (*of train*)

撤销 **chèxiāo** cancel; get
rid of

车站 **chēzhàn** bus stop;
station

车子 **chēzi** bicycle; car

吃 **chī** eat

池 **chí** pool; pond

迟 **chí** late

匙 **chí** spoon

齿 **chǐ** tooth

翅膀 **chìbǎng** wing

吃饱了 **chī bǎo le** full up

吃不消 **chībùxiāo** unbearable

吃醋 **chīcù** be jealous

尺寸 **chǐcùn** dimension; measurement

迟到 **chídào** be late

赤道 **chìdào** equator

尺度 **chǐdù** measure; standard; rule

迟钝 **chídùn** clumsy

吃饭 **chīfàn** eat; have a meal

迟缓 **chíhuǎn** slow; hesitant

赤脚 **chìjiǎo** barefoot

吃惊 **chījīng** be surprised

吃亏 **chīkuī** disadvantaged

齿轮 **chǐlún** gear

耻辱 **chǐrǔ** disgrace

池塘 **chítáng** pond

持续 **chíxù** continue

吃药 **chīyào** take medicine

迟早 **chízǎo** sooner or later

斥责 **chìzé** reprimand

尺子 **chǐzi** ruler *(to measure)*

赤子 **chìzǐ** newborn child

赤字 **chìzì** deficit

冲 **chōng** push forward; attack; flush

虫 **chóng** insect

宠爱 **chǒng'ài** dote on

崇拜 **chóngbài** worship

充当 **chōngdāng** serve as

充电 **chōngdiàn** charge; recharge

重迭 **chóngdié** overlap

充分 **chōngfèn** full; ample

重逢 **chóngféng** meet again

重复 **chóngfù** repetition; duplicate ◊ repeat

崇高 **chónggāo** lofty

虫害 **chónghài** plague of insects

崇敬 **chóngjìng** revere

冲突 **chōngtū** conflict

宠物 **chǒngwù** pet *(animal)*

冲洗 **chōngxǐ** develop *photographs*; flush

重新 **chóngxīn** again

虫牙 **chóngyá** decayed tooth

充裕 **chōngyù** abundant

虫子 **chóngzi** insect; worm

充足 **chōngzú** sufficient

抽出 **chōu chū** pull out; draw

稠 **chóu** thick; dense

愁 **chóu** worry

仇 **chóu** enemy; hatred

丑 **chǒu** ugly

臭 **chòu** stinking

酬报 **chóubào** reward; payment

筹备 **chóubèi** arrange

仇敌 **chóudí** enemy

丑恶 chǒu'è revolting

仇恨 chóuhèn hatred; enmity

筹集 chóují raise *money*

抽筋 chōujīn cramp

丑角 chǒujué clown

抽空 chōukòng find time

丑陋 chǒulòu ugly, hideous

愁闷 chóumèn worried; down

臭名昭著 chòumíng zhāozhù infamous

抽泣 chōuqì sob

臭气 chòuqì stink

抽屉 chōuti drawer

丑闻 chǒuwén scandal

抽象 chōuxiàng abstract

抽烟 chōuyān smoke

抽样 chōuyàng sampling

出 chū go out; out

橱 chú cupboard

除 chú remove; except; divide MATH

锄 chú hoe

雏 chú young (*bird*)

除…外 chú ... wài apart from ...

穿 chuān wear; penetrate

传 chuán pass on

船 chuán boat

喘 chuǎn breathe heavily

串 chuàn string together ◊ *measure word for strings of things*

传播 chuánbō spread

船舱 chuáncāng cabin

穿戴 chuāndài wear; dress

传单 chuándān leaflet

传递 chuándì pass on; convey

传动 chuándòng transmission

窗 chuāng window

床 chuáng bed

床单 chuángdān sheet

床垫 chuángdiàn mattress

窗户 chuānghu window

创建 chuàngjiàn found

窗口 chuāngkǒu hatch; window; contact

创立 chuànglì found

窗帘 chuānglián curtains

创始人 chuàngshǐrén founder

窗台 chuāngtái window sill

创造 chuàngzào create

创作 chuàngzuò create ◊ creation

传话 chuánhuà pass on a message

传教 chuánjiào do missionary work

船票 chuánpiào ticket (*for ship*)

传奇 chuánqí legend

喘气 chuǎnqì gasp

传染 chuánrǎn infect ◊ contagious

传授 chuánshòu teach

传说 chuánshuō legend; legend has it...; it is said

传统 chuántǒng tradition ◊ traditional ◊ traditionally

传闻 chuánwén hearsay ◊ it is said

船坞 chuánwù dock

船舷 chuánxián side of a ship

传讯 chuánxùn summons

船员 chuányuán sailor

传真 chuánzhēn fax

传真机 chuánzhēnjī fax machine

穿着 chuānzhuó clothing

出版 chūbǎn publish; come out

出版社 chūbǎnshè publisher

储备 chǔbèi store; reserve ◊ stock up on; stockpile

出差 chūchāi go on a business trip

出丑 chūchǒu make a spectacle of oneself

橱窗 chúchuāng display window

初次 chūcì the first time

出点子 chū diǎnzi give advice

出发 chūfā departure ◊ leave

厨房 chúfáng kitchen

处方 chǔfāng prescribe ◊ prescription

除非 chúfēi unless

出国 chūguó go abroad

出汗 chūhàn sweat

储户 chǔhù depositor

出乎意料 chūhū yìliào unexpected ◊ strangely enough

吹 chuī blow

锤 chuí hammer

吹干 chuīgān blow-dry

吹鼓手 chuīgǔshǒu musicians

吹口哨 chuī kǒushào whistle

垂柳 chuíliǔ weeping willow

吹牛 chuīniú boast; talk big

吹嘘 chuīxū show off

垂直 chuízhí perpendicular; vertical

雏鸡 chújī baby chicken

出家人 chūjiārén Buddhist monk; Buddhist nun

出借 chūjiè lend

出境 chūjìng leave the country

初级小学 chūjí xiǎoxué lower elementary school

处决 chǔjué execute

出口 chūkǒu export ◊ exit

出口处 chūkǒuchù exit

出来 chūlái come out

除了 chúle except

处理 chǔlǐ deal with

出路 chūlù way out

出卖 chūmài sell; sell out

出名 chūmíng well-known

春 chūn spring

纯 chún pure; neat *drink*; net *price*

唇 chún lip

蠢 chún stupid

出纳员 chūnàyuán cashier

唇膏 chúngāo lipstick

春季 chūnjì spring

春节 Chūnjié Chinese New Year

纯洁 chúnjié innocent

纯净 chúnjìng clean

春卷 chūnjuǎn spring roll

纯熟 chúnshú proficient; skillful

春天 chūntiān spring

处女 chǔnǚ virgin (*female*)

纯正 chúnzhèng pure

绰号 chuòhào nickname

出钱 chūqián chip in; fork out

出去 chūqù go out

出身 chūshēn family background

出神 chūshén fascinated

出生 chūshēng be born

畜生 chùsheng beast; brute

出生地 chūshēng dì birthplace

出生年份 chūshēng niánfèn year of birth

出示 chūshì show

出事 chūshì go wrong; have an accident

厨师 chúshī chef

出售 chūshòu put up for sale

锄头 chútou pickax; hoe

出席 chūxí attend

除夕 Chúxī Chinese New Year's Eve

出现 chūxiàn appear

储蓄 chǔxù save; deposit

出血 chūxuè bleed

处于 chǔyú be (*in a situation*)

初中 **chūzhōng** junior high school

出租 **chūzū** rent ◊ for rent

磁 **cí** magnetism ◊ magnetic

瓷 **cí** porcelain; china

词 **cí** term; word

慈 **cí** kind

雌 **cí** female

此 **cǐ** this

刺 **cì** prick (pain); thorn; splinter ◊ stab

次 **cì** time

辞别 **cíbié** say goodbye

磁带 **cídài** cassette; tape

词典 **cídiǎn** dictionary

刺耳 **cì'ěr** shrill

此后 **cǐhòu** henceforth

伺候 **cìhòu** serve

词汇 **cíhuì** vocabulary

此刻 **cǐkè** right now

此路不通 **cǐ lù bù tōng** no thoroughfare

磁盘 **cípán** disk

瓷器 **cíqì** porcelain; china

瓷器厂 **cíqìchǎng** porcelain factory

慈善 **císhàn** benevolent; charitable

次数 **cìshù** frequency

祠堂 **cítáng** ancestral temple

辞退 **cítuì** fire

此外 **cǐwài** besides; also

刺猬 **cìwei** hedgehog

慈祥 **cíxiáng** kind; loving

刺绣品 **cìxiùpǐn** embroidery

次序 **cìxù** order

次要 **cìyào** minor; peripheral

赐予 **cìyǔ** bestow

辞职 **cízhí** resign ◊ resignation

此致 **cǐzhì** yours truly; best regards

葱 **cōng** scallion

匆 **cōng** hasty

丛 **cóng** bushes

从 **cóng** from

从不 **cóng bù** never

从此 **cóngcǐ** from now on

从来 **cónglái** ever

从来不 **cónglái bù** never

匆忙 **cōngmáng** in a hurry

聪明 **cōngmíng** intelligent ◊ intelligence

从前 **cóngqián** in the past

从容 **cóngróng** calm ◊ leisurely

从事 **cóngshì** engage in; deal with

从小 **cóngxiǎo** from childhood

从中 **cóngzhōng** from

among; between

凑合 còuhe rough it; make the best of ◊ so-so, average

凑巧 còuqiǎo by chance

粗 cū rough

醋 cù vinegar

粗笨 cūbèn crude

粗糙 cūcāo coarse

催 cuī urge

脆 cuì fragile; brittle

催促 cuīcù hurry up; press for

摧毁 cuīhuǐ destroy; devastate

脆弱 cuìruò weak; frail

促进 cùjìn further; stimulate ◊ boost

粗略 cūlüè rough; cursory

村 cūn village

存 cún exist; store

寸 cùn Chinese inch

存储器 cúnchǔqì memory

存货 cúnhuò stock

存折 cúnzhé bank book

错 cuò wrong

锉 cuò file

错觉 cuòjué misconception; illusion

磋商 cuōshāng consult

措施 cuòshī step

错误 cuòwù mistake

挫折 cuòzhé setback; failure

错综复杂 cuòzōng-fùzá complicated

促使 cùshǐ impel; spur; cause to happen

粗心 cūxīn careless

粗壮 cūzhuàng stocky

D

答 dá reply

打 dǎ hit; get; play

大 dà big

答案 dá'àn answer

大白菜 dàbáicài Chinese cabbage

打扮 dǎbàn dress up; put on make-up

打包 dǎbāo package; pack; bale

大便 dàbiàn defecate ◊ shit; feces

搭便车 dā biànchē hitch a ride

大不列颠 Dà Bùlièdiǎn Great Britain ◊ British

搭车 **dāchē** thumb a ride; take a cab

大葱 **dàcōng** leek

大胆 **dàdǎn** bold

搭档 **dādàng** partner

达到 **dádào** reach

打电话 **dǎ diànhuà** call, phone

打动 **dǎdòng** touch; move

大豆 **dàdòu** soybean

打断 **dǎduàn** interrupt

大多数 **dà duōshù** bulk, majority; most

大发雷霆 **dà fā léitíng** fly off the handle

答复 **dáfù** answer; respond ◊ response

打嗝 **dǎgé** burp

大哥 **dàgē** eldest brother; *a term of address for a man of similar age to oneself*

大公无私 **dàgōng-wúsī** selfless

打鼓 **dǎgǔ** beat a drum

打鼾 **dǎ hān** snore

打哈欠 **dǎ hāqian** yawn

打火机 **dǎhuǒjī** (cigarette) lighter

带 **dài** bring ◊ belt; area

戴 **dài** wear

贷 **dài** loan ◊ borrow; lend

代表团 **dàibiǎotuán** delegation

逮捕 **dàibǔ** arrest

大夫 **dàifu** doctor

贷款 **dàikuǎn** loan

代理 **dàilǐ** represent

带领 **dàilǐng** lead; guide

袋泡茶 **dàipàochá** teabag

代替 **dàitì** substitute

呆一会儿 **dāi yíhuìr** stick around

带子 **dàizi** belt; tape; strip

袋子 **dàizi** bag

打架 **dǎjià** fight

大家 **dàjiā** everyone

打搅 **dǎjiǎo** disturb

打交道 **dǎ jiāodào** have dealings with

大姐 **dàjiě** eldest sister

搭救 **dājiù** rescue

打击 **dǎjī** blow ◊ hit; deal a blow to

打开 **dǎkāi** open; turn on

打量 **dǎliang** size up

打猎 **dǎliè** hunt

大理石 **dàlǐshí** marble

大陆 **dàlù** mainland

大麻 **dàmá** hemp; marijuana

大麦 **dàmài** barley

大门 **dàmén** door; gate

单 **dān** simple; only; single;

odd *number*

胆 **dǎn** gall bladder

蛋 **dàn** egg

淡 **dàn** faint; light; pale

弹 **dàn** bullet; bomb

蛋白 **dànbái** white (*of egg*)

担保 **dānbǎo** guarantee; sponsor

担保人 **dānbǎorén** guarantor; sponsor

蛋炒饭 **dànchǎofàn** egg fried rice

诞辰 **dànchén** birthday

单程 **dānchéng** one-way

单纯 **dānchún** simple; pure ◊ alone

单词 **dāncí** word

单调 **dāndiào** monotonous

单独 **dāndú** alone; independently

单方面 **dān fāngmiàn** unilateral

当 **dāng** work as ◊ when

党 **dǎng** political party

挡 **dǎng** block ◊ gear (*engine*)

荡 **dàng** shake; swing

胆敢 **dǎn'gǎn** dare

档案 **dàng'àn** file; records

档案室 **dàng'ànshì** archives

蛋糕 **dàngāo** cake

当场 **dāngchǎng** immediately

当代 **dāngdài** contemporary ◊ the present era

党代会 **dǎngdàihuì** party conference

当地 **dāngdì** local

当今 **dāngjīn** nowadays

当局 **dāngjú** the authorities

当前 **dāngqián** present

荡秋千 **dàng qiūqiān** swing; rock

当然 **dāngrán** of course

当天 **dàngtiān** on the same day

党委 **dǎngwěi** party committee

当心 **dāngxīn** be careful

当中 **dāngzhōng** in the middle

党中央 **dǎng-zhōngyāng** Party Central Committee

蛋黄 **dànhuáng** yolk

担架 **dānjià** stretcher

胆量 **dǎnliàng** guts; nerve

胆怯 **dǎnqiè** cowardly

单人床 **dānrénchuáng** single bed

单人房间 **dānrén fángjiān** single room

单人沙发 **dānrén shāfā**

armchair

单色 **dānsè** plain, all one color

单身 **dānshēn** single

诞生 **dànshēng** be born ◊ birth

单身汉 **dānshēn hàn** bachelor

但是 **dànshì** but

淡水 **dànshuǐ** fresh water

耽误 **dānwù** delay

担心 **dānxīn** worry ◊ worried

单行道 **dānxíng dào** one-way street

弹药 **dànyào** ammunition

但愿 **dànyuàn** hopefully

胆汁 **dǎnzhī** bile

刀 **dāo** knife

岛 **dǎo** island

道 **dào** way; road; path; Tao

倒 **dào** fall; pour ◊ upside down

到 **dào** arrive; reach ◊ to; up to

盗 **dào** steal ◊ thief

盗版 **dàobǎn** pirate copy

倒闭 **dǎobì** go bankrupt

倒彩 **dàocǎi** catcall; boo

到处 **dàochù** everywhere

到达 **dàodá** arrive ◊ arrival

捣蛋 **dǎodàn** get up to mischief

倒档 **dàodǎng** reverse gear

道德 **dàodé** morals, ethics

稻谷 **dàogǔ** rice paddy

道教 **Dàojiào** Taoism

道理 **dàolǐ** sense; reason; principle; truth

道路 **dàolù** road

捣乱 **dǎoluàn** create unrest

倒霉 **dǎoméi** have bad luck

悼念 **dàoniàn** mourn

到期 **dàoqī** become due; mature; expire

道歉 **dàoqiàn** apologize ◊ apology

盗窃 **dàoqiè** steal

倒数第二 **dàoshǔ dì'er** penultimate

倒塌 **dǎotā** collapse

倒下 **dǎoxià** fall down

导线 **dǎoxiàn** (electrical) wire; cable

倒叙 **dàoxù** flashback

导演 **dǎoyǎn** director (*film*) ◊ direct ◊ direction

岛屿 **dǎoyǔ** island

打喷嚏 **dǎ pēntì** sneeze

打扫 **dǎsǎo** sweep

大厦 **dàshà** high-rise building

打闪 dǎshǎn flash (of lightning)

大赦 dàshè amnesty

大使 dàshǐ ambassador

大使馆 dàshǐguǎn embassy

打手势 dǎ shǒushì gesticulate

打算 dǎsuàn intend; plan

大蒜 dàsuàn garlic

打听 dǎtīng inquire about

大厅 dàtīng hall

打通 dǎtōng TEL get through

大腿 dàtuǐ thigh

大象 dàxiàng elephant

大西洋 dàxīyáng Atlantic

大学 dàxué university

大衣 dàyī overcoat

答应 dāying reply; agree

打印机 dǎyìnjī printer

大约 dàyuē around ◊ thereabouts

打招呼 dǎ zhāohu greet

大众 dàzhòng masses

打字 dǎzì type

打字机 dǎzìjī typewriter

德 dé virtue

得到 dédào get

德国 Déguó German ◊ Germany

德国人 Déguórén German

灯 dēng lamp

登 dēng climb

等 děng wait; grade

凳 dèng stool

等待 děngdài wait for ◊ hang on

登广告 dēng guǎnggào advertise

等候 děnghòu wait

登记 dēngjì check in; register ◊ registration

等级 děngjí class; classification; grade

等价 děngjià of equivalent value

灯笼 dēnglong lantern

灯泡 dēngpào light bulb

登山 dēngshān mountaineering

灯芯绒 dēngxīnróng corduroy

等于 děngyú equal

凳子 dèngzi stool

得体 détǐ proper; tactful

得罪 dézuì insult; offend

滴 dī drop ◊ drip

堤 dī dike

低 dī low

敌 dí enemy

底 dǐ bottom

地 dì earth; land; ground

点 **diǎn** measure word for time

点 **diǎn** dot; (decimal) point

碘 **diǎn** iodine

电 **diàn** electric ◊ electricity

垫 **diàn** cushion; mat

店 **diàn** shop

电报 **diànbào** telegram

颠簸 **diānbǒ** jolt ◊ bumpy

点菜 **diǎncài** order (in restaurant)

电车 **diànchē** streetcar; trolleybus

电池 **diànchí** battery

颠倒 **diāndǎo** reverse

电灯 **diàndēng** electric light

电饭锅 **diànfànguō** rice cooker

淀粉 **diànfěn** starch; cornstarch

垫付 **diànfù** pay for someone else

电工 **diàngōng** electrician

电话 **diànhuà** telephone

电话磁卡 **diànhuà cíkǎ** phonecard

电缆 **diànlǎn** electricity cable

典礼 **diǎnlǐ** ceremony ◊ ceremonial

电流 **diànliú** electric current

电气 **diànqì** electricity

电器 **diànqì** electrical appliance

电扇 **diànshàn** electric fan

电视 **diànshì** television

电视机 **diànshìjī** television set

电梯 **diàntī** elevator

电筒 **diàntǒng** flashlight

点心 **diǎnxin** dim sum

典型 **diǎnxíng** characteristic; classic; representative; typical ◊ typically

电压 **diànyā** voltage

电影 **diànyǐng** movie

电影院 **diànyǐng yuàn** movie theater

店员 **diànyuán** sales clerk

垫子 **diànzi** cushion; padding

电子 **diànzǐ** electronic

电子表 **diànzǐbiǎo** quartz watch

电子邮件 **diànzǐ yóujiàn** e-mail

刁 **diāo** wily

掉 **diào** fall; drop; lose

吊 **diào** hang; suspend

碉堡 **diāobǎo** fortress

调查 **diàochá** investigate; survey ◊ investigation

调动 diàodòng transfer

钓竿 diàogān fishing rod

调换 diàohuàn exchange

刁难 diāonàn create
difficulties

吊桥 diàoqiáo suspension
bridge

掉色 diàoshǎi fade

调头 diàotóu turn around

吊唁 diàoyàn offer one's
condolences

钓鱼 diàoyú go fishing

底层 dǐcéng first floor, *Br*
ground floor

低沉 dīchén low and heavy

地带 dìdài area

抵挡 dǐdǎng resist; repel

弟弟 dìdi younger brother

地点 dìdiǎn place

蝶 dié butterfly

跌倒 diēdǎo fall over

跌价 diējià price drop

第二点 dì'èrdiǎn secondly

蝶泳 diéyǒng butterfly
stroke

地方 dìfang place

低估 dīgū underestimate

低级 dījí low; crude

地基 dìjī foundations

递交 dìjiāo hand over

地窖 dìjiào vaults

缔结 dìjié conclude *contract*

抵抗 dǐkàng resist ◊
resistance

地理 dìlǐ geography

叮 dīng sting; stab

钉 dīng nail; staple

丁 dīng cube

盯 dīng stare

顶 dǐng measure word for
hats, umbrellas

顶 dǐng top

定 dìng set

订 dìng order; subscribe

钉 dìng nail

顶点 dǐngdiǎn summit

定额 dìng'é quota; target

顶风 dǐngfēng against the
wind

订户 dìnghù customer;
subscriber

订婚 dìnghūn engaged ◊ get
engaged ◊ engagement

订货 dìnghuò order goods

定金 dìngjīn deposit

订机票 dìng jīpiào book
a flight

定居 dìngjū settle down

定期 dìngqī regular ◊
periodically

盯梢 dīngshāo tail

订书机 dìngshūjī stapler

丁香 **dīngxiāng** lilac

定义 **dìngyì** definition

订阅 **dìngyuè** subscribe to

顶住 **dǐngzhù** resist

订桌 **dìngzhuō** book a table

钉子 **dīngzi** nail

地皮 **dìpí** plot of land to build on

底片 **dǐpiàn** negative PHOT

地平线 **dìpíngxiàn** horizon

地区 **dìqū** region ◊ regional

敌人 **dírén** enemy

第三 **dìsān** third

第三世界 **Dìsān Shìjiè** Third World

递送 **dìsòng** deliver

地毯 **dìtǎn** carpet

地铁 **dìtiě** subway

迪厅 **dítīng** disco

地图 **dìtú** map

地图册 **dìtúcè** atlas

丢掉 **diūdiào** throw away

丢失 **diūshī** lose

地下 **dìxià** underground

抵押 **dǐyā** mortgage

第一 **dìyī** first

第一流 **dìyīliú** first-class

地狱 **dìyù** hell

地震 **dìzhèn** earthquake

地址 **dìzhǐ** address

笛子 **dízi** flute

东 **dōng** east

冬 **dōng** winter

懂 **dǒng** understand

洞 **dòng** hole; cave

动 **dòng** move

冻 **dòng** freeze

栋 **dòng** *measure word for houses*

东北 **dōngběi** northeast

动产 **dòngchǎn** moveable assets

冻疮 **dòngchuāng** chilblain

动词 **dòngcí** verb

东道主 **dōngdàozhǔ** host

东方人 **dōngfāng rén** Oriental

东方 **dōngfāng** east; the East; the Orient ◊ eastern

冬菇 **dōnggū** winter mushroom

懂行 **dǒngháng** expert

恫吓 **dònghè** threaten; intimidate

动画片 **dònghuà piān** animated cartoon

动力 **dònglì** driving force; motivation

动乱 **dòngluàn** unrest; upheaval

动脉 **dòngmài** artery

冬眠 **dōngmián** hibernation

◊ hibernate

东南 **dōngnán** southeast

东南亚 **Dōngnán Yà** Southeast Asia ◊ Southeast Asian

动人 **dòngrén** moving

动身 **dòngshēn** set off

董事 **dǒngshì** director

懂事 **dǒngshì** sensible

董事会 **dǒngshì huì** board of directors

动手 **dòngshǒu** get to work

动手术 **dòng shǒushù** operate MED

冬天 **dōngtiān** winter

动物 **dòngwù** animal

动物园 **dòngwù yuán** zoo

东西 **dōngxi** thing

洞穴 **dòngxué** cave

动摇 **dòngyáo** waver

动作 **dòngzuò** movement

陡 **dǒu** steep

豆 **dòu** bean

逗 **dòu** cheer up

抖动 **dǒudòng** schütteln shake

兜风 **dōufēng** drive

豆腐 **dòufu** tofu

逗号 **dòuhào** comma

逗留 **dòuliú** stay; stop over; linger

抖落 **dǒuluò** shake off

斗篷 **dǒupeng** cape

豆芽 **dòuyá** beansprouts

斗争 **dòuzhēng** battle; struggle; fight for

都 **dū** city; capital

督 **dū** supervise

读 **dú** read

毒 **dú** poison; narcotics

独 **dú** alone

堵 **dǔ** block

赌 **dǔ** gamble

度 **dù** degree

妒 **dù** envy

渡 **dù** cross *water*; ferry

妒 **dù** envy

端 **duān** end; extremity ◊ carry

短 **duǎn** short

缎 **duàn** satin

断 **duàn** break

短处 **duǎnchù** shortcoming

断定 **duàndìng** conclude; decide

断绝 **duànjué** break off

短裤 **duǎnkù** shorts

锻炼 **duànliàn** exercise ◊ gymnastics; workout

短路 **duǎnlù** short circuit

段落 **duànluò** paragraph

短篇小说 **duǎnpiān xiǎoshuō** short story

短缺 duǎnquē shortage

短袜 duǎnwà sock

端午节 Duānwǔjié Dragon Boat Festival

锻造 duànzào forge

赌博 dǔbó bet; gamble ◊ gambling

赌场 dǔchǎng casino

堵车 dǔchē traffic jam

都城 dūchéng capital city

渡船 dùchuán ferry

督促 dūcù urge; press

度过 dùguò pass; spend *time*

堆 duī heap

对 duì right ◊ against

队 duì team

兑 duì exchange

对比 duìbǐ compare

对不起 duìbùqǐ I'm sorry

对称 duìchèn symmetric ◊ symmetry

对待 duìdài treat ◊ treatment

对方 duìfāng opposite side

对付 duìfu handle; 对付 X **duìfu X** have X to reckon with

对话 duìhuà dialog

兑换 duìhuàn exchange

堆积 duījī pile up

对面 duìmiàn opposite

对手 duìshǒu opponent

对外贸易 duìwài màoyì foreign trade

队伍 duìwǔ troops; ranks

兑现 duìxiàn cash *check*

对象 duìxiàng target; boyfriend; girlfriend

对照 duìzhào contrast

妒忌 dùjì envy

度假 dùjià spend vacation

独立 dúlì independence ◊ independent ◊ independently

蹲 dūn squat

吨 dūn ton

钝 dùn blunt

炖 dùn stew

顿 dùn *measure word for meals*

多 duō many; much; more

夺 duó take by force

朵 duǒ *measure word for flowers*

躲 duǒ hide

舵 duò helm; rudder

跺 duò stamp *foot*

躲避 duǒbì dodge; elude

躲藏 duǒcáng hide

多次 duōcì time and again

多亏 duōkuī fortunately

堕落 duòluò degenerate

多么 **duōme** how (*for emphasis*)

夺取 **duóqǔ** conquer

堕入 **duòrù** sink into

多少 **duōshao** how much

多数 **duōshù** majority; most

堕胎 **duòtāi** abortion

多谢 **duōxiè** thanks very much

多余 **duōyú** spare; superfluous

多雨 **duōyǔ** rainy

多云 **duōyún** overcast

毒品 **dúpǐn** drugs

肚脐 **dùqí** navel

堵塞 **dǔsè** block; jam

都市 **dūshì** metropolis

毒死 **dúsǐ** kill with poison

独特 **dútè** unique

读物 **dúwù** reading material

毒药 **dúyào** poison

独有 **dúyǒu** exclusive

读者 **dúzhě** reader

赌咒 **dǔzhòu** swear; take an oath

杜撰 **dùzhuàn** make up; invent

肚子 **dùzi** stomach

独自 **dúzì** alone; by itself; by myself etc

度 **dù** degree ◊ spend, pass *time*

E

额 **é** volume (*of business*)

鹅 **é** goose

蛾 **é** moth

恶 **è** evil

饿 **è** hunger ◊ hungry

恶毒 **èdú** malevolent

恶化 **èhuà** deteriorate

恶劣 **èliè** vile

俄罗斯 **Éluósī** Russia ◊ Russian

恶梦 **èmèng** nightmare

恶魔 **èmó** devil; demon

恩 **ēn** favor; kindness

而 **ér** and; but

儿 **ér** child; son

耳 **ěr** ear

二 **èr** two

耳背 **ěrbèi** hard of hearing

儿歌 **érgē** nursery rhyme

耳光 **ěrguāng** clip round the ear

耳环 **ěrhuán** earring

二流 **èrliú** second-rate
二十 **èrshí** twenty
二手 **èrshǒu** secondhand
儿童 **értóng** children
儿媳妇 **érxífu** daughter-in-law
二月 **èryuè** February
儿子 **érzi** son

扼杀 **èshā** strangle
额外 **éwài** extra
恶习 **èxí** vice
恶心 **èxin** nausea ◊ revolting
恶性 **èxìng** malignant; virulent
鳄鱼 **èyú** crocodile
蛾子 **ézi** moth

F

阀 **fá** valve
罚 **fá** punish
乏 **fá** lack ◊ exhausted
筏 **fá** raft
法 **fǎ** law; method
发 **fà** hair
发表 **fābiǎo** publish; issue
发愁 **fāchóu** worry
发达 **fādá** developed
发达国家 **fādá guójiā** developed country
发呆 **fādāi** be in a daze
法典 **fǎdiǎn** code; statutes
法定 **fǎdìng** legal; statutory
发动机 **fādòngjī** motor
发抖 **fādǒu** shake
发奋 **fāfèn** make an effort
发疯 **fāfēng** go crazy
法官 **fǎguān** judge

发光 **fāguāng** shine
法国 **Fǎguó** France ◊ French
发慌 **fāhuāng** feel nervous
发火 **fāhuǒ** erupt; get angry
发货 **fāhuò** send goods
发奖 **fājiǎng** award prizes
发酵 **fājiào** ferment ◊ fermentation
发掘 **fājué** find
罚款 **fákuǎn** fine
乏力 **fálì** weak
法律 **fǎlǜ** law ◊ legal
发霉 **fāméi** go moldy
发明 **fāmíng** invent ◊ invention
帆 **fān** sail
烦 **fán** annoyed
返 **fǎn** back
饭 **fàn** cooked rice

翻版 fānbǎn reprint

反驳 fǎnbó contradict

帆布 fānbù canvas

帆布篷 fānbùpéng tarpaulin

饭菜 fàncài food

帆船 fānchuán sailboat

饭店 fàndiàn hotel

反对 fǎnduì oppose ◊ opposition

反复 fǎnfù repeated

方 fāng square; direction

防 fáng prevent

纺 fǎng spin

访 fǎng visit

放 fàng put; release

妨碍 fáng'ài hinder; obstruct

方案 fāng'àn plan; program

反感 fǎngǎn aversion; dislike

方便 fāngbiàn convenience ◊ convenient

放大 fàngdà amplify; enlarge; magnify

房东 fángdōng landlord

方法 fāngfǎ method

方格 fānggé check (pattern); box (on form)

防护 fánghù protect

防火 fánghuǒ fire prevention

放假 fàngjià be on leave; have a day off

房间 fángjiān room

房客 fángkè roomer; tenant

方面 fāngmiàn aspect; side

放弃 fàngqì give up

放晴 fàngqíng clear up (of weather)

放射 fàngshè radiate

方式 fāngshì way; manner

防水 fángshuǐ waterproof

放肆 fàngsì impertinent

放松 fàngsōng relax ◊ relaxed

方糖 fāngtáng sugar cubes

反光 fǎnguāng reflect

翻滚 fāngǔn roll

防卫 fángwèi defend; protect

访问 fǎngwèn pay a visit

方向 fāngxiàng direction

放心 fàngxīn put one's mind at rest

方言 fāngyán dialect

防御 fángyù defend ◊ defensive ◊ defense

仿造 fǎngzào copy ◊ imitation

仿照 fǎngzhào copy

方针 fāngzhēn policy; guideline

防止 **fángzhǐ** guard against

纺织品 **fángzhīpǐn** textiles

房子 **fángzi** house

房租 **fángzū** rent

返回 **fǎnhuí** return; turn back

反抗 **fǎnkàng** revolt

泛滥 **fànlàn** overflow; flood

烦劳 … **fánláo** …would you mind …?

繁忙 **fánmáng** busy

反面 **fǎnmiàn** reverse (side)

烦恼 **fánnǎo** annoyance ◊ annoyed

蕃茄 **fānqié** tomato

繁荣 **fánróng** thriving

反响 **fǎnxiǎng** echo; repercussion

翻译 **fānyì** translate ◊ translation; translator

反应 **fǎnyìng** react ◊ reaction

翻阅 **fānyuè** leaf through

反正 **fǎnzhèng** in any case; anyway

繁殖 **fánzhí** reproduce ◊ reproduction ◊ reproductive

犯罪 **fànzuì** commit a crime

反作用 **fǎnzuòyòng** reaction

发胖 **fāpàng** put on weight

发票 **fāpiào** invoice

发卡 **fàqiǎ** hairpin

法人 **fǎrén** legal person; legal entity

发烧 **fāshāo** have a fever

发射 **fāshè** launch; blast off

发生 **fāshēng** happen

发誓 **fāshì** swear

法庭 **fǎtíng** (law) court

乏味 **fáwèi** tasteless

发现 **fāxiàn** discover ◊ discovery

发信 **fāxìn** send off a letter

发型 **fàxíng** hairstyle

法学 **fǎxué** law

发炎 **fāyán** inflammation

发音 **fāyīn** pronounce ◊ pronunciation

发育 **fāyù** grow ◊ growth

发源 **fāyuán** spring

法院 **fǎyuàn** court; courthouse

发展 **fāzhǎn** develop; grow ◊ development; growth

飞 **fēi** fly

非 **fēi** not

非…非… **fēi … fēi …** neither …nor …

非…即… **fēi … jí …** either… or …

肥 féi fat; fertile ◊ fertilizer

费 fèi cost; fee

肺 fèi lung

吠 fèi bark (of dog)

废 fèi useless

诽谤 fěibàng defamation ◊ defamatory

非常 fēicháng extraordinary ◊ very

废除 fèichú abolish; repeal

非典 fēidiǎn SARS

非法 fēifǎ illegal

飞机 fēijī airplane

飞机场 fēijīchǎng airport

费劲 fèijìn strenuous

飞快 fēikuài quick as a flash

费力 fèilì effort ◊ laborious

肥料 féiliào fertilizer; manure

菲律宾 Fēilǜbīn the Philippines

废品 fèipǐn trash

废气 fèiqì exhaust fumes

废弃 fèiqì abandon ◊ disused; waste

沸腾 fèiténg boil

肥沃 féiwò fertile ◊ fertility

飞行 fēixíng flight; flying ◊ fly

肺炎 fèiyán pneumonia

费用 fèiyòng fee; costs

肥皂 féizào soap

非正式 fēi zhèngshì informal; unofficial

废纸 fèizhǐ wastepaper

非洲 Fēizhōu Africa ◊ African

分 fēn divide; split ◊ cent

坟 fén grave

粉 fěn powder

粪 fèn excrement

份 fèn measure word for portions, newspapers

粉笔 fěnbǐ chalk

分别 fēnbié separate ◊ respectively; separately

奋斗 fèndòu struggle

份额 fèn'é share

粪肥 fènféi manure

疯 fēng mad

风 fēng wind

峰 fēng summit

封 fēng measure word for letters

缝 féng sew

风暴 fēngbào storm

封闭 fēngbì seal

奉承 fèngchéng flatter; suck up to ◊ flattery

讽刺 fěngcì mock; deride

丰富 fēngfù abundance ◊ abundant ◊ enrich

风格 **fēnggé** method; style

风寒 **fēnghán** cold

缝合 **fénghé** sew up

凤凰 **fènghuáng** phoenix

风景 **fēngjǐng** view; landscape

锋利 **fēnglì** sharp

丰满 **fēngmǎn** busty; plump; rounded

蜂蜜 **fēngmì** honey

封面 **fēngmiàn** (front) cover

奉陪 **fèngpéi** accompany

奉劝 **fèngquàn** advise

缝纫 **féngrèn** sew; sewing

丰盛 **fēngshèng** rich

风湿 **fēngshī** rheumatism

丰收 **fēngshōu** good harvest

封锁 **fēngsuǒ** blockade ◊ seal off

缝隙 **fèngxì** crack

风险 **fēngxiǎn** risk

风筝 **fēngzheng** kite

分号 **fēnhào** semicolon

粉红 **fěnhóng** pink

分居 **fēnjū** separate

分开 **fēnkāi** break; part; separate; detach

分裂 **fēnliè** division ◊ divide

分泌 **fēnmì** secrete ◊ secretion

分娩 **fēnmiǎn** childbirth

坟墓 **fénmù** tomb

愤怒 **fènnù** anger ◊ angry

分配 **fēnpèi** assign; distribute ◊ distribution

分批 **fēnpī** in groups

分歧 **fēnqí** difference; gulf

分期付款 **fēnqī fùkuǎn** pay in installments

焚烧 **fénshāo** burn

粉饰 **fěnshì** gloss over

分手 **fēnshǒu** split up; break up ◊ breakup; separation ◊ separated

分数 **fēnshù** fraction; mark

粉丝 **fěnsī** Chinese vermicelli

分析 **fēnxī** analysis ◊ analyze

分子 **fēnzǐ** numerator MATH; molecule ◊ molecular

佛 **Fó** Buddha

佛教 **Fójiào** Buddhism ◊ Buddhist

否 **fǒu** no; not

否定 **fǒudìng** negate

否决 **fǒujué** overrule; throw out; veto

否认 **fǒurèn** denial ◊ deny; disclaim

否则 **fǒuzé** or else

佛爷 **Fóye** Buddha

夫 **fū** husband

敷 **fū** apply

孵 **fū** hatch

肤 **fū** skin

扶 **fú** hold up; support

福 **fú** happiness

服 **fú** take *medicine*

斧 **fǔ** ax

腐 **fǔ** rotten; stale

付 **fù** pay

父 **fù** father

富 **fù** rich

腹 **fù** abdomen

负 **fù** negative; minus

妇 **fù** wife

副本 **fùběn** copy

浮标 **fúbiāo** buoy

副标题 **fùbiāotí** subheading

服从 **fúcóng** obey; comply ◊ obedience

附带 **fùdài** incidental; supplementary ◊ incidentally

负担 **fùdān** load; burden

辅导 **fúdǎo** tuition

复发 **fùfā** relapse

夫妇 **fūfù** married couple

覆盖 **fùgài** cover

讣告 **fùgào** obituary

符号 **fúhào** symbol

符合 **fúhé** tally with; conform to ◊ compatible

复活节 **Fùhuójié** Easter

附加 **fùjiā** add ◊ additional

附件 **fùjiàn** accessory; enclosure; attachment

附近 **fùjìn** close by

付款 **fùkuǎn** pay ◊ payment

腐烂 **fǔlàn** decay; rot ◊ rotten

福利 **fúlì** welfare

俘虏 **fúlǔ** capture ◊ prisoner; captive

附录 **fùlù** appendix

覆灭 **fùmiè** demise

抚摩 **fǔmó** caress

父母 **fùmǔ** parents

妇女 **fùnǚ** woman

福气 **fúqi** happiness

肤浅 **fūqiǎn** superficial; sketchy

父亲 **fùqīn** father

夫人 **fūrén** wife

富人 **fùrén** the rich; rich person

附入 **fùrù** enclose; add

肤色 **fūsè** skin color

负伤 **fùshāng** injured

敷设 **fūshè** lay *cable etc*

辐射 **fúshè** radiate ◊ radiation

服饰 **fúshì** clothes and accessories

复数 fùshù plural
复述 fùshù relate
伏特 fútè volt
伏特加 fútèjiā vodka
伏天 fútiān dog days
服贴 fútiē obedient;
  manageable
斧头 fŭtou ax
富翁 fùwēng rich man
服务 fúwù serve ◊ service
服务台 fúwùtái reception
服务员 fúwùyuán waiter
腹泻 fùxiè diarrhea
复写纸 fùxiězhǐ carbon
paper
抚养 fŭyǎng raise
副业 fùyè sideline
复印 fùyìn copy
富裕 fùyù affluent; well-off
复杂 fùzá complicated
负载 fùzài load ELEC
负责 fùzé be responsible for
  ◊ responsible
付账 fùzhàng pay the bill
负重 fùzhòng burden
服装 fúzhuāng dress; clothes
副作用 fùzuòyòng side
  effect

G

该 gāi should
改 gǎi change; correct
盖 gài cover ◊ lid
钙 gài calcium
改变 gǎibiàn change
改革 gǎigé reform
改建 gǎijiàn convert
改进 gǎijìn improve ◊
  improvement
概况 gàikuàng survey;
  overview
概括 gàikuò summarize
概念 gàiniàn concept
改期 gǎiqī postpone
改善 gǎishàn improve
概述 gàishù sum up ◊
  summary
改写 gǎixiě rewrite
概要 gàiyào outline
盖章 gàizhāng stamp
改正 gǎizhèng amend
盖住 gàizhù cover up
盖子 gàizi lid; cap
咖喱 gālí curry
干 gān dry ◊ dried
肝 gān liver

杆 **gān** pole

甘 **gān** sweet

敢 **gǎn** dare

赶 **gǎn** drive out; rush; 赶
时髦 **gǎn shímáo** keep up
with the latest fashions

秆 **gǎn** stalk

擀 **gǎn** roll out

感 **gǎn** feel ◊ sense

干 **gàn** do

干杯 **gānbēi** cheers!

干部 **gànbù** cadre

干草 **gāncǎo** hay

感到 **gǎndào** feel

感到无聊 **gǎndào wúliáo**
feel bored

感动 **gǎndòng** move

钢 **gāng** steel

缸 **gāng** earthenware vessel

刚 **gāng** just

港 **gǎng** harbor

尴尬 **gān'gà** embarrassed

钢笔 **gāngbǐ** fountain pen

港币 **gǎngbì** Hong Kong
dollar

刚才 **gāngcái** just now

杠杆 **gànggǎn** lever

刚好 **gānghǎo** just right

港口 **gǎngkǒu** port; harbor

肛门 **gāngmén** anus

钢琴 **gāngqín** piano

岗哨 **gǎngshào** guard

岗位 **gǎngwèi** guard

港务局 **gǎngwùjú** port
authorities

缸子 **gāngzi** beaker; cup

干旱 **gānhàn** drought

干涸 **gānhé** dry out; dry up

感激 **gǎnjī** appreciation ◊
appreciate; feel grateful

赶集 **gǎnjí** go to market

赶紧 **gǎnjǐn** hurry

干净 **gānjìng** clean

感觉 **gǎnjué** feeling;
sensation; sense ◊ feel

赶快 **gǎnkuài** hurry ◊
quickly

橄榄 **gǎnlǎn** olive

干酪 **gānlào** cheese

感冒 **gǎnmào** cold ◊ catch
a cold

擀面杖 **gǎnmiànzhàng**
rolling pin

感情 **gǎnqíng** feeling;
emotion

感染 **gǎnrǎn** contract, pick
up; infect; influence; affect;
become infected ◊ infected;
infectious; septic

干扰 **gānrǎo** interference ◊
interfere with

感人 **gǎnrén** moving,

touching

赶上 gǎnshàng catch up

干涉 gānshè interfere;
meddle ◊ interference

干洗 gānxǐ drycleaning

感谢 gǎnxiè thanks ◊ say
thanks

甘心 gānxīn willingly ◊
resign oneself to

感性 gǎnxìng sensory

感兴趣 gǎn xìngqù be
interested

肝炎 gānyán hepatitis

敢于 gǎnyú dare

肝藏 gānzàng liver

干燥 gānzào dry

甘蔗 gānzhe sugar cane

赶走 gǎnzǒu chase away;
banish

高 gāo big; tall; high ◊ top
(gear)

膏 gāo ointment; cream

糕 gāo cake

告别 gàobié say goodbye

高超 gāochāo masterly

高潮 gāocháo climax;
high tide

高大 gāodà enormous

高等 gāoděng higher;
advanced; elite

高等教育 gāoděng jiàoyù

higher education

糕点 gāodiǎn cakes and
pastries

高度 gāodù height

高尔夫球 gāo'ěrfūqiú golf

告发 gàofā inform; inform
on

高贵 gāoguì noble

高级 gāojí high-quality

稿件 gǎojiàn manuscript;
article

高楼大厦 gāolóu dàshà
high-rise buildings

告密 gàomì sneak; inform
on

高尚 gāoshàng noble

高烧 gāoshāo high fever

告诉 gàosu tell

高速公路 gāosù gōnglù
expressway

睾丸 gāowán testicles

高兴 gāoxìng happy ◊
happily

高压 gāoyā high pressure

羔羊 gāoyáng lamb

膏药 gāoyao plaster;
Bandaid®

高原 gāoyuán plateau

高涨 gāozhǎng upturn

告知 gàozhī inform

个 ge general measure word

哥 gē elder brother

歌 gē song

鸽 gē dove; pigeon

格 gé grid; grating; square

革 gé leather

嗝 gé hiccups

个 gè general measure word

隔壁 gébì next door

个别 gèbié individual

戈壁滩 Gēbìtān Gobi Desert

胳膊 gēbo arm

胳膊肘儿 gēbozhǒur elbow

歌词 gēcí lyrics

疙瘩 gēda boil

隔断 géduàn separate

哥哥 gēge elder brother

给 gěi give

歌剧 gējù opera

隔绝 géjué cut off; isolate

阁楼 gélóu attic; loft

革命 gémìng revolution ◊ revolutionary

根 gēn root

跟 gēn follow ◊ with ◊ and

根本 gēnběn ultimate; underlying ◊ at all; fundamentally ◊ base; foundation

耕 gēng plow

耕地 gēngdì plow ◊ arable land

更多 gèngduō more

更改 gènggǎi alter

耕牛 gēngniú draft ox

更新 gèngxīn renew; replace

更衣室 gēngyī shì cubicle

根据 gēnjù basis ◊ according to

跟随 gēnsuí follow

根源 gēnyuán origin; source ◊ originate

跟踪 gēnzōng stalk; rail

歌曲 gēqǔ song

个人 gèrén individual ◊ personal

格式 géshì layout

格式设定 géshì shèdìng format

歌手 gēshǒu singer

个体 gètǐ freelance; self-employed

格外 géwài particularly

个性 gèxìng personality; character

隔音 géyīn soundproof

革制品 gézhìpǐn leather goods

各种各样 gèzhǒnggèyàng mixed; miscellaneous

鸽子 gēzi dove; pigeon

弓 gōng bow

工 **gōng** worker ◊ work

攻 **gōng** attack

功 **gōng** merit; service

供 **gōng** supply; provide

恭 **gōng** respectful

公 **gōng** public; male

宫 **gōng** palace

共 **gòng** common; joint; mutual

公安局 **Gōng'ān jú** Public Security Bureau

公布 **gōngbù** announce; declare

共产党 **Gòngchǎndǎng** Communist Party

工厂 **gōngchǎng** factory

共产主义 **Gòngchǎn zhǔyì** communism ◊ communist

工程 **gōngchéng** construction

工程师 **gōngchéngshī** engineer

供词 **gòngcí** confession

公道 **gōngdào** justice

工地 **gōngdì** building site

宫殿 **gōngdiàn** palace

公共 **gōnggòng** public

公共汽车 **gōnggòng qìchē** bus

公关 **gōngguān** public relations

公害 **gōnghài** environmental damage

公函 **gōnghán** official letter

恭贺 **gōnghè** congratulate

共和国 **gònghé guó** republic

工会 **gōnghuì** labor union

公鸡 **gōngjī** rooster

攻击 **gōngjī** attack

供给 **gōngjǐ** supply

公斤 **gōngjīn** kilogram

恭敬 **gōngjìng** respect

工具 **gōngjù** tool

公开 **gōngkāi** public; open

功劳 **gōngláo** merit; service

公里 **gōnglǐ** kilometer

公路 **gōnglù** highway; road

公民 **gōngmín** citizen ◊ civic; civil

公墓 **gōngmù** cemetery

功能 **gōngnéng** function

公牛 **gōngniú** bull

供暖 **gōngnuǎn** heating

贡品 **gòngpǐn** tribute

公婆 **gōngpó** in-laws (*husband's parents*)

公顷 **gōngqǐng** hectare

工人 **gōngrén** worker

供认 **gòngrèn** confess

工伤 **gōngshāng** industrial accident

公社 **gōngshè** commune

公式 **gōngshì** formula

供水 **gōngshuǐ** water supply

公司 **gōngsī** company ◊ incorporated

共同 **gòngtóng** collective; common; joint

共同体 **gòngtóngtǐ** community

恭维 **gōngwéi** compliment; flatter

公物 **gōngwù** public property

恭喜 **gōngxǐ** congratulations

贡献 **gòngxiàn** contribute; devote ◊ contribution

工业 **gōngyè** industry ◊ industrial

工艺 **gōngyì** craft; technology

工艺美术 **gōngyì měishù** arts and crafts

供应 **gōngyìng** provide ◊ provision

公寓 **gōngyù** apartment

公园 **gōngyuán** park

公约 **gōngyuē** pact; convention

公正 **gōngzhèng** fair; impartial

公证 **gōngzhèng** authenticate; witness

公证人 **gōngzhèngrén** notary

公职人员 **gōngzhí rényuán** official

公众 **gōngzhòng** public

公主 **gōngzhǔ** princess

工资 **gōngzī** wage

工作 **gōngzuò** work; job

沟 **gōu** trench; ditch

钩 **gōu** hook

狗 **gǒu** dog

购 **gòu** buy

够 **gòu** enough

构成 **gòuchéng** comprise

购买 **gòumǎi** purchase

沟通 **gōutōng** communicate ◊ communication

购物 **gòuwù** shopping ◊ do one's shopping

勾引 **gōuyǐn** pick up; seduce

构造 **gòuzào** construction; design

钩针 **gōuzhēn** crochet hook

钩子 **gōuzi** hook

姑 **gū** aunt

估 **gū** estimate

孤 **gū** orphaned; lonely

鼓 **gǔ** drum

古 **gǔ** ancient

骨 **gǔ** bone

谷 gǔ valley; grain

雇 gù employ

顾 gù look around

瓜 guā melon

刮 guā scrape; shave

挂 guà hang; drape

寡妇 guǎfù widow

呱呱叫 guāguājiào great

挂号信 guàhào xìn registered letter

乖 guāi good; well-behaved

拐 guǎi turn

怪 guài strange

拐棍 guǎigùn walking stick

拐角 guǎijiǎo turning

拐骗 guǎipiàn kidnap

怪人 guàirén freak, weirdo; crank; nerd

拐弯 guǎiwān turn corner

怪物 guàiwu monster

怪相 guàixiàng grimace

关 guān close; turn off

官 guān official

鳏 guān widowed

观 guān look at; observe

罐 guàn jar; can

灌 guàn pour into

鹳 guàn stork

惯 guàn used to; accustomed

关闭 guānbì close (down)

贯彻 guànchè implement;

carry out

管道 guǎndào pipeline; tube

观点 guāndiǎn point of view

官方 guānfāng formal; official ◇ officially

鳏夫 guānfū widower

光 guāng light

广 guǎng wide

逛 guàng wander; stroll

灌溉 guàngài irrigate ◇ irrigation

广播 guǎngbō broadcast

光彩 guāngcǎi brilliance

广场 guǎngchǎng square (in city)

广度 guǎngdù scope; range

广而言之 guǎng ér yán zhī in general

广泛 guǎngfàn wide ◇ widely

广告 guǎnggào advertisement

光滑 guānghuá smooth; glossy

广阔 guǎngkuò wide

光明 guāngmíng bright

光盘 guāngpán CD-ROM; CD

光荣 guāngróng honor; glory

逛商店 guàng shāngdiàn

walk around the shops

光秃秃 guāng tūtū bare; bald

观光 guāngguāng look around; go sightseeing

光线 guāngxiàn light; ray

光学 guāngxué optics

关怀 guānhuái show concern for

关节 guānjié joint

冠军 guànjūn champion; championship

观看 guānkàn watch

管理 guǎnlǐ manage; operate; run ◊ administration; management

惯例 guànlì custom; habit

官僚制度 guānliáo zhìdù bureaucracy

灌木 guànmù bush

关税 guānshuì customs duty

罐头 guàntóu can

关系 guānxi connection; relationship

管弦乐 guǎnxiányuè orchestral music

管弦乐队 guǎnxián yuèduì orchestra

关心 guānxīn care about

盥洗室 guànxǐshì washroom

关押 guānyā lock up

关于 guānyú with reference to

观众 guānzhòng audience

管子 guǎnzi pipe; tube

馆子 guǎnzi restaurant

挂毯 guàtǎn tapestry; wall hanging

挂衣钩 guàyīgōu coat hook

瓜子 guāzǐ melon seed

古巴 Gǔbā Cuba ◊ Cuban

古代 gǔdài antiquity

孤单 gūdān alone; solitary

古典 gǔdiǎn classical

固定 gùdìng fasten; fix ◊ fixed

股东 gǔdōng stockholder

古董 gǔdǒng antique

孤独 gūdú lonely; solitary

孤儿 gū'ér orphan

孤儿院 gū'ér yuàn orphanage

股份公司 gǔfèn gōngsī joint-stock company

辜负 gūfù disappoint

故宫 gùgōng the former imperial palace in Beijing

古怪 gǔguài odd; eccentric

骨灰 gǔhuī ashes (after cremation)

骨灰盒 gǔhuīhé urn (for

ashes)

归 **guī** return

龟 **guī** turtle

鬼 **guǐ** ghost

贵 **guì** expensive; noble

跪 **guì** kneel

贵宾 **guìbīn** guest of honor

轨道 **guǐdào** track; orbit

规定 **guīdìng** stipulation ◊ stipulate

规格 **guīgé** specifications

归功 **guīgōng** owing to

鬼鬼祟祟 **guǐguǐ suìsuì** shifty-looking; sneaky

规划 **guīhuà** plan ◊ planning

归还 **guīhuán** give back; return

规模 **guīmó** scale

桂皮 **guìpí** cinnamon

归属 **guīshǔ** belong to

归途 **guītú** way back

贵重 **guìzhòng** valuable

柜子 **guìzi** cabinet

刽子手 **guìzishǒu** executioner

估计 **gūjì** calculate; estimate; assess

古迹 **gǔjì** antiquities

顾及 **gùjí** take into account

故居 **gùjū** former residence

顾客 **gùkè** client; customer

古老 **gǔlǎo** ancient

鼓励 **gǔlì** encourage ◊ encouragement

谷粒 **gǔlì** grain

估量 **gūliáng** weigh up

顾虑 **gùlǜ** misgivings

滚 **gǔn** roll ◊ get lost!

滚动 **gǔndòng** roll

姑娘 **gūniang** girl

牤牛 **gūniú** bull

棍子 **gùnzi** stick; rod

锅 **guō** pan; wok

国谷 **guó** state; country

果 **guǒ** fruit; result

裹 **guǒ** wrap

过 **guò** pass

锅铲 **guōchǎn** spatula

过程 **guòchéng** process

过错 **guòcuò** mistake

过道 **guòdào** corridor

过度 **guòdù** excess ◊ excessive

果断 **guǒduàn** decisive

过分 **guòfèn** excessive; unreasonable

果脯 **guǒfǔ** candied fruit

过高 **guògāo** exorbitant; too high

国歌 **guógē** national anthem

过火 **guòhuǒ** exaggerated ◊ exaggerate

国籍 **guójí** citizenship; nationality

国际 **guójì** international ◊ internationally

国家 **guójiā** country; nation; state ◊ national

国家队 **guójiāduì** national team

果酱 **guǒjiàng** jam

过节 **guòjié** celebrate (a festival)

过境 **guòjìng** be in transit (between countries)

过境签证 **guòjìng qiānzhèng** transit visa

锅炉 **guōlú** boiler

过滤 **guòlǜ** filter; strain

过滤器 **guòlǜqì** filter; strainer

过滤嘴香烟 **guòlǜzuǐ xiāngyān** filter-tipped cigarette

国民 **guómín** national

过敏 **guòmǐn** allergy ◊ hypersensitive

国内 **guónèi** domestic; internal

过年 **guònián** celebrate Chinese New Year

国旗 **guóqí** national flag

国庆节 **Guóqìngjié** National Day

过剩 **guòshèng** surplus

果实 **guǒshí** fruit

过时 **guòshí** old-fashioned; out-of-date

果树 **guǒshù** fruit tree

国外 **guówài** abroad; foreign

国王 **guówáng** king

国务院 **guówùyuàn** State Council

过夜 **guòyè** stay the night

国营 **guóyíng** state-run

果汁 **guǒzhī** fruit juice

股票 **gǔpiào** stocks and shares

故事 **gùshì** story; narrative; joke

骨髓 **gǔsuǐ** bone marrow

固体 **gùtǐ** solid

骨头 **gútou** bone

顾问 **gùwèn** adviser; consultant

股息 **gǔxī** dividend

故乡 **gùxiāng** home town; native place

故意 **gùyì** deliberate; willful ◊ deliberately

雇佣 **gùyōng** employ

固有 **gùyǒu** inherent

雇员 **gùyuán** employee; staff

鼓掌 **gǔzhǎng** applaud ◊

applause

故障 **gùzhàng** breakdown;
defect

骨折 **gǔzhé** break a bone;

fracture ◊ broken

固执 **gùzhí** inflexible;
stubborn

雇主 **gùzhǔ** employer

H

哈 **hā** exhale ◊ ha (ha)

还 **hái** still; as well as

海 **hǎi** sea

害 **hài** harm

海岸 **hǎi'àn** coast

海报 **hǎibào** poster

害虫 **hàichóng** pest; vermin

害处 **hàichu** damage

海带 **hǎidài** seaweed

海关 **hǎiguān** customs

海军 **hǎijūn** navy ◊ naval

海绵 **hǎimián** sponge; foam
rubber

海鸥 **hǎi'ōu** seagull

害怕 **hàipà** fear ◊ be afraid

海平面 **hǎipíngmiàn** sea
level

海滩 **hǎitān** beach

海外 **hǎiwài** overseas

害羞 **hàixiū** shy

海洋 **hǎiyáng** ocean ◊
marine

海员 **hǎiyuán** sailor

海蜇 **hǎizhé** jellyfish

孩子 **háizi** child

蛤蟆 **háma** toad

寒 **hán** cold

函 **hán** letter

喊 **hǎn** shout

汗 **hàn** sweat

旱 **hàn** dryness

焊 **hàn** weld

汉堡包 **hànbǎobāo**
hamburger

汉朝 **Hàncháo** Han Dynasty

行 **háng** line; row; trade;
profession

航班 **hángbān** flight

行家 **hángjia** expert

航空 **hángkōng** aviation

航空邮件 **hángkōng
yóujiàn** airmail

航天 **hángtiān** space flight

航线 **hángxiàn** flight route

航向 **hángxiàng** course

行业 **hángyè** trade;

profession

旱季 hànjì dry season

罕见 hǎnjiàn rare ◊ seldom seen

喊叫声 hǎnjiàoshēng yell; scream

含酒精 hán jiǔjīng alcoholic

寒冷 hánlěng icy cold

含量 hánliàng content

汗淋淋 hànlínlín sweaty

寒流 hánliú stream of cold air

汗衫 hànshān T-shirt

函授 hánshòu correspondence course

寒暑表 hánshǔbiǎo thermometer

寒酸 hánsuān shabby

汉学 Hànxué Sinology

汉语 Hànyǔ Chinese

旱灾 hànzāi drought

汉族 Hànzú the Han people

蚝 háo oyster

毫 háo milli-; in the least

好 hǎo good; well; very

耗 hào use; consume

号 hào number

好 hào like

好吃 hǎochī delicious

好处 hǎochù advantage

耗费 hàofèi spend; use

好感 hǎogǎn fondness; affection

豪华 háohuá luxury ◊ luxurious; de luxe; plush

好看 hǎokàn good-looking

好客 hàokè hospitable

号码 hàomǎ number

毫米 háomǐ millimeter

好奇 hàoqí curious ◊ curiously

好强 hàoqiáng ambitious

好听 hǎotīng melodious; nice-sounding

毫无 háowú not in the least

好象 hǎoxiàng seem; resemble ◊ apparently ◊ as if

好笑 hǎoxiào amusing

好心 hǎoxīn kind-hearted

号召 hàozhào call; call up

好转 hǎozhuǎn improve ◊ improvement

哈腰 hāyāo stoop; bow

喝 hē drink

和 hé and

盒 hé box

颌 hé jaw

核 hé core

河 hé river

褐 hè brown

贺 hè congratulate

荷包蛋 hébao dàn fried egg
合并 hébìng merge ◊ merger
喝采 hēcǎi applaud; cheer
合成 héchéng synthesis
喝倒彩 hè dàocǎi boo
合得来 hédelái get on well
核对 héduì check
荷尔蒙 hé'ěrméng hormone
合法 héfǎ legal; legitimate
荷花 héhuā lotus (flower)
黑 hēi black; dark
黑暗 hēi'àn darkness
黑白片 hēibáipiàn black and white movie
黑板 hēibǎn blackboard
黑客 hēikè hacker
黑啤酒 hēipíjiǔ dark beer
黑市 hēishì black market
黑手党 hēishǒudǎng Mafia
核计 héjì calculate
合计 héjì add up
和解 héjiě make up
河马 hémǎ hippopotamus
褐煤 hèméi brown coal
和睦 hémù harmony
很 hěn very; quite
狠 hěn hard-hearted
恨 hèn hate ◊ hatred
狠毒 hěndú malicious; venomous
横 héng horizontal

横贯 héngguàn cross
衡量 héngliáng consider; weigh up
恒心 héngxīn stamina; persistence
痕迹 hénjì evidence; trail; traces
很快 hěnkuài soon
和气 héqì polite; friendly
和尚 héshàng Buddhist monk
合身 héshēn fit
核实 héshí verification ◊ verify
合适 héshì suitable; appropriate
合算 hésuàn profitable
喝汤 hētāng drink soup
核桃 hétáo walnut
合同 hétóng contract ◊ contractual
贺喜 hèxǐ congratulate
和谐 héxié harmonious
核心 héxīn core; kernel
贺信 hèxìn letter of congratulation
合意 héyì please; appeal to
合影 héyǐng group photo
和约 héyuē peace treaty
喝醉了 hēzuìle drunken
红 hóng red

虹 **hóng** rainbow

哄 **hōng** coax

红宝石 **hóng bǎoshí** ruby

红茶 **hóngchá** black tea

宏大 **hóngdà** great

轰动 **hōngdòng** cause a
  sensation

轰击 **hōngjī** shoot at;
  bombard

烘烤 **hōngkǎo** toast

洪亮 **hóngliàng** sonorous

红绿灯 **hónglǜdēng** traffic
  light

轰鸣 **hōngmíng** roar

哄骗 **hōngpiàn** deceive;
  swindle

红薯 **hóngshǔ** sweet potato

洪水 **hóngshuǐ** flood

红外线 **hóngwàixiàn** infra-
  red rays

宏伟 **hóngwěi** grandiose

轰炸 **hōngzhà** bomb

猴 **hóu** monkey

喉 **hóu** throat

吼 **hǒu** roar

后 **hòu** back; behind

厚 **hòu** thick

候车室 **hòuchēshì** waiting
  room

后代 **hòudài** offspring

后跟 **hòugēn** heel

后果 **hòuguǒ** consequence;
  effect

喉结 **hóujié** Adam's apple

候机室 **hòujī shì** departure
  lounge

侯爵 **hóujué** marquis

后来 **hòulái** after; later

喉咙 **hóulóng** throat

后面 **hòumiàn** behind

候鸟 **hòuniǎo** migratory
  bird; migrant

后天 **hòutiān** the day after
  tomorrow

候选人 **hòuxuǎnrén**
  candidate

厚颜无耻 **hòuyán-wúchǐ**
  outrageous; impertinent

猴子 **hóuzi** monkey

壶 **hú** jug; kettle; pot

湖 **hú** lake

糊 **hú** stick

煳 **hú** burnt

虎 **hǔ** tiger

糊 **hù** mush

花 **huā** flower; blossom ◊
  spend; cost

划 **huá** row

滑 **huá** slide; slip ◊ slippery

画 **huà** draw; paint ◊
  drawing; painting

话 **huà** talk; speech

划 huà stroke

画报 huàbào magazine

哗变 huábiàn mutiny

滑冰 huábīng skate ◊ skating

滑冰场 huábīngchǎng ice rink

划船 huáchuán row; paddle

华尔兹 huá'ěrzī waltz

花费 huāfèi spend

化肥 huàféi artificial fertilizer

划分 huàfēn divide

花粉热 huāfěn rè hay fever

花岗岩 huāgāngyán granite

化工 huàgōng chemical industry

踝 huái ankle

坏 huài bad

坏处 huàichù disadvantage

怀旧 huáijiù nostalgia ◊ nostalgic ◊ reminisce

怀念 huáiniàn long for

坏人 huàirén rogue

坏事 huàishì evil (thing)

怀疑 huáiyí doubt; suspect; question

怀孕 huáiyùn pregnant

滑稽 huájī comical ◊ funnily

画家 huàjiā artist; painter

花椒 huājiāo Sichuan pepper

花轿 huājiào bridal palanquin

画廊 huàláng art gallery

还 huán return

环 huán ring

缓 huǎn leisurely

换 huàn change; swap

换班 huànbān change shifts

环保 huánbǎo environmental protrection

患病 huànbìng suffer from an illness

欢畅 huānchàng cheerful

幻灯 huàndēng slide show

幻灯片 huàndēngpiàn slide

荒 huāng desolate

慌 huāng nervous

黄 huáng yellow

谎 huǎng lie

晃 huàng swing; wave

蝗虫 huángchóng locust

荒诞 huāngdàn absurd; grotesque

黄道带 huángdào dài zodiac

皇帝 huángdì emperor ◊ imperial

晃动 huàngdòng shake; waggle

黄豆 huángdòu soybean

荒废 **huāngfèi** lie fallow

皇宫 **huánggōng** imperial palace

黄瓜 **huángguā** cucumber

黄河 **Huánghé** Yellow River

皇后 **huánghòu** empress; queen

谎话 **huǎnghuà** lie

黄昏 **huánghūn** dusk

黄金 **huángjīn** gold

荒凉 **huāngliáng** bleak; deserted

慌忙 **huāngmáng** hurried

黄色 **huángsè** yellow; pornographic

黄色人种 **huángsè rénzhǒng** the yellow race

荒疏 **huāngshū** lose the knack

黄铜 **huángtóng** brass

环顾 **huángù** look around

黄油 **huángyóu** butter

慌张 **huāngzhāng** nervous; lacking composure

缓和 **huǎnhé** détente; respite ◊ lighten

还击 **huánjī** hit back

环境 **huánjìng** environment; surroundings; setting

环境污染 **huánjìng wūrǎn** environmental pollution

欢聚 **huānjù** convivial get-together

欢乐 **huānlè** happy; cheerful

缓慢 **huǎnmàn** leisurely

化脓 **huànóng** fester

唤起 **huànqǐ** evoke; arouse

换钱 **huànqián** change money

还清 **huánqīng** pay off

环绕 **huánrào** surround

涣散 **huànsàn** loose; limp

换算 **huànsuàn** convert

幻想 **huànxiǎng** illusion; fantasy

唤醒 **huànxǐng** wake; rouse

欢迎 **huānyíng** welcome ◊ reception

花盆 **huāpén** flowerpot

花瓶 **huāpíng** vase

华侨 **Huáqiáo** overseas Chinese

花哨 **huāshao** flashy, gaudy

花生 **huāshēng** peanut

华氏 **huáshì** Fahrenheit

花束 **huāshù** bouquet

划算 **huásuàn** be worthwhile

滑梯 **huátī** slide

话题 **huàtí** topic of conversation

话务员 **huàwùyuán**

switchboard operator

化纤 huàxiān synthetic fiber

滑翔 huáxiáng glide

滑翔机 huáxiángjī glider

滑雪 huáxuě ski ◊ skiing

化学 huàxué chemistry ◊ chemical

化验室 huàyànshì laboratory

花园 huāyuán garden

画展 huàzhǎn exhibition of paintings

花招 huāzhāo trick

化妆 huàzhuāng put on make-up

化妆品 huàzhuāng pǐn make-up; cosmetics

划子 huázi rowboat

湖滨 húbīn lakeside

蝴蝶 húdié butterfly

蝴蝶结 húdié jié bow (knot)

煳饭 húfàn burnt rice

胡蜂 húfēng wasp

呼喊 hūhǎn call

呼唤 hūhuàn call

灰 huī ash; dust

回 huí return; go back

喙 huì beak; snout

会 huì be able to; meet ◊ meeting

回避 huíbì evade; duck

回车健 huíchē jiàn return key COMPUT

灰尘 huīchén dust

回答 huídá answer

挥动 huīdòng swing; wield

汇兑 huìduì transfer money

挥发 huīfā evaporate

恢复 huīfù recover; restore

回顾 huígù look back ◊ retrospective

汇合 huìhé join

会合 huìhé meet

悔恨 huǐhèn regret

绘画 huìhuà paint ◊ painting; picture

辉煌 huīhuáng brilliant; glorious

挥霍 huīhuò wasteful ◊ squander

回家 huíjiā go home

会见 huìjiàn meeting

灰浆 huījiāng mortar

回教 huíjiào Islam

灰烬 huījìn ash

汇款 huìkuǎn transfer money

汇率 huìlǜ exchange rate

会面 huìmiàn meet

毁灭 huǐmiè wreck; obliterate

汇票 huìpiào bill of

exchange

回去 huíqù go back

灰色 huīsè gray

会谈 huìtán have a conversation

诙谐 huīxié humorous

灰心 huīxīn discouraged

回形针 huíxíngzhēn paper clip

回信 huíxìn reply

会演 huìyǎn festival

回忆 huíyì recollect ◊ recollection

会议 huìyì conference; congress

徽章 huīzhāng badge

绘制 huìzhì draw

胡椒 hújiāo pepper

胡椒薄荷 hújiāo bòhé peppermint

呼救 hūjiù emergency call

狐狸 húli fox

护理 hùlǐ nurse

忽略 hūlüè neglect ◊ overlook

胡萝卜 hú luóbo carrot

荤 hūn meat or fish

混 hùn mix

昏暗 hūn'àn dark; dim

胡闹 húnào make trouble

fool around

混合 hùnhé mix; combine

婚礼 hūnlǐ wedding

混乱 hùnluàn chaos; muddle ◊ chaotic; turbulent

昏迷 hūnmí unconscious

混凝土 hùnníngtǔ concrete

馄饨 húntun won ton

混淆 hùnxiáo confuse ◊ confusion

混血儿 hùnxuè'ér half-caste

婚姻 hūnyīn marriage ◊ marital

婚约 hūnyuē engagement

浑浊 húnzhuó cloudy; muddy

或 huò or

火 huǒ fire

活 huó live ◊ alive

祸 huò accident

获 huò achieve

货 huò goods

伙伴 huǒbàn buddy; partner

货币 huòbì currency ◊ monetary

火柴 huǒchái match

火车 huǒchē train; van

火车头 huǒchētóu locomotive

火车站 huǒchēzhàn train station

货船 huòchuán freighter

获得 huòdé get; achieve; capture

活动 huódòng activity ◊ move

火锅 huǒguō hot pot

火花 huǒhuā spark

火化 huǒhuà cremate ◊ cremation

火鸡 huǒjī turkey

火箭 huǒjiàn rocket

火警 huǒjǐng fire alarm

火炬 huǒjù torch

霍乱 huòluàn cholera

活泼 huópo lively

活塞 huósāi piston

火山 huǒshān volcano

获胜 huòshèng win ◊ winning ◊ winner

祸首 huòshǒu instigator

火腿 huǒtuǐ ham

货物 huòwù goods

获悉 huòxī discover

或许 huòxǔ perhaps

火焰 huǒyàn flame

活跃 huóyuè active; vivid

货运站 huòyùnzhàn freight depot

或者 huòzhě or

糊墙纸 húqiángzhǐ wallpaper

忽然 hūrán suddenly

忽视 hūshì neglect

护士 hùshì nurse

胡同 hútòng alley

户头 hùtóu account

糊涂 hútu confused

呼吸 hūxī breath; breathing ◊ breathe

互相 hùxiāng reciprocal; mutual; one another

弧形 húxíng arched

护照 hùzhào passport

胡子 húzi beard; mustache

J

鸡 jī chicken

机 jī machine

奇 jī odd *number*

集 jí collect

极 jí extreme ◊ extremely

急 jí impatient; in a hurry; urgent

及 jí and

几 jǐ some; a few; several ◊ how many?

寄 jì send

季 jì season

记 jì remember

系 jì button up; tie up

既…又… jì … yòu … both ... and ...

加 jiā add ◊ plus

家 jiā home; family

痂 jiā scab

颊 jiā cheek

假 jiǎ false; bogus

价 jià price

假 jià vacation

加班 jiābān work overtime

甲板 jiǎbǎn deck

加倍 jiābèi double

甲虫 jiǎchóng beetle

家畜 jiāchù domestic animal

假定 jiǎdìng assume

假发 jiǎfà wig

价格 jiàgé price; cost

加工 jiāgōng process; embellish

加固 jiāgù fasten; secure

家伙 jiāhuo guy

嘉奖 jiājiǎng praise

佳节 jiājié happy celebration

家具 jiājù furniture

加剧 jiājù intensify

茄克 jiākè jacket; coat

肩 jiān shoulder

尖 jiān point

奸 jiān traitor

简 jiān straightforward

剪 jiǎn cut

减 jiǎn minus ◊ reduce

捡 jiǎn collect; pick up

件 jiàn *measure word for baggage, clothes etc*

键 jiàn key

见 jiàn see; meet

溅 jiàn splash; splatter

剑 jiàn sword

腱 jiàn tendon

舰 jiàn warship

箭 jiàn arrow

件 jiàn *measure word for items, clothing, furniture*

建 jiàn build; put up

加拿大 Jiānádà Canada ◊ Canadian

肩膀 jiānbǎng shoulder

鉴别 jiànbié differentiate

剪裁 jiǎncái cut to size; cut out

检查 jiǎnchá check; examine ◊ examination; inspection

检察 jiǎnchá prosecute

检察官 jiǎncháguān prosecuting attorney

简称 jiǎnchēng abbreviation

坚持 jiānchí maintain; carry

on; stand by

简单 **jiǎndān** simple ◊
  simply

剪刀 **jiǎndāo** scissors

间谍 **jiàndié** spy

坚定 **jiāndìng** firm;
  determined

鉴定 **jiàndìng** survey; assess

监督 **jiāndū** supervise;
  monitor

简短 **jiǎnduǎn** brief

尖端产品 **jiānduān chǎnpǐn**
  top-quality product

减肥 **jiǎnféi** diet; lose weight

姜 **jiāng** ginger

缰 **jiāng** rein

桨 **jiǎng** paddle; oar

讲 **jiǎng** speak; tell

奖 **jiǎng** award; prize

降 **jiàng** lower; sink

酱 **jiàng** paste; sauce

奖杯 **jiǎngbēi** trophy

降低 **jiàngdī** decline; lower;
  reduce

间隔 **jiàngé** interval;
  distance

讲话 **jiǎnghuà** speak

讲价 **jiǎngjià** haggle

讲解 **jiǎngjiě** explain

将近 **jiāngjìn** almost

奖金 **jiǎngjīn** bonus

僵局 **jiāngjú** deadlock;
  stalemate

将军 **jiāngjūn** general

讲课 **jiǎngkè** teach

将来 **jiānglái** in the future

奖励 **jiǎnglì** award; reward

降落 **jiàngluò** land

降落伞 **jiàngluòsǎn**
  parachute

奖品 **jiǎngpǐn** prize

缰绳 **jiāngshéng** lead; reins

讲师 **jiǎngshī** lecturer

讲述 **jiǎngshù** relate; tell

坚固 **jiāngù** strong; resistant

见怪 **jiànguài** take offense

降温 **jiàngwēn** drop in
  temperatue

奖学金 **jiǎngxuéjīn**
  scholarship

讲演 **jiǎngyǎn** lecture

将要 **jiāngyào** about to

僵硬 **jiāngyìng** stiff

酱油 **jiàngyóu** soy sauce

疆域 **jiāngyù** territory

奖章 **jiǎngzhāng** medal

讲座 **jiǎngzuò** lecture

简化 **jiǎnhuà** simplify

监护人 **jiānhùrén** guardian

减价 **jiǎnjià** reduce the price

渐渐 **jiànjiàn** gradually

建交 **jiànjiāo** establish

diplomatic relations

间接 **jiànjiē** indirect ◊ indirectly

坚决 **jiānjué** determined; decided; strong

健康 **jiànkāng** fit; healthy ◊ fitness; health

尖刻 **jiānkè** cutting; bitter

艰苦 **jiānkǔ** difficult; strenuous

尖利 **jiānlì** sharp; piercing

建立 **jiànlì** establish; set up; found

健美锻炼 **jiànměi duànliàn** aerobics; bodybuilding

见面 **jiànmiàn** meet

简明 **jiǎnmíng** concise

键盘 **jiànpán** keyboard

剪票 **jiǎnpiào** punch a ticket

柬埔寨 **Jiǎnpǔzhài** Cambodia ◊ Cambodian

坚强 **jiānqiáng** strong; tough

减轻 **jiǎnqīng** relieve; lighten; ease

尖锐 **jiānruì** sharp; shrill

减少 **jiǎnshǎo** reduce

建设 **jiànshè** build

健身中心 **jiànshēn zhōngxīn** fitness center

坚实 **jiānshí** solid

监视 **jiānshì** oversee; watch

见识 **jiànshí** experience; common sense

减速 **jiǎnsù** decelerate; slow down

健谈 **jiàntán** talkative

监听 **jiāntīng** listen in on; tap; bug

健忘 **jiànwàng** forgetful

奸污 **jiānwū** rape

见习 **jiànxí** become familiar with one's work; train

间隙 **jiànxì** gap

见效 **jiànxiào** effective

艰辛 **jiānxīn** suffering; hardship

饯行 **jiànxíng** have a farewell meal

检验 **jiǎnyàn** test

简要 **jiǎnyào** succinct

检疫 **jiǎnyì** quarantine

建议 **jiànyì** suggest ◊ suggestion

坚硬 **jiānyìng** rigid; hard

监狱 **jiānyù** prison

鉴于 **jiànyú** in view of

建造 **jiànzào** build ◊ building (activity)

见证人 **jiànzhèngrén** witness

简直 **jiǎnzhí** simply; utterly

剪纸 **jiǎnzhǐ** paper cut

建筑 **jiànzhù** building

健壮 **jiànzhuàng** robust

建筑学 **jiànzhù xué** architecture

剪子 **jiǎnzi** scissors

胶 **jiāo** glue

教 **jiāo** teach

浇 **jiāo** pour

交 **jiāo** hand over; cross

焦 **jiāo** burnt

嚼 **jiáo** chew

脚 **jiǎo** foot; bottom

角 **jiǎo** corner; jiao (*Chinese money*)

搅 **jiǎo** stir

叫 **jiào** call; ask

较 **jiào** relatively

教 **jiào** teach

骄傲 **jiāo'ào** proud

搅拌 **jiǎobàn** stir; whisk

脚步 **jiǎobù** footstep

交叉 **jiāochā** intersect

轿车 **jiàochē** car

搅动 **jiǎodòng** stir; move

角度 **jiǎodù** angle

娇惯 **jiāoguàn** spoil; indulge

狡猾 **jiǎohuá** crafty

交换 **jiāohuàn** exchange; barter; trade

教诲 **jiàohuì** explain; instruct ◊ explanation; instruction

交货 **jiāohuò** deliver goods

交互式 **jiāohùshì** interactive

焦急 **jiāojí** anxious ◊ anxiety

交际 **jiāojì** communication; contact

脚尖 **jiǎojiān** tip of the toe; tiptoe

交界 **jiāojiè** border (on)

胶卷 **jiāojuǎn** film

教科书 **jiàokēshū** textbook

教练 **jiàoliàn** coach

较量 **jiàoliàng** compete; compare

教练员 **jiàoliànyuán** trainer

交流 **jiāoliú** exchange; flow

交流电 **jiāoliúdiàn** alternating current

角落 **jiǎoluò** corner

角膜 **jiǎomó** cornea

酵母 **jiàomǔ** yeast

娇嫩 **jiāonèn** tender; sensitive

娇气 **jiāoqì** squeamish; fragile

郊区 **jiāoqū** suburbs; outskirts ◊ suburban

绞肉机 **jiǎoròujī** meat grinder

矫揉造作 **jiǎoróu zàozuò**

jiātíng fùnǔ

affected

礁石 **jiāoshí** reef

教师 **jiàoshī** teacher

教室 **jiàoshì** classroom

教授 **jiàoshòu** professor

教书 **jiāoshū** teach

教唆 **jiàosuō** instigate

交谈 **jiāotán** talk

焦炭 **jiāotàn** coke

教堂 **jiàotáng** church

交通 **jiāotōng** traffic

交通工具 **jiāotōng gōngjù** means of transportation

脚腕 **jiǎowàn** ankle

交往 **jiāowǎng** mingle; mix with; contact ◊ dealings

交响乐 **jiāoxiǎngyuè** symphony

胶鞋 **jiāoxié** sneakers

矫形 **jiǎoxíng** orthopedic

叫醒 **jiàoxǐng** wake

教训 **jiàoxùn** lesson

教养 **jiàoyǎng** manners; breeding

交易 **jiāoyì** deal; transaction ◊ transact

交易会 **jiāoyìhuì** trade fair

交易所 **jiāoyìsuǒ** exchange

郊游 **jiāoyóu** excursion

教育 **jiàoyù** education ◊ educational

校正 **jiàozhèng** correct; correction

脚趾 **jiǎozhǐ** toe

脚注 **jiǎozhù** footer; footnote

饺子 **jiǎozi** Chinese dumpling

叫做 **jiàozuò** be called

家谱 **jiāpǔ** family tree

假期 **jiàqī** vacation; leave

加强 **jiāqiáng** reinforce; strengthen

加热 **jiārè** heat up

家人 **jiārén** family members

假日 **jiàrì** public holiday

加入 **jiārù** add; join

假设 **jiǎshè** suppose ◊ assuming

加深 **jiāshēn** deepen

夹生 **jiāshēng** half-done

驾驶 **jiàshǐ** drive; fly; sail ◊ driving

驾驶员 **jiàshǐyuán** driver

驾驶执照 **jiàshǐ zhízhào** driver's license

家属 **jiāshǔ** family members

加速 **jiāsù** accelerate; speed up ◊ acceleration

家庭 **jiātíng** family ◊ domestic

家庭妇女 **jiātíng fùnǔ**

housewife

家庭作业 **jiātíng zuòyè** homework

家兔 **jiātù** rabbit

家务 **jiāwù** housework; chores

家乡 **jiāxiāng** home; home town

假想 **jiǎxiǎng** imaginary

假牙 **jiǎyá** dentures

加油 **jiāyóu** fill up; refuel ◊ come on!

加油站 **jiāyóuzhàn** gas station

家长 **jiāzhǎng** head of household; parent

假肢 **jiǎzhī** artificial limb

价值 **jiàzhí** value; worth

假装 **jiǎzhuāng** pretend; put on ◊ masquerade

架子 **jiàzi** stand; frame; shelf; airs

几百美元 **jǐbǎi měiyuán** a few hundred dollars

基本 **jīběn** basic, fundamental

级别 **jíbié** rank; level

疾病 **jíbìng** disease; illness; sickness

机场 **jīchǎng** airport; airfield

继承 **jìchéng** inherit

计程表 **jìchéngbiǎo** meter

继承人 **jìchéngrén** heir

基础 **jīchǔ** basis; foundation

挤出 **jǐchū** squeeze out

鸡蛋 **jīdàn** (hen's) egg

记得 **jìde** remember

激动 **jīdòng** excite; inflame ◊ feverish; impassioned

嫉妒 **jídù** jealousy ◊ be jealous

极度 **jídù** extreme ◊ extremely

忌妒 **jìdù** envy ◊ envious

季度 **jìdù** quarter ◊ quarterly

基督教 **Jīdūjiào** Christianity ◊ Christian

饥饿 **jī'è** starvation; hunger ◊ hungry

街 **jiē** street

结 **jiē** bear *fruit*

揭 **jiē** take off *lid*

接 **jiē** contact; call for; collect

结 **jié** knot

节 **jié** festival; knot; verse

解 **jiě** untie

姐 **jiě** elder sister

借 **jiè** borrow; lend ◊ loan

界 **jiè** border; limit

结巴 **jiēba** stammer

接班人 **jiēbānrén** successor

戒备 jièbèi vigilance ◊ vigilant

结冰 jiébīng freeze

阶层 jiēcéng (social) class

劫持 jiéchí hijack; abduct

杰出 jiéchū brilliant; eminent

戒除 jièchú remove; get rid off; kick *habit*

接触 jiēchù encounter

接待 jiēdài greet; receive

街道 jiēdào street

解冻 jiědòng thaw

阶段 jiēduàn stage

揭发 jiēfā uncover; discover

解放 jiěfàng liberate ◊ liberation; the 1949 Communist victory in China

借方 jièfāng debit ◊ debtor

姐夫 jiěfū brother-in-law

结构 jiégòu structure

解雇 jiěgù dismiss; lay off ◊ dismissal

结果 jiéguǒ result ◊ end up; put away *animal*

结核病 jiéhé bìng tuberculosis

结婚 jiéhūn marry; get married

结婚证书 jiéhūn zhèngshū marriage certificate

节俭 jiéjiǎn economical

接近 jiējìn near ◊ access ◊ verge on

洁净 jiéjìng clean

劫机者 jiéjīzhě hijacker

结局 jiéjú outcome; ending

解决 jiějué solve; settle; sort out

借口 jièkǒu excuse

揭露 jiēlù expose; reveal

结论 jiélùn conclusion

睫毛 jiémáo eyelash

姐妹 jiěmèi sisters

芥末 jièmò mustard

节目 jiémù program; show

节能 jiénéng save energy

节拍 jiépāi rhythm; beat

接壤 jiērǎng border (on)

节日 jiérì festival; (public) holiday

介绍 jièshào introduce ◊ introduction; profile

节省 jiéshěng economize on; save ◊ economical

结实 jiēshi sturdy; firm

解释 jiěshì explain ◊ explanation

接收 jiēshōu receive

接受 jiēshòu accept; take; receive; admit ◊ acceptance

结束 **jiéshù** end

阶梯 **jiētī** steps; stairs

接替 **jiētì** replace; relieve

接吻 **jiēwěn** kiss

界限 **jièxiàn** border

介意 **jièyì** mind; object to

节育 **jiéyù** birth control

节约 **jiéyuē** save

解约 **jiéyuē** cancel a contract

戒指 **jièzhǐ** ring (*on finger*)

接种 **jiēzhòng** vaccinate

节奏 **jiézòu** rhythm; beat

杰作 **jiézuò** masterpiece

挤干 **jǐgān** squeeze dry

及格 **jígé** pass (*in exam*)

机构 **jīgòu** organization; institution; structure; mechanism

籍贯 **jíguàn** home; birthplace

激光唱片 **jīguāng chàngpiān** compact disc

记号 **jìhao** mark

集合 **jíhé** meet; assemble

激化 **jīhuà** intensify; increase

计划 **jìhuà** plan; project; figure on; structure ◊ planning; program; project

机 坏 **jīhuài** rotten

饥荒 **jīhuāng** famine

计划生育 **jìhuà shēngyù** family planning

击毁 **jīhuǐ** destroy

机会 **jīhuì** chance

集会 **jíhuì** meeting; assembly

击剑 **jījiàn** fencing

即将 **jíjiāng** about to; soon

寄件人 **jìjiànrén** sender

季节 **jìjié** season

激进 **jījìn** radical

寂静 **jìjìng** quiet

基金会 **jījīnhuì** foundation

急救 **jíjiù** first aid

积极性 **jījíxìng** initiative; dynamism; activity

急剧 **jíjù** rapid; abrupt

疾苦 **jíkǔ** suffering

积累 **jīlěi** accumulate; pile up

激励 **jīlì** boost; spur; stimulation

吉利 **jílì** favorable; lucky

剂量 **jìliàng** dose

激烈 **jīliè** intense; fierce

机灵 **jīlíng** smart; sharp

记录 **jìlù** record; note ◊ minutes; log

纪律 **jìlǜ** discipline

急忙 **jímáng** hurried

寂寞 **jìmò** lonely

继母 **jìmǔ** stepmother

金 jīn gold

巾 jīn cloth

今 jīn now; today; the present

筋 jīn tendon

斤 jīn one jin *(500 grams)*

紧 jǐn tight; tense; taut

锦 jǐn brocade

仅 jǐn only

近 jìn close

进 jìn go in; enter

浸 jìn soak

禁 jìn prohibit

挤奶 jǐnǎi milk

锦标赛 jǐnbiāo sài championship; tournament

进步 jìnbù advance; progress ◊ progressive

禁地 jìndì restricted area

筋斗 jīndǒu somersault

技能 jìnéng technique; skills

茎 jīng stem

京 jīng capital city

井 jǐng well

景 jǐng landscape; scenery

颈 jǐng neck; throat

净 jìng clean ◊ net

镜 jìng mirror

静 jìng quiet

敬 jìng respect ◊ respectful

金刚石 jīngāngshí diamond

警报 jǐngbào alarm

精彩 jīngcǎi wonderful

警察 jǐngchá police; police officer

经常 jīngcháng often ◊ frequent; habitual

境地 jìngdì situation; position

经度 jīngdù longitude

惊愕 jīng'è dismay

胫骨 jìnggǔ shin; shinbone

经过 jīngguò pass ◊ through

净化 jìnghuà purify

惊慌 jīnghuāng alarmed

经济 jīngjì economy ◊ economic; economical

竞技 jìngjì athletics; sports

警戒 jǐngjiè warn

经纪人 jīngjìrén broker; middleman

京剧 Jīngjù Peking Opera

警觉 jǐngjué alert

镜框 jìngkuàng frame

境况 jìngkuàng circumstances

经理 jīnglǐ manager

经历 jīnglì career; experience; background ◊ go through

痉挛 jìngluán cramp

静脉 jìngmài vein

精明 jīngmíng clever

敬佩 jìngpèi respect

精辟 jīngpì profound

惊奇 jīngqí be amazed

精确 jīngquè precise

井然 jǐngrán neat; proper

惊人 jīngrén amazing

径赛 jìngsài track event

景色 jǐngsè scenery

精神 jīngshén soul; spirit ◊ mental

精神病 jīngshénbìng mental illness

经受 jīngshòu undergo; suffer

景泰蓝 jǐngtàilán cloisonné

惊叹 jīngtàn admire

晶体 jīngtǐ crystal

警惕 jǐngtì watchful ◊ warily

晶体管收音机 jīngtǐguǎn shōuyīnjī transistor radio

精通 jīngtōng be expert at; master ◊ proficient ◊ mastery

镜头 jìngtóu shot; photograph; lens

尽管 jǐnguǎn although; despite

惊吓 jīngxià startle

竞选活动 jìngxuǎn huódòng election campaign

惊讶 jīngyà astonishment ◊ be astonished

经验 jīngyàn experience

敬仰 jìngyǎng admire; worship

敬意 jìngyì respect; deference

经营 jīngyíng manage; run ◊ running ◊ managerial

鲸鱼 jīngyú whale

竞争 jìngzhēng compete; contend for ◊ competition

竞争者 jìngzhēngzhě rival

精致 jīngzhì exquisite

净重 jìngzhòng net weight

镜子 jìngzi mirror

今后 jīnhòu in future

纪念 jìniàn commemorate ◊ memorial

纪念碑 jìniànbēi memorial; monument

纪念品 jìniàn pǐn souvenir

紧急 jǐnjí urgent; imperative ◊ urgency

进口 jìnkǒu import

尽快 jǐnkuài as soon as possible

近来 jìnlái recent ◊ recently

进来 jìnlai come in

尽量 jǐnliàng as well as

one can

禁令 jìnlìng ban

今年 jīnnián this year

金牌 jīnpái gold medal

浸泡 jìnpào soak

筋疲力尽 jīnpí lìjìn exhausted

紧迫 jǐnpò extremely urgent

进去 jìnqu go in

禁区 jìnqū no-go area

进入 jìnrù enter ◊ entrance; entry

谨慎 jǐnshèn cautious; discreet ◊ caution; tact

近视 jìnshì shortsighted

金属 jīnshǔ metal

金属丝 jīnshǔsī wire

近似 jìnsì almost; roughly

今天 jīntiān today

津贴 jīntiē subsidy; allowance

劲头 jìntóu enthusiasm

浸透 jìntòu soak

激怒 jīnù infuriate; provoke ◊ enraged

妓女 jìnǚ prostitute

继女 jìnǚ stepdaughter

进行 jìnxíng carry out; execute; move on

进修 jìnxiū continue one's education

金鱼 jīnyú goldfish

尽早 jìnzǎo as early as possible

进展 jìnzhǎn proceed

紧张 jǐnzhāng nervous; tense ◊ nervousness; tension

禁止 jìnzhǐ ban

鸡皮疙瘩 jīpí gēda gooseflesh

祭品 jìpǐn sacrifice

击破 jípò strike down; fell

急迫 jípò urgent

激起 jīqǐ excite; work up

机器 jīqì machine; machinery

极其 jíqí extremely

技巧 jìqiǎo skill; knack

急切 jíqiè eager

激情 jīqíng passion

机器人 jīqìrén robot

既然 jìrán since

鸡肉 jīròu chicken (meat)

肌肉 jīròu muscle

及时 jíshí prompt; timely ◊ promptly; in time

即时 jíshí immediately

即使 jíshǐ even if

几时 jǐshí when; what time

集市广场 jíshì guǎngchǎng market place

棘手 jíshǒu tricky

奇数 jīshù odd number

技术 jìshù skill; technology ◊ technological

技术员 jìshùyuán technician

祭祀 jìsì sacrifice

计算 jìsuàn calculate; count

计算机 jìsuànjī computer; calculator

吉他 jítā guitar

祭坛 jìtán altar

集体 jítǐ collective

集团 jítuán group; clique

阄 jiū lot; ticket in a draw

酒 jiǔ alcoholic drink

九 jiǔ nine

久 jiǔ a long time

旧 jiù old

救 jiù save

就 jiù right; directly; then

酒吧 jiǔbā bar

臼齿 jiùchǐ molar

纠纷 jiūfēn dispute; quarrel

纠葛 jiūgé dispute; involvement

酒鬼 jiǔguǐ drunk; alcoholic

救护车 jiùhùchē ambulance

酒会 jiǔhuì cocktail party

旧货 jiùhuò second-hand goods

究竟 jiūjìng actually

酒精 jiǔjīng alcohol

舅舅 jiùjiu uncle

旧历 jiùlì Chinese lunar calendar

救命！jiùmìng! help!

就寝 jiùqǐn go to bed

救生衣 jiùshēng yī life jacket

九十 jiǔshí ninety

就是说 jiùshìshuō that is to say

酒席 jiǔxí banquet

就医 jiùyī go to the doctor

九月 jiǔyuè September

纠正 jiūzhèng correct

酒钻 jiǔzuān corkscrew

就座 jiùzuò take a seat

鸡尾酒 jīwěijiǔ cocktail

挤向 jǐxiàng crowd

迹象 jìxiàng mark; sign

讥笑 jīxiào scoff; laugh at

机械 jīxiè machinery; mechanism

急性 jíxìng acute

记性 jìxing memory

积蓄 jīxù save up; keep

继续 jìxù continue

鸡眼 jīyǎn corn; bunion

给养 jǐyǎng provisions

记忆 jìyì remember ◊

memory

集邮 jíyóu stamp-collecting

基于 jīyú because of; on the basis of

机遇 jīyù chance; stroke of luck

纪元 jìyuán era

妓院 jìyuàn brothel

记载 jìzǎi record

及早 jízǎo early; premature

机长 jīzhǎng captain (of aircraft)

记者 jìzhě reporter

急诊医生 jízhěn yīshēng emergency doctor

机智 jīzhì tact; wit ◊ witty; resourceful

集中 jízhōng concentrate ◊ cluster; focus (of attention)

脊柱 jǐzhù spine ◊ spinal

记住 jìzhù remember; memorize

脊椎 jǐzhuī vertebra

机组 jīzǔ air crew

驹 jū foal

局 jú office; bureau

举 jǔ raise; hold up

锯 jù saw

聚 jù assemble

剧 jù drama; play; theater

捐 juān donate; contribute

卷 juǎn roll; coil ◊ frizzy

卷 juàn volume

圈 juàn pen; enclosure

卷尺 juǎnchǐ tape measure

卷发 juǎnfà curly hair

绢纺 juànfǎng silk spinning

捐款 juānkuǎn donation; contribution

卷心菜 juǎnxīn cài cabbage

捐赠 juānzèng donate; contribute

举办 jǔbàn organize; hold

具备 jùbèi own; have

剧本 jùběn (stage) play

局部 júbù partial ◊ partially

巨大 jùdà enormous

掘 jué dig

觉察 juéchá perceive

觉得 juéde feel; think

决定 juédìng decide ◊ decision

绝对 juéduì absolute; total ◊ definitely; absolutely

绝妙 juémiào sensational; magic

诀窍 juéqiào knack

决赛 juésài final SPORT

角色 juésè part

绝食 juéshí hunger strike

爵士音乐 juéshì yīnyuè jazz

爵士乐队 juéshì yuèduì

jazz band

决算 juésuàn balance (sheet)

掘土机 juétǔjī excavator

绝望 juéwàng despair

决心 juéxīn determination

决议 juéyì decision; resolution

鞠躬 jūgōng bow

句号 jùhào period

聚会 jùhuì gathering; get-together

聚集 jùjí assemble; gather

拘谨 jūjǐn reserved

拒绝 jùjué refuse; reject ◊ refusal; rejection

俱乐部 jùlèbù club

距离 jùlí distance ◊ apart

拘留 jūliú detain; intern ◊ detention

居留 jūliú stay; reside

居留证 jūliúzhèng residence permit

局面 júmiàn situation

居民 jūmín inhabitant; resident

军 jūn army

均 jūn same; equal

军备 jūnbèi armament

均等 jūnděng equal ◊ equality

军队 jūnduì army; the military; troops

军官 jūnguān officer MIL

军舰 jūnjiàn warship

峻岭 jùnlǐng high mountains

军人 jūnrén serviceman

军事 jūnshì military

均匀 jūnyún even ◊ evenly

君子 jūnzǐ gentleman

巨人 jùrén giant

沮丧 jǔsàng depressed

拘束 jūshù awkward; constrained; unnatural

据说 … jùshuō … it is said (that)…; they say (that) …

具体 jùtǐ concrete; definite

举行 jǔxíng organize; hold

具有 jùyǒu own; have

剧院 jùyuàn theater; opera house

举止 jǔzhǐ conduct; behavior

居住 jūzhù live

橘子 júzi mandarin orange

句子 jùzi sentence GRAM

锯子 jùzi saw

K

卡 kǎ card

卡车 kǎchē truck

咖啡 kāfēi coffee

咖啡馆 kāfēiguǎn café

开 kāi open; turn on; start; drive; boil

揩 kāi wipe

开车 kāichē drive (a car)

开端 kāiduān start

开发 kāifā develop

开关 kāiguān switch

揩汗 kāihàn wipe away perspiration

开花 kāihuā bloom; blossom

开会 kāihuì hold a meeting

开阔 kāikuò extensive

开朗 kāilǎng outgoing; cheerful

开幕 kāimù open

开头 kāitóu start

开拓 kāituò pioneering

开玩笑 kāi wánxiào make a joke

凯旋 kǎixuán triumph

开业 kāiyè open a business

开支 kāizhī expenditure; expenses

砍 kǎn fell; chop

看 kàn see

看病 kànbìng see a doctor

看穿 kànchuān see through

砍伐 kǎnfá fell *trees*

看法 kànfǎ view; idea

康采恩 kāngcǎi'ēn group; concern

康复 kāngfù recuperate

抗菌素 kàngjūnsù antibiotic

慷慨 kāngkǎi generous

抗体 kàngtǐ antibody

看管 kānguǎn guard; look after

抗议 kàngyì protest

看护 kānhù look after; nurse

看见 kànjiàn see

看望 kànwàng visit

刊物 kānwù publication; periodical

烤 kǎo barbecue; broil; roast; bake ◊ barbecued; broiled; roasted; baked

考 kǎo test *student*; take *exam*

靠 kào lean against; be near;

rely on

靠岸 kào'àn dock

靠背 kàobèi back

考查 kǎochá examine

靠窗座位 kàochuāng zuòwèi window seat

考古学 kǎogǔ xué archeology

靠拢 kàolǒng move closer; close up

烤炉 kǎolú oven

考虑 kǎolǜ consider; think over

考试 kǎoshì exam

卡片 kǎpiàn card

棵 kē measure word for trees

颗 kē measure word for small round things

科 kē department

壳 ké shell

渴 kě thirst ◊ thirsty

可 kě can; may ◊ -able

课 kè class; lesson; subject

克 kè gram

客 kè guest

可爱 kě'ài delightful; lovable; cute

课本 kèběn textbook

可变 kěbiàn changeable

客车 kèchē passenger train

课程 kèchéng course

curriculum

客店 kèdiàn guest house; inn

刻度 kèdù scale

克服 kèfú overcome

可观 kěguān substantial

客观 kèguān objective

可贵 kěguì valuable; praiseworthy

科技 kējì science and technology

可敬 kějìng worthy; venerable

可靠 kěkào reliable

可可 kěkě cocoa

可口 kěkǒu tasty

刻苦 kèkǔ hard-working

可怜 kělián pitiful; pitiable

科目 kēmù subject

啃 kěn chew; gnaw; nibble

肯定 kěndìng certain; positive GRAM ◊ certainly ◊ it's a certainty (that)...

可能 kěnéng possibility ◊ possible ◊ possibly; maybe

可能性 kěnéngxìng possibility; probability

坑 kēng ditch; pit

坑道 kēngdào gallery; tunnel

恳求 kěnqiú implore; plead for ◊ plea

可怕 **kěpà** terrible; formidable

客气 **kèqi** polite; friendly

客人 **kèrén** visitor; guest

瞌睡 **kēshuì** sleepy

咳嗽 **késou** cough

课堂 **kètáng** classroom; lecture theater

客厅 **kètīng** living room

磕头 **kētóu** kowtow

渴望 **kěwàng** crave; long for ◊ craving; longing ◊ eager; wistful

可恶 **kěwù** horrible

可惜 **kěxī** what a shame; unfortunately

可笑 **kěxiào** ridiculous; comical

可信 **kěxìn** credible; reliable

科学 **kēxué** science ◊ scientific

科学家 **kēxuéjiā** scientist

可疑 **kěyí** suspicious

可以 **kěyǐ** can; may ◊ not bad ◊ OK

克制 **kèzhì** control oneself

空 **kōng** empty; bare; vacant

恐 **kǒng** be afraid; fear

空 **kòng** spare time

空白 **kòngbái** gap; hole; empty space

恐怖 **kǒngbù** terror

空洞 **kōngdòng** empty

空腹 **kōngfù** empty stomach

控告 **kònggào** charge; sue

恐慌 **kǒnghuāng** panic

空间 **kōngjiān** space; room

恐惧 **kǒngjù** fear

空军 **kōngjūn** air force

恐龙 **kǒnglóng** dinosaur

恐怕 **kǒngpà** I'm afraid ◊ perhaps

孔雀 **kǒngquè** peacock

控诉 **kòngsù** bring charges

空调 **kōngtiáo** air-conditioning

空闲 **kòngxián** leisure; leisure time ◊ unoccupied; at a loose end

空想 **kōngxiǎng** daydream

空心 **kōngxīn** hollow

空虚 **kōngxū** empty

控制 **kòngzhì** control

空中小姐 **kōngzhōng xiǎojie** air hostess

孔子 **Kǒngzǐ** Confucius

口 **kǒu** mouth

扣 **kòu** button up

口吃 **kǒuchī** stutter

扣除 **kòuchú** subtract; deduct

口袋 **kǒudài** pocket

口号 **kǒuhào** slogan

口渴 **kǒukě** thirsty

口令 **kǒulìng** password

扣人心弦 **kòu rén xīnxián** gripping

口水 **kǒushuǐ** saliva

口头 **kǒutóu** oral

口香糖 **kǒuxiāng táng** chewing gum

口译 **kǒuyì** interpret ◊ interpretation

口音 **kǒuyīn** accent

口语 **kǒuyǔ** colloquial language

扣子 **kòuzi** button

哭 **kū** cry

枯 **kū** dried up; parched

苦 **kǔ** bitter ◊ bitterness

库 **kù** storehouse; warehouse

裤 **kù** pants

夸 **kuā** praise; exaggerate

胯 **kuà** hip

酷爱 **kù'ài** love passionately

块 **kuài** piece; *measure word for money*

快 **kuài** quick; sharp ◊ quickly; soon

快餐 **kuàicān** fast food; quick snack

快车 **kuàichē** fast train

快感 **kuàigǎn** pleasurable feeling; thrill

会计 **kuàijì** accounting ◊ accountant

快乐 **kuàilè** joy ◊ happy

筷子 **kuàizi** chopsticks

夸奖 **kuājiǎng** praise

宽 **kuān** broad

款 **kuǎn** sum of money; article

宽敞 **kuānchang** spacious

宽度 **kuāndù** width

筐 **kuāng** basket

框 **kuàng** frame

矿藏 **kuàngcáng** mineral resources

矿工 **kuànggōng** miner

旷工 **kuànggōng** skip work

狂欢节 **kuánghuānjié** carnival

旷课 **kuàngkè** play truant

况且 **kuàngqiě** furthermore

矿泉水 **kuàngquánshuǐ** mineral water

狂热 **kuángrè** feverish

矿山 **kuàngshān** mine

矿石 **kuàngshí** ore

狂妄 **kuángwàng** arrogant; presumptuous

矿物 **kuàngwù** mineral

宽阔 **kuānkuò** wide

宽容 **kuānróng** lenient

宽恕 **kuānshù** forgive

跨越 **kuàyuè** pass; exceed

夸张 **kuāzhāng** exaggerate ◊ exaggerated

裤衩 **kùchǎ** underpants

库存 **kùcún** inventory

裤兜 **kùdōu** pants pocket

亏 **kuī** sustain losses

盔 **kuī** helmet

葵花 **kuíhuā** sunflower

傀儡 **kuǐlěi** puppet

亏损 **kuīsǔn** deficit; loss ◊ make a loss

溃疡 **kuìyáng** ulcer

馈赠 **kuìzèng** give a present

捆 **kǔn** bundle

困 **kùn** tired

苦恼 **kǔnǎo** worry

哭闹纠缠 **kūnào jiūchán** whine

昆虫 **kūnchóng** insect

困惑 **kùnhuò** confused; perplexed ◊ perplexity

困倦 **kùnjuàn** sleepy

困难 **kùnnan** difficult ◊ difficulty

阔 **kuò** wide; rich

扩大 **kuòdà** expand; enlarge ◊ expansion; enlargement

括号 **kuòhào** parenthesis

扩建 **kuòjiàn** extend *house*

扩军 **kuòjūn** arm; build up the army

阔气 **kuòqi** wealthy

哭诉 **kūsù** moan

枯萎 **kūwěi** wilting

枯燥 **kūzào** boring

裤子 **kùzi** pants

L

拉 **lā** pull; draw; drag

辣 **là** spicy

蜡 **là** wax

喇叭 **lǎba** loudspeaker; horn

拉肚子 **lādùzi** diarrhea

来 **lái** come

来回 **láihuí** back and forth

来历 **láilì** origin

来临 **láilín** approach; come

来往 **láiwǎng** contact; dealings

来由 **láiyóu** reason

来源 **láiyuán** source

垃圾 **lājī** garbage

辣椒 **làjiāo** chili pepper

拉链 **lāliàn** zipper

喇嘛 lǎma lama

栏 lán railing; hurdle

拦 lán block

蓝 lán blue

篮 lán basket

懒 lǎn lazy

缆 lǎn cable; rope

滥 làn excessive

烂 làn decayed

蓝宝石 lánbǎoshí sapphire

缆车 lǎnchē cable car

懒惰 lǎnduò lazy

狼 láng wolf

浪 làng wave

栏杆 lángān railings

朗读 lǎngdú read aloud

浪费 làngfèi waste

浪漫 làngmàn romantic ◊ romance

朗诵 lǎngsòng read out

榔头 lángtou hammer

懒汉 lǎnhàn bum

拦河坝 lánhébà dam

烂泥 lànní mud

篮球 lánqiú basketball

阑尾炎 lánwěiyán appendicitis

懒洋洋 lǎnyángyáng unenthusiastic; listless

蓝眼睛 lányǎnjīng blue eyes ◊ blue-eyed

滥用 lànyòng misuse; abuse

篮子 lánzi basket

牢 láo prison ◊ solid; sturdy

老 lǎo old

老板 lǎobǎn boss

劳动 láodòng work; labor

劳动日 láodòngrì working day

牢固 láogù solid; durable

老虎 lǎohǔ tiger

老虎机 lǎohǔjī slot machine

老虎钳 lǎohǔqián pliers; pincers

老家 lǎojiā home town

老年 lǎonián geriatric ◊ old age

老前辈 lǎoqiánbèi senior citizen; senior partner

老人 lǎorén old person

老实 lǎoshi honest

老师 lǎoshī teacher

老是 lǎoshì always

老鼠 lǎoshǔ rat; mouse

劳损 láosǔn strain

邋遢 lāta messy person; scruffy

蜡烛 làzhú candle

勒 lè rein in; check

乐 lè joy; happiness

乐观 lèguān optimistic; positive ◊ optimism

雷 léi thunder

累 léi accumulate

泪 lèi tear

累 lèi tired

类 lèi sort

肋骨 lèigǔ rib

雷鸣 léimíng thunder

类似 lèisì similar

类型 lèixíng type

雷雨 léiyǔ thunderstorm

雷阵雨 léizhènyǔ thundery shower

累赘 léizhui cumbersome

棱 léng edge

冷 lěng cold

冷淡 lěngdàn chilly; indifferent

冷冻 lěngdòng freeze ◊ frozen

冷静 lěngjìng calm

冷酷 lěngkù cold-blooded

冷却 lěngquè cool ◊ cooling

冷烫 lěngtàng cold wave

冷饮 lěngyǐn cold drinks

棱锥体 léngzhuītǐ pyramid

乐趣 lèqù enjoyment; fun

勒索 lèsuǒ extort; blackmail

乐意 lèyì willingly

乐园 lèyuán paradise; amusement park

乐于助人 lèyú zhùrén

obliging

梨 lí pear

犁 lí plow

离 lí leave

礼 lǐ rite; ritual; etiquette

里 lǐ in; inside ◊ li (measure of distance = 500m)

力 lì strength; power

立 lì stand

俩 liǎ both; two

连 lián link

脸 liǎn face

炼 liàn refine

练 liàn practice; train

链 liàn chain

恋爱 liàn'ài love

联邦 liánbāng federation; union

凉 liáng cool; cold

良 liáng good

量 liáng measure

两 liǎng two

量 liàng capacity; quantity; volume

亮 liàng bright; light; clear

辆 liàng measure word for vehicles

量 liàng capacity

炼钢厂 liàngāngchǎng steelworks

亮度 liàngdù brightness

谅解 **liàngjiě** understand; forgive

量具 **liángjù** measuring instrument

凉快 **liángkuai** pleasantly cool

两栖 **liǎngqī** amphibious

踉跄 **liàngqiàng** stagger; sway

粮食 **liángshi** grain; cereal

凉台 **liángtái** balcony

凉鞋 **liángxié** sandal

良心 **liángxīn** conscience

两种 **liǎngzhǒng** two kinds

联合 **liánhé** unite; form an alliance ◊ alliance; union ◊ united

脸红 **liǎnhóng** blush

连接 **liánjiē** connect

联接 **liánjiē** connect

连裤袜 **liánkùwà** pantyhose

连累 **liánlèi** cause difficulty for

联盟 **liánméng** coalition; alliance

怜悯 **liánmǐn** sympathize with

脸盆 **liǎnpén** washbasin

莲蓬头 **liánpengtóu** shower head

连日 **liánrì** lasting for days

炼乳 **liànrǔ** condensed milk

联系 **liánxì** contact; connect ◊ connection

练习 **liànxí** practice

连续 **liánxù** continuous; uninterrupted

连衣裙 **liányīqún** dress

帘子 **liánzi** curtain

料 **liào** material

了不起 **liǎobuqǐ** terrific

疗法 **liáofǎ** therapy

了结 **liǎojié** deal with; settle

了解 **liǎojiě** understand; know

料理 **liàolǐ** take care of ◊ Japanese cooking

聊天 **liáotiān** chat

疗养 **liáoyǎng** convalesce

疗养院 **liáoyǎngyuàn** sanitarium

篱笆 **líba** fence

离别 **líbié** separate; part from

立场 **lìchǎng** standpoint

列 **liè** list ◊ column; row ◊ *measure word for trains*

裂 **liè** crack; split

烈 **liè** intense

劣 **liè** inferior; poor

列车 **lièchē** train

裂缝 **lièfèng** crack

裂痕 lièhén crack

烈酒 lièjiǔ spirits

列举 lièjǔ enumerate

猎枪 lièqiāng shotgun

猎区 lièqū hunting ground

猎人 lièrén hunter

烈士 lièshì martyr

理发 lǐfà haircut; hairdressing ◊ style hair

立法 lìfǎ legislate ◊ legislation ◊ legislative

立方米 lìfāngmǐ cubic meter

理发师 lǐfàshī hairdresser

理发厅 lǐfàtīng hairdressing salon; barber shop

利害 lìhai severe; tough

离合器 líhéqì clutch

离婚 líhūn divorce; get divorced ◊ divorced

痢疾 lìjí dysentery

立即 lìjí immediate ◊ immediately

理解 lǐjiě understand; perceive ◊ understanding

离开 líkāi leave; quit

利率 lìlǜ interest rate

理论 lǐlùn theory ◊ theoretical

厘米 límǐ centimeter

黎明 límíng daybreak

林 lín forest

临 lín overlook ◊ be about to

铃 líng bell

零 líng zero

另 lìng other ◊ in addition

令 lìng order

灵车 língchē hearse

凌晨 língchén early morning

领带 lǐngdài necktie

领导 lǐngdǎo leader; head ◊ lead

领导人 lǐngdǎorén leader

领海 lǐnghǎi territorial waters

领会 lǐnghuì grasp; comprehend

灵魂 línghún soul; spirit

灵活 línghuó flexible

领结 lǐngjié bow tie

伶俐 línglì nimble

陵墓 língmù mausoleum

零钱 língqián change (coins)

灵巧 língqiǎo deft; quick

令人恶心 lìngrén ěxin disgusting

零食 língshí snacks; candy

领事 lǐngshì consul

领事馆 lǐngshì guǎn consulate

零售 língshòu retail

另外 lìngwài other ◊ in addition; apart from that

零星 língxīng scattered

领袖 lǐngxiù leader

零用钱 língyòng qián allowance

领域 lǐngyù territory; field

林火 línhuǒ forest fire

邻居 línjū neighbor

林区 línqū forestry district

吝啬 lìnsè miserly

吝啬鬼 lìnsèguǐ miser

临时 línshí provisional; temporary; casual

临时工 línshígōng temp

林荫道 línyīndào avenue

淋浴 línyù shower

礼炮 lǐpào salute

礼品 lǐpǐn gift

离奇 líqí strange; uncanny

离奇 líqí strange

沥青 lìqīng asphalt

例如 lìrú for example

利润 lìrùn profit

历史 lìshǐ history

历史性 lìshǐxìng historic; historical

理所当然 lǐsuǒdāngrán naturally; of course

礼堂 lǐtáng (ceremonial) hall; church

立体声装置 lìtǐshēng zhuāngzhì stereo system

流 liú flow; run

硫 liú sulfur

留 liú stay

柳 liǔ willow

六 liù six

流产 liúchǎn miscarriage

流畅 liúchàng smooth; fluent

流传 liúchuán spread

留话 liúhuà leave a message

留念 liúniàn keep as a memento

流逝 liúshì slip away; pass

六十 liùshí sixty

流亡 liúwáng exile

流行 liúxíng fashionable; popular

流行病 liúxíngbìng epidemic

流行歌曲 liúxíng gēqǔ pop song

留学 liúxué study abroad

留言 liúyán leave a message

流言蜚语 liúyán fēiyǔ gossip; scandal

六月 liùyuè June

流走 liúzǒu drain; flow away

例外 lìwài exception

利息 lìxī interest

理性 lǐxìng reason; sense

力学 lìxué mechanics

利益 **lìyì** interest; advantage; benefit

利用 **lìyòng** use, take advantage of

鲤鱼 **lǐyú** carp

理智 **lǐzhì** reason (*faculty*)

荔枝 **lìzhī** lychee

李子 **lǐzi** plum

里子 **lǐzi** lining

例子 **lìzi** example; case

聋 **lóng** deaf ◊ deafness

垄断 **lǒngduàn** monopolize ◊ monopoly

龙卷风 **lóngjuǎn fēng** tornado

龙虾 **lóngxiā** lobster

隆重 **lóngzhòng** festive

笼子 **lóngzi** cage

楼 **lóu** building; floor, story

搂 **lǒu** hug

漏 **lòu** leak

楼层 **lóucéng** floor, story

漏洞 **lòudòng** leak; loophole

楼房 **lóufáng** building

楼梯 **lóutī** stairs

炉 **lú** oven

路 **lù** *measure word for bus routes*

鹿 **lù** deer

路 **lù** road; way; possibility

驴 **lǘ** donkey

铝 **lǚ** aluminum

氯 **lǜ** chlorine

绿 **lǜ** green

率 **lǜ** level; amount; rate (*of pay*)

卵 **luǎn** (human) egg

乱 **luàn** in a mess ◊ chaos

路标 **lùbiāo** landmark; roadsign

铝箔 **lǚbó** aluminum foil

绿茶 **lǜchá** green tea

旅程 **lǚchéng** itinerary

露出 **lùchū** expose, reveal

陆地 **lùdì** land; mainland ◊ terrestrial

旅店 **lǚdiàn** inn

路过 **lùguò** pass by

绿化 **lǜhuà** plant up

鹿角 **lùjiǎo** antlers

旅客 **lǚkè** passenger

履历 **lǚlì** résumé

陆路 **lùlù** track; overland route

轮 **lún** wheel; round (*of drinks*)

轮船 **lúnchuán** ship

论点 **lùndiǎn** thesis

轮换 **lúnhuàn** alternate

论据 **lùnjù** argument (*reasoning*)

轮廓 **lúnkuò** contour,

outline; silhouette

轮流 lúnliú alternate

轮胎 lúntāi tire

论文 lùnwén treatise

轮椅 lúnyǐ wheelchair

锣 luó gong

裸 luǒ naked

落 luò fall; sink; land (of ball etc); set (of sun)

萝卜 luóbo turnip; radish

落后 luòhòu backward; behind, trailing ◊ be behind

逻辑 luójí logic ◊ logical

罗马数字 luómǎ shùzì Roman numerals

螺母 luómǔ nut (for bolt)

络腮胡子 luòsāi húzi full beard

螺丝 luósī screw

螺丝刀 luósīdāo screwdriver

裸体 luǒtǐ naked

裸体像 luǒtǐxiàng nude (painting)

骆驼 luòtuo camel

螺纹 luówén thread (of screw)

螺旋 luóxuán spiral

录取 lùqǔ admit

律师 lùshī attorney

露水 lùshuǐ dew

芦笋 lúsǔn asparagus

露天 lùtiān open-air

芦苇 lúwěi reed

录像 lùxiàng video; video recording

录像带 lùxiàng dài video cassette

录像机 lùxiàngjī video recorder, VCR

履行 lǚxíng fulfill ◊ fulfillment

旅行 lǚxíng travel

旅行社 lǚxíng shè travel agency

旅行支票 lǚxíng zhīpiào traveler's check

陆续 lùxù one after the other

录音 lùyīn recording; record ◊ audio

录音机 lùyīnjī cassette player; cassette recorder; tape recorder

旅游业 lǚyóu yè tourism

旅游者 lǚyóuzhě tourist

旅游指南 lǚyóu zhīnán guidebook

炉子 lúzi stove; furnace

M

妈 mā mom

抹 mā wipe

麻 má hemp

马 mǎ horse

骂 mà curse

马表 mǎbiǎo stopwatch

抹布 mābù cloth; dish cloth

马达 mǎdá motor; engine

麻烦 máfán bother

吗啡 mǎfēi morphine

埋 mái bury

买 mǎi buy

卖 mài sell

脉 mài blood vessel

脉搏 màibó pulse

迈步 màibù stride

埋藏 máicáng bury

卖方 màifāng seller

麦克风 màikèfēng microphone

麦片 màipiàn rolled oats

卖俏 màiqiào flirt

麦乳精 màirǔjīng malted milk

卖艺 màiyì work as a performer

卖淫 màiyín prostitute onself

埋葬 máizàng bury

买主 mǎizhǔ purchaser; customer

麦子 màizi wheat

麻将 májiàng mah-jong

马克思主义 Mǎkèsīzhǔyì Marxism ◊ Marxist

马来西亚 Mǎláixīyà Malaysia ◊ Malaysian

马拉松 mǎlāsōng marathon

马力 mǎlì horsepower

马路 mǎlù street

妈妈 māma mom

马马虎虎 mǎmǎhūhū average

瞒 mán conceal

满 mǎn full

慢 màn slow

满不在乎 mǎn bú zàihu not care at all

盲 máng blind

忙 máng busy ◊ be in a rush

芒果 mángguǒ mango

忙碌 mánglù be busy

盲目 mángmù blind

盲人 mángrén blind person

盲文 mángwén braille

漫画 mànhuà comic

蔓生植物 mànshēng zhíwù climbing plant

馒头 mántou steamed bun

慢性 mànxìng chronic

蔓延 mànyán spread; sprawl (of city); be overrun with ◊ contagious; sprawling

满意 mǎnyì satisfied

满月 mǎnyuè full moon

慢走 mànzǒu goodbye

满足 mǎnzú satisfied ◊ satisfy

猫 māo cat

锚 máo anchor

毛 máo hair; bristles; wool; mao (Chinese money)

矛 máo spear

铆 mǎo rivet

冒 mào give off

毛笔 máobǐ writing brush

毛虫 máochóng caterpillar

冒充 màochōng impersonate

冒号 màohào colon GRAM

毛巾 máojīn towel; washcloth

冒浓烟 mào nóngyān give off smoke

毛皮 máopí coat

茂盛 màoshèng flourishing

毛毯 máotǎn blanket

猫头鹰 māotóuyīng owl

毛线 máoxiàn knitting wool

冒险 màoxiǎn take a risk ◊ risky

冒险家 màoxiǎnjiā adventurer

毛衣 máoyī sweater

贸易 màoyì trade

贸易关系 màoyì guānxi trade relations

毛毡 máozhān felt

麻雀 máquè sparrow

骂人话 màrénhuà swearword

马上 mǎshàng immediately, right now

马蹄 mǎtí hoof

码头 mǎtóu dock; wharf; pier

马尾辫 mǎwěibiàn pigtail

马戏团 mǎxìtuán circus

蚂蚁 mǎyǐ ant

麻油 máyóu sesame oil

马掌 mǎzhǎng horseshoe

麻醉 mázuì anesthetize ◊ anesthesia

麻醉剂 mázuìjì anesthetic; narcotic

煤 méi coal

霉 méi mold

没 méi not ◊ have not

眉 méi eyebrow

每 měi every; each; per

美 měi lovely

妹 mèi younger sister

每次 měicì each time

梅毒 méidú syphilis

每个人 měigèrén everyone

没关系 méi guānxi it
  doesn't matter

玫瑰 méigui rose

美国 Měiguó America,
  USA ◊ American

美国人 Měiguórén
  American

美好 měihǎo wonderful;
  good

美化 měihuà beautify;
  brighten up

美丽 měilì beautiful

魅力 mèilì attraction; charm;
  glamor

眉毛 méimao eyebrow

美貌 měimào looks

妹妹 mèimei younger sister

美妙 měimiào wonderful

煤气 méiqì coal gas

煤气灶 méiqìzào gas stove

美容 měiróng cosmetic

美术片 měishùpiān

animation

每天 měitiān daily ◊ every
  day

每晚 měiwǎn every evening

美味 měiwèi tidbit

美学 měixué esthetics

煤油 méiyóu paraffin;
  kerosene

没有 méiyǒu not have ◊
  without

美元 měiyuán US dollar

每月 měiyuè monthly

闷 mēn stuffy

门 mén door

梦 mèng dream

蒙蔽 méngbì deceive ◊
  deception

蒙古 Měnggǔ Mongolia ◊
  Mongolian

梦见 mèngjiàn dream about

猛烈 měngliè fierce; violent;
  passionate

蒙蒙细雨 méngméng xìyǔ
  drizzle

蒙骗 méngpiàn deceive

梦想 mèngxiǎng dream

门槛 ménkǎn threshold

门牌号 ménpáihào house
  number

门票 ménpiào entrance
  ticket

闷热 **mēnrè** clammy; sultry

门闩 **ménshuān** bolt; latch

闷 **mèn stickig** bored

门诊部 **ménzhěnbù** outpatients

门诊治疗 **ménzhěn zhìliáo** outpatient treatment

门柱 **ménzhù** goalpost

迷 **mí fan**

米 **mǐ** rice; meter

密 **mì** thick; close

蜜 **mì** honey

棉 **mián** cotton

免 **miǎn** avoid; prohibit

面 **miàn** face; side; flour; noodle

面包 **miànbāo** bread

面包店 **miànbāo diàn** bakery

免费 **miǎnfèi** free (no charge)

棉花 **miánhua** cotton

面积 **miànjī** area; proportions

面具 **miànjù** mask

面孔 **miànkǒng** face

勉励 **miǎnlì** encourage

面貌 **miànmào** face; appearance

面前 **miànqián** in front of

勉强 **miǎnqiǎng** reluctant ◊ reluctance ◊ reluctantly

面纱 **miànshā** veil

面食 **miànshí** pasta; pastry

面试 **miànshì** (job) interview

面熟 **miànshú** seem familiar

免税 **miǎnshuì** tax free; dutyfree

面条 **miàntiáo** noodle

面团 **miàntuán** dough

绵羊 **miányáng** sheep

免疫 **miǎnyì** immune ◊ immunity

苗 **miáo** young plant

秒 **miǎo** second

庙 **miào** temple; temple market

妙 **miào** wonderful

描绘 **miáohuì** portray; describe

妙极了 **miàojíle** fantastic

苗圃 **miáopǔ** nursery (for plants)

苗条 **miáotiao** slim

描写 **miáoxiě** describe

瞄准 **miáozhǔn** aim ◊ be aimed at

弥补 **míbǔ** make up for; recoup; rectify ◊ compensation

灭 miè put out

灭火 mièhuǒ put out a fire

灭火器 mièhuǒqì fire extinguisher

灭绝 mièjué wipe out

灭亡 mièwáng go under; be ruined

蜜蜂 mìfēng bee

密封 mìfēng close; seal

猕猴桃 míhóutáo kiwi fruit

迷惑 míhuo mislead; confuse

米酒 mǐjiǔ rice wine

迷路 mílù lose one's way

秘密 mìmì secret ◊ secretly

密谋 mìmóu conspire, plot

民 mín people; folk

名 míng name

明 míng bright; light

命 mìng life

敏感 mǐngǎn sensitive ◊ sensitivity

明白 míngbai understand ◊ clear

名称 míngchēng name; designation

民歌 míngē folk song

明亮 míngliàng bright ◊ brightly ◊ brightness

命令 mìnglìng command

命名 mìngmíng name

明年 míngnián next year

名牌 míngpái well-known brand

名片 míngpiàn card

名人 míngrén prominent figure; celebrity

名声 míngshēng reputation

名胜 míngshèng scenic spot

明天 míngtiān tomorrow

明显 míngxiǎn clear ◊ clearly

明星 míngxīng star (movie etc)

明信片 míngxìnpiàn postcard

名誉 míngyù fame; reputation

命运 mìngyùn fate

名字 míngzi name

民航 mínháng civil aviation

民间 mínjiān civil; folk

敏捷 mǐnjié quick

民意调查 mínyì diàochá poll

民乐 mínyuè folk music

民众 mínzhòng the people

民主 mínzhǔ democracy ◊ democratic

民族 mínzú people; ethnic group; nation; nationality

密切 mìqiè intimate, close

秘书 mìshū secretary ◊ secretarial

迷信 míxìn superstitious

谜语 míyǔ riddle

蜜月 mìyuè honeymoon

摸 mō feel

磨 mó grind

末 mò end

没 mò sink

墨 mò ink

末班车 mòbānchē last bus

漠不关心 mò bù guānxīn indifference ◊ indifferent; nonchalant

摩擦 mócā friction ◊ rub

模范 mófàn example ◊ exemplary

模仿 mófǎng imitate; forge ◊ imitation; forgery

磨坊 mòfáng mill

蘑菇 mógū mushroom

魔鬼 móguǐ devil

模糊 móhu vague; indistinct; fuzzy; misty ◊ blur ◊ mist over

魔力 mólì magic

茉莉 mòli jasmine

莫名其妙 mò míng qí miào mysterious

陌生 mòshēng strange

没收 mòshōu confiscate

摸索 mōsuǒ grope

模特儿 mótèr model (fashion)

摩天大楼 mótiān dàlóu skyscraper

摩托 mótuō motor; engine

摩托车 mótuōchē motorcycle

某 mǒu certain; some

某人 mǒurén someone

谋杀 móushā murder

末尾 mòwěi end

模型 móxíng model; prototype; cast

墨鱼 mòyú cuttlefish

母 mǔ mother ◊ female

木 mù wood

墓 mù grave

目 mù eye

牧 mù tend livestock

暮 mù evening

母爱 mǔ'ài motherly love

墓碑 mùbēi gravestone

目标 mùbiāo target

木柴 mùchái firewood

牧场 mùchǎng pasture

目的 mùdì purpose

木耳 mù'ěr wood-ear mushroom

木筏 mùfá raft

木工 mùgōng carpenter

目光 mùguāng look

母鸡 mǔjī hen

募捐 mùjuān collect
donations

木刻 mùkè wood engraving

目录 mùlù catalog;
directory; list; table of
contents

牧民 mùmín herdsman

母牛 mǔniú cow

木偶 mù'ǒu puppet

目前 mùqián at present

母亲 mǔqīn mother

暮色降临 mùsè jiànglín
get dark

穆斯林 Mùsīlín Muslim

木炭 mùtàn charcoal

母语 mǔyǔ mother tongue

拇指 mǔzhǐ thumb

母猪 mǔzhū sow (pig)

N

拿 ná carry (in hand); hold

哪个 nǎge which; which one

那个 nàge that ◊ that one

奶 nǎi milk

耐久 nàijiǔ durable

耐力 nàilì stamina

奶奶 nǎinai grandma

耐心 nàixīn patience ◊
patiently

耐用 nàiyòng hard-wearing
◊ wear well

奶油 nǎiyóu cream

奶嘴 nǎizuǐ pacifier; nipple

哪里 nǎli where

那里 nàli there

南 nán south ◊ southern;
southerly

难 nán difficult

男 nán man ◊ male

南边 nánbiān south; the
south side

南部 nánbù south

南方 nánfāng south

南风 nánfēng southerly
wind

难过 nánguò sad

男孩 nánhái boy

南极 nánjí South Pole

难堪 nánkān embarrassed

难看 nánkàn ugly

难免 nánmiǎn hard to avoid

男朋友 nánpéngyou
boyfriend

男人 nánrén man, male

难受 **nánshòu** feel ill-at-ease

难为情 **nánwéiqíng** ashamed; embarrassed

男性 **nánxìng** male

南亚 **Nán Yà** South Asia

脑 **nǎo** brain

闹 **nào** noisy

恼怒 **nǎonù** annoyed

闹事 **nàoshì** make a scene; riot

脑髓 **nǎosuǐ** brain

脑震荡 **nǎozhèndàng** concussion

闹钟 **nàozhōng** alarm clock

纳税人 **nàshuìrén** taxpayer

哪些 **nǎxiē** which; which ones

那些 **nàxiē** those

拿走 **názǒu** remove

内 **nèi** inside ◊ inner; internal

内部 **nèibù** inside ◊ internal; inner ◊ internally

内地 **nèidì** interior; inland

内阁 **nèigé** cabinet POL

内疚 **nèijiù** guilt; guilty conscience ◊ guilty

内科医生 **nèikē yīshēng** internist

内容 **nèiróng** content

内衣 **nèiyī** underwear

内政 **nèizhèng** domestic policy; domestic affairs

嫩 **nèn** tender

能干 **nénggàn** capable

能力 **nénglì** ability

能手 **néngshǒu** expert

泥 **ní** mud

你 **nǐ** you (*singular*)

年 **nián** year ◊ annual

念 **niàn** think of; read (out loud); study

年初 **niánchū** start of the year

年底 **niándǐ** end of the year

酿 **niàng** ferment; brew

酿酒厂 **niàngjiǔchǎng** distillery; winery

粘合剂 **niánhéjì** adhesive

粘糊糊 **niánhūhū** sticky

年龄 **niánlíng** age

年青 **niánqīng** young

碾碎 **niǎnsuì** grind

念头 **niàntou** thought, idea

粘土 **niántǔ** clay

粘液 **niányè** mucus

鸟 **niǎo** bird

尿 **niào** urine

鸟笼 **niǎolóng** birdcage

尿片 **niàopiàn** diaper

昵称 **nìchēng** pet name

你的 **nǐde** your ◊ yours

(singular)

拟订 nǐdìng draft

捏造 niēzào invent

尼姑 nígū Buddhist nun

你好 nǐ hǎo hi

霓虹灯管 níhóngdēngguǎn neon strip

你们 nǐmen you (plural)

您 nín you (polite)

拧 níng twist; pinch

拧干 nínggān wring

凝固 nínggù freeze; congeal

宁静 níngjìng peace ◊ peaceful

柠檬 níngméng lemon

柠檬汽水 níngméng qìshuǐ lemonade

凝视 níngshì gaze; peer; gaze at ◊ stare; gaze

宁愿 nìngyuàn would rather

牛 niú cattle; cow

牛犊 niúdú calf

牛奶 niúnǎi (cow's) milk

牛奶加工 niúnǎi jiāgōng dairy

牛肉 niúròu beef

扭伤 niǔshāng sprain

泥瓦工 níwǎgōng bricklayer

脓 nóng pus

弄 nòng do; make; obtain

脓包 nóngbāo pimple

农村 nóngcūn countryside

弄错 nòngcuò be mistaken

浓厚 nónghòu thick; strong

农户 nónghù farm

弄坏 nònghuài break

弄清 nòngqīng make clear

农田 nóngtián field

农业 nóngyè agriculture ◊ agricultural

怒 nù anger; rage

女 nǚ female; feminine

暖 nuǎn warm

暖房 nuǎnfáng hothouse

暖和 nuǎnhuo warm

暖气 nuǎnqì central heating

疟疾 nüèjí malaria

女儿 nǚ'ér daughter

女孩 nǚhái girl

怒号 nùháo howl; roar

怒吼 nùhǒu howl; roar; bellow

女皇 nǚhuáng empress

奴隶 núlì slave

努力 nǔlì attempt; endeavor ◊ laborious ◊ struggle; work hard

懦夫 nuòfū coward

糯米 nuòmǐ glutinous rice

女朋友 nǚpéngyou girlfriend

女人 nǚrén woman; female

女神 nǔshén goddess
女生 nǔshēng female
  student
女士 nǔshì lady ◊ ma'am

◊ Ms
女王 nǔwáng queen
女巫 nǔwū witch
女性 nǔxìng female

O

藕 ǒu lotus root
偶尔 ǒu'ěr occasionally
欧化 ǒuhuà westernize
偶然 ǒurán by chance;

occasionally
呕吐 ǒutù vomit
欧洲 Ōuzhōu Europe ◊
  European

P

爬 pá climb; crawl
耙 pá rake
怕 pà fear
拍 pāi take *photograph*;
  shoot *movie*; clap
牌 pái plate; board; brand;
  card
排 pái line; tier ◊ rank (*in
  order*); discharge
派别 pàibié group; sect
排斥 páichì exclude; push
  away
排除 páichú eliminate; cut
  out; rule out ◊ removal
派出所 pàichūsuǒ police

station
排队 páiduì stand in line
排练 páiliàn rehearse ◊
  rehearsal
拍卖 pāimài auction
排尿 páiniào urinate
排球 páiqiú volleyball
拍摄 pāishè film;
  photograph
拍手 pāishǒu applaud
排水 páishuǐ drainage
排水工程 páishuǐ
  gōngchéng sewerage
排水沟 páishuǐgōu gutter
拍照 pāizhào photograph

拍子 pāizi bat; racket; club; stick

牌子 páizi sign; nameplate; brand

盘 pán dish; plate; set (tennis); measure word for cassettes

盼 pàn hope for; expect

盘点 pándiǎn check; take stock

判断 pànduàn judge; make a judgment; pass judgment on

旁 páng side

胖 pàng fat

旁边 pángbiān side

庞大 pángdà enormous

旁观 pángguān watch

胖乎乎 pànghūhū plump

庞然大物 pángrán dàwù monster

螃蟹 pángxiè crab

胖子 pàngzi fatso

判决 pànjué pass judgment ◊ judgment, verdict

叛逆 pànnì rebel

叛徒 pàntú traitor

盘旋 pánxuán twist; circle

攀缘 pānyuán climb

盘子 pánzi plate

抛 pāo throw

跑 pǎo run; run away

泡 pào bubble

炮 pào gun

炮兵 pàobīng artillery

跑步 pǎobù run; jog

泡茶 pàochá make tea

刨出 páochū dig up

跑道 pǎodào runway; racetrack; lane

抛锚 pāomáo break down

泡沫 pàomò foam; suds; lather

泡沫塑料 pàomò sùliào foam (material)

抛弃 pāoqì abandon; discard

跑腿 pǎotuǐ run errands

爬行 páxíng creep; crawl

耙子 pázi rake

赔 péi pay compensation

陪 péi accompany

配 pèi match, go together

陪伴 péibàn accompany

赔本 péiběn make a loss

赔偿 péicháng compensate ◊ compensation

佩服 pèifú admire

配合 pèihé cooperate

配给 pèijǐ ration

赔礼 péilǐ apologize

配偶 pèi'ǒu spouse

陪同 péitóng escort

accompany

陪同者 **péitóngzhě** escort; companion

培训 **péixùn** train ◊ training

培养 **péiyǎng** raise; develop; cultivate

配音 **pèiyīn** dub *movie*

培植 **péizhí** cultivate *plants*

喷 **pēn** spray

盆 **pén** bowl; plant pot; *measure word for potted plants*

盆地 **péndì** basin GEOG

喷发胶 **pēnfà jiāo** hair spray

碰 **pèng** touch; knock; push; bump into; meet

碰杯 **pèngbēi** clink glasses

碰见 **pèngjiàn** meet

蓬乱 **péngluàn** unkempt; disheveled

碰碰车 **pèngpèngchē** bumper car

碰巧 **pèngqiǎo** by chance

烹调 **pēngtiáo** cook ◊ cookery ◊ culinary

碰头 **pèngtóu** meet

朋友 **péngyǒu** friend

膨胀 **péngzhàng** expand; bulge; inflate ECON ◊ expansion ◊ puffy

喷壶 **pēnhú** watering can

盆景 **pénjǐng** bonsai

喷气式飞机 **pēnqìshì fēijī** jet plane

喷泉 **pēnquán** fountain

喷嚏 **pēntì** sneeze

披 **pī** put on; drape

脾 **pí** spleen

皮 **pí** skin; hide; leather; shell

癖 **pǐ** addiction; obsession

匹 **pǐ** *measure word for horses*

屁 **pì** fart

篇 **piān** piece of writing; *measure word for paper, books etc*

骗 **piàn** cheat

片 **piàn** slice (*of bread etc*); stretch (*of land etc*); *measure word for pills, slices etc*

偏差 **piānchā** deviation

偏见 **piānjiàn** prejudice

骗局 **piànjú** deceipt; deception; fraud

片刻 **piànkè** moment

偏离 **piānlí** deviate; differ

片面 **piànmiàn** biased

偏僻 **piānpì** remote

偏偏 **piānpiān** deliberately; of all people; just

偏袒 **piāntǎn** bias (*in favor*)

◊ biased

偏头痛 piāntóutòng migraine

便宜 piányi cheap

篇章 piānzhāng chapter

骗子 piànzi cheat; fraud; crook

票 piào ticket

飘荡 piāodàng drift; float

漂亮 piàoliang lovely

飘泼大雨 piáopō dàyǔ cloudburst

飘扬 piāoyáng flutter; flap; blow

皮包骨 píbāogǔ skinny

疲惫 píbèi exhausted

皮带 pídài leather belt

皮蛋 pídàn preserved egg

匹敌 pídí equal; evenly matched

撇号 piēhào apostrophe

瞥见 piējiàn glimpse

批发 pīfā wholesale

皮肤 pífū skin

皮革 pígé leather

皮革制品 pígé zhìpǐn leather goods

屁股 pìgu butt

癖好 pīhào mania; passion

啤酒 píjiǔ beer

啤酒厂 píjiǔchǎng brewery

啤酒花 píjiǔhuā hops

疲倦 píjuàn tire ◊ fatigue ◊ tired; run-down

劈开 pīkāi split

疲劳 píláo exhausted

皮毛 pímáo fur; skin; fleece

品尝 pǐncháng taste; sample

频繁 pínfán frequently

瓶 píng bottle; jar; *measure word for bottles, jars etc*

平 píng even

平安到达 píng'ān dàodá arrive safe and sound

平常 píngcháng usually; normally ◊ common; conventional

平等 píngděng equal ◊ equality

平凡 píngfán usual; normal

平方 píngfāng square MATH

苹果 píngguǒ apple

平局 píngjú tie; deuce (*in tennis*)

凭据 píngjù evidence

平均 píngjūn average

凭空 píngkōng unfounded

评论 pínglùn review; commentary ◊ review; remark

平民 píngmín civilian

屏幕 píngmù screen

乒乓球 **pīngpāngqiú** table tennis

平时 **píngshí** ordinarily; usually

平坦 **píngtǎn** flat

平息 **píngxī** appease; calm down

平行 **píngxíng** parallel

评语 **píngyǔ** comment; assessment

平原 **píngyuán** plain

瓶子 **píngzi** bottle

贫瘠 **pínjí** barren

贫困 **pínkùn** poor ◊ poverty

频率 **pínlǜ** frequency

拼盘 **pīnpán** cold platter

贫穷 **pínqióng** poor

品位 **pǐnwèi** taste

品行 **pǐnxíng** behavior

贫血 **pínxuè** anemia ◊ anemic

拼音 **pīnyīn** pinyin

品种 **pǐnzhǒng** breed

批评 **pīpíng** criticism ◊ criticize

脾气 **píqi** temperament; temper

皮鞋 **píxié** leather shoes

皮衣 **píyī** leather garment

批准 **pīzhǔn** approve ◊ approval

坡 **pō** slope

破 **pò** break ◊ broken

破产 **pòchǎn** go bankrupt ◊ bankruptcy

破坏 **pòhuài** destroy

破裂 **pòliè** burst

婆婆 **pópo** mother-in-law

迫切 **pòqiè** pressing

破伤风 **pòshāngfēng** tetanus

迫使 **pòshǐ** force

破碎 **pòsuì** break ◊ broken

剖腹产 **pōufùchǎn** Cesarean

剖面 **pōumiàn** profile; section

破晓 **pòxiǎo** dawn

铺 **pū** spread; unfold ; pave

普遍 **pǔbiàn** general; universal

瀑布 **pùbù** waterfall

铺床 **pūchuáng** make the bed

扑粉 **pūfěn** powder

曝光 **pùguāng** expose ◊ exposure

普及 **pǔjí** generalize; popularize ◊ widespread; universal

扑克 **pūkè** poker; playing cards

谱曲 pǔqǔ compose

菩萨 Púsà Bodhisattva;
  Buddha

铺设 pūshè pave; lay

朴素 pǔsù simple

葡萄 pútáo grape; vine

葡萄干 pútáo gān raisin

葡萄酒 pútaojiǔ wine

葡萄糖 pútaotáng glucose

普通 pǔtōng ordinary

普通话 Pǔtōnghuà
  Mandarin Chinese

Q

漆 qī paint

七 qī seven

期 qī period

妻 qī wife

鳍 qí fin

旗 qí flag

骑 qí ride; pedal

其 qí his; her; its

起 qǐ get up

汽 qì vapor; steam

器 qì utensil; device

气 qì air; gas

迄 qì until; by

恰当 qiàdàng appropriate

千 qiān thousand

铅 qiān lead (metal)

牵 qiān pull

签 qiān sign

前 qián before; in front of
  ◊ former

钱 qián money

潜 qián dive; submerge ◊
  hidden

浅 qiǎn shallow

欠 qiàn owe ◊ owed

钱包 qiánbāo billfold; purse

前辈 qiánbèi senior; elder

前臂 qiánbì forearm

浅薄 qiǎnbó shallow

虔诚 qiánchéng devout;
  ardent; pious

签订 qiāndìng sign;
  conclude contract

前额 qián'é forehead; brow

签发 qiānfā issue

潜伏 qiánfú latent; potential

枪 qiāng gun

强 qiáng strong

墙 qiáng wall

抢 qiǎng snatch

墙报 qiángbào wall news-
  sheet

枪毙 qiāngbì shoot

墙壁 qiángbì wall

强大 qiángdà powerful

强盗 qiángdào robber;
bandit

强调 qiángdiào emphasize

强奸 qiángjiān rape

抢劫 qiǎngjié rob; hold up ◊
robbery; holdup; raid

抢救 qiǎngjiù rescue;
recover; save

踉跄 qiàngliàng stumble

钳工 qiángōng fitter

强迫 qiǎngpò force;
compel

牵挂 qiānguà worry about

墙纸 qiángzhǐ wallpaper

强壮 qiángzhuàng strong;
sound; hardy

前景 qiánjǐng view;
prospects

迁就 qiānjiù accommodate

迁居 qiānjū move house

千克 qiānkè kilogram

牵连 qiānlián involve

千米 qiānmǐ kilometer

前面 qiánmian front ◊ in
front; ahead

签名 qiānmíng sign ◊
signature

前任 qiánrèn predecessor

潜入 qiánrù submerge

歉收 qiànshōu crop failure

签署 qiānshǔ sign

潜水 qiánshuǐ dive ◊ diving

潜水艇 qiánshuǐtǐng
submarine

潜水员 qiánshuǐyuán diver

前提 qiántí prerequisite;
condition

前天 qiántiān the day before
yesterday

前途 qiántú future;
prospects

欠妥 qiàntuǒ inappropriate

前夕 qiánxī eve

前行 qiánxíng proceed

谦虚 qiānxū modest

前言 qiányán foreword;
preface

迁移 qiānyí move; migrate;
transfer

潜意识 qiányìshí
subconscious

欠债 qiànzhài be in debt

签证 qiānzhèng visa

钳子 qiánzi forceps; pliers;
tongs

前奏 qiánzòu overture;
prelude

敲 qiāo knock

桥 qiáo bridge

瞧 qiáo look

巧 qiǎo skillful; coincidental

瞧不起 qiáobuqǐ look
  down on

侨居 qiáojū live abroad

巧克力 qiǎokèlì chocolate

巧妙 qiǎomiào clever; subtle

敲诈 qiāozhà blackmail

恰如其分 qià rú qí fèn
  applicable; accurate

洽商 qiàshāng negotiate

洽谈 qiàtán discuss;
  negotiate

器材 qìcái equipment

汽车 qìchē automobile

启程 qìchéng leave

气冲冲 qìchōngchōng
  furious

起初 qǐchū at first

气喘 qìchuǎn gasp ◊ asthma

起床 qǐchuáng get up

期待 qīdài expect

祈祷 qídǎo pray; wish for

起点 qǐdiǎn starting point

企鹅 qǐ'é penguin

切 qiē cut; carve meat

窃 qiè steal

怯场 qièchǎng stage fright

切除 qièchú remove; cut out

切断 qiēduàn cut off

切合实际 qièhé shíjì
  realistic

窃听 qiètīng eavesdrop

窃听器 qiètīngqì bug

茄子 qiézi eggplant

起飞 qǐfēi take off ◊ takeoff

气氛 qìfēn atmosphere; tone

气愤 qìfèn outraged

乞丐 qǐgài beggar

汽缸 qìgāng cylinder
  (engine)

漆革 qīgé patent leather

气功 qìgōng qigong
  (Chinese system of breath
  control)

奇怪 qíguài odd ◊ oddly

器官 qìguān organ

启航 qǐháng sail

漆黑 qīhēi pitch black

起哄 qǐhòng jeer

气候 qìhòu climate

奇迹 qíjī miracle ◊
  miraculously

迄今 qìjīn yet, so far

期刊 qīkān periodical;
  magazine

起立 qǐlì stand, rise

起码 qǐmǎ at least

起锚 qǐmáo weigh anchor

奇妙 qímiào wonderful

器皿 qìmǐn vessel; container

亲 qīn kiss ◊ intimate ◊

relatives

侵 qīn invade

禽 qīn bird

亲爱 qīn'ài dear; darling

芹菜 qíncài celery

侵犯 qīnfàn encroach; breach; violate

勤奋 qínfèn hard-working; industrious

氢 qīng hydrogen

轻 qīng light ◊ lightness

清 qīng clear; pure

情 qíng feeling

晴 qíng sunny; clear

请 qǐng please ◊ ask

庆 qìng celebrate

清白 qīngbái pure; clear; flawless

情报 qíngbào intelligence; information; news

轻便 qīngbiàn handy

清偿 qīngcháng settle; pay off

清晨 qīngchén early morning

清楚 qīngchu clear ◊ clearly

青春 qīngchūn youth

清淡 qīngdàn weak; plain

倾倒 qīngdǎo tip over; overturn

轻浮 qīngfú flighty

情妇 qíngfù mistress (lover)

请假 qǐngjià ask for leave

请教 qǐngjiào ask for advice

清洁 qīngjié cleanse ◊ clean

情节 qíngjié plot

请客 qǐngkè invite guests; pick up the tab

情况 qíngkuàng situation; scenario

晴朗 qínglǎng sunny; clear

清凉 qīngliáng refreshing

情侣 qínglǚ couple

青年 qīngnián youth

青年旅社 qīngnián lǚshè youth hostel

青年人 qīngniánrén young people; young person

轻拍 qīngpāi pat

情人 qíngrén lover

青少年 qīngshàonián teenager ◊ teenage

轻视 qīngshì despise; scorn; put down

轻率 qīngshuài impetuous; indiscreet ◊ indiscretion

轻松 qīngsōng relaxed

青苔 qīngtái moss

请帖 qǐngtiě invitation

倾听 qīngtīng listen

蜻蜓 qīngtíng dragonfly

青铜 qīngtóng bronze

青蛙 qīngwā frog

请问 qǐngwèn excuse me; may I ask

请勿吸烟 qǐng wù xīyān no smoking

清洗 qīngxǐ rinse; flush

倾向于 qīngxiàng yú incline toward; tend toward

倾斜 qīngxié slope; tilt; lurch; dip ◊ slanting

轻信 qīngxìn credulous

情绪 qíngxù mood; spirits ◊ sentimental

轻音乐 qīngyīnyuè light music

晴雨表 qíngyǔ biǎo barometer

清真寺 qīngzhēnsì mosque

庆祝 qìngzhù celebrate

庆祝活动 qìngzhù huódòng celebration

勤快 qínkuai hardworking

勤劳 qínláo hardworking

侵略 qīnlüè invade ◊ invasion

亲密 qīnmì close; intimate ◊ intimacy

亲戚 qīnqi relatives

亲切 qīnqiè kind; familiar; genial

侵入 qīnrù intrude

亲手 qīnshǒu in person; with one's own hands

亲属关系 qīnshǔ guānxi relations ◊ related

侵吞 qīntūn embezzle

亲吻 qīnwěn kiss

亲自 qīnzì in person; personally

穷 qióng poor

穷人 qióngrén the poor; poor person

旗袍 qípáo cheongsam

欺骗 qīpiàn deceit; deception ◊ deceive; trick

气球 qìqiú balloon

齐全 qíquán complete

七十 qīshí seventy

汽水 qìshuǐ carbonated mineral water; soda

起水疱 qǐ shuǐpào blister

起诉 qǐsù sue; prosecute

其他 qítā other

乞讨 qǐtǎo beg

奇特 qítè original; unique; strange

气体 qìtǐ gas

汽艇 qìtǐng motor boat

企图 qìtú try

秋 qiū fall

球 qiú ball

求 qiú implore

球队 **qiúduì** team

囚犯 **qiúfàn** prisoner

求婚 **qiúhūn** propose ◊ proposal

求救 **qiújiù** call for help

丘陵 **qiūlíng** hill

秋千 **qiūqiān** swing

秋天 **qiūtiān** fall

蚯蚓 **qiūyǐn** earthworm

气味 **qìwèi** smell

气温 **qìwēn** temperature

期限 **qīxiàn** deadline; time limit

气象 **qìxiàng** weather

气象学 **qìxiàngxué** meteorology ◊ meteorological

气压 **qìyā** air pressure

企业 **qǐyè** enterprise

企业家 **qǐyèjiā** entrepreneur

起义 **qǐyì** uprising

汽油 **qìyóu** gas

其余 **qíyú** the rest

起源 **qǐyuán** origin

七月 **qīyuè** July

其中 **qízhōng** among; among which; of which

起重机 **qǐzhòngjī** crane; hoist

妻子 **qīzi** wife

旗子 **qízi** flag

骑自行车 **qí zìxíngchē** cycle ◊ cycling

区 **qū** district; zone

蛆 **qū** maggot

取 **qǔ** take; fetch; get

曲 **qǔ** tune; song; music

去 **qù** go

圈 **quān** circle

拳 **quán** fist ◊ punch

泉 **quán** spring; stream

权 **quán** right; power; authority

全 **quán** whole

犬 **quǎn** dog

劝 **quàn** persuade

全部 **quánbù** all; entire

劝导 **quàndǎo** teach; advise; instruct

劝告 **quàngào** advise

权衡 **quánhéng** weigh up

拳击 **quánjī** box ◊ boxing; fight

拳击比赛 **quánjī bǐsài** boxing match

权力 **quánlì** power; authority

权利 **quánlì** right

全面 **quánmiàn** comprehensive

全球 **quánqiú** global

全权 **quánquán** power of

attorney; full powers

泉水 quánshuǐ spring water

劝说 quànshuō persuade

蜷缩 quánsuō writhe;
double up

圈套 quāntào trap; noose

全体 quántǐ all; whole ◊
totality

拳头 quántou fist

权威 quánwēi authority

痊愈 quányù recuperate;
convalesce

劝阻 quànzǔ advise against

区别 qūbié distinguish ◊
distinction

驱除 qūchú remove; drive
out

渠道 qúdào drain

取得 qǔdé gain; achieve

曲调 qǔdiào tune

去掉 qùdiào remove; get
rid of

驱动器 qūdòngqì disk drive

缺 quē lack; miss

瘸 qué lame

雀 què sparrow

雀斑 quèbān freckle

缺点 quēdiǎn disadvantage;
weakness

确定 quèdìng confirm

◊ final

缺乏 quēfá shortage ◊ lack;
be lacking

确切 quèqiè exact

确认 quèrèn confirm

确实 quèshí in fact

缺席 quēxí absent ◊ absence

缺陷 quēxiàn defect;
downside

确信 quèxìn be convinced

瘸子 quézi cripple

驱赶 qūgǎn chase away;
dispel

取决于 qǔjuéyú depend on

群 qún group; crowd; flock;
cluster; *measure word for
crowds*

去年 qùnián last year

取暖 qǔnuǎn warm up

群众 qúnzhòng the masses

裙子 qúnzi skirt

趋势 qūshì tendency, trend

去世 qùshì die ◊ demise

躯体 qūtǐ body

曲线 qūxiàn curve

取消 qǔxiāo cancel

区域 qūyù area

取之不尽 qǔ zhī bú jìn
inexhaustible

驱逐 qūzhú expel; deport

R

燃 rán burn; ignite

染 rǎn color; dye

然而 rán'ér but

染发 rǎnfà dye one's hair

让 ràng let; give way

让步 ràngbù give way ◊ concession

让路 rànglù give way

然后 ránhòu then; next; afterwards

燃料 ránliào fuel

燃烧 ránshāo burn

绕道 ràodào go round; detour

热 rè hot; warm ◊ heat ◊ warm up

热爱 rè'ài love passionately

热带 rèdài tropics

热浪 rèlàng heatwave

热烈 rèliè enthusiastic; heated *discussion*; wild *applause*

人 rén person; people; man

忍 rěn endure

认 rèn recognize

热闹 rènao exciting; lively ◊ hustle and bustle

人道 réndào humane ◊ humanity

扔 rēng throw; throw away; drop; dump

仍 réng still

人格 réngé personality

仍然 réngrán still

任何 rènhé any

认可 rènkě acknowledgment

人口 rénkǒu population

人类 rénlèi human race ◊ human

人力 rénlì labor; manpower

人们 rénmen people

人民 rénmín the people

任命 rènmìng appointment ◊ appoint

人民解放军 rénmín jiěfàngjūn People's Liberation Army

忍耐 rěnnài endure

人权 rénquán human rights

人参 rénshēn ginseng

认生 rènshēng be scared of strangers

认识 rènshi know; get to know

人事部 **rénshìbù** personnel
(department)

人世间 **rénshìjiān** the world
◊ earthly

忍受 **rěnshòu** put up with;
endure

认为 **rènwéi** consider;
reckon; figure

任务 **rènwù** assignment; job

人性 **rénxìng** human ◊
humanity

任性 **rènxìng** headstrong

人行道 **rénxíngdào**
sidewalk

人行横道 **rénxíng héngdào**
(pedestrian) crosswalk

任意 **rènyì** arbitrary

人员 **rényuán** personnel

人造 **rénzào** synthetic

人造卫星 **rénzào wèixīng**
satellite

认真 **rènzhēn** serious;
earnest; conscientious

人质 **rénzhì** hostage

热情 **rèqíng** warm;
enthusiastic

热水袋 **rèshuǐdài** hot-water
bottle

热水瓶 **rèshuǐpíng** vacuum
flask

热心 **rèxīn** enthusiastic;
warm-hearted

热衷于 **rèzhōng yú** be wild
about

日 **rì** sun; day

日报 **rìbào** daily paper

日本 **Rìběn** Japan ◊
Japanese

日本人 **Rìběnrén** Japanese

日常 **rìcháng** everyday; daily

日出 **rìchū** sunrise

日光灯 **rìguāngdēng**
fluorescent light

日记 **rìjì** diary

日历 **rìlì** calendar

日落 **rìluò** sunset

日期 **rìqī** date

绒 **róng** down

荣 **róng** honor

熔化 **rónghuà** smelt

融化 **rónghuà** thaw

容积 **róngjī** volume

溶解 **róngjiě** dissolve

容量 **róngliàng** volume;
capacity

绒毛 **róngmáo** down

容纳 **róngnà** hold

容器 **róngqì** container

融洽 **róngqià** peaceable

容忍 **róngrěn** tolerate;
stand for

容许 róngxǔ allow

溶液 róngyè solution

荣誉 róngyù glory; honor

揉 róu rub

肉 ròu meat

柔道 róudào judo

肉店 ròudiàn butcher shop

柔和 róuhé soft; mild; mellow

肉末 ròumò ground meat

柔软 róuruǎn soft; supple

肉体 ròutǐ flesh

肉汁 ròuzhī gravy

如 rú like; similar to

乳 rǔ breast; milk

入 rù enter

乳癌 rǔ'ái breast cancer

软 ruǎn soft; tender ◊ tenderness

软骨 ruǎngǔ gristle

软件 ruǎnjiàn software

软木塞 ruǎnmùsāi cork (stopper)

软盘 ruǎnpán floppy disk

软卧 ruǎnwò soft sleeper (on train)

如此 rúcǐ thus; in this way

蠕动 rúdòng squirm

锐不可当 ruì bù kě dāng inexorable; irresistible

如今 rújīn nowadays; at present

入境 rùjìng enter country

入口 rùkǒu access; entry; way in; entrance

入迷 rùmí be fascinated

润肤膏 rùnfūgāo moisturizer

润滑 rùnhuá lubricate ◊ lubrication

闰年 rùnnián leap year

弱 ruò weak

弱点 ruòdiǎn weakness

若干 ruògān some; a certain number

入神 rùshén be engrossed

乳霜 rǔshuāng cream

入睡 rùshuì fall asleep

如同 rútóng just like

乳牙 rǔyá milk tooth

如愿 rúyuàn as planned; as hoped

乳制品 rǔzhì pǐn dairy products

S

撒 sǎ scatter

洒 sǎ sprinkle

撒谎 sāhuǎng lie

塞 sāi stick in; stuff; plug

赛 sài competition

赛马 sàimǎ horse race

赛跑 sàipǎo race (on foot)

塞子 sāizi plug

三 sān three

伞 sǎn umbrella

散步 sànbù stroll ◊ take a stroll

散布 sànbù spread

散步者 sànbùzhě stroller (person)

三等仓 sānděngcāng third-class cabin

散发 sànfā distribute

丧礼 sānglǐ funeral service

丧命 sàngmìng die

桑拿浴 sāngnáyù sauna

丧失 sàngshī loss ◊ lose

桑树 sāngshù mulberry tree

嗓子 sǎngzi throat

三角形 sānjiǎo xíng triangle ◊ triangular

三十 sānshí thirty

散文 sānwén prose

三心二意 sānxīn-èryì indecisive; half-hearted

三月 sānyuè March

搔 sāo scratch

扫 sǎo sweep; drag

骚乱 sāoluàn commotion; turmoil

扫兴 sǎoxìng be disappointed

搔痒 sāoyǎng scratch

扫帚 sàozhou broom

撒种 sǎzhǒng sow

色 sè color

色彩 sècǎi color

色盲 sèmáng color-blind

森林 sēnlín forest

色情 sèqíng pornographic; erotic

沙 shā sand

纱 shā thread

杀 shā kill

傻 shǎ dumb

纱布 shābù gauze

刹车 shāchē brake ◊ brakes

沙发 shāfā sofa

傻瓜 shǎguā idiot

杀害 **shāhài** kill

筛 **shāi** sift

晒 **shài** expose to the sun

晒太阳 **shài tàiyáng** sunbathe; bask

筛子 **shāizi** sieve

色子 **shǎizi** dice

沙龙 **shālóng** salon

沙漠 **shāmò** desert

山 **shān** mountain; mount

扇 **shàn** fan; *measure word for doors and windows*

善 **shàn** kind-hearted

擅长 **shàncháng** excel at

闪电 **shǎndiàn** lightning

煽动 **shāndòng** incite; rouse

山峰 **shānfēng** peak

商 **shāng** commercial

伤 **shāng** injure ◊ injury

上 **shàng** on ◊ at the top; up ◊ get on

上岸 **shàng'àn** go ashore

伤疤 **shāngbā** scar

上班 **shàngbān** go to work; be at work

上臂 **shàngbì** upper arm

商标 **shāngbiāo** brand name; trademark

上部 **shàngbù** top part

商场 **shāngchǎng** department store; bazaar

上床 **shàngchuáng** go to bed

上等货 **shàngděnghuò** top-quality goods

上帝 **shàngdì** God

商店 **shāngdiàn** store

上吊 **shàngdiào** hang oneself

商定 **shāngdìng** agree; arrange

伤风 **shāngfēng** catch a cold

伤害 **shānghài** hurt

伤寒 **shānghán** typhoid (fever)

商会 **shānghuì** chamber of commerce

伤口 **shāngkǒu** wound; injury

商量 **shāngliang** discuss

上面 **shàngmian** top ◊ at the top; up ◊ upper

商品 **shāngpǐn** commodity; goods

商人 **shāngrén** businessman

上色 **shàngshǎi** tint

上身 **shàngshēn** upper body

上升 **shàngshēng** rise; climb

赏识 **shǎngshí** have great respect for

上述 shàngshù above-mentioned

上司 shàngsi boss

上诉 shàngsù appeal

商讨 shāngtǎo discuss

山谷 shāngǔ valley

闪光灯 shǎnguāngdēng flash; flashlight

上午 shàngwǔ morning ◊ in the morning

伤心 shāngxīn heart-broken

上学 shàngxué go to school

上演 shàngyǎn perform

商业 shāngyè business; commerce ◊ commercial

上瘾 shàngyǐn be addicted to

伤员 shāngyuán casualty

善良 shànliáng generous; kind

山脉 shānmài mountain range

山坡 shānpō hill

山区 shānqū mountainous area

闪烁 shǎnshuò flash; glint; blink; gleam

山羊 shānyáng goat

赡养 shànyǎng support

闪耀 shǎnyào sparkle; twinkle; glare

善意 shànyì goodwill

善于 shànyú be good at

扇子 shànzi fan (handheld)

擅自 shànzì unauthorized

烧 shāo burn

少 shǎo few

少 shào young

少不得 shǎobude essential

烧毁 shāohuǐ burn down

烧开 shāokāi boil

少量 shǎoliàng small amount

少年 shàonián young person (in early teens)

烧伤 shāoshāng burn

少数 shǎoshù few; minority

少数民族 shǎoshù mínzú ethnic minority

稍微 shāowēi slightly

少许 shǎoxǔ a little

哨子 shàozi whistle

沙丘 shāqiū dune

杀人犯 shārénfàn murderer

沙滩 shātān sandy beach

鲨鱼 shāyú shark

砂质土壤 shāzhì tǔrǎng sandy soil

蛇 shé snake

舌 shé tongue

设备 shèbèi equipment

奢侈 shēchǐ extravagant

社会 **shèhuì** society ◊ social

社会学 **shèhuì xué** sociology

社会主义 **shèhuì zhǔyì** socialism ◊ socialist

谁 **shéi** who; whoever

射击 **shèjī** shoot

涉及 **shèjí** involve; concern ◊ reference

设计 **shèjì** plan

设立 **shèlì** set up

社论 **shèlùn** editorial

赦免 **shèmiǎn** pardon; amnesty ◊ absolve

深 **shēn** deep ◊ dearly (love)

身 **shēn** body

伸 **shēn** stretch

神 **shén** god; deity ◊ divine; spiritual

肾 **shèn** kidney

渗 **shèn** seep; leak

申辩 **shēnbiàn** defend oneself

身材 **shēncái** build; figure

审查 **shēnchá** check; examine

深度 **shēndù** depth

身分 **shēnfen** identity; status

生 **shēng** give birth to; grow; live ◊ raw; unripe

升 **shēng** rise; hoist ◊ liter

声 **shēng** sound

绳 **shéng** cord; rope

省 **shěng** province ◊ provincial

剩 **shèng** remain

身高 **shēngāo** height

生病 **shēngbìng** fall ill ◊ sick

生产 **shēngchǎn** produce ◊ production

生产线 **shēngchǎnxiàn** production line

生产者 **shēngchǎnzhě** manufacturer

声称 **shēngchēng** claim; profess

牲畜 **shēngchu** livestock

生存 **shēngcún** exist; live

圣诞节 **Shèngdàn Jié** Christmas; Christmas Day

圣诞老人 **Shèngdàn Lǎorén** Santa Claus

圣诞树 **shèngdàn shù** Christmas tree

生动 **shēngdòng** vivid

省会 **shěnghuì** provincial capital

生活 **shēnghuó** life

生活水平 **shēnghuó shuǐpíng** standard of living

牲口 **shēngkou** livestock

胜利 **shènglì** victory ◊ victorious

省略 **shěnglüè** leave out

声明 **shēngmíng** declaration; statement ◊ declare; state

生命 **shēngmìng** life

生气 **shēngqì** angry ◊ get angry ◊ anger

圣人 **shèngrén** saint; sage

生日 **shēngrì** birthday

声望 **shēngwàng** popularity; reputation; standing

生物学 **shēngwù xué** biology

剩下 **shèngxia** remain

盛夏 **shèngxià** height of summer

声响 **shēngxiǎng** sound

生肖 **shēngxiào** the twelve animals of the Chinese horoscope

盛行 **shèngxíng** prevailing

生涯 **shēngyá** career

生锈 **shēngxiù** get rusty

生意 **shēngyi** business

声音 **shēngyīn** sound; noise; voice

生育 **shēngyù** bear *child*

声誉 **shēngyù** reputation; fame

剩余 **shèngyú** rest

生长 **shēngzhǎng** grow

升值 **shēngzhí** revalue

生殖器 **shēngzhíqì** genitals

绳子 **shéngzi** cord

深厚 **shēnhòu** deep

神话 **shénhuà** myth

肾结石 **shènjiéshí** kidney stone

神经 **shénjīng** nerve ◊ screwed up

神经崩溃 **shénjīng bēngkuì** nervous breakdown

神经过敏 **shénjīng guòmǐn** neurotic

伸懒腰 **shēn lǎnyāo** stretch

渗漏 **shènlòu** leak; drip

什么 **shénme** what ◊ anything

神秘 **shénmì** mysterious

申明 **shēnmíng** declare

审判 **shěnpàn** trial ◊ try

神奇 **shénqí** supernatural

申请 **shēnqǐng** apply for ◊ application

神圣 **shénshèng** holy; sacred ◊ sanctity

申诉 **shēnsù** lodge complaint ◊ objection

审问 **shěnwèn** question

审讯 **shěnxùn** examine; hear

深夜 **shēnyè** in the dead of night

呻吟 **shēnyín** groan; moan

深渊 **shēnyuān** abyss

深远 **shēnyuǎn** far-reaching

深造 **shēnzào** continue one's education

伸展 **shēnzhǎn** stretch; extend; spread

伸展四肢 **shēnzhǎn sìzhī** stretch

甚至 **shènzhì** even

慎重 **shènzhòng** careful

舍弃 **shěqì** abandon

设施 **shèshī** facilities

摄氏 **shèshì** Celsius; centigrade

射手 **shèshǒu** marksman

舌头 **shétou** tongue

摄像机 **shèxiàngjī** video camera; camcorder

摄影 **shèyǐng** photography

诗 **shī** poem; verse; poetry

湿 **shī** wet; damp

狮 **shī** lion

师 **shī** master

失 **shī** lose

十 **shí** ten

实 **shí** real; solid

石 **shí** stone

时 **shí** time; hour

食 **shí** food ◊ eat

识 **shí** know; recognize

史 **shǐ** history

始 **shǐ** begin

使 **shǐ** send; make

事 **shì** matter

是 **shì** yes

室 **shì** room

市 **shì** city; market

试 **shì** try

示 **shì** show; indicate

失败 **shībài** fail; lose ◊ failure; defeat

事变 **shìbiàn** incident

识别 **shíbié** recognize; distinguish

时差 **shíchā** time difference

视察 **shìchá** inspect ◊ inspection

时常 **shícháng** often

市场 **shìchǎng** market

试车 **shìchē** test drive

使吃亏 **shǐ chīkuī** put at a disadvantage

时代 **shídài** age; generation

适当 **shìdàng** suitable

食道 **shídào** gullet

是的 **shìde** yes; that's right

湿度 **shīdù** humidity

适度 **shìdù** mildly; moderately; in moderation

十二 **shí'èr** twelve

十二月 **shí'èryuè** December

释放 **shìfàng** release

施肥 **shīféi** fertilize

是否 **shìfǒu** whether or not

师傅 **shīfu** master

石膏 **shígāo** plaster

尸骨 **shīgǔ** skeleton

事故 **shìgù** accident; crash

使馆 **shǐguǎn** embassy

嗜好 **shìhào** hobby; addiction

适合 **shìhé** suit; fit; be in accordance with

事后 **shìhòu** subsequent ◊ subsequently

石灰 **shíhuī** lime

实际 **shíjì** real; practical; substantive

世纪 **shìjì** century

时间 **shíjiān** time

实践 **shíjiàn** practice

事件 **shìjiàn** event; incident; business

市郊 **shìjiāo** suburbs

世界 **shìjiè** world

世界地图 **shìjiè dìtú** map of the world

世界观 **shìjièguān** world view

世界冠军 **shìjiè guànjūn** world champion

世界记录 **shìjiè jìlù** world record

世界著名 **shìjiè zhùmíng** world-famous

什锦 **shíjǐn** mixed; miscellaneous

诗句 **shījù** verse

时刻 **shíkè** moment ◊ constantly

时刻表 **shíkèbiǎo** schedule

石窟 **shíkū** grotto

实况转播 **shíkuàng zhuānbō** live transmission

湿冷 **shīlěng** cold and damp

势力 **shìlì** strength, power

视力 **shìlì** sight

失恋 **shīliàn** be jilted

失灵 **shīlíng** out of order; out of action

石榴 **shíliu** pomegranate

时髦 **shímáo** fashionable

失眠 **shīmián** insomnia

市民 **shìmín** city dweller

失明 **shīmíng** go blind

使命 **shǐmìng** mission; vocation

室内 **shìnèi** indoors; inside

食品 **shípǐn** food

识破 **shípò** see through

食谱 **shípǔ** recipe; cookbook

时期 **shíqī** term; period

拾起 **shíqǐ** pick up

事情 **shìqing** issue; matter

失去 **shīqù** lose

拾取 **shíqǔ** pick up

市区 **shìqū** city area

诗人 **shīrén** poet

施舍 **shīshě** give alms

失事 **shīshì** have an accident

时事 **shíshì** current events

事实 **shìshí** fact; truth

逝世 **shìshì** pass away

失算 **shīsuàn** miscalculate

食堂 **shítáng** cafeteria; canteen

尸体 **shītǐ** corpse

湿透 **shītòu** soaked

石头 **shítou** stone

室外 **shìwài** outdoors; outside ◊ outdoor

失望 **shīwàng** disappointment ◊ disappointed

视网膜 **shìwǎngmó** retina

示威游行 **shìwēi yóuxíng** demonstration

失误 **shīwù** mistake

食物 **shíwù** food; diet

事物 **shìwù** thing

实习 **shíxí** work as an intern ◊ internship

世袭 **shìxí** hereditary; inherited

实现 **shíxiàn** fulfill; realize; come true ◊ realization

事先 **shìxiān** beforehand ◊ prior

失信 **shīxìn** break one's promise

时新 **shíxīn** stylish

实行 **shíxíng** carry out

失修 **shīxiū** run-down

实验 **shíyàn** experiment

誓言 **shìyán** oath; vow

试验 **shìyàn** test; experiment; trial

试样 **shìyàng** sample

式样 **shìyàng** style; type

失业 **shīyè** unemployed ◊ unemployment

诗意 **shīyì** poetic

十一 **shíyī** eleven

十亿 **shíyì** billion

适宜 **shìyí** suitable

示意 **shìyì** give a sign

石英 **shíyīng** quartz

适应 **shìyìng** adapt; acclimatize; readjust

石英钟 **shíyīngzhōng** quartz clock

十一月 **shíyīyuè** November

实用 **shíyòng** practical;
useful

使用 **shǐyòng** access; use

适用 **shìyòng** applicable
◊ apply

使用说明书 **shǐyòng
shuōmíngshū** instructions
for use

食油 **shíyóu** cooking oil

食欲 **shíyù** appetite

十月 **shíyuè** October

施展 **shīzhǎn** display; put to
good use

市长 **shìzhǎng** mayor

湿疹 **shīzhěn** eczema

食指 **shízhǐ** forefinger

实质 **shízhì** essence

始终 **shǐzhōng** from start
to finish

始终不渝 **shǐzhōng bù yú**
consistent ◊ consistently

时装表演 **shízhuāng
biǎoyǎn** fashion show

虱子 **shīzi** louse

狮子 **shīzi** lion

师资 **shīzī** teachers

柿子 **shìzi** persimmon

十字架 **shízìjià** cross

十字路口 **shízì lùkǒu**
crossroads; intersection

狮子舞 **shīziwǔ** lion dance

氏族 **shìzú** family; clan

收 **shōu** receive; accept

手 **shǒu** hand

守 **shǒu** keep watch; guard;
abide by

瘦 **shòu** thin; lean

兽 **shòu** beast; animal

售 **shòu** sell

受 **shòu** receive; accept

售报亭 **shòubàotíng**
newsstand

手表 **shǒubiǎo** wristwatch

收成 **shōuchéng** harvest

首都 **shǒudū** capital

手段 **shǒuduàn** means

守法 **shǒufǎ** comply with
the law

手风琴 **shǒufēngqín**
accordion

手工 **shǒugōng** manual ◊
handiwork

手工业 **shǒugōngyè** craft

手工业者 **shǒugōngyèzhě**
craftsman

收购 **shōugòu** purchase ◊
purchasing

受害 **shòuhài** sustain
damage; suffer an injury

守护 **shǒuhù** look after

售货员 **shòuhuòyuán** sales

clerk

收集 **shǒují** collect

手机 **shǒují** cell phone

售价 **shòujià** retail price

收件人 **shōujiànrén**
addressee

手巾 **shǒujīn** towel

收据 **shōujù** receipt

手绢 **shǒujuàn** handkerchief

首领 **shǒulǐng** leader

守门员 **shǒuményuán**
goalkeeper

售票处 **shòupiàochù** ticket
office

手枪 **shǒuqiāng** handgun

授权 **shòuquán** authorize ◊
authority

收入 **shōurù** income;
revenue

首饰 **shǒushì** jewelry

手势 **shǒushì** gesture

手术 **shǒushù** surgery;
operation

收缩 **shōusuō** shrink

手套 **shǒutào** glove

手提包 **shǒutí bāo** bag;
handbag

手提行李 **shǒutí xíngli**
hand baggage

手推车 **shǒutuīchē**
wheelbarrow

手腕 **shǒuwàn** wrist

守卫 **shǒuwèi** guard

首先 **shǒuxiān** in the first
place

首相 **shǒuxiàng** prime
minister

手写 **shǒuxiě** handwritten ◊
write by hand

手续 **shǒuxù** procedure

收养 **shōuyǎng** adopt

收益 **shōuyì** return

兽医 **shòuyī** veterinary
surgeon

收音机 **shōuyīnjī** radio

授予 **shòuyǔ** grant; present;
confer

守则 **shǒuzé** rules

手掌 **shǒuzhǎng** palm

手指 **shǒuzhǐ** finger

手镯 **shǒuzhuó** bracelet

书 **shū** book

梳 **shū** comb

熟 **shú** cooked; ripe; familiar

赎 **shú** redeem

数 **shǔ** count

鼠 **shǔ** mouse; rat

束 **shù** *measure word for
flowers*

树 **shù** tree

竖 **shù** vertical

数 **shù** number

束 **shù** bundle

刷 **shuā** clean ◊ brush

摔 **shuāi** fall; drop; throw down

摔倒 **shuāidǎo** fall; throw down

摔跤 **shuāijiāo** wrestle

摔跤比赛 **shuāijiāo bǐsài** wrestling match

衰落 **shuāiluò** go downhill

拴 **shuān** tie up

双 **shuāng** both; even; double; dual; twin ◊ measure word for pairs

霜 **shuāng** frost

双胞胎 **shuāng bāo tāi** twins

双边 **shuāngbiān** bilateral

双重 **shuāngchóng** double

霜冻 **shuāngdòng** frost

双方 **shuāngfāng** both sides

孀妇 **shuāngfù** widow

双击 **shuāngjī** double click

双人床 **shuāngrén chuáng** double bed

双数 **shuāngshù** even number

栓剂 **shuānjì** suppository

刷牙 **shuāyá** brush one's teeth

刷子 **shuāzi** brush

书包 **shūbāo** schoolbag; satchel

鼠标 **shǔbiāo** mouse

数不清 **shǔbuqīng** countless

蔬菜 **shūcài** vegetable

输出 **shūchū** output; export

书店 **shūdiàn** bookstore

数额 **shù'é** amount

书法 **shūfǎ** calligraphy

舒服 **shūfu** comfortable ◊ well

束缚 **shùfù** tie; bind

疏忽 **shūhū** oversight

谁 **shuí** who

水 **shuǐ** water

睡 **shuì** sleep

税 **shuì** tax; duty; tariff

水彩 **shuǐcǎi** watercolor

水彩画 **shuǐcǎihuà** watercolor (painting)

水池 **shuǐchí** basin

水电站 **shuǐdiànzhàn** hydroelectric power plant

水管 **shuǐguǎn** water pipe

水果 **shuǐguǒ** fruit

睡过头 **shuì guòtóu** oversleep

睡觉 **shuìjiào** sleep; go to bed

水坑 **shuǐkēng** puddle

水冷却 **shuǐlěngquè** water-cooling

水龙头 **shuǐlóngtóu** faucet

睡眠 **shuìmián** sleep

水墨画 **shuǐmòhuà** ink wash painting

水泥 **shuǐní** cement

水牛 **shuǐniú** water buffalo

水平 **shuǐpíng** level ◊ horizontal

水平面 **shuǐpíngmiàn** water level; level surface

水上运动 **shuǐshàng yùndòng** watersports

税收 **shuìshōu** tax revenue

水桶 **shuǐtǒng** bucket

税务局 **shuìwùjú** tax office

睡醒 **shuìxǐng** wake up

睡衣 **shuìyī** nightdress; pajamas; pajama jacket

水银 **shuǐyín** mercury

水域 **shuǐyù** waters; area of water

睡着 **shuìzháo** fall asleep

水族馆 **shuǐzú guǎn** aquarium

书籍 **shūjí** books

暑假 **shǔjià** summer vacation

赎金 **shújīn** ransom

数据 **shùjù** data

数据保护 **shùjù bǎohù** data

protection

数据库 **shùjù kù** database

数据载体 **shùjù zàitǐ** data carrier

熟客 **shúkè** regular visitor

漱口 **shùkǒu** gargle

熟练 **shúliàn** proficient; practised

数量 **shùliàng** amount

树林 **shùlín** wood

数码照相机 **shùmǎ zhàoxiàngjī** digital camera

书面 **shūmiàn** written ◊ in writing

数目 **shùmù** number; sum

吮 **shǔn** suck

顺便 **shùnbiàn** passing ◊ in passing

顺从 **shùncóng** obedient

顺风 **shùnfēng** tail wind

枢纽 **shūniǔ** hub; center of

瞬间 **shùnjiān** moment

顺利 **shùnlì** smooth ◊ smoothly

顺心 **shùnxīn** satisfactory

顺序 **shùnxù** sequence

说 **shuō** talk; speak; say

说定 **shuōdìng** agree on; arrange

说服 **shuōfú** persuade

说明 **shuōmíng** explain ◊

explanation

说明书 shuōmíngshū
instruction manual

树皮 shùpí bark

述评 shùpíng comment ◊
commentary

竖起 shùqǐ erect ◊ erection

书签 shūqiān bookmark

熟人 shúrén acquaintance

树梢 shùshāo treetop

舒适 shūshì cozy

熟食 shúshí cooked meal

叔叔 shūshu uncle

输送 shūsòng transport

熟悉 shúxī know; be
familiar with

书信往来 shūxìn wǎnglái
correspondence

输血 shūxuè blood
transfusion

数学 shùxué mathematics ◊
mathematical

输血者 shūxuèzhě blood
donor

输液 shūyè infusion

鼠疫 shǔyì plague

属于 shǔyú belong; belong
to

术语 shùyǔ terminology;
term

疏远 shūyuǎn drift

apart; distance oneself ◊
estranged

树枝 shùzhī branch

树脂 shùzhī resin

书桌 shūzhuō desk

梳子 shūzi hairbrush; comb

数字 shùzì digit ◊ digital

撕 sī tear (up)

思 sī think; consider

私 sī private

丝 sī silk

死 sǐ die ◊ death ◊ dead

寺 sì Buddhist temple

四 sì four

似 sì resemble, be like; seem

丝绸 sīchóu silk

丝绸之路 Sīchóu zhī lù
Silk Road

司法 sīfǎ justice ◊ judicial

四方形 sìfāng xíng square

丝瓜 sīguā loofah

似乎 sìhū look like; seem

死胡同 sǐ hútòng dead end

司机 sījī driver; chauffeur

四季豆 sìjìdòu green bean

撕开 sīkāi slit; rip open

思考 sīkǎo think about

饲料 sìliào fodder

司炉 sīlú stoker

思念 sīniàn miss

私人 sīrén private; intimate

私人财产 **sīrén cáichǎn** private property

私生活 **sīshēnghuó** private life

私生子 **sīshēngzǐ** illegitimate child

四十 **sìshí** forty

撕碎 **sīsuì** tear to pieces

死亡 **sǐwáng** death; fatality

私下 **sīxià** privately

撕下 **sīxià** tear out; tear off

思想 **sīxiǎng** thought; idea

死刑 **sǐxíng** death penalty; execution

嘶哑 **sīyǎ** hoarse

饲养 **sìyǎng** breed ◊ breeding

私语 **sīyǔ** whisper

寺院 **sìyuàn** temple

四月 **sìyuè** April

死者 **sǐzhě** the deceased

四肢 **sìzhī** limbs

丝织品 **sīzhīpǐn** silk products

四周 **sìzhōu** all around

松 **sōng** pine ◊ loose ◊ loosely

送 **sòng** deliver; give; escort

松弛 **sōngchí** slack; flabby ◊ slacken

松动 **sōngdong** loose ◊

work loose; loosen up

耸肩 **sǒngjiān** shrug

耸立 **sǒnglì** tower; rise

送礼 **sònglǐ** give a present

松手 **sōngshǒu** let go

松鼠 **sōngshǔ** squirrel

松树 **sōngshù** pine (tree)

搜捕 **sōubǔ** search

搜索 **sōusuǒ** search; scan

宿 **sù** stay overnight

酸 **suān** acid ◊ acidic

算 **suàn** count

蒜 **suàn** garlic

算出 **suànchū** calculate; charge

算命 **suànmìng** fortune-telling

酸奶 **suānnǎi** yogurt

算盘 **suànpan** abacus

算术 **suànshù** arithmetic; sum

酸味 **suānwèi** acidity; sourness

素菜 **sùcài** vegetarian dish

酥脆 **sūcuì** crisp

苏打 **sūdá** soda

速冻 **sùdòng** quick-freeze ◊ quick-frozen

速度 **sùdù** pace; tempo

穗 **suì** ear (of corn)

碎 **suì** shatter ◊ shattered

岁 suì year; years old

随便什么 suíbiàn shénme anything; something

隧道 suìdào tunnel

随后 suíhòu afterward

碎块 suìkuài fragment

碎裂 suìliè break up; crumble

碎片 suìpiàn broken pieces; fragment

虽然 suīrán although

随时 suíshí at any time

碎石 suìshí gravel

随意 suíyì as one likes

诉苦 sùkǔ complain

塑料 sùliào plastic

塑料袋 sùliàodài plastic bag

笋 sǔn bamboo shoot

损害 sǔnhài harm, damage

损耗 sǔnhào wear (and tear)

孙女 sūnnǚ granddaughter

损失 sǔnshī damage; loss; toll

孙子 sūnzi grandson

锁 suǒ lock

索道 suǒdào cable railway

缩短 suōduǎn shorten

锁骨 suǒgǔ collarbone

缩水 suōshuǐ shrink

所谓 suǒwèi alleged; so-called

缩小 suōxiǎo reduce

缩写 suōxiě abbreviate ◊ abbreviation

所以 suǒyǐ therefore

所在地 suǒzàidì seat; site

俗气 súqì tasteless, tacky

速溶咖啡 sùróng kāfēi instant coffee

素食 sùshí vegetarian

诉讼 sùsòng lawsuit

塑像 sùxiàng statue

苏醒 sūxǐng come to ◊ revival

宿营地 sùyíngdì quarters

酥油 sūyóu butter; cream

塑造 sùzào shape

素质 sùzhì quality

T

他 tā he; him

她 tā she; her

它 tā it

塔 tǎ tower

踏 tà step
踏板 tàbǎn pedal
塌方 tāfāng landslide
太 tài too; very
台布 táibù tablecloth
态度 tàidu attitude
胎儿 tāi'ér embryo; fetus
泰国 Tàiguó Thailand ◊ Thai
胎记 tāijì birthmark
太空 tàikōng (outer) space
太平洋 Tàipíngyáng the Pacific Ocean
台球 táiqiú snooker; billiards
台湾 Táiwān Taiwan ◊ Taiwanese
太阳 tàiyáng sun
太阳镜 tàiyángjìng sunglasses
他们 tāmen they; them
谈 tán talk
痰 tán phlegm; sputum
坦白 tǎnbái confess ◊ frankly ◊ open
探测 tàncè probe
摊贩 tānfàn street trader
汤 tāng broth
糖 táng sugar; candy
躺 tǎng lie
淌 tǎng run (of nose etc)
烫 tàng hot

汤匙 tāngchí spoon
搪瓷 tángcí enamel
糖醋 tángcù sweet and sour
烫发 tàngfà have a perm
糖果 tángguǒ candy
糖浆 tángjiāng molasses
糖尿病 tángniào bìng diabetes ◊ diabetic
唐三彩 tángsāncǎi Tang ceramics glazed in three colors
趟水 tāngshuǐ wade
躺下 tǎngxia lie down
躺椅 tǎngyǐ deck chair; lounge chair
谈话 tánhuà talk
瘫痪 tānhuàn paralysis ◊ paralyze
弹簧 tánhuáng spring
坦克 tǎnkè tank MIL
贪婪 tānlán greedy; acquisitive
谈判 tánpàn negotiate ◊ negotiations
叹气 tànqì sigh
贪食 tānshí gluttony ◊ gluttonous
坦率 tǎnshuài open ◊ openly ◊ candor
碳酸 tànsuān carbonic acid
贪污 tānwū embezzle ◊

embezzlement

弹性 tánxìng elasticity;

探照灯 tànzhàodēng
searchlight

摊子 tānzi stall, booth

逃避 táobì escape; shirk ◊
evasion

讨价还价 tǎojià huánjià
bargain ◊ haggle

讨论 tǎolùn discuss ◊
discussion

逃跑 táopǎo run away ◊
flight; getaway

陶器 táoqì ceramics; pottery;
earthenware

淘气 táoqì naughty

淘汰 táotài eliminate

讨脱 táotuō escape

讨厌 tǎoyàn disgusting;
tiresome ◊ detest; loathe ◊
what a nuisance!

桃子 táozi peach

套子 tàozi housing; case

逃走 táozǒu run away

太阳穴 tàiyángxué temple

特别 tèbié particular ◊
particularly

特产 tèchǎn specialty

特点 tèdiǎn characteristic

特技 tèjì trick; stunt

疼痛 téngtòng pain ◊

painful

特殊 tèshū special;
exceptional

特务 tèwu secret agent

特性 tèxìng quality; trait

特征 tèzhēng characteristic

踢 tī kick

蹄 tí hoof

题 tí subject

剃 tì shave

替 tì replace; substitute

天 tiān sky; heaven; day

甜 tián sweet

田 tián field

舔 tiǎn lick; lap up

填表 tiánbiǎo fill in a form

甜菜 tiáncài sugar beet

田地 tiándì field; farmland

天鹅 tiān'é swan

天鹅绒 tiān'éróng velvet

天份 tiānfèn gift; flair

天赋 tiānfù gift

天花 tiānhuā smallpox

天花板 tiānhuābǎn ceiling

添加 tiānjiā add

田径 tiánjìng track and field;
athletics

天空 tiānkōng sky

填满 tiánmǎn fill

天气 tiānqì weather

天气预报 tiānqì yùbào weather

weather forecast

天然 **tiānrán** natural ◊ naturally

天然气 **tiānrán qì** natural gas

天生 **tiānshēng** naturally ◊ innate

天使 **tiānshǐ** angel

甜食 **tiánshí** confectionery

田鼠 **tiánshǔ** vole

天坛 **Tiāntán** Temple of Heaven

天文 **tiānwén** astronomy

天线 **tiānxiàn** antenna; aerial

天性 **tiānxìng** disposition

天衣无缝 **tiān yī wú fèng** perfect

天真 **tiānzhēn** naïve

天主教 **Tiānzhǔjiào** (Roman) Catholic

条 **tiáo** strip; item; *measure word for long thin things*

跳 **tiào** jump; hop; skip

跳板 **tiàobǎn** springboard; gangway

挑拨 **tiǎobō** provoke

挑动 **tiǎodòng** stir up

跳动 **tiàodòng** beat

跳高 **tiàogāo** high jump

调羹 **tiáogēng** spoon

条件 **tiáojiàn** condition ◊ conditional

调节 **tiáojié** adjust

调解 **tiáojiě** mediate; reconcile ◊ mediation; reconciliation

条款 **tiáokuǎn** clause; provision

调料 **tiáoliào** spice; herb; condiment; ingredient

调皮 **tiáopí** naughty; rude

调情 **tiáoqíng** flirt

挑三拣四 **tiāosān-jiǎnsì** choosy

跳水 **tiàoshuǐ** dive; diving

调味 **tiáowèi** season

跳舞 **tiàowǔ** dance

挑衅 **tiǎoxìn** provoke ◊ provocation ◊ provocative

挑选 **tiāoxuǎn** choose

跳远 **tiàoyuǎn** long jump

条约 **tiáoyuē** treaty, pact

挑战 **tiǎozhàn** challenge

体操 **tǐcāo** gymnastics

提倡 **tíchàng** advocate

提出 **tíchū** bring up; advance

题词 **tící** dedication ◊ dedicate

提到 **tídào** mention

铁 **tiě** iron

贴边 **tiēbiān** hem; seam; edge

铁路 **tiělù** railroad

铁锹 **tiěqiāo** shovel; spade

提高 **tígāo** raise; increase; improve ◊ rise

提供 **tígōng** supply

替换 **tìhuàn** substitute; replace

剃胡子 **tì húzi** shave

体积 **tǐjī** volume

题目 **tímù** topic

听 **tīng** listen (to)

停 **tíng** stop

亭 **tíng** pavilion

挺 **tǐng** very; quite

听从 **tīngcóng** obey; respond

停电 **tíngdiàn** power cut

停放车 **tíngfàng chē** park

听话 **tīnghuà** listen; obey ◊ obedient

听筒 **tīngtǒng** receiver TEL

停业 **tíngyè** shut down

听止 **tíngzhǐ** stop; let up

听众 **tīngzhòng** audience; listeners

停住 **tíngzhù** stop

亭子 **tíngzi** kiosk

提前 **tíqián** early

提神 **tíshén** freshen up; refresh oneself

提升 **tíshēng** promote

提示 **tíshì** point out

体现 **tǐxiàn** embody

提醒 **tíxǐng** remind

剃须刀 **tìxū dāo** razor

提议 **tíyì** suggest

体育场 **tǐyùchǎng** stadium

体育运动 **tǐyù yùndòng** sport ◊ sporting

体质 **tǐzhì** physique; constitution

体制 **tǐzhì** system

体重 **tǐzhòng** (body) weight

梯子 **tīzi** ladder

铜 **tóng** copper

同 **tóng** same ◊ with ◊ and

童 **tóng** child

桶 **tǒng** barrel; tub; pail

痛 **tòng** pain; sore

同伴 **tóngbàn** partner

铜版画 **tóngbǎnhuà** copperplate

同胞 **tóngbāo** fellow citizen; fellow countryman

统舱 **tǒngcāng** lower deck

通常 **tōngcháng** normal ◊ normally

同等价值 **tóngděng jiàzhí** of equal value

通风 **tōngfēng** air; ventilate ◊ airy; drafty ◊ ventilation

同感 **tónggǎn** sympathy

通过 **tōngguò** pass ◊ via

童话 **tónghuà** fairy tale

通货膨胀 **tōnghuò péngzhàng** inflation

统计 **tǒngjì** statistics ◊ statistical

同居 **tóngjū** cohabit

瞳孔 **tóngkǒng** pupil

痛哭 **tòngkū** bawl

痛苦 **tòngkǔ** suffering; distress

同盟 **tóngméng** alliance

童年 **tóngnián** childhood

同年 **tóngnián** same year ◊ of the same age

通气 **tōngqì** air

同情 **tóngqíng** pity; sympathize with ◊ compassion

同时 **tóngshí** simultaneously; in the meantime ◊ simultaneous

同事 **tóngshì** colleague

通宵 **tōngxiāo** throughout the night

同性恋 **tóngxìngliàn** homosexual; lesbian

通行证 **tōngxíngzhèng** pass

同学 **tóngxué** classmate

通讯员 **tōngxùnyuán** correspondent

同样 **tóngyàng** same

同意 **tóngyì** agree; sanction

统一 **tǒngyī** unite ◊ unification

通知 **tōngzhī** inform; report ◊ circular; notice

同志 **tóngzhì** comrade

统治 **tǒngzhì** reign; rule

偷 **tōu** steal

头 **tóu** head

投 **tóu** hurl; throw in

投递 **tóudì** deliver ◊ delivery

头顶 **tóudǐng** top of the head

头发 **tóufa** hair

头巾 **tóujīn** (head)scarf

透镜 **tòujìng** lens

偷懒 **tōulǎn** laze about; goof off

投篮 **tóulán** shoot (at the basket)

头颅 **tóulú** skull

头路 **tóulù** part (in hair)

透露 **tòulù** leak out; disclose

透明 **tòumíng** transparent

头皮屑 **tóupíxiè** dandruff

偷窃 **tōuqiè** steal

投入 **tóurù** plunge into

透入 **tòurù** penetrate

偷税 **tōushuì** evade taxes

头痛 **tóutòng** headache

偷偷 tōutōu furtive
头衔 tóuxián title
投降 tóuxiáng yield; surrender ◇ submission
投影仪 tóuyǐngyí projector
头晕 tóuyūn dizzy
投资 tóuzī invest ◇ investment
涂 tú apply
图 tú picture
途 tú path; road; way
土 tǔ earth; land
吐 tù vomit
兔 tù rabbit; hare
图案 tú'àn pattern; design
团结 tuánjié unite ◇ united
团体 tuántǐ group
团圆 tuányuán reunion; get-together
团子 tuánzi dumpling
突变 tūbiàn sudden change
涂层 túcéng coat
突出 tūchū stick out ◇ prominent
吐出 tùchū spit (out)
秃顶 tūdǐng bald
图钉 túdīng thumbtack
土豆 tǔdòu potato
图画 túhuà picture
推 tuī push; jolt
腿 tuǐ leg

退 tuì move backward; retreat; retire
退步 tuìbù go backward; fall behind
推测 tuīcè suspect; assume; guess
退潮 tuìcháo ebb tide
推迟 tuīchí postpone
退出 tuìchū withdraw; exit
推辞 tuīcí decline
推动 tuīdòng push forward; promote; boost; budge
推断 tuīduàn conclude ◇ conclusion
推荐 tuījiàn recommendation; reference ◇ recommend
蜕皮 tuìpí peel; shed its skin
退让 tuìràng retreat
退烧 tuìshāo subside (of fever)
推行 tuīxíng implement; pursue
退休 tuìxiū retire ◇ retired ◇ retirement
退休金 tuìxiūjīn pension
退休者 tuìxiūzhě pensioner
途经 tújīng via
途径 tújìng way
徒劳 túláo in vain
吞 tūn swallow

吞并 **tūnbìng** annex

臀部 **túnbù** buttocks; rump; hip

囤积 **túnjī** hoard

吞食 **tūnshí** devour

吞咽 **tūnyàn** gulp

拖 **tuō** drag; pull

拖把 **tuōbǎ** mop

驼背 **tuóbèi** hunchback; hump

拖车 **tuōchē** trailer

托儿所 **tuō'érsuǒ** day-nursery; crèche

脱轨 **tuōguǐ** be derailed

脱臼 **tuōjiù** dislocation

拖拉机 **tuōlājī** tractor

脱离 **tuōlí** break away

脱落 **tuōluò** come off; fall out

陀螺 **tuóluó** (spinning) top

唾沫 **tuòmo** spittle

鸵鸟 **tuóniǎo** ostrich

拖盘 **tuōpán** tray

拖鞋 **tuōxié** slippers

妥协 **tuǒxié** compromise

脱衣服 **tuō yīfu** undress

托运 **tuōyùn** send, ship

突破 **tūpò** breakthrough; penetration

突然 **tūrán** suddenly ◊ sudden

土壤 **tǔrǎng** soil

屠杀 **túshā** massacre; slaughter

图书馆 **túshūguǎn** library

吐痰 **tǔtán** spit

徒刑 **túxíng** prison sentence

图形学 **túxíngxué** graphics

涂油漆 **tú yóuqī** paint

屠宰 **túzǎi** slaughter

屠宰场 **túzǎichǎng** slaughterhouse

图章 **túzhāng** seal

途中 **túzhōng** en route

土著 **tǔzhù** native

兔子 **tùzi** rabbit; hare

W

挖 **wā** dig; extract

蛙 **wā** frog

瓦 **wǎ** roof tile

袜 **wà** socks; stockings

歪 **wāi** leaning; crooked

外 **wài** outside ◊ external; foreign; outward ◊ externally; outwardly

外表 wàibiǎo exterior; facade; veneer ◊ outward

外部 wàibù exterior ◊ outer; external

外出 wàichū go out

外公 wàigōng (maternal) grandfather

外观 wàiguān exterior; appearance; look

外国 wàiguó foreign country ◊ abroad ◊ foreign

外国人 wàiguórén foreigner

外行 wàiháng layman

外号 wàihào nickname

外汇 wàihuì foreign currency, foreign exchange

外交部 wàijiāobù Ministry of Foreign Affairs

外科医师 wàikē yīshī surgeon

外来语 wàiláiyǔ foreign loan word

外贸 wàimào foreign trade

外面 wàimiàn outside ◊ external

外婆 wàipó (maternal) grandmother

歪曲 wāiqū misrepresent

外甥 wàisheng nephew

外甥女 wàishengnǚ niece

外衣 wàiyī coat

外语 wàiyǔ foreign language

挖掘 wājué excavate ◊ excavation

挖空 wākōng excavate

瓦砾 wǎlì rubble

弯 wān bend ◊ bent

完 wán finish ◊ finished; complete

玩 wán play

碗 wǎn bowl

晚 wǎn late ◊ evening; night

万 wàn ten thousand

晚安 wǎn'ān good night

完毕 wánbì finished

晚餐 wǎncān dinner

完成 wánchéng complete; accomplish ◊ completion

晚点 wǎndiǎn delayed

豌豆 wāndòu pea

晚饭 wǎnfàn supper

王 wáng king

网 wǎng net; web; network

往 wǎng to; toward ◊ past

忘 wàng forget

望 wàng look ahead; expect

往返 wǎngfǎn there and back

王国 wángguó kingdom

王后 wánghòu queen

忘记 wàngjì forget

旺季 wàngjì high season

往来 **wǎnglái** contact;
dealings; relations

网络 **wǎngluò** network;
Internet

王牌 **wángpái** trump card

网球 **wǎngqiú** tennis; tennis
ball

往事 **wǎngshì** the past

顽固 **wángù** obstinate; set ◊
obstinacy

王位 **wángwèi** throne

望远镜 **wàngyuǎn jìng**
telescope; binoculars

网址 **wǎngzhǐ** web site;
web page

王子 **wángzǐ** prince

晚会 **wǎnhuì** party;
(evening) function

万金油 **wànjīnyóu** balm

玩具 **wánjù** toy

完美 **wánměi** perfect;
beautiful ◊ impeccably ◊
perfection

顽强 **wánqiáng** stubborn;
tenacious

完全 **wánquán** complete;
total ◊ completely

完全一样 **wánquán yīyàng**
exactly the same

完善 **wánshàn** perfect

晚上 **wǎnshang** evening

晚上好 **wǎnshang hǎo**
good evening

弯身 **wānshēn** bend;
double up

玩世不恭 **wán shì bù gōng**
cynically

玩耍 **wánshuǎ** enjoy oneself

玩童 **wántóng** urchin

玩笑 **wánxiào** joke

万幸 **wànxìng** fortunate

弯腰 **wānyāo** bend down

完整 **wánzhěng** complete ◊
completely

瓦特 **wǎtè** watt

蛙泳 **wāyǒng** breaststroke

袜子 **wàzi** socks; stockings

微 **wēi** small; micro-

围 **wéi** surround; besiege

唯 **wéi** only

喂 **wèi** hello TEL; hey! ◊ feed

为 **wèi** for

味 **wèi** taste

胃 **wèi** stomach

位 **wèi** position

未 **wèi** not yet; not

尾巴 **wěiba** tail

违背 **wéibèi** violate

微薄 **wēibó** sparse; scanty ◊
sparsely; scantily

微波炉 **wēibōlú** microwave
oven

未曾 wèicéng never

维持 wéichí maintain; get by; hold out

为此 wèicǐ for this reason

伟大 wěidà great ◊ greatness

味道 wèidao taste; flavor

尾灯 wěidēng tail light

纬度 wěidù latitude

违法 wéifǎ illicit; illegal ◊ illegally

违反 wéifǎn break

桅杆 wéigān mast

危害 wēihài damage

威吓 wēihè intimidate

维护 wéihù protect, look after

未婚 wèihūn unmarried

未婚夫 wèihūnfū fiancé

未婚妻 wèihūnqī fiancée

危机 wēijī crisis

危急 wēijí critical; desperate ◊ critically

围巾 wéijīn scarf

味精 wèijīng monosodium glutamate

胃口 wèikǒu appetite

围困 wéikùn besiege ◊ siege

未来 wèilái future

为了 wèile for; in order to; because of

喂奶 wèinǎi breast-feed

围棋 Wéiqí Go

围裙 wéiqún apron

围绕 wéirǎo surround ◊ around

围绕着 wéiràozhe revolve around

委任 wěirèn appoint

伪善 wěishàn hypocrisy

卫生 wèishēng hygienic ◊ hygiene

卫生带 wèishēngdài sanitary napkin

卫生间 wèishēngjiān rest room

维生素 wéishēngsù vitamin

卫生纸 wèishēngzhǐ toilet paper

为什么 wèishénme why

威士忌 wēishìjì whiskey

畏缩 wèisuō recoil; shy away

胃痛 wèitòng stomach ache

威望 wēiwàng prestige

微温 wēiwēn lukewarm

危险 wēixiǎn danger ◊ dangerous

微小 wēixiǎo tiny

微笑 wēixiào smile

威胁 wēixié threat; intimidation ◊ threaten; intimidate

猥亵 wěixiè obscene

卫星 **wèixīng** satellite

卫星电视 **wèixīng diànshì** satellite TV

维修 **wéixiū** repair

喂养 **wèiyǎng** feed

偎依 **wēiyī** snuggle; cling

唯一 **wéiyī** sole ◊ solely

位于 **wèiyú** be (situated)

伪造 **wěizào** forge; falsify

位置 **wèizhi** location, position

胃灼痛 **wèizhuótòng** heartburn

位子 **wèizi** seat

闻 **wén** smell

吻 **wěn** kiss

稳 **wěn** stable

稳定 **wěndìng** stability ◊ stabilize ◊ stable

温度 **wēndù** temperature

温度表 **wēndùbiǎo** thermometer

嗡嗡作响 **wēngwēng zuòxiǎng** hum; buzz

问好 **wènhǎo** ask after; send greetings

问号 **wènhào** question mark

温和 **wēnhé** mild; moderate; mellow

ask after

文化 **wénhuà** culture ◊ cultural

文件 **wénjiàn** document; papers; file

闻名 **wénmíng** famous

文明 **wénmíng** civilization; culture

温暖 **wēnnuǎn** warm

文凭 **wénpíng** qualification; diploma; certificate

温柔 **wēnróu** gentle

温室 **wēnshì** greenhouse

问题 **wèntí** problem; question; matter

温习 **wēnxí** brush up; revise

文学 **wénxué** literature ◊ literary

问讯 **wènxùn** ask; inquire

问讯处 **wènxùnchù** information office

瘟疫 **wēnyì** epidemic; plague

文艺 **wényì** literature and art

文章 **wénzhāng** article

蚊帐 **wénzhàng** mosquito net

稳重 **wěnzhòng** sedate; sober

蚊子 **wénzi** mosquito

文字 **wénzì** writing; text

窝 wō nest

我 wǒ I; me

握 wò grasp

卧 wò lie down

卧车 wòchē sleeping car

卧倒 wòdǎo lie flat; drop to the ground

涡轮机 wōlúnjī turbine

我们 wǒmen we; us

蜗牛 wōniú snail

窝棚 wōpeng shed; hangar; hovel

卧铺 wòpù place to sleep; bed

卧室 wòshì bedroom

握手 wòshǒu handshake ◊ shake hands

乌 wū black ◊ crow

屋 wū house

无 wú nothing ◊ not ◊ no

五 wǔ five

午 wǔ midday

舞 wǔ dance

雾 wù fog; mist

勿 wù do not

物 wù thing

五百 wǔbǎi five hundred

舞伴 wǔbàn (dance) partner

无比 wúbǐ incomparable

五彩 wǔcǎi colorful

舞场 wǔchǎng dance floor

无产阶级 wúchǎn jiējí proletariat

无耻 wúchǐ outrageous, shameless

无处 wúchù nowhere

舞蹈家 wǔdǎojiā dancer

屋顶 wūdǐng roof

午饭 wǔfàn lunch

无根据 wúgēnjù unfounded

污垢 wūgòu dirt

无辜 wúgū innocent ◊ innocently

乌龟 wūguī tortoise; turtle

舞会 wǔhuì dance; prom

误会 wùhuì misunderstanding

误解 wùjiě misunderstand; misread ◊ misunderstanding

无可奈何 wúkě nàihé helpless

无可指摘 wúkě zhǐzhāi irreproachable

无愧 wúkuì worthy

无力 wúlì feeble

物理 wùlǐ physics

无聊 wúliáo boredom ◊ boring; bored

诬蔑 wūmiè smear

无名指 wúmíngzhǐ ring finger

无能 **wúnéng** incompetent; incapable; unable ◊ inability

物品 **wùpǐn** object; item

武器 **wǔqì** weapon

雾气 **wùqì** mist, haze

无情 **wúqíng** ruthless; callous

舞曲 **wǔqǔ** dance music

无权 **wúquán** unauthorized

污染 **wūrǎn** pollution ◊ pollute

侮辱 **wǔrǔ** insult

无声 **wúshēng** silent; mute ◊ silently

五十 **wǔshí** fifty

无数 **wúshù** countless

武术 **wǔshù** martial arts

污水 **wūshuǐ** sewage

午睡 **wǔshuì** afternoon nap

无所谓 **wúsuǒwèi** indifferent ◊ all the same

舞台 **wǔtái** stage; platform

物体 **wùtǐ** object

舞厅 **wǔtīng** ballroom; dancehall

无痛 **wútòng** painless

乌托邦 **wūtuōbāng** utopia

无味 **wúwèi** insipid; dull

无限 **wúxiàn** infinite

无线 **wúxiàn** cordless, wireless

无线电 **wúxiàndiàn** radio

无限制 **wúxiànzhì** unlimited

无效 **wúxiào** invalid; futile

无心 **wúxīn** unintentionally

五星红旗 **wǔxīng hóngqí** Chinese flag

五星级饭店 **wǔxīngjí fàndiàn** five-star hotel

午休 **wǔxiū** lunch break

乌鸦 **wūyā** crow; raven

屋檐 **wūyán** eaves

无疑 **wúyí** doubtless; easily

无意 **wúyì** unintentional ◊ unintentionally

无意识 **wúyìshí** unconscious ◊ unconsciously

无用 **wúyòng** useless

无忧无虑 **wúyōu wúlǜ** carefree

五月 **wǔyuè** May

无与伦比 **wú yǔ lúnbǐ** unique

乌云 **wūyún** dark clouds

无知 **wúzhī** ignorance ◊ ignorant

物质 **wùzhì** matter

无止境 **wúzhǐjìng** endless ◊ endlessly

武装 **wǔzhuāng** arms ◊ arm ◊ armed

X

膝 xī knee

吸 xī inhale; smoke; suck

稀 xī rare; sparse; thin

锡 xī tin

西 xī west ◊ western

溪 xī stream

熄 xī extinguish

席 xí mat; seat; place; feast

洗 xǐ wash; shuffle *cards*; develop *photographs*

喜 xǐ pleasure; joy

铣 xǐ mill

系 xì system; department ◊ tie

细 xì thin; fine

瞎 xiā blind

虾 xiā prawn; shrimp

下 xià down, downward ◊ below; under ◊ next ◊ get off; come down; lay; finish

吓 xià scare

夏 xià summer

下巴 xiàba chin

下班 xiàbān finish work; go off duty

下车 xiàchē alight

下沉 xiàchén sink; settle

下次 xiàcì next time

峡谷 xiágǔ canyon; gorge; glen

喜爱 xǐ'ài like; love ◊ beloved; fond ◊ favor; fondness

夏季 xiàjì summer

下降 xiàjiàng decrease; decline; drop

下来 xiàlái come down; descend ◊ descent

夏令时 xiàlìngshí summer time; daylight saving time

下流 xiàliú indecent; sleazy

下面 xiàmiàn underneath; below

先 xiān first

鲜 xiān fresh

弦 xián chord; string

咸 xián salty; savory

闲 xián idle ◊ leisure

线 xiàn line; thread; cord

县 xiàn county

馅 xiàn filling

腺 xiàn gland

现场 xiànchǎng on the spot ◊ scene of the crime

县城 **xiànchéng** county town

现存 **xiàncún** existing; in existence; in stock

现代 **xiàndài** modern; contemporary ◊ modern times

现代化 **xiàndàihuà** modernize ◊ modernization

限定 **xiàndìng** limit

限度 **xiàndù** limit

宪法 **xiànfǎ** constitution ◊ constitutional

箱 **xiāng** box; crate; case

香 **xiāng** incense; perfume ◊ fragrant; tasty

乡 **xiāng** countryside; hometown

详 **xiáng** details

响 **xiǎng** sound ◊ loud

想 **xiǎng** think; want

向 **xiàng** to; toward

象 **xiàng** elephant

像 **xiàng** look like

香槟酒 **xiāngbīn jiǔ** champagne

相册 **xiàngcè** photo album

香肠 **xiāngcháng** sausage

相当 **xiāngdāng** quite ◊ parallel; match

想到 **xiǎngdào** think of

想法 **xiǎngfa** thought, idea

相反 **xiāngfǎn** opposite

相反方向 **xiāngfǎn fāngxiàng** opposite direction

相符 **xiāngfú** correspond, match

香港 **Xiānggǎng** Hong Kong

香蕉 **xiāngjiāo** banana

橡胶 **xiàngjiāo** rubber

项链 **xiàngliàn** necklace

相连接 **xiāngliánjiē** be connected; hang together

相貌 **xiàngmào** features (facial)

项目 **xiàngmù** item; project

想念 **xiǎngniàn** miss

相配 **xiāngpèi** match; complement

橡皮 **xiàngpí** rubber; eraser

相片 **xiàngpiàn** photo

橡皮筋 **xiàngpíjīn** elastic band

香气 **xiāngqì** scent

想起 **xiǎngqǐ** remember; think of

象棋 **xiàngqí** Chinese chess

向前 **xiàngqián** forward; onward

向日葵 **xiàngrìkuí** sunflower

向上 **xiàngshàng** up

响声 **xiǎngshēng** sound

相识 **xiāngshí** know each other

享受 **xiǎngshòu** enjoy

橡树 **xiàngshù** oak tree

香水 **xiāngshuǐ** perfume

乡思 **xiāngsī** homesickness

相似 **xiāngsì** similar ◊ be alike ◊ similarity

相同 **xiāngtóng** equal; equivalent ◊ equally

闲逛 **xiánguàng** wander; stroll; hang about

向外 **xiàngwài** outward

详细 **xiángxì** full ◊ fully; minutely

向下 **xiàngxià** down ◊ downward ◊ underneath

想象 **xiǎngxiàng** imagine; envisage ◊ imagination

相信 **xiāngxìn** believe; believe in; trust

香烟 **xiāngyān** cigarette

享有 **xiǎngyǒu** enjoy

香皂 **xiāngzào** toilet soap

象征 **xiàngzhēng** emblem ◊ symbolize

相撞 **xiāngzhuàng** collide; knock together

箱子 **xiāngzi** box; chest; crate

显赫 **xiǎnhè** influential

鲜花 **xiānhuā** fresh flowers

先进 **xiānjìn** advance ◊ advanced; progressive

现金 **xiànjīn** cash

现今 **xiànjīn** nowadays

陷阱 **xiànjǐng** pitfall; trap

闲聊 **xiánliáo** chatter; gossip

线路 **xiànlù** circuit; line

鲜美 **xiānměi** delicious

羡慕 **xiànmù** envy

仙女 **xiānnǚ** fairy

先驱 **xiānqū** pioneer; forerunner

线圈 **xiànquān** coil

显然 **xiǎnrán** obvious ◊ apparently

仙人掌 **xiānrénzhǎng** cactus

献身于 **xiànshēn yú** dedicate oneself to

显示 **xiǎnshì** display; show

现实 **xiànshí** realistic ◊ reality

显示器 **xiǎnshìqì** indicator; monitor

咸水 **xiánshuǐ** salt water

线索 **xiànsuǒ** clue; thread

纤维素 **xiānwéisù** cellulose

现象 **xiànxiàng** phenomenon

献血 **xiànxuè** donate blood

显眼 **xiǎnyǎn** conspicuous ◊ stand out ◊ conspicuously

嫌疑 **xiányí** suspicion

现有 **xiànyǒu** available; in existence

陷于 **xiànyú** get into

弦乐器 **xiányuèqì** stringed instrument

现在 **xiànzài** now; at the moment

限制 **xiànzhì** restriction ◊ restrict; qualify *remark*

显著 **xiǎnzhù** prominent

削 **xiāo** peel

小 **xiǎo** small; young

笑 **xiào** laugh

校 **xiào** school

小便 **xiǎobiàn** urine ◊ urinate

小吃店 **xiǎochīdiàn** snack bar

消除 **xiāochú** eliminate

哮喘 **xiàochuǎn** asthma

小刀 **xiǎodāo** pocket knife

消毒 **xiāodú** sterilize ◊ sterile

小儿麻痹症 **xiǎo'ér mábìzhèng** polio

消防队 **xiāofángduì** fire department

消费 **xiāofèi** expense; consumption ◊ consume

小费 **xiāofèi** tip

消费者 **xiāofèizhě** consumer

效果 **xiàoguǒ** effect

小孩 **xiǎohái** child

消耗 **xiāohào** use; consume; fritter away ◊ consumption

消化 **xiāohuà** digest ◊ digestion

笑话 **xiàohua** joke

小伙子 **xiǎohuǒzi** young man

消极 **xiāojí** negative

小姐 **xiǎojie** Miss ◊ young woman

销路 **xiāolù** sales; circulation

效率 **xiàolǜ** efficiency

小马 **xiǎomǎ** pony

小米 **xiǎomǐ** millet

消灭 **xiāomiè** destroy; exterminate

消磨时间 **xiāomó shíjiān** pass the time

小朋友 **xiǎo péngyǒu** children

小气 **xiǎoqì** mean; mean-spirited

消遣 **xiāoqiǎn** amuse oneself ◊ pastime

小人书 **xiǎorénshū** picture-book

消失 **xiāoshī** disappear; go away

小时 **xiǎoshí** hour

小事 **xiǎoshì** trivial matter

消瘦 **xiāoshòu** emaciated

销售 **xiāoshòu** market ◊ marketing

小说 **xiǎoshuō** novel; fiction

萧条 **xiāotiáo** (economic) depression ◊ depressed

小提琴 **xiǎo tíqín** violin

小偷 **xiǎotōu** thief; burglar

小屋 **xiǎowū** hut

消息 **xiāoxi** news

肖像 **xiàoxiàng** portrait

小心 **xiǎoxīn** be careful ◊ carefully

小学 **xiǎoxué** elementary school

小学生 **xiǎoxuéshēng** schoolchild

校长 **xiàozhǎng** principal (of school)

下水 **xiàshuǐ** launch ◊ downstream

下水道 **xiàshuǐ dào** drains

下塌 **xiàtà** stay

下午 **xiàwǔ** afternoon

下陷 **xiàxiàn** drop; subside

下雪 **xiàxuě** snow

下意识 **xiàyìshí** subconscious

下雨 **xiàyǔ** rain

狭窄 **xiázhǎi** confined

瞎子 **xiāzi** blind person

稀薄 **xībó** thin

西餐 **xīcān** Western cuisine

细长 **xìcháng** narrow; slim

吸尘器 **xīchénqì** vacuum cleaner

洗涤 **xǐdí** wash; erase *tape*

吸毒者 **xīdúzhě** drug addict

斜 **xié** oblique; diagonal

鞋 **xié** shoe; footwear

携 **xié** carry; hold

写 **xiě** write

谢 **xiè** thank

卸 **xiè** unload

蟹 **xiè** crab

鞋带 **xiédài** shoelace; strap

携带 **xiédài** take (along)

鞋底 **xiédǐ** sole

鞋店 **xiédiàn** shoestore

协定 **xiédìng** agreement

邪恶 **xié'è** evil; spiteful

鞋跟 **xiégēn** heel

协会 **xiéhuì** association

卸货 **xièhuò** unload

鞋匠 **xiéjiang** shoemaker

泄密 **xièmì** reveal a secret

斜坡 **xiépō** slope; gradient

斜视 **xiéshì** squint; look sideways

鞋刷 **xiéshuā** shoe brush

斜体 **xiétǐ** italic

卸下 **xièxià** unload

谢谢 **xièxie** thanks

泻药 **xièyào** laxative

鞋油 **xiéyóu** shoe polish

楔子 **xiēzi** wedge

写作 **xiězuò** write ◊ writing

洗发剂 **xǐfàjì** shampoo

稀饭 **xīfàn** congee

西方 **xīfāng** western ◊ West

西风 **xīfēng** westerly wind

西服 **xīfú** suit

媳妇 **xífù** daughter-in-law

膝盖骨 **xīgàigǔ** kneecap

西瓜 **xīguā** watermelon

吸管 **xīguǎn** drinking straw

习惯 **xíguàn** custom; habit ◊ be accustomed to

希罕 **xīhan** rare ◊ rarity

西红柿 **xīhóngshì** tomato

喜欢 **xǐhuan** like, be fond of

袭击 **xíjī** attack; strike

细节 **xìjié** detail

喜剧 **xǐjù** comedy

戏剧 **xìjù** drama ◊ dramatic

细菌 **xìjùn** germ

戏剧性 **xìjùxìng** drama ◊ dramatic

系列 **xìliè** series; range; installment

喜马拉雅山 **Xīmǎlāyǎshān** Himalayas

熄灭 **xīmiè** put out; quench; go out

心 **xīn** heart; mind; center

新 **xīn** new; unused

信 **xìn** faith; letter ◊ believe; trust

信封 **xìnfēng** envelope

星 **xīng** star

行 **xíng** go ◊ expedition ◊ OK; you're on!

醒 **xǐng** awake ◊ rouse

擤 **xǐng** blow one's nose

杏 **xìng** apricot

性 **xìng** nature; character; gender; sex

姓 **xìng** surname

性别 **xìngbié** gender

形成 **xíngchéng** form; come into existence ◊ formation

行动 **xíngdòng** act ◊ action

刑法 **xíngfǎ** criminal law

兴奋 **xīngfèn** excited ◊ excitement ◊ get excited

幸福 **xìngfú** happy ◊ happiness

性格 **xìnggé** nature

型号 xínghào model

猩红热 xīnghóngrè scarlet fever

性急 xìngjí impatient

性交 xìngjiāo sexual intercourse ◊ have sex

幸亏 xìngkuī fortunately

行李 xíngli baggage

星期 xīngqī week

星期二 xīngqī'èr Tuesday

星期六 xīngqīliù Saturday

性情 xìngqíng temperament

星期日 xīngqīrì Sunday

星期三 xīngqīsān Wednesday

星期四 xīngqīsì Thursday

星期五 xīngqīwǔ Friday

星期一 xīngqīyī Monday

兴趣 xìngqù interest

行人 xíngrén pedestrian

行人区 xíngrén qū pedestrian precinct

形容 xíngróng describe

行善者 xíngshànzhě benefactor

行使 xíngshǐ exercise right

行驶 xíngshǐ drive; go; travel

刑事 xíngshì criminal

形势 xíngshì situation

形式上 xíngshì shàng formal ◊ formally

兴旺 xīngwàng flourish ◊ flourishing

行为 xíngwéi behavior; deed

醒悟 xǐngwù awaken; realize

星象 xīngxiàng horoscope

形象 xíngxiàng image

行星 xíngxīng planet

形形色色 xíngxíng-sèsè varied

性欲 xìngyù sexual desire, lust

幸运 xìngyùn fortunate ◊ fortunately ◊ good fortune

幸灾乐祸 xìngzāi-lèhuò malicious delight

行政 xíngzhèng administration ◊ administrative

性质 xìngzhì quality; character

形状 xíngzhuàng form

信号 xìnhào signal

信笺 xìnjiān writing paper

信教 xìnjiào devout

新加坡 Xīnjiāpō Singapore

心肌梗塞 xīnjī gěngsè heart attack

辛苦 xīnkǔ arduous

信赖 xìnlài trust; rely on

新郎 xīnláng bridegroom

心理学 xīnlǐxué psychology

◊ psychological

心满意足 **xīnmǎn yìzú** happy

新年 **Xīnnián** New Year

信念 **xìnniàn** belief

新娘 **xīnniáng** bride

心情 **xīnqíng** mood

信任 **xìnrèn** trust ◊ trusting

欣赏 **xīnshǎng** appreciate ◊ appreciation

新式 **xīnshì** up-to-date

信使 **xìnshǐ** courier

新手 **xīnshǒu** beginner; rookie

薪水 **xīnshuǐ** salary

新闻广播 **xīnwén guǎngbo** newscast

欣喜 **xīnxǐ** jubilant

信息 **xìnxī** information

新鲜 **xīnxiān** fresh ◊ freshness

信箱 **xìnxiāng** mailbox

新西兰 **Xīnxīlán** New Zealand

信心 **xìnxīn** confidence

信息学 **xìnxī xué** information science

信仰 **xìnyǎng** belief, faith

信用卡 **xìnyòngkǎ** credit card

心脏病 **xīnzàng bìng** heart disease

胸 **xiōng** chest; bust

凶 **xiōng** fierce; terrible; evil

熊 **xióng** bear

雄 **xióng** male

兄弟 **xiōngdì** brothers

兄弟般 **xiōngdìban** fraternal ◊ like brothers

熊猫 **xióngmāo** panda

胸腔 **xiōngqiāng** thorax

凶杀 **xiōngshā** murder

凶手 **xiōngshǒu** murderer

雄伟 **xióngwěi** imposing; majestic ◊ majestically

胸罩 **xiōngzhào** bra

喜鹊 **xǐque** magpie

牺牲品 **xīshēng pǐn** victim

稀释 **xīshì** water down

吸收 **xīshōu** absorb

稀疏 **xīshū** sparse

蟋蟀 **xīshuài** cricket

习俗 **xísú** custom

系统 **xìtǒng** system

羞 **xiū** shame; embarrass

修 **xiū** repair

锈 **xiù** rust

嗅 **xiù** sniff

修补 **xiūbǔ** mend; darn

羞耻 **xiūchǐ** shame

修道院 **xiūdàoyuàn** abbey; convent; monastery

修改 xiūgǎi correct; amend ◊ correction; amendment

休假 xiūjià vacation ◊ take a vacation

休克 xiūkè shock

羞愧 xiūkuì ashamed

修理 xiūlǐ repair

秀丽 xiùlì beautiful; dainty

修理车间 xiūlǐ chējiān workshop; garage

修女 xiūnǚ nun

羞怯 xiūqiè shy; sheepish

修缮 xiūshàn renovate

休息 xiūxi take a break ◊ recess

休养 xiūyǎng recover

袖珍本 xiùzhēnběn paperback

袖子 xiùzi sleeve

希望 xīwàng hope; wish

细心 xìxīn careful; considerate

吸烟车厢 xīyān chēxiāng smoking car

吸烟者 xīyānzhě smoker

洗衣店 xǐyī diàn laundry (place)

洗衣粉 xǐyīfěn detergent

洗衣机 xǐyījī washing machine

吸引 xīyǐn attract; fascinate

习以为常 xí yǐ wéi cháng usual ◊ used to

稀有 xīyǒu rare

西藏 Xīzàng Tibet ◊ Tibetan

洗澡 xǐzǎo bathe; shower

西装上衣 xīzhuāng shàngyī suit jacket

席子 xízi mat

选 xuǎn choose

选拔赛 xuǎnbásài qualifier

宣布 xuānbù declare ◊ declaration

宣传 xuānchuán promotion; propaganda ◊ promote; publicize

旋风 xuànfēng whirlwind

宣告 xuāngào announce ◊ announcement

选举 xuǎnjǔ election ◊ elect

选举权 xuǎnjǔ quán right to vote

选民 xuǎnmín voter

喧闹 xuānnào racket ◊ noisy; tumultuous ◊ blare out

悬念 xuánniàn suspense

悬赏 xuánshǎng offer a reward

宣誓 xuānshì swear an oath

选手 xuǎnshǒu competitor

旋涡 xuánwō whirlpool

选择 **xuǎnzé** choice ◊ choose

旋转 **xuánzhuǎn** revolve ◊ revolution

许多 **xǔduō** many

学 **xué** study; learn

雪 **xuě** snow

血 **xuè** blood

雪白 **xuěbái** snow-white

雪崩 **xuěbēng** avalanche

血管 **xuèguǎn** blood vessel

学会 **xuéhuì** learn ◊ academy

雪茄 **xuějiā** cigar

血淋淋 **xuè línlín** bloody

学期 **xuéqī** semester

雪橇 **xuěqiāo** sled

雪球 **xuéqiú** snowball

雪人 **xuěrén** snowman

削弱 **xuēruò** impaired ◊ weaken

学生 **xuésheng** student

学说 **xuéshuō** doctrine

学徒 **xuétú** apprentice

学位 **xuéwèi** (university) degree

穴位 **xuéwèi** acupuncture point

学问 **xuéwen** knowledge

学习 **xuéxí** study; learn ◊ studying; learning

学校 **xuéxiào** school

学校假期 **xuéxiào jiàqī** school vacation

血型 **xuèxíng** blood group

血压 **xuèyà** blood pressure

血液循环 **xuèyè xúnhuán** circulation

学院 **xuéyuàn** college

学者 **xuézhě** scholar

血肿 **xuèzhǒng** hematoma

靴子 **xuēzi** boot

续集 **xùjí** sequel

许久 **xǔjiǔ** a long time

酗酒 **xùjiǔ** drink

许可 **xǔkě** permission ◊ permit

畜牧 **xùmù** raise livestock

序幕 **xùmù** prologue

熏 **xūn** smoke

训斥 **xùnchì** reprimand

驯服 **xùnfú** tame, docile

训练 **xùnliàn** train ◊ training

训练班 **xùnliàn bān** training course

许诺 **xǔnuò** promise

询问 **xúnwèn** inquire; interrogate ◊ inquiry; interrogation

勋章 **xūnzhāng** medal; decoration

寻找 **xúnzhǎo** look for

需求 **xūqiú** demand

序曲 **xùqǔ** overture

虚弱 **xūruò** weak ◊ weakness

叙述 **xùshù** tell ◊ account

序言 **xùyán** introduction

需要 **xūyào** need; cost; take; entail ◊ need

Y

压 **yā** press; crush ◊ pressure

鸭 **yā** duck

牙 **yá** tooth

哑 **yǎ** mute

牙齿 **yáchǐ** tooth ◊ dental

牙膏 **yágāo** toothpaste

押金 **yājīn** deposit, security

哑口无言 **yǎkǒu wúyán** speechless

压力 **yālì** pressure; stress

哑铃 **yǎlíng** dumbbell

亚麻布 **yàmá bù** linen

烟 **yān** smoke

腌 **yān** salt; pickle; cure

盐 **yán** salt

沿 **yán** along

眼 **yǎn** eye

咽 **yàn** swallow

砚 **yàn** inkstone

烟草 **yāncǎo** tobacco

延长 **yáncháng** lengthen; prolong ◊ lengthy

烟囱 **yāncōng** chimney;

ship's funnel

烟斗 **yāndǒu** pipe (for smoking)

厌烦 **yànfán** be fed up

羊 **yáng** sheep

洋 **yáng** ocean

阳 **yáng** yang (opposite of yin)

痒 **yǎng** itch

仰 **yǎng** look up

养 **yǎng** rear

样本 **yàngběn** sample

养蚕业 **yǎngcányè** silkworm breeding

洋葱 **yángcōng** onion

严格 **yángé** strict ◊ strictness ◊ strictly

羊倌 **yángguān** shepherd

阳光 **yángguāng** sunshine

养老院 **yǎnglǎo yuàn** old people's home

样品 **yàngpǐn** specimen

氧气 **yǎngqì** oxygen

阳伞 yángsǎn parasol

养神 yǎngshén relax

扬声器 yángshēngqì loudspeaker

样式 yàngshì pattern

杨树 yángshù poplar tree

阳台 yángtái balcony

验光 yànguāng eye test

仰望 yǎngwàng look up

仰卧 yǎngwò lie on one's back

阳性 yángxìng positive *result*

仰泳 yǎngyǒng backstroke

烟盒 yānhé cigarette case

咽喉 yānhóu gullet; larynx

延缓 yánhuǎn postpone

宴会 yànhuì dinner party; banquet

烟灰缸 yānhuī gāng ashtray

眼睛 yǎnjīng eye

眼镜 yǎnjìng glasses

研究 yánjiū study; research

厌倦 yànjuàn be tired of

眼泪 yǎnlèi teardrop

淹没 yānmò flood; submerge

颜色 yánsè color; coloring

延伸 yánshēn stretch

岩石 yánshí rock

掩饰 yǎnshì cover up

淹死 yānsǐ drown

严肃 yánsù serious ◊ seriously ◊ severity

燕尾服 yànwěifú tail coat

厌恶 yànwù hate

演戏 yǎnxì put on a play; perform

眼下 yǎnxià at present

延续 yánxù last

验血 yànxuè blood test

眼药水 yǎnyàoshuǐ eyedrops

谚语 yànyǔ saying

演员 yǎnyuán actor; actress

严重 yánzhòng severe, serious ◊ seriousness

燕子 yànzi swallow (*bird*)

演奏 yǎnzòu perform ◊ performance

腰 yāo waist

摇 yáo shake

咬 yǎo bite

舀 yǎo scoop

药 yào drug; medication

要 yào want; need; must ◊ if

摇摆 yáobǎi roll, sway

腰带 yāodài belt; girdle

要道 yàodào main street

药店 yàodiàn pharmacy

摇动 yáodòng wave; shake; flap

妖怪 yāoguài monster; ghost

摇晃 yáohuàng rock; tremble

药剂师 yàojì shī pharmacist

遥控 yáokòng remote control

药片 yàopiàn tablet

药品 yàopǐn medicine

邀请 yāoqǐng invite ◊ invitation

要求 yāoqiú ask for; demand

钥匙 yàoshi key

腰痛 yāotòng lumbago

药丸 yàowán pill

药物 yàowù drug

谣言 yáoyán rumor

耀眼 yàoyǎn dazzle ◊ dazzling

遥远 yáoyuǎn far away

鸦片 yāpiàn opium

牙签 yáqiān toothpick

牙刷 yáshuā toothbrush

压缩空气 yāsuō kōngqì compressed air

牙痛 yátòng toothache

牙医 yáyī dentist

牙龈 yáyín gum

压韵 yāyùn rhyme

压制 yāzhì suppress

亚洲 Yàzhōu Asia ◊ Asian

亚洲人 Yàzhōurén Asian

也 yě too

野 yě wild

夜 yè night

页 yè page

夜班 yèbān night shift

野餐 yěcān picnic

野地 yědì wilderness

夜间 yèjiān at night

冶炼厂 yěliàn chǎng iron and steel works

野兽 yěshòu wild beast

液体 yètǐ liquid

夜晚 yèwǎn night

腋窝 yèwō armpit

夜校 yèxiào night school

也许 yěxǔ perhaps

野丫头 yěyātou tomboy

爷爷 yéye (paternal) grandfather

夜莺 yèyīng nightingale

业余时间 yèyú shíjiān spare time

野猪 yězhū wild boar

椰子 yēzi coconut

叶子 yèzi leaf

夜总会 yèzǒnghuì nightclub; nightspot

一 yī one

姨 yí (maternal) aunt

疑 yí doubt; suspect

倚 yǐ lean on; depend on

已 yǐ already

易 yì easy ◊ change; exchange

亿 yì hundred million

译 yì translate

一般 yìbān usual; mediocre ◊ usually, generally

一半 yíbàn half

遗产 yíchǎn estate; legacy

异常 yìcháng exceptional; unusual ◊ exceptionally; unusual

溢出 yìchū overflow; slop

遗传 yíchuán genetic; hereditary ◊ heredity ◊ pass on

一次 yícì once

依次 yīcì in turn

以此 yǐcǐ for this reason; consequently; hence

依从 yīcóng obey

意大利 Yìdàlì Italy ◊ Italian

一点儿 yìdiǎnr a little

一定 yídìng definitely

移动 yídòng move; shift; remove ◊ removal; cell phone

移动电话 yídòng diànhuà cellular phone

衣服 yīfu clothes

衣钩 yīgōu coat hook

衣柜 yīguì closet

异国 yìguó foreign country

遗憾 yíhàn sad ◊ regret

颐和园 Yíhéyuán Summer Palace

以后 yǐhòu later, afterward

议会 yìhuì parliament

以及 yǐjí and

衣架 yījià coathanger

意见 yìjiàn opinion; suggestion; complaint

已经 yǐjīng already

依据 yījù basis; grounds

一开始 yìkāishǐ from the start

依靠 yīkào rely on ◊ support

倚靠 yǐkào lean against

一刻钟 yíkèzhōng quarter of an hour

依赖 yīlài depend on ◊ dependent ◊ dependence

医疗保险 yīliáo bǎoxiǎn health insurance

一流 yìliú first-class, first-rate

遗留 yíliú leave behind; bequeath

一律 yílǜ without exception

一路平安 yílù píng'ān have a good trip

衣帽间 yīmào jiān checkroom (for coats)

移民 yímín immigrate; emigrate ◊ immigrant; emigrant; immigration; emigration

因 yīn because ◊ reason

阴 yīn yin (opposite of yang) ◊ overcast

银 yín silver

阴暗 yīn'àn gloomy

疑难 yínán problematic

引爆装置 yǐnbào zhuāngzhì detonator

音标 yīnbiāo phonetics

隐藏 yǐncáng hide

阴沉 yīnchén overcast

因此 yīncǐ so; therefore; thus

阴道 yīndào vagina ◊ vaginal

引导 yǐndǎo lead

引渡 yǐndù extradite ◊ extradition

印度 Yìndù India ◊ Indian

印度洋 yìndùyáng Indian Ocean

音符 yīnfú note

鹰 yīng eagle

赢 yíng win; beat

硬 yìng hard

硬币 yìngbì coin

应承 yìngchéng promise

赢得 yíngdé gain; win

硬度 yìngdù hardness

婴儿 yīng'ér baby

应该 yīnggāi should; ought to

英格兰 Yīnggélán England ◊ English

英国 Yīngguó Britain ◊ British

硬件 yìngjiàn hardware COMPUT

迎接 yíngjiē greet, welcome

盈利 yínglì profit; surplus

英明 yīngmíng brilliant; wise

影射 yǐngshè allude to

樱桃 yīngtáo cherry (fruit)

鹦鹉 yīngwǔ parrot

影响 yǐngxiǎng influence; impact ◊ influence; affect

英雄 yīngxióng hero

营养 yíngyǎng nourishment; nutrition

硬要 yìngyào impose (oneself)

营业时间 yíngyè shíjiān business hours

应用 yìngyòng use; apply ◊ applied

英语 Yīngyǔ English

影子 yǐngzi shadow

银行 **yínháng** bank FIN

引号 **yǐnhào** quotation mark

银婚 **yínhūn** silver wedding (anniversary)

音节 **yīnjié** syllable

引进 **yǐnjìn** introduce ◊ introduction

阴茎 **yīnjīng** penis

音量 **yīnliàng** volume (*of radio etc*)

饮料 **yǐnliào** drink

淫乱 **yínluàn** indecent

隐瞒 **yǐnmán** conceal; disguise

阴谋 **yīnmóu** plot

银幕 **yínmù** screen

引起 **yǐnqǐ** cause; produce; inspire; arouse

引人注目 **yǐn rén zhùmù** stand out; attract attention ◊ spectacular; striking

印刷厂 **yìnshuā chǎng** printing works

饮水 **yìnshuǐ** water *animals*

因素 **yīnsù** ingredient; factor

因特网 **yīntèwǎng** Internet

因特网接口 **yīntèwǎng jiēkǒu** Internet connection

引退 **yǐntuì** resign

因为 **yīnwèi** because ◊ on account of

引文 **yǐnwén** quote

阴险 **yīnxiǎn** devious; insidious ◊ deviously; insidiously

印象 **yìnxiàng** impression

印象深刻 **yìnxiàng shēnkè** impressive

阴性 **yīnxìng** feminine GRAM; negative *results*

隐形眼镜 **yǐnxíng yǎnjìng** contact lens

引用 **yǐnyòng** quote

饮用水 **yǐnyòng shuǐ** drinking water

引诱 **yǐnyòu** seduce ◊ seduction

音乐 **yīnyuè** music ◊ musical

音乐会 **yīnyuèhuì** concert

音乐家 **yīnyuèjiā** musician

引证 **yǐnzhèng** cite

银质 **yínzhì** silver

印子 **yìnzi** imprint

一起 **yìqǐ** together ◊ along

仪器 **yíqì** apparatus; instrument

以前 **yǐqián** before; formerly; previously ◊ former; past

一切 **yíqiè** everything; all

易燃 **yìrán** combustible

医生 **yīshēng** doctor

遗失 **yíshī** lose

仪式 **yíshì** ceremony; ritual

意识 **yìshí** awareness

意识到 **yìshí dào** realize

艺术 **yìshù** art ◊ artistic

艺术家 **yìshùjiā** artist

艺术品 **yìshù pǐn** work of art

意思 **yìsi** meaning; interest

伊斯兰教 **Yīsīlán jiào** Islam ◊ Islamic

一条裤子 **yìtiáo kùzi** a pair of pants

意图 **yìtú** intention

意外 **yìwài** accidental ◊ unexpectedly

疑问 **yíwèn** doubt; query

译文 **yìwén** translation

义务 **yìwù** obligation; duty ◊ voluntary *work*

以下 **yǐxià** under; following

一下子 **yíxiàzi** all at once; in one go

一些 **yìxiē** some, a few

疑心 **yíxīn** suspicion

医学 **yīxué** medicine ◊ medical

一样 **yíyàng** just as; just the same

一言为定 **yī yán wéi dìng** it's a deal

意义 **yìyì** meaning; point

异议 **yìyì** objection

医院 **yīyuàn** hospital, infirmary

议员 **yìyuán** representative; congressman

译员 **yìyuán** interpreter

一月 **yīyuè** January

依仗 **yīzhàng** count on

译者 **yìzhě** translator

一直 **yìzhí** all the time, all along

抑制 **yìzhì** restrain; refrain

移植 **yízhí** transplant; graft

遗址 **yízhǐ** ruin

一致 **yízhì** uniform; unanimous ◊ uniformly; unanimously

意志 **yìzhì** will, willpower

以至于 **yǐzhìyú** so that

遗嘱 **yízhǔ** legacy; will

椅子 **yǐzi** chair

用 **yòng** use; apply ◊ with

拥抱 **yōngbào** cuddle; embrace; hug

涌出 **yǒngchū** pour

勇敢 **yǒnggǎn** brave ◊ bravery

用户 **yònghù** user; consumer

拥挤 **yǒngjǐ** crowd; jostle ◊ crowded

佣金 yòngjīn commission

用量 yòngliàng dose

勇气 yǒngqì courage; spirit

佣人 yōngrén servant

用途 yòngtú use

永远 yǒngyuǎn for ever

用早餐 yòng zǎocān have breakfast

油 yóu oil; fat; grease

有 yǒu have; there is; there are

右 yòu right ◊ on the right

又 yòu again

幽暗 yōu'àn dark

有别于 yǒubiéyú differ from

油菜 yóucài rape

幼虫 yòuchóng larva

邮戳 yóuchuō postmark

由此 yóucǐ from this

优待 yōudài favor; special treatment

邮递 yóudì mail delivery

优点 yōudiǎn merit

邮递员 yóudìyuán mailman

幼儿 yòu'ér infant

诱饵 yòu'ěr bait, decoy

幼儿园 yòu'éryuán kindergarten

有轨电车 yǒuguǐ diànchē streetcar

有规律 yǒu guīlǜ regular ◊ regularly

有害元素 yǒuhài yuánsù harmful substance

友好 yǒuhǎo friendly; kind ◊ goodwill

油画 yóuhuà oil painting

邮汇 yóuhuì money order

有机 yǒujī organic ◊ organically

邮件 yóujiàn mail

有价证券 yǒujià zhèngquàn bond, security

邮局 yóujú post office

由来 yóulái origin

游览 yóulǎn visit; tour; go sightseeing

游乐场 yóulèchǎng amusement park

有理 yǒulǐ reasonable; rational; in the right

有利 yǒulì advantageous; favorable

忧虑 yōulǜ worry ◊ worried; distracted

优美 yōuměi graceful; dainty ◊ grace

幽默 yōumò humor

油腻 yóunì greasy; rich

右派 yòupài right; right

winger

邮票 yóupiào stamp

尤其 yóuqí especially

有趣 yǒuqù fun, amusing, entertaining; interesting

优势 yōushì superiority

有时 yǒushí sometimes

有失体统 yǒu shī tǐtǒng offensive

幼兽 yòushòu cub

犹太人 Yóutàirén Jew

有弹性 yǒu tánxìng springy, elastic; supple

油田 yóutián oil field

游戏 yóuxì play; game

优先 yōuxiān preferential, priority ◊ take priority

有线电视 yǒuxiàn diànshì cable TV

邮箱 yóuxiāng mailbox

优先权 yōuxiān quán priority

有些 yǒuxiē some

游行 yóuxíng march, parade

优秀 yōuxiù excellent; excellence

有益 yǒuyì beneficial; useful

友谊 yǒuyì friendship

有意 yǒuyì deliberate ◊ deliberately

游泳 yóuyǒng swim ◊ swimming

有用 yǒuyòng useful

游泳池 yóuyǒngchí swimming pool

游泳裤 yóuyǒngkù swimming shorts

游泳衣 yóuyǒng yī swimsuit

忧郁 yōuyù gloom ◊ gloomy

由于 yóuyú with; through ◊ because of; due to

犹豫 yóuyù hesitate ◊ hesitation ◊ tentative

犹豫不定 yóuyù búdìng indecisive

优越 yōuyuè superior

邮政编码 yóuzhèng biānmǎ zip code

幼稚 yòuzhì childish; naive ◊ childishness; child

邮资 yóuzī postage

柚子 yòuzi pomelo

鱼 yú fish

与 yǔ and ◊ with

雨 yǔ rain

玉 yù jade

欲 yù desire

圆 yuán round ◊ circle

元 yuán yuan (Chinese currency)

园 yuán garden

远 yuǎn far; distant

愿 **yuàn** wish

远处 **yuǎnchù** distant place

元旦 **Yuándàn** New Year's Day

园丁 **yuándīng** gardener

远东 **Yuǎndōng** Far East

原告 **yuángào** claimant; plaintiff

园规 **yuánguī** compass

远见 **yuǎnjiàn** vision

原来 **yuánlái** original ◊ originally

原谅 **yuánliàng** forgive ◊ forgiveness

原料 **yuánliào** raw material; ingredient

圆盘 **yuánpán** disk

原始 **yuánshǐ** primitive

远视 **yuǎnshì** long-sighted

元素 **yuánsù** element CHEM

愿望 **yuànwàng** wish

圆形 **yuánxíng** round

园艺 **yuányì** gardening; horticulture

愿意 **yuànyì** willing ◊ willingness ◊ want

原因 **yuányīn** cause

元音 **yuányīn** vowel

原则 **yuánzé** principle

援助 **yuánzhù** support, help

圆珠笔 **yuánzhūbǐ** ballpoint pen

院子 **yuànzi** yard; courtyard

原子弹 **yuánzǐ dàn** atom bomb

原子能 **yuánzǐ néng** atomic energy

远足 **yuǎnzú** excursion; hike

预报 **yùbào** forecast

预备 **yùbèi** prepare

愚蠢 **yúchǔn** stupid ◊ stupidity

鱼刺 **yúcì** fishbone

遇到 **yùdào** meet, run into

预定 **yùdìng** book ◊ booking

约 **yuē** arrange

月 **yuè** month

乐 **yuè** music

越…越… **yuè…yuè…** the more…the more…

约定 **yuēdìng** agree; arrange to meet

阅读 **yuèdú** read ◊ reading

乐队 **yuèduì** band; orchestra

岳父 **yuèfù** father-in-law

月光 **yuèguāng** moonlight

越过 **yuèguò** exceed, pass; get over

月经 **yuèjīng** period; menstruation

月经带 **yuèjīngdài** sanitary napkin

越来越 **yuèláiyuè** increasingly

阅览室 **yuèlǎnshì** reading room

月亮 **yuèliàng** moon ◊ lunar

岳母 **yuèmǔ** mother-in-law

越南 **Yuènán** Vietnam ◊ Vietnamese

月票 **yuèpiào** monthly ticket

乐器 **yuèqì** musical instrument

约束 **yuēshù** restrain; curb; bind; restrict ◊ restriction

越野 **yuèyě** cross-country

乐音 **yuèyīn** tone

语法 **yǔfǎ** grammar

预防 **yùfáng** prevent ◊ prevention

预防措施 **yùfáng cuòshī** precaution; preventive measure

预付 **yùfù** advance ◊ pay in advance

鱼竿 **yúgān** fishing pole

鱼肝油 **yúgānyóu** cod-liver oil

预告 **yùgào** forecast

宇航 **yǔháng** space travel

宇航员 **yǔhángyuán** astronaut

愈合 **yùhé** heal

预计 **yùjì** estimate; plan

预见 **yùjiàn** foresee

遇见 **yùjian** meet

浴巾 **yùjīn** bath towel

郁金香 **yùjīnxiāng** tulip

愉快 **yúkuài** happy

娱乐 **yúlè** entertainment; pleasure; recreation

预料 **yùliào** expect; foretell ◊ anticipation

羽毛 **yǔmáo** feather; plume

羽毛球 **yǔmáoqiú** badminton; shuttlecock

玉米 **yùmǐ** corn

玉米花 **yùmǐhuā** popcorn

渔民 **yúmín** fisherman

云 **yún** cloud

熨 **yùn** iron

晕 **yùn** dizzy

运 **yùn** transport

晕船 **yùnchuán** seasick ◊ get seasick

运动 **yùndòng** move; movement; campaign; sport; exercise

运动场 **yùndòng chǎng** playing field

运动员 **yùndòngyuán** sportsman; sportswoman; athlete; player

熨斗 **yùndǒu** iron

孕妇 **yùnfù** pregnant woman

运河 **yùnhé** canal

晕机 **yùnjī** airsickness

愚弄 **yúnòng** tease

云雀 **yúnquè** lark

运输 **yùnshū** transportation

运输公司 **yùnshū gōngsī** shipping company

允许 **yǔnxǔ** allow

浴盆 **yùpén** bathtub

语气 **yǔqì** tone

雨伞 **yǔsǎn** umbrella

于是 **yúshì** then; consequently

浴室 **yùshì** bathroom

预算 **yùsuàn** calculate ◊ budget

欲望 **yùwàng** desire; longing

雨靴 **yǔxuē** rain boot

语言 **yǔyán** language ◊ linguistic

预言 **yùyán** prophecy; prediction ◊ predict

渔业 **yúyè** fishing industry

雨衣 **yǔyī** raincoat

浴衣 **yùyī** bathrobe

预约 **yùyuē** arrange; reserve ◊ advance booking

预兆 **yùzhào** sign

宇宙 **yǔzhòu** universe

Z

杂草 **zácǎo** weed

杂货店 **záhuò diàn** grocery store

栽 **zāi** plant

在 **zài** at; in; on

再 **zài** again; further

在…里 **zài…lǐ** inside...

在…旁 **zài…páng** beside...

在…上面 **zài…shàngmian** on...; above...

在…同时 **zài…tóngshí** during...

在…下面 **zài…xiàmiàn** under...

在…之间 **zài…zhījiān** between...

在…之前 **zài…zhīqián** before...

在场 **zàichǎng** presence ◊ be present

灾害 **zāihài** disaster

在乎 **zàihu** mind; care

灾祸 **zāihuò** disaster

再见 **zàijiàn** goodbye

灾难 zāinàn disaster

栽培 zāipéi cultivation

再说 zàishuō besides; moreover

再一次 zàiyícì once more

杂技 zájì acrobatics

杂乱无章 záluàn-wúzhāng disorder; mess ◊ messy

暂 zàn temporary

赞成 zànchéng approve; agree with ◊ favorable, agreeable ◊ approval

脏 zāng dirty

葬礼 zànglǐ funeral; burial

脏物 zāngwù dirt

赞美 zànměi praise; compliment ◊ complimentary

咱们 zánmen us; we

赞赏 zànshǎng appreciate

暂时 zànshí temporarily ◊ temporary

赞同 zàntóng agree with; approve

暂行 zànxíng temporary ◊ temporary

赞助 zànzhù support; patronage; sponsorship

凿 záo chisel

早 zǎo morning ◊ early ◊ beforehand

灶 zào stove; hearth

早餐 zǎocān breakfast

早产 zǎochǎn premature birth

早晨 zǎochén morning ◊ in the morning

遭到 zāodào meet with

造反 zàofǎn revolt

糟糕 zāogāo bad ◊ badly

早就 zǎojiù for a long time; a long time ago

早上好 zǎoshang hǎo good morning

遭受 zāoshòu suffer

噪音 zàoyīn noise

凿子 záozi chisel

枣子 zǎozi Chinese date

杂志 zázhì magazine

责备 zébèi blame; reproach; reprimand

责骂 zémà scold

憎恨 zēnghèn hate

增加 zēngjiā increase ◊ raise ◊ increasing

增刊 zēngkān supplement

增强 zēngqiáng strengthen

赠送 zèngsòng give ◊ complimentary

曾孙 zēngsūn great-grandchild

增长 zēngzhǎng grow

growth

增值 **zēngzhí** increase in value

增值税 **zēngzhí shuì** value-added tax

曾祖父 **zēngzǔfù** great-grandfather

曾祖母 **zēngzǔmǔ** great-grandmother

怎么 **zěnme** how

责任 **zérèn** responsibility, duty; blame

闸 **zhá** lock; sluice

炸 **zhà** blow up; explode

榨出 **zhàchū** extract; squeeze out ◊ extraction

炸弹 **zhàdàn** bomb

轧辊 **zhágǔn** roller

摘 **zhāi** pick

窄 **zhǎi** narrow

债 **zhài** debt

摘录 **zhāilù** extract

债券 **zhàiquàn** promissory note; bond

债权人 **zhàiquánrén** creditor

债务 **zhàiwù** debt

栅栏 **zhàlán** fence; railings; bars

蚱蜢 **zhàměng** grasshopper

粘 **zhān** stick

毡 **zhān** felt

占 **zhàn** occupy; take; constitute; make up

站 **zhàn** stand ◊ stop; station

展出 **zhǎnchū** exhibit; display

战斗 **zhàndòu** combat; fight

战俘 **zhànfú** prisoner of war

章 **zhāng** chapter

长 **zhǎng** grow ◊ head

障碍 **zhàng'ài** obstacle; barrier

障碍物 **zhàng'àiwù** barrier

涨潮 **zhǎngcháo** incoming tide ◊ come in (of tide)

章程 **zhāngchéng** rules; statutes

长大 **zhǎngdà** grow up; develop

账单 **zhàngdān** check; invoice

丈夫 **zhàngfu** husband

涨价 **zhǎngjià** price rise

张开 **zhāngkāi** open, unfold

樟脑 **zhāngnǎo** camphor

帐篷 **zhàngpeng** tent

掌声 **zhǎngshēng** applause

掌握 **zhǎngwò** grasp; master; control

展览 **zhǎnlǎn** display, exhibit

展览会 zhǎnlǎnhuì
exhibition

占领 zhànlǐng capture;
occupy ◊ occupation

战胜 zhànshèng conquer ◊
victorious

战士 zhànshì soldier;
warrior; fighter

站台 zhàntái platform

粘贴 zhāntiē stick

站位 zhànwèi standing room

占线 zhànxiàn busy ◊ the
line is busy

战线 zhànxiàn front; battle
line

战役 zhànyì battle

占有 zhànyǒu own; take

占有者 zhànyǒuzhě owner

战争 zhànzhēng war;
conflict; hostilities

站住 zhànzhù stop

辗转 zhǎnzhuǎn toss and
turn

找 zhǎo look for; ask for

招待 zhāodài entertain;
serve customer

招待会 zhāodài huì
reception

照顾 zhàogù look after;
tend ◊ care

照管 zhàoguǎn look after

着急 zháojí worry

召集 zhàojí call

召开 zhàokāi convene, hold

照看 zhàokàn watch, keep
an eye on

照明 zhàomíng illuminate,
light ◊ lighting

照片 zhàopiàn photograph

招聘 zhāopìn recruit ◊
recruitment

招认 zhāorèn confess

招手 zhāoshǒu wave;
beckon

朝霞 zhāoxiá dawn

照相 zhàoxiàng take a
photo

照像机 zhàoxiàngjī camera

照耀 zhàoyào shine

罩衣 zhàoyī coverall

沼泽 zhǎozé swamp

眨眼 zhǎyǎn blink; wink

炸药 zhàyào dynamite;
gunpowder; explosive

这 zhè this; the

这次 zhècì this time

折叠 zhédié fold ◊ folding

折断 zhéduàn break; break
off; fracture

这个 zhège this ◊ this one

折扣 zhékòu discount;
rebate

这里 zhèlǐ here

折磨 zhémó torture

针 zhēn needle

真 zhēn real

珍宝 zhēnbǎo treasure; gem

侦察 zhēnchá reconnoiter ◊ reconnaissance

震颤 zhènchàn throb; tremble; twitch

真诚 zhēnchéng sincere ◊ sincerely ◊ sincerity

针刺 zhēncì acupuncture

镇定 zhèndìng calm

震动 zhèndòng shudder; vibrate ◊ vibration; tremor

振动 zhèndòng vibrate ◊ vibration

蒸 zhēng steam

正 zhèng positive; plus; upright; just

挣 zhèng earn; struggle

政策 zhèngcè policy

正常 zhèngcháng normal ◊ normally ◊ normality

正常运转 zhèngcháng yùnzhuǎn normal operation

争吵 zhēngchǎo quarrel

证词 zhèngcí testimony

正当 zhèngdàng proper; legitimate; right

挣得 zhèngde earn

正点 zhèngdiǎn on schedule

争斗 zhēngdòu fight

整顿 zhěngdùn regulation; arrangement

蒸发 zhēngfā evaporate; steam

正方形 zhèngfāng xíng square

征服 zhēngfú conquer ◊ conquest

政府 zhèngfǔ government

正好 zhènghǎo just right

证件 zhèngjiàn ID

整洁 zhěngjié neat, tidy

拯救 zhěngjiù save ◊ salvation

证据 zhèngjù evidence; proof

整理 zhěnglǐ arrange; sort out; clear up

争论 zhēnglùn argue; dispute ◊ argument; controversy

正面 zhèngmiàn front; façade

证明 zhèngmíng certify; prove

正派 zhèngpài decent; law-abiding; straight ◊ decency

蒸汽 zhēngqì steam

整齐 zhěngqí neat, tidy

挣钱 zhèngqián earn money

蒸汽机车 zhēngqì jīchē steam locomotive

政权 zhèngquán regime

正确 zhèngquè correct ◊ correctly

证人 zhèngrén witness

证实 zhèngshí confirm

正式 zhèngshì formal; official ◊ formally; officially

征收 zhēngshōu impose; collect

证书 zhèngshū certificate; qualification

整体 zhěngtǐ whole

正义 zhèngyì just ◊ justice

证章 zhèngzhāng badge

正直 zhèngzhí be right ◊ decent

政治 zhèngzhì politics ◊ political

政治家 zhèngzhìjiā politician

症状 zhèngzhuàng symptom

正字法 zhèngzìfǎ spelling

震撼 zhènhàn shake

赈济 zhènjì charity

贞洁 zhēnjié chaste ◊ virginity

震惊 zhènjīng shock

镇静 zhènjìng composed ◊ composure

真理 zhēnlǐ truth

珍品 zhēnpǐn gem

真实 zhēnshí real; true ◊ really

诊所 zhěnsuǒ clinic

侦探 zhēntàn detective

侦探片 zhēntànpiàn detective movie

枕套 zhěntào pillowcase

镇痛 zhèntòng analgesic

枕头 zhěntou pillow

真相 zhēnxiàng fact; truth

阵雨 zhènyǔ shower (of rain)

真正 zhēnzhèng authentic; real ◊ really

针织品 zhēnzhīpǐn knitwear

珍珠 zhēnzhū pearl

榛子 zhēnzi hazelnut

这些 zhèxiē these

哲学 zhéxué philosophy

这样 zhèyàng like this; so ◊ such

遮阴 zhēyīn shade ◊ shady

汁 zhī juice

织 zhī weave

直 zhí straight

只 zhǐ only

纸 zhǐ paper

指 zhǐ finger ◊ point to

至 zhì to; up to ◊ reach

纸板 zhǐbǎn cardboard

纸板盒 zhǐbǎn hé cardboard box

纸币 zhǐbì bill

织布机 zhībùjī loom

支撑 zhīchēng support; sustain

支持 zhīchí support

支出 zhīchū pay ◊ expenditure

直达 zhídá direct

知道 zhīdào know

直到 zhídào until

指导 zhǐdǎo guide; instruct; coach ◊ instructions; guidance; directory

值得 zhídé deserve; be worthwhile ◊ desirable; recommended

制动 zhìdòng brake

制度 zhìdù system

至多 zhìduō at most

脂肪 zhīfáng fat

支付 zhīfù pay

制服 zhìfú uniform

支付手段 zhīfù shǒuduàn means of payment

制革 tan zhìgé leather

职工 zhígōng workforce

智慧 zhìhuì wisdom; intelligence

支架 zhījià upright; support

指甲 zhījia fingernail

指甲油 zhījia yóu nail polish

直接 zhíjiē direct ◊ directly

至今 zhìjīn until now

直径 zhíjìng diameter

指控 zhǐkòng accuse; charge ◊ allegation

智力 zhìlì intellect; intelligence ◊ intellectual

质量 zhìliàng quality

治疗 zhìliáo treatment; therapy ◊ treat

支流 zhīliú tributary

直流电 zhíliúdiàn direct current

支路 zhīlù side road

芝麻 zhīma sesame

芝麻油 zhīmayóu sesame oil

殖民地 zhímíndì colony ◊ colonial

知名 zhīmíng famous; prominent

指明 zhǐmíng point out

致命 zhìmìng fatal ◊ fatally

指南针 zhǐnánzhēn compass

执拗 zhíniù stubborn

侄女 zhínǚ niece

支票 **zhīpiào** check FIN

志气 **zhìqi** ambition

支气管炎 **zhīqìguǎnyán** bronchitis

支取 **zhīqǔ** withdraw

掷骰子 **zhì shǎizi** throw dice

至少 **zhìshǎo** at least

直升飞机 **zhíshēng fēijī** helicopter

知识 **zhīshi** knowledge; learning

指示 **zhǐshì** indicate; instruct ◊ indication; directions

肢体语言 **zhītǐ yǔyán** body language

制图 **zhìtú** make maps

职位 **zhíwèi** position

质问 **zhìwèn** question, challenge

植物 **zhíwù** plant ◊ botanical

职务 **zhíwù** duties; job

植物学 **zhíwùxué** botany

窒息 **zhìxī** suffocate ◊ suffocation

支线 **zhīxiàn** branch line

直线 **zhíxiàn** straight line

志向 **zhìxiàng** ambition

致谢 **zhìxiè** extend one's thanks

执行 **zhíxíng** carry out

秩序 **zhìxù** order

止血 **zhǐxuè** stop bleeding ◊ styptic

只要 **zhǐyào** provided that; so long as

职业 **zhíyè** business; profession; occupation ◊ vocational; occupational; professional

致意 **zhìyì** greeting

指引 **zhǐyǐn** guide, show

只有 **zhǐyǒu** only if; nothing but

治愈 **zhìyù** cure

职员 **zhíyuán** employee

志愿者 **zhìyuànzhě** volunteer

制造 **zhìzào** manufacture ◊ manufacturing

指责 **zhǐzé** rebuke; reproach ◊ disapproval ◊ reproachful

执照 **zhízhào** license

指针 **zhǐzhēn** needle (on dial); hand (on clock)

制止 **zhìzhǐ** prevent; deter; stem, block

蜘蛛 **zhīzhū** spider

侄子 **zhízi** nephew

知足 **zhīzú** undemanding

制作 **zhìzuò** produce ◊ production

钟 **zhōng** clock; bell

中 zhōng middle; medium; China

肿 zhōng swell ◊ swollen

种 zhòng plant

仲裁 zhòngcái arbitrate ◊ arbitration

中餐 zhōngcān Chinese food

忠诚 zhōngchéng faithful

重大 zhòngdà serious

终点 zhōngdiǎn finish, end

重点 zhòngdiǎn stress; key point; emphasis

终点站 zhōngdiǎnzhàn terminus

中东 Zhōngdōng Middle East

中毒 zhòngdú poisoning

中断 zhōngduàn interrupt; break off ◊ interruption

中耳炎 zhōng'ěryán middle ear infection

中饭 zhōngfàn lunch

中风 zhòngfēng stroke MED

重工业 zhònggōngyè heavy industry

中国 Zhōngguó China ◊ Chinese

中国人 Zhōngguórén Chinese (person)

中华人民共和国 Zhōng-huá Rénmín Gònghéguó People's Republic of China, PRC

中间 zhōngjiān middle ◊ halfway

终究 zhōngjiū finally

中肯 zhòngkěn apt ◊ aptly

肿块 zhǒngkuài lump

种类 zhǒnglèi kind; species

中立 zhōnglì disinterested; neutral

重力 zhònglì gravity PHYS

重量 zhòngliàng weight

肿瘤 zhǒngliú tumor

中年 zhōngnián middle age ◊ middle-aged

中篇小说 zhōngpiān xiǎoshuō novella

中秋节 Zhōngqiūjié Mid-Autumn Festival, Moon Festival

终身 zhōngshēn lifelong; for life

终身伴侣 zhōngshēn bànlǚ life partner

忠实 zhōngshí devoted

重视 zhòngshì value

中世纪 Zhōngshìjì Middle Ages ◊ medieval

众所周知 zhòngsuǒ zhōuzhī well-known

中文 **Zhōngwén** Chinese

中午 **zhōngwǔ** midday

中心 **zhōngxīn** center; heart

衷心 **zhōngxīn** sincere; warm

中学 **zhōngxué** middle school; junior high school

中央 **zhōngyāng** central ◊ middle

重要 **zhòngyào** important

重要性 **zhòngyàoxìng** importance

终于 **zhōngyú** in the end

肿胀 **zhǒngzhàng** swell up ◊ swollen ◊ swelling

中止 **zhōngzhǐ** cease

中指 **zhōngzhǐ** middle finger

终止 **zhōngzhǐ** end

种植 **zhòngzhí** plant; cultivate

种植园 **zhòngzhíyuán** plantation

种子 **zhǒngzi** seed

洲 **zhōu** continent

周 **zhōu** week

粥 **zhōu** rice porridge

轴 **zhóu** shaft; axle

皱 **zhòu** crease

周到 **zhōudao** considerate; tactful

周末 **zhōumò** weekend ◊ on the weekend

周期 **zhōuqī** cycle; period

周围 **zhōuwéi** around ◊ surrounding ◊ surroundings

皱纹 **zhòuwén** crease

绉纹纸 **zhòuwénzhǐ** crepe paper

猪 **zhū** pig

竹 **zhú** bamboo

煮 **zhǔ** boil (cook)

住 **zhù** live; stop

柱 **zhù** pillar

祝 **zhù** wish

爪 **zhuǎ** claw

砖 **zhuān** brick; tile

转 **zhuǎn** turn; transfer ◊ turning

转变 **zhuǎnbiàn** shift ◊ swing; changeover

转播 **zhuǎnbō** relay *signal*

转车 **zhuǎnchē** change (trains/buses)

转达 **zhuǎndá** pass on

转达问候 **zhuǎndá wènhòu** send one's regards

转动 **zhuàndòng** turn

桩 **zhuāng** stake; peg

装 **zhuāng** pack

撞 **zhuàng** hit

壮 **zhuàng** strong

装扮 **zhuāngbàn** disguise

oneself; dress up

装备 zhuāngbèi equipment
◊ equip; furnish

撞翻 zhuàngfān knock over

庄稼 zhuāngjia crops

状况 zhuàngkuàng state

装饰 zhuāngshì decorate ◊
decorative

装载 zhuāngzài load

装作 zhuāngzuò pretend;
pose as

传记 zhuànjì biography

专家 zhuānjiā expert,
specialist

专科医生 zhuānkē yīshēng
specialist (doctor)

专利 zhuānlì patent

专门 zhuānmén special

转让 zhuǎnràng entrust;
transfer

转身 zhuǎnshēn turn
around

转弯处 zhuǎnwānchù
curve; corner

转向 zhuǎnxiàng change
direction; turn around;
move on ◊ change of
direction; U-turn

专心 zhuānxīn concentrate
◊ concentration; devotion

专有知识 zhuānyǒu zhīshi

know-how

专业 zhuānyè professional ◊
professionally ◊ field

专业知识 zhuānyè zhīshi
specialized knowledge

抓住 zhuāzhù grab, grasp

爪子 zhuǎzi claw; paw

珠宝 zhūbǎo jewel; jewelry

珠宝商 zhūbǎoshāng
jeweler

逐步 zhúbù progressively;
step by step

住处 zhùchù residence;
lodging

贮存 zhùcún store

住房 zhùfáng housing

逐个 zhúgè one by one

主观 zhǔguān subjective

主管 zhǔguǎn be in charge
of ◊ supervisor

祝贺 zhùhè congratulate

追求 zhuīqiú seek; pursue

追溯 zhuīsù date back to;
backdate ◊ retroactive

逐渐 zhújiàn gradual ◊
gradually

主角 zhǔjué leading role

著名 zhùmíng famous

准 zhǔn allow ◊ accurate

准备 zhǔnbèi plan; prepare;
fix ◊ preparation

准确 zhǔnquè accurate; precise

准确性 zhǔnquèxìng accuracy

准时 zhǔnshí punctual ◊ punctually

准许 zhǔnxǔ approve

准予 zhǔnyǔ grant

桌布 zhuōbù tablecloth

着陆 zhuólù land ◊ landing

啄木鸟 zhuómùniǎo woodpecker

捉弄 zhuōnòng take in

啄食 zhuóshí peck at one's food

着想 zhuóxiǎng consider

卓有成效 zhuō yǒu chéngxiào effective; successful

卓越 zhuōyuè outstanding; remarkable; notable ◊ remarkably

桌子 zhuōzi table

捉住 zhuōzhù catch, capture

主人 zhǔrén host; owner

猪肉 zhūròu pork

侏儒 zhūrú dwarf

注射 zhùshè inject ◊ injection

注视 zhùshì gaze ◊ gaze at

注释 zhùshì note; gloss

助手 zhùshǒu assistant

竹笋 zhúsǔn bamboo shoots

主题 zhǔtí subject, topic ◊ topical

铸铁 zhùtiě cast iron

助听器 zhùtīngqì hearing aid

主席 zhǔxí chair

助学金 zhùxuéjīn grant (for studies)

主要 zhǔyào main ◊ mainly

主意 zhǔyì idea

注意 zhùyì notice; pay attention to

铸造 zhùzào cast

主张 zhǔzhāng cause; position ◊ advocate; stand up for; represent

柱子 zhùzi pillar

字 zì word; character; handwriting

自 zì self ◊ from

资本 zīběn capital

资本主义 zīběn zhǔyì capitalism ◊ capitalist

滋补 zībǔ nutritious

资产 zīchǎn asset FIN

资产阶级 zīchǎn jiējí bourgeoisie

自从 zìcóng since

子弹 zǐdàn bullet; cartridge;

pellet

字典 **zìdiǎn** dictionary

自动 **zìdòng** automatic ◊ automatically; by itself

自发 **zìfā** spontaneous

自负 **zìfù** pompous; arrogant; conceited ◊ arrogance; conceit

资格 **zīgé** qualification

子宫 **zǐgōng** womb

自豪 **zìháo** pride ◊ proud ◊ proudly

自己 **zìjǐ** self; oneself ◊ own ◊ by oneself

紫禁城 **Zǐjìnchéng** Forbidden City

自来水 **zìláishuǐ** running water

自来水笔 **zìláishuǐbǐ** fountain pen

字面 **zìmiàn** literal ◊ literally

字母 **zìmǔ** letter (of alphabet)

字幕 **zìmù** subtitle

字母表 **zìmǔbiǎo** alphabet

自然 **zìrán** nature ◊ natural ◊ naturally, of course

自然保护 **zìrán bǎohù** conservation

自然灾害 **zìrán zāihài** natural disaster

紫色 **zìsè** purple

自杀 **zìshā** suicide ◊ commit suicide

姿势 **zīshì** position; posture

自私自利 **zìsī-zìlì** selfish

字体 **zìtǐ** font; typeface

滋味 **zīwèi** flavor; taste

自卫 **zìwèi** self-defense

自我控制 **zìwǒ kòngzhì** self-control

仔细 **zǐxì** careful ◊ closely

自信 **zìxìn** confident; self-confident; assertive ◊ self-confidence

自行车 **zìxíngchē** bicycle

自信心 **zìxìnxīn** self-confidence

自选 **zìxuǎn** self-service ◊ optional

咨询 **zīxún** advice; consultancy

自由 **zìyóu** freedom, liberty ◊ free; liberal

自愿 **zìyuàn** voluntary ◊ of one's own accord

自助餐 **zìzhùcān** buffet, self-service meal

自尊心 **zìzūnxīn** self-respect

总 **zǒng** total; general; main; gross FIN ◊ always

总部 **zǒngbù** head office

总裁 **zǒngcái** president

总共 **zǒnggòng** altogether

纵横交错 **zònghéng jiāocuò** checkered

总机 **zǒngjī** telephone exchange

踪迹 **zōngjì** trace

总计 **zǒngjì** total

宗教 **zōngjiào** religion ◊ religious

总结 **zǒngjié** summary

总理 **zǒnglǐ** premier; prime minister

棕榈树 **zōnglǘshù** palm tree

棕色 **zōngsè** brown

总是 **zǒngshì** always

总数 **zǒngshù** total; sum

总统 **zǒngtǒng** president ◊ presidential

走 **zǒu** walk; go; move; leave; run; navigate COMPUT

奏 **zòu** play *instrument*

揍 **zòu** beat up; punch

走过来 **zǒu guòlai** approach

走进 **zǒujìn** enter

走开 **zǒukāi** buzz off; walk away

走廊 **zǒuláng** corridor; passageway

走私 **zǒusī** smuggle ◊

smuggling

走运 **zǒuyùn** be lucky

租 **zū** rent; hire; lease

足 **zú** foot ◊ enough

组 **zǔ** group; team, crew

阻碍 **zǔ'ài** hinder; frustrate ◊ setback

钻孔 **zuānkǒng** bore a hole

钻头 **zuàntóu** bit

组成 **zǔchéng** comprise

阻挡 **zǔdǎng** obstruct; keep, detain ◊ tackle

祖父母 **zǔfùmǔ** grandparents

足够 **zúgòu** ample ◊ amply

祖国 **zǔguó** native country, homeland

嘴 **zuǐ** mouth; spout

罪 **zuì** crime

醉 **zuì** drunk

最 **zuì** most, *used to form superlatives*

最初 **zuìchū** first; original

嘴唇 **zuǐchún** lip

最多 **zuìduō** maximum ◊ at most

罪犯 **zuìfàn** criminal; culprit; offender

最高 **zuìgāo** highest; topmost; tallest

最好 **zuìhǎo** best

最后 **zuìhòu** last; ultimate ◊ lastly; in the end

最近 **zuìjìn** recent; closest ◊ recently; soon

罪人 **zuìrén** sinner; offender

最小 **zuìxiǎo** least

罪行 **zuìxíng** crime; offense

最终 **zuìzhōng** eventual; final ◊ eventually; finally

租金 **zūjīn** rental

遵从 **zūncóng** comply with ◊ compliance

尊敬 **zūnjìng** respect ◊ esteemed

遵守 **zūnshǒu** abide by ◊ observauuce

遵循 **zūnxún** follow

尊严 **zūnyán** dignity

尊重 **zūnzhòng** respect; honor

左 **zuǒ** left

坐 **zuò** sit; sit down; catch

作 **zuò** make; do

做 **zuò** make; do; perform, carry out

作伴 **zuòbàn** keep company

左边 **zuǒbian** left, the left-hand side ◊ left-hand

做出反应 **zuòchū fǎnyìng** respond

作坊 **zuòfang** workshop

作废 **zuòfèi** expire

作家 **zuòjiā** writer

作料 **zuóliào** seasoning

坐落在 **zuòluòzài** be situated

做梦 **zuòmèng** dream

琢磨 **zuómo** ponder

左派 **zuǒpài** the left

作品 **zuòpǐn** work; production

作曲家 **zuòqǔ jiā** composer

左手 **zuǒshǒu** left hand

昨天 **zuótiān** yesterday

昨天晚上 **zuótiān wǎnshang** last night

作为 **zuòwéi** as; by way of

座位 **zuòwèi** place, seat

坐下 **zuòxià** sit down

作业 **zuòyè** job, task; homework; assignment

作用 **zuòyòng** function

作者 **zuòzhě** author, writer

作证 **zuòzhèng** testify

足球 **zúqiú** soccer

阻塞 **zǔsè** block ◊ traffic jam

祖先 **zǔxiān** ancestor; ancestry

租用 **zūyòng** lease

阻止 **zǔzhǐ** stop, prevent; block

诅咒 **zǔzhòu** curse

A

a, an *no translation*

abandon pāoqì 抛弃; *car* líqì 离弃; *plan* fàngqì 放弃

abbreviation suōxiě 缩写

ability nénglì 能力

able: *be ~ to* néng 能

abolish fèichú 废除

abortion réngōng liúchǎn 人工流产

about 1 *prep* (*concerning*) guānyú ...关于...; *what's it ~?* jiǎng shénme? 讲什么的？**2** *adv* (*roughly*) dàyuē 大约; *be ~ to ...* zhèng zhǔnbèi ...正准备...

above 1 *prep* bǐ ...gāo 比...高; (*more than*) bǐ ...duō 比...多; *~ all* zuì zhòngyào 最重要 **2** *adv* zài shàngtóu 在上头

abroad *live* guówài 国外; *go ~* chūguó 出国

abrupt *departure* tūrán 突然; *manner* shēngyìng 生硬

absent *adj* quēxí 缺席

absent-minded xīnbú zàiyān 心不在焉

absolutely (*completely*) wánquán 完全

absorb xīshōu 吸收

abstain (*in vote*) qìquán 弃权

abstract *adj* chōuxiàng 抽象

absurd huāngtáng 荒唐

abuse *n* (*insults*) rǔmà 辱骂

academic *n* xuézhě 学者

accelerate 1 *v/i* jiāsù 加速 **2** *v/t output* jiākuài 加快

accent kǒuyīn 口音; (*emphasis*) zhòngyīn 重音

accept *v/t offer* jiēshòu 接受

acceptance jiēshòu 接受

access *n* (*to building*) rùkǒu 入口

accident shìgù 事故; (*not done on purpose*) bùxiǎoxīn 不小心

accommodations zhùsuǒ 住所

accompany péitóng 陪同

MUS bànzòu 伴奏

accomplice bāngxiōng 帮凶

according: ~ to gēnjù 根据

account n FIN zhàngmù 帐目; (description) xùshù 叙述

accountant kuàijì 会计

accounts zhàngmù 帐目

accumulate v/t & v/i lěijī 累积

accuracy zhǔnquèxìng 准确性

accurate zhǔnquè 准确

accusation zéguài 责怪; (public) qiǎnzé 谴责

accuse zhǐkòng 指控; (publicly) qiǎnzé 谴责

accused: the ~ LAW bèigào 被告

ache n & v/i tòng 痛

achieve huòdé 获得

achievement (of ambition) huòdé 获得; (thing achieved) chéngjiù 成就

acid n suān 酸

acknowledge chéngrèn 承认

acknowledg(e)ment rènkě 认可

acquaintance (person) shúrén 熟人

acquire skill huòdé 获得;

property qǔdé 取得

acquit LAW xuānpàn wúzuì 宣判无罪

acrobat zájì yǎnyuán 杂技演员

across 1 prep (on other side of) zài ... de língyìbiān 在 ...的另一边 ◊ (to other side of) héngguò 横过; (of street etc) guòlái 过来 2 adv (to other side) guòlái 过来

act 1 v/i THEA biǎoyǎn 表演; ~ as línshí dānrèn 临时担任 2 n (deed) xíngdòng 行动; (of play) mù 幕; (in vaudeville) jiémù 节目; (pretense) jiǎzhuāng 假装

acting 1 n (profession) biǎoyǎn yè 表演业; (performance) biǎoyǎn 表演 2 adj (temporary) dàilǐ 代理

action xíngdòng 行动

active huóyuè 活跃

activity huódòng 活动

actor yǎnyuán 演员

actress nǚyǎnyuán 女演员

actual shíjì 实际

acupuncture zhēnjiǔ 针灸

acute pain jùliè 剧烈

adapt 1 v/t (for TV etc)

gǎibiān 改编; *machine* gǎiyòng 改用 2 *v/i (of person)* shìyìng 适应

adapter ELEC shìpèiqì 适配器

add *v/t* jiā 加

addict *n* chéngyǐnzhě 成瘾者

addiction yǐn 瘾

addition MATH jiāfǎ 加法; *(to list etc)* bǔchōng 补充

additional fùjiā 附加

additive tiānjiājì 添加剂

address *n* dìzhǐ 地址

address book tōngxùn lù 通讯录

adequate chōngfèn 充分; *(satisfactory)* jǐn gòu mǎnyì 仅够满意

adhesive yǒu niánxìng 有粘性

adjourn *v/i (of meeting)* xiūhuì 休会

adjust *v/t* tiáozhěng 调整

administration xíngzhèng 行政; *(of country)* zhìlǐ 治理; *(government)* zhèngfǔ 政府

administrative xíngzhèng 行政

admiration qīnpèi 钦佩

admire qīnpèi 钦佩

admission *(confession)* chéngrèn 承认; ~ *free* miǎnfèi rùchǎng 免费入场

admit *(to hospital etc)* jiēnà 接纳; *(confess)* chéngrèn 承认

adolescent *n* qīngshàonián 青少年

adopt *child* lǐngyǎng 领养; *plan* cǎinà 采纳

adult chéngrén 成人

adultery sītōng 私通

advance *n (money)* tòuzhī 透支; *(in science etc)* xiānjìn 先进; MIL jìngōng 进攻; *in* ~ yùxiān 预先

advanced *country* xiānjìn 先进; *level* gāoděng 高等; *learner* gāojí 高级

advantage hǎochù 好处

adventure màoxiǎn 冒险

advertise *v/t & v/i* dēng guǎnggào 登广告

advertisement guǎnggào 广告

advice zīxún 咨询

advisable kěqǔ 可取

advise *person* quàngào 劝告; *caution etc* zhōnggào 忠告; ~ *X to* ... jiànyì X zuò ... 建议X做 ...

adviser gùwèn 顾问

aerobics jiànměicāo 健美操

affair (*matter*) shì 事；
(*business*) shìwù 事务；
(*love*) liàn'ài 恋爱

affect yǐngxiǎng 影响；MED
qīnxí 侵袭

affection àimù 爱慕

affectionate shì'ài biǎoshì'ài 示爱

afford (*financially*) fùdān de
qǐ 负担得起

afraid: *be ~* (*of*) hàipà 害怕

Africa Fēizhōu 非洲

African 1 *adj* Fēizhōu 非洲
2 *n* Fēizhōurén 非洲人

after 1 *prep* zhīhòu 之后；
~ all bìjìng 毕竟；*it's ten
~ two* liǎngdiǎn shífēn 两
点十分 **2** *adv* (*afterward*)
hòulái 后来；*the day ~*
dì'èrtiān 第二天

afternoon xiàwǔ 下午

aftershave xūhòushuǐ 须
后水

afterward hòulái 后来

again zài 再

against lean kào 靠；*X ~ Y* SP
X duì Y X 对 Y；*I'm ~ the
idea* wǒ fǎnduì zhège zhǔyì
我反对这个主意

age *n* (*of person, object*)
niánjì 年纪；(*era*) shídài
时代

agency dàilǐchù 代理处

agenda yìchéng 议程

agent dàilǐrén 代理人

aggressive hào xúnxìn 好
寻衅

agitated jiāolù bù'ān 焦
虑不安

ago: *2 days ~* liǎngtiān qián
两天前；*long ~* hěnjiǔ
yǐqián 很久以前

agree *v/i* tóngyì 同意

agreement (*consent*) tóngyì
同意；(*contract*) xiéyì 协议

agriculture nóngyè 农业

ahead: *be ~ of* lǐngxiān 领先

Aids àizìbìng 艾滋病

aim 1 *n* (*in shooting*)
miáozhǔn 瞄准；(*objective*)
mùbiāo 目标 **2** *v/i*: *~ to do
X* lìqiú zuò X 力求做 X

air *n* kōngqì 空气；*by ~*
travel zuò fēijī 坐飞机；
send mail hángkōng 航空

air-conditioned
kōngtiáo 有空调

airport jīchǎng 机场

alarm *n* jǐngbào 警报

alarm clock nàozhōng 闹钟

album (*for photos*) yǐngjí 影

集; (*record*) chàngpiàn 唱片

alcohol jiǔ 酒

alcoholic 1 *n* xùjiǔzhě 酗酒者 **2** *adj* hán jiǔjīng 含酒精

alert *adj* jījǐng 机警

alien *n* (*foreigner*) wàiguórén 外国人

alike *adj*: **be ~** xiāngsì 相似

alimony shànyǎng fèi 赡养费

alive: **be ~** huózhe 活着

all 1 *adj* dōu 都; **~ Chinese cities** Zhōngguó suǒyǒude chéngshì 中国所有的城市 **2** *pron*: **~ of them** tāmen dōu 他们都; **that's ~, thanks** jiù zhèixiē, xièxie 就这些, 谢谢; **not ~ alike** gēnběn búxiàng 根本不像; **~!** yìdiǎnr yě bù! 一点儿也不!; **two ~** (*in score*) èrpíng 二平

allergic: **be ~ to ...** duì ... guòmǐn 对...过敏

allergy guòmǐn 过敏

alliance tóngméng 同盟

allow (*permit*) yǔnxǔ 允许; (*calculate for*) jìsuàn 计算

allowance (*money*) jīntiē 津贴

ally *n* tóngméngzhě 同盟者

almost jīhū 几乎

alone dāndú 单独

along 1 *prep*: **~ this path** yánzhe zhètiáo xiǎolù 沿着这条小路 **2** *adv*: **~ with** hé 和

aloud chūshēngdi 出声地

alphabet zìmǔ biǎo 字母表

already yǐjīng 已经

alright: **that's ~** (*doesn't matter*) méi guānxi 没关系; (*when s.o. says thank you*) búxiè 不谢; (*is quite good*) búcuò 不错; **I'm ~** (*not hurt*) wǒ méi shìr 我没事儿; **can I?** **– ~** kěyǐ ma? – kěyǐ 可以吗? – 可以

also yě 也

alter *v/t* gǎibiàn 改变

alteration gēnggǎi 更改

alternate 1 *v/i* jiāotì 交替 **2** *adj* měigé 每隔

alternative 1 *n* xuǎnzé 选择 **2** *adj* lìngyī kě xuǎnzé yòng yīqī de xuǎnzé 另一可选择用以期的选择; *lifestyle, music etc* bùtóng zhǒng 不同种

alternatively huòzhě 或者

although jǐnguǎn 尽管

altitude hǎibá 海拔; (*of plane*) gāodù 高度)

altogether (*completely*)

wánquán 完全; (*in all*) yīgòng 一共

aluminum lǚ 铝

always zǒngshì 总是

amateur *n* yèyú àihàozhě 业余爱好者

amaze shǐ dàwéi chījīng 使大为吃惊

amazement jīngqí 惊奇

amazing jīngrén 惊人; (*very good*) méizhíle 没治了

ambassador dàshǐ 大使

ambiguous hánhú 含糊

ambition zhìxiàng 志向; *pej* yěxīn 野心

ambitious *plan* xióngxīn bóbó 雄心勃勃

ambulance jiùhùchē 救护车

amendment xiūgǎi 修改

amends: make ~ bǔguò 补过

America Měiguó 美国

American 1 *adj* Měiguó 美国 **2** *n* Měiguórén 美国人

ammunition jūnhuǒ 军火

amnesty *n* shèmiǎn 赦免

among(st) zài ...zhīzhōng 在...之中

amount shùliàng 数量; (*sum of money*) jīn'é 金额

♦ **amount to** děngyú 等于

amplifier fàngdàqì 放大器

amputate jiézhī 节肢

amuse (*make laugh*) dòuxiào 逗笑; (*entertain*) yúlè 娱乐

amusement lèqù 乐趣; (*entertainment*) yúlè 娱乐

amusing yǒuqù 有趣

analysis fēnxī 分析

analyze fēnxī 分析

anatomy jiěpōu 解剖

ancestor zǔxiān 祖先

ancient *adj* gǔlǎo 古老

and ◊ (*joining nouns*) hé 和 ◊ (*joining adjectives*) yòu ...yòu ... 又...又...◊ (~ *then*) ránhòu 然后 ◊ (*when listing, not translated*): **two beers ~ a coffee** liǎngge píjiǔ yíge kāfēi 两个啤酒一个咖啡

anemic: be ~ pínxuè 贫血

anesthetic *n* mázuì 麻醉

anger *n* fènnù 愤怒

angle *n* jiǎodù 角度

angry fènnù 愤怒; be ~ with X duì X fānnù 对X生气

animal dòngwù 动物

animated cartoon dònghuà piān 动画片

animosity díyì 敌意

ankle jiǎowàn 脚腕

annex 1 n (building) kuòjiàn bùfen 扩建部分 **2** v/t state tūnbìng 吞并

anniversary (wedding ~) zhōunián 周年

announce xuānbù 宣布

announcement xuāngào 宣告

announcer TV, RAD bōyīnyuán 播音员

annoy shǐ fánnǎo 使烦恼

annual adj (once a year) nián nián年; (of a year) niándù 年度

anonymous nímíng 匿名

another adj & pron (different) lìng yíge 另一个; (additional) yòu yíge 又一个; **can I have ~ ...** wǒ kěyǐ zài lái yíge ...ma? 我可以再来一个...吗？; **one** ~ hùxiāng 互相

answer 1 n dáfù 答复; (to problem, question) dá'àn 答案 **2** v/t dáfù 答复; question huídá 回答

answerphone lùyīn diànhuà 录音电话

antenna (of insect) chùjiǎo 触角; (for TV) tiānxiàn 天线

antibiotic n kàngjūnsù 抗

菌素

anticipate yùliào 预料

antiseptic n kàngjūnjì 抗菌剂

anxiety jiāojí 焦急

anxious (worried) jiāojí 焦急

any 1 adj: **are there ~ glasses?** yǒuméiyǒu bēizi? 有没有杯子？**2** pron: **do you have ~?** nǐ yǒu méiyǒu?你有没有？

anybody rènhérén 任何人◊ (with negatives): **there wasn't ~ there** méirén zài nàr 没人在那儿◊ (in questions, conditionals) shéi

anyhow (summarizing) zǒngzhī 总之; (at least) zhìshǎo 至少

anyone → **anybody**

anything shénme 什么

anyway → **anyhow**

anywhere wúlùn nǎli 无论哪里; **I can't find it ~** wǒ nǎr dōu zhǎobùzháo 我哪儿都找不着

apart (in distance) jùlí 距离; **live ~** fēnjū 分居

apartment gōngyù 公寓

apartment block gōngyù dàshà 公寓大厦

apologize dàoqiàn 道歉

apology dàoqiàn 道歉

apparently hǎoxiàng 好像

appeal n (charm) xīyǐn lì 吸引力; (for funds etc) hūyù 呼吁; LAW shàngsù 上诉

appear chūxiàn 出现; (look, seem) xiǎndé 显得

appearance (arrival) dàolái 到来; (look) wàibiǎo 外表

appendicitis lánwěiyán 阑尾炎

appetite wèikǒu 胃口; fig yùwàng 欲望

applaud v/i gǔzhǎng 鼓掌

applause gǔzhǎng 鼓掌

apple píngguǒ 苹果

appliance qìxiè 器械

applicant shēnqǐngzhě 申请者

application (for job, visa etc) shēnqǐng 申请

apply (of rule) shìyòng 适用

♦ **apply for** shēnqǐng 申请

appoint rènmìng 任命

appointment (to position) rènmìng 任命; (meeting) yuēhuì 约会

appreciate 1 v/t (value) xīnshǎng 欣赏; (be grateful for) gǎnjī 感激 2 v/i FIN tígāo jiàzhí 提高价值

apprehensive dānxīn 担心

approach 1 n línjìn 临近; (offer, proposal) tíyì 提议; (to problem) fāngshì 方式 2 v/t (get near to) línjìn 临近; (contact) liánxì 联系; problem chǔlǐ 处理

appropriate adj qiàdàng 恰当

approve 1 v/i zànchéng 赞成 2 v/t pīzhǔn 批准

approximate adj dàyuē 大约

April sìyuè 四月

Arab 1 adj Ālābó 阿拉伯 2 n Ālābórén 阿拉伯人

archeologist kǎogǔ xué jiā 考古学家

archeology kǎogǔ xué 考古学

architect jiànzhù shī 建筑师

architecture jiànzhù xué 建筑学

archives dǎng'àn 档案

area (region) dìqū 地区; (of activity, study) fànwéi 范围; (square feet etc) miànjī 面积

area code TELEC qūhào 区号

argue 1 *v/i (fight)* chǎojià 吵架 **2** *v/t: ~ that* jiānchí 坚持

argument chǎojià 吵架; *(reasoning)* zhēnglùn 争论

arise *(of situation, problem)* chéngxiàn 呈现

arithmetic suànshù 算术

arm *n* shǒubì 手臂; *(of chair)* fúshǒu 扶手

armchair fúshǒu yǐ 扶手椅

armed wǔzhuāng 武装

armed robbery chíxiè qiǎngjié 持械抢劫

arms *(weapons)* wǔqì 武器

army jūnduì 军队

around 1 *prep (in circle)* wéirào 围绕; *(roughly)* dàyuē 大约 **2** *adv (in the area)* zài zhèr 在这儿; *(encircling)* zhōuwéi 周围; *(near)* zài fùjìn 在附近

arouse *suspicion etc* yǐnqǐ 引起; *(sexually)* jīfā 激发

arrange *(put in order)* zhěnglǐ 整理; *furniture* bùzhì 布置; *flowers* chā 插; *music* gǎibiān 改编; *meeting, time etc* ānpái 安排

arrangement *(plan)* ānpái 安排; *(agreement)* xiéyì 协议;

(of furniture etc) bùzhì 布置; *(of flowers)* chāhuā 插花; *(of music)* gǎibiān 改编

arrest *n & v/t* dàibǔ 逮捕

arrive dàodá 到达

arrogance àomàn 傲慢

arrogant jiāo'ào zìdà 骄傲自大

art yìshù 艺术

artery MED dòngmài 动脉

article wùjiàn 物件; *(in newspaper)* wénzhāng 文章

artificial rénzào 人造

artist *(painter)* huàjiā 画家

artistic yǒu yìshùxìng 有艺术性; *skills* yìshù 艺术

as 1 *conj* ◊ *(while, when)* dāng ...de shíhou 当 ... 的时候 ◊ *(like)* xiàng 像; **~ if** hǎoxiàng 好像; **~ usual** rútóng wǎngcháng 如同往常 **2** *adv:* **~ high** ... hé ... yíyàng gāo 和 ... 一样高 **3** *prep* zuòwéi 作为; **~ a child** zuòwéi háizi 作为孩子

ashamed xiūkuì 羞愧; **be ~ of** wèi ... diūliǎn 为 ... 丢脸

ashore zài ànshàng 在岸上

ashtray yānhuī gāng 烟灰缸

Asia Yàzhōu 亚洲

Asian

Asian 1 *adj* Yàzhōu 亚洲
2 *n* Yàzhōurén 亚洲人

aside yībiān 一边；**~** *from*
(*excepting*) chúle 除了；(*in addition to*) cǐwài 此外

ask *v/t person* wèn 问；
(*invite*) jiào 叫；*question* tíwèn 提问；*favor* qǐngqiú 请求；**~** *X for X* gēn X yào ...跟 X 要...；**~** *X to* yào X ...要 X ...

♦ ask for yāoqiú 要求；
person zhǎo 找

♦ ask out yuēhuì 约会

asleep: *be* **~** shúshuì 熟睡；
fall **~** shuizháo le 睡着了

aspect fāngmiàn 方面

aspirin āsīpǐlín 阿司匹林

assassinate ànshā 暗杀

assault *n* gōngjī 攻击；
(*physical*) ōudǎ 殴打；
(*verbal*) wēixié 威胁

assemble 1 *v/t parts* zǔzhuāng 组装 **2** *v/i* (*of people*) jízhóng 集合

assembly zǔzhuāng 组装；
POL yìhuì 议会

assertive *person* zìxìn 自信

assess pínggū 评估

asset FIN zīchǎn 资产；*fig* bǎobèi 宝贝

assignment rènwù 任务

assist bāngzhù 帮助

assistant zhùshǒu 助手

associate 1 *v/i*: **~** *with* jiéjiāo 结交 **2** *n* tóngshì 同事

association xiéhuì 协会；
in **~** *with* yǔ ...hézuò 与 ...合作

assume (*suppose*) jiǎshè 假设

assumption shèxiǎng 设想

assurance bǎozhèng 保证；
(*confidence*) xìnxīn 信心

assure (*reassure*) shǐ quèxìn 使确信

asthma xiàochuǎn 哮喘

astonish shǐ jīngyà 使惊讶

astonishing lìngrén jīngyà 令人惊讶

astonishment jīngyà 惊讶

astronomical *price etc* jùdà 巨大

asylum (*political*) bìhù 庇护

at (*with places*) zài 在；**~** *Joe's* zài Qiáo jiālǐ 在乔家里；**~** *10 dollars* biāojià shí měiyuán 标价十美元；**~** *5 o'clock* wǔ diǎnzhōng 五点钟；*be good* **~** *X* shàncháng yú X 擅长于X

atheist wú shén lùnzhě 无

神论者

athlete yùndòngyuán 运动员

athletics tiánjìng yùndòng 田径运动

Atlantic Dàxīyáng 大西洋

ATM (= *automated teller machine*) qǔkuǎnjī 取款机

atmosphere (*of earth*) dàqì 大气; (*ambiance*) qìfēn 气氛

atomic yuánzǐ 原子

atrocity bàoxíng 暴行

attach shuānláo 栓牢

attack n & v/t (*physical*) ōudǎ 殴打; MIL xíjī 袭击; (*verbal*) pēngjī 抨击

attempt 1 n chángshì 尝试 **2** v/t shìtú 试图

attend cānjiā 参加

attendance chūqín 出勤

attention zhùyìlì 注意力; *pay* ~ zhùyì 注意

attitude tàidu 态度

attorney lǜshī 律师

attract *person, attention* xīyǐn 吸引

attraction xīyǐn lì 吸引力; (*romantic*) mèilì 魅力

attractive yǒu xīyǐn lì 有

吸引力

audible tīngdejiàn 听得见

audience (*at concert*) tīngzhòng 听众; THEA, TV guānzhòng 观众

audiovisual shìtīng 视听

audition n & v/i shìyǎn 试演

auditor shěnjì shī 审计师

August bāyuè 八月

aunt (*own, paternal*) gū 姑; (*own, maternal*) yí 姨; (*somebody else's*) āyí 阿姨

Australia Áodàlìyà 澳大利亚

Australian 1 adj Áodàlìyà 澳大利亚 **2** n Áodàlìyà rén 澳大利亚人

authentic *antique* zhēnzhèng 真正; *accent* dìdao 地道

author zuòzhě 作者

authority quánwēi 权威; (*permission*) xǔkě 许可

authorize shòuquán 授权; *be ~d to ...* shòuquán ... 授权

auto n MOT qìchē 汽车

autobiography zìzhuàn 自传

authority quánwēi 权威; (*permission*) xǔkě 许可

automate shǐ zìdònghuà 使自动化

automatic adj & n zìdòng 自动

automatically zìdòng 自动
automobile qìchē 汽车
available *product* kě dédào 可得到; *person* yǒukōng 有空
avenue dàdào 大道
average 1 *adj* píngjūn 平均; (*ordinary*) pǔtōng 普通 **2** *n* píngjūn shuǐzhǔn 平均水准; **on ~** píngjūn láishuō 平均来说
avoid bìmiǎn 避免
awake *adj* xǐng 醒
award 1 *n* (*prize*) jiǎnglì 奖励 **2** *v/t* jiǎnglì 奖励; *damages* pàngěi 判给
aware: **be ~ of X** zhīdào X 知道 X; **become ~ of X** dézhī X 得知 X
awareness yìshí 意识
away: **be ~** (*traveling, sick etc*) búzài 不在; **walk / run ~** zǒu / pǎo kāi 走 / 跑开; **it's 2 miles ~** liǎng yīnglǐ yuǎn 两英里远
awesome F (*terrific*) gàilemàole 盖了帽了
awful zāogāo 糟糕
awkward (*clumsy*) bènzhuō 笨拙; (*difficult*) nányí duìfù 难以对付; (*embarrassing*) gāngà 尴尬
ax 1 *n* fǔ 斧 **2** *v/t* *project, jobs* xiāojiǎn 削减

B

baby *n* yīng'ér 婴儿
baby-sitter línshí bǎomǔ 临时保姆
bachelor dānshēn hàn 单身汉
back 1 *n* (*of person*) hòubèi 后背; (*of car, bus*) hòubù 后部; (*of paper, jacket, house, book*) bèimiàn 背面; (*of chair*) kàobèi 靠背; SP hòuwèi 后卫; **in ~** zài hòumian 在后面; **~ to front** qiánhòu diāndǎo 前后颠倒 **2** *adj* hòu 后; **~ road** xiǎolù 小路 **3** *adv*: **please stand ~** qǐng hòutuì 请后退; **give X ~ to Y** jiāng X huángěi Y 将X还给Y; **she'll be ~ tomorrow** tā míngtiān huílái 她明天

回来 4 v/t (support) zhīchí 支持;car dǎochē 倒车

♦ **back down** fàngqì 放弃

♦ **back up 1** v/t (support) zhīchí 支持;claim, argument zhèngshí 证实;file bèifèn 备份

backdate zhuīsù 追溯

backer zànzhùrén 赞助人

background bèijīng 背景;(of person) jīnglì 经历

backing (support) zhīchí 支持;(musicians) bànzòu 伴奏;(singers) bànchàng 伴唱

backpacker bēibāo lǚxíngzhě 背包旅行者

backward adj child chídùn 迟钝;society luòhòu 落后;glance xiànghòu 向后

bacon xūn xiánròu 熏咸肉

bacteria xìjūn 细菌

bad bùhǎo 不好;weather èliè 恶劣;headache jùliè 剧烈;mistake, accident yánzhòng 严重;(rotten) huài 坏;it's not ~ hái kě yǐ 还可以

badge zhèngzhāng 证章

badly behave bùhǎo 不好;injured, damaged yánzhòng 严重;perform chà 差

bad-tempered bàozào 暴躁

baffle shǐ kùnhuò 使困惑

bag (plastic, paper) dàizi 袋子;(for school, traveling) bāo 包;(purse) shǒutí bāo 手提包

baggage xíngli 行李

bake v/t kǎo 烤

balance 1 n pínghéng 平衡;(remainder) chā'é 差额;(of bank account) jiécún 结存 **2** v/t & v/i pínghéng 平衡

balance sheet juésuàn biǎo 决算表

balcony yángtái 阳台;(in theater) lóutíng 楼厅

bald man tūdǐng 秃顶

ball qiú 球

ballet bālěiwǔ 芭蕾舞

balloon (child's) qìqiú 气球;(for flight) rè qìqiú 热气球

ballot n tóupiào 投票

ballpoint (pen) yuánzhū bǐ 圆珠笔

bamboo zhúzi 竹子

bamboo shoots zhúsǔn 竹笋

ban 1 n jìnlìng 禁令 **2** v/t jìnzhǐ 禁止

banana xiāngjiāo 香蕉

band (*musical*) yuèduì 乐队

bandage n bēngdài 绷带

Band-Aid® chuàngkětiē 创可贴

bang 1 n (*noise*) hōngde yīshēng 轰的一声; (*blow*) měngjī 猛击 **2** v/t *door* shuāi 摔; (*hit*) zhuàng 撞

bank¹ n (*of river*) hé'àn 河岸

bank² n FIN yínháng 银行

bank account yínháng zhànghù 银行帐户

bankrupt adj pòchǎn 破产; *go ~* pòchǎn 破产

baptize xǐlǐ 洗礼

bar¹ n (*iron, chocolate*) tiáo 条; (*for drinks*) jiǔbā 酒吧; (*counter*) guìtái 柜台

bar² v/t jìnzhǐ 禁止

barbecue 1 n shāokǎo huì 烧烤会; (*equipment*) kǎojià 烤架 **2** v/t kǎo 烤

barbed wire yǒucì tiěsī 有刺铁丝

barber tìtóu jiàng 剃头匠

bare adj (*naked*) guāng 光; *room* kōng 空; *hillside, floor* guāngtū 光秃秃

barefoot *be ~* guāngjiǎo 光脚

barefoot doctor chìjiǎo yīshēng 赤脚医生

barely jǐnjǐn 仅仅

bargain 1 n (*deal*) jiāoyì 交易; (*good buy*) piányí huò 便宜货 **2** v/i tǎojià huánjià 讨价还价

bark n & v/i (*of dog*) fèi 吠

barracks MIL yíngfáng 营房

barrel (*container*) tǒng 桶

barricade n lùzhàng 路障

barrier lángān 栏杆; (*cultural*) zhàng'ài 障碍

base 1 n (*bottom end*) dǐbù 底部; (*underside*) dǐzuò 底座; (*center,* MIL) jīdì 基地 **2** v/t yī ...wéi jīchǔ 以...为基础

baseball (*ball*) bàngqiú 棒球; (*game*) bàngqiú yùndòng 棒球运动

baseball cap bàngqiú mào 棒球帽

basement dìxiàshì 地下室; (*of store*) dǐcéng 底层

basic (*rudimentary*) jīběn 基本; (*fundamental*) zhǔyào 主要

basically jīběnshang 基本上

basics: *the ~* jīběn yuánlǐ 基本原理

basin (*for washing*) shuǐchí

水池

basis jīchǔ 基础; *(of argument)* gēnjù 根据

basket lánzi 篮子; *(in basketball)* wǎng 网

basketball lánqiú 篮球

bass *adj* nán dīyīn 男低音

bat[1] *n (for baseball)* qiúgùn 球棍; *(for table tennis)* qiúpāi 球拍

bat[2] *(animal)* biānfú 蝙蝠

bath zǎopén 澡盆; *have a ~* xǐzǎo 洗澡

bathrobe yùyī 浴衣

bathroom xǐzǎo jiān 洗澡间; *(toilet)* xǐshǒu jiān 洗手间

bathtub yùgāng 浴缸

battery diànchí 电池

be ◊ shì 是; *there is, there are* yǒu 有; *~ careful* xiǎoxīn 小心; *don't ~ sad* bié shāngxīn 别伤心; *I've never been to Beijing* wǒ cóngméi qùguò Běijīng 我从没去过北京 ◊ *(passive)* bèi 被; *he was killed* tā bèi shāsǐ le 他被杀死了

beach hǎitān 海滩

beam 1 *n (in roof)* héngliáng 横梁 2 *v/i (smile)* xiàoróng

mǎnmiàn 笑容满面

bean curd dòufu 豆腐

beansprouts dòuyá 豆芽

bear *v/t weight* chéngshòu 承受; *costs* chéngdān 承担; *(tolerate)* rěnshòu 忍受

bearable kě róngrěn 可容忍

beard húzi 胡子

beat 1 *n (of heart)* tiàodòng 跳动; *(of music)* jiézòu 节奏 2 *v/t (in game)* jībài 击败; *(hit)* dǎ 打

beating *(physical)* dǎ 打

beautiful *woman, house, day* měilì 美丽; *meal* fēngshèng kěkǒu 丰盛可口; *vacation* wánměi 完美; *story, movie* dòngrén 动人

beauty měilì 美丽

because yīnwèi 因为; *~ of* yóuyú 由于

become biànchéng 变成; *what's ~ of her?* tā jiūjìng zěnmeyàng? 她究竟怎么样?

bed chuáng 床; *(of flowers)* tán 坛; *(of sea, river)* chuáng 床; *go to ~* shuìjiào 睡觉

bedroom wòshì 卧室

beef *n* niúròu 牛肉

beer píjiǔ 啤酒

before 1 *prep & conj* zhīqián 之前 2 *adv* yǐqián 以前; *the week / day* ~ qián yīgè xīngqī / tiān 前一个星期/天

beforehand shìxiān 事先

beg *v/i* yàofàn 要饭

begin *v/t & v/i* kāishǐ 开始

beginner chūxuézhě 初学者

beginning kāishǐ 开始; (*origin*) qǐyuán 起源

behalf: *on* or *in* ~ *of* dàibiǎo 代表

behave *v/i* biǎoxiàn 表现; ~ (*oneself*) shǒu guījǔ 守规矩

behavior xíngwéi 行为

behind 1 *prep* zài ... hòumiàn 在 ... 后面; (*in progress, order*) luòhòu 落后; *be* ~ ... (*responsible for*) zài ... bèihòu 在 ... 背后; (*support*) zhīchí 支持 2 *adv* (*at the back*) zài hòumiàn 在后面; *leave, stay* liúxià 留下

Beijing Běijīng 北京

being (*existence*) shēngcún 生存; (*creature*) shēngwù 生物

belief (*trust*) xìnrèn 信任; (*religion*) xìnyǎng 信仰; (*opinion*) kànfǎ 看法

believe xiāngxìn 相信
♦ believe in xiāngxìn 相信; *ghosts* xìn 信; *person* xìnrèn 信任

bell (*on bike, door*) líng 铃; (*in church, school*) zhōng 钟

bellhop shìzhě 侍者

belly dùzi 肚子

belong *v/i* shǔyú 属于
♦ belong to shǔyú 属于; *club, organization* shì ... chéngyuán 是 ... 成员

belongings suǒyǒu wù 所有物

below 1 *prep* zài ... de xiàmian 在 ... 的下面; (*in amount*) dīyú 低于 2 *adv* zài xiàmian 在下面; *10 degrees* ~ língxià shídù 零下十度

belt yāodài 腰带

bend 1 *n* wānqū 弯曲 2 *v/t* wān 弯 3 *v/i* wān 弯; (*of person*) wānshēn 弯身
♦ bend down wānyāo 弯腰

beneath 1 *prep* zài ... xiàmiàn 在...下面; *(in status, value)* dīyú 低于 **2** *adv* xiàbiān 下边

beneficial yǒuyì 有益

benefit 1 *n* hǎochù 好处 **2** *v/t* yǒuyì yú 有益于

beside zài ...pángbiān 在 ...旁边

besides 1 *adv* zàishuō 再说 **2** *prep (apart from)* chúle 除了

best 1 *adj & adv* zuìhǎo 最好 **2** *n:* **do one's ~** jìnlì érwéi 尽力而为; **the ~** zuìhǎo 最好

best before date zàicǐ rìqí qián shǐyòng 在此日期 前使用

best man *(at wedding)* nán bīnxiàng 男傧相

bet 1 *n* dǔzhù 赌注 **2** *v/i* dǔbó 赌博

betray bèipàn 背叛

better 1 *adj* gènghǎo 更 好; **get ~** gǎijìn 改进; *(in health)* hǎozhuǎn 好 转; **he's ~** *(in health)* tā hǎodiǎnr le 他好点儿 了 **2** *adv* gènghǎo 更好; **I'd really ~ not** wǒ háishì

bùyào le 我还是不要了

better off *adj* fùyù 富裕

between *prep* zài ...zhījiān 在...之间

beware: ~ of xiǎoxīn 小心

beyond 1 *prep (in space)* yuǎnyú 远于; *(in degree, extent)* chāochū 超出 **2** *adv* gěngyuǎn 更远

bias(s)ed piānjiàn 偏见; *(in favor of)* piāntǎn 偏袒

Bible shèngjīng 圣经

bicycle *n* zìxíng chē 自行车

bid *n (at auction)* chūjià 出价

big *adj* dà 大; *(tall)* gāo 高

bike *n* zìxíng chē 自行车

bill *n* zhàngdān 账单; *(money)* chāopiào 钞票

billboard guǎnggào pái 广 告牌

billfold qiánbāo 钱包

billion shíyì 十亿

bind *v/t (tie)* bǎngbǎng 绑绑; *(oblige)* yuēshù 约束

binding *adj agreement* yǒu yuēshù lì 有约束力

binoculars wàngyuǎn jìng 望远镜

biography zhuànjì 传记

biological shēngwù 生物

biology shēngwù xué 生物学

biotechnology shēngwù gōngyì xué 生物工艺学

bird niǎo 鸟

birth (of child) chūshēng 出生; (labor) fēnmiǎn 分娩; **date of ~** chūshēng rìqī 出生日期

birth certificate chūshēng zhèng 出生证

birth control jiéyù 节育

birthday shēngrì 生日; **happy ~!** shēngrì kuàile! 生日快乐！

bit n (piece) xiǎokuàir 小块儿; (length) xiǎoduànr 小段儿; (part) bùfen 部分; **a ~** (a little) yǒudiǎnr 有点儿; (of time) yīhuìr 一会儿; **a ~ of** (a little) yīdiǎn 一点

bitch n (dog) mǔgǒu 母狗; F (woman) pōfù 泼妇

bite n & v/t (of dog, snake) yǎo 咬; (of mosquito) dīng 叮

bitter kǔ 苦; person chōngmǎn yuànhèn 充满怨恨

black 1 adj hēi 黑; coffee etc wúnǎi 无奶 **2** n (color) hēisè 黑色; (person) hēirén 黑人

blackboard hēibǎn 黑板

black box hēi xiázi 黑匣子

black eye qīngzhǒng yǎnkuàng 青肿眼眶

blackmail n & v/t xiépò 胁迫

black market hēishì 黑市

blackout n diàntíng 停电; MED hūnmí 昏迷

blade (of knife, sword) rèn 刃

blame 1 n zébèi 责备; (responsibility) zérèn 责任 **2** v/t zéguài 责怪

blank adj page, tape kòngbái 空白; look máorán 茫然

blanket n tǎnzi 毯子

blast n (explosion) bàozhà 爆炸; (gust) yīgǔ 一股

blatant míngxiǎn 明显

blaze n (fire) huǒyàn 火焰

bleach 1 n piǎobáijì 漂白剂 **2** v/t hair shǐ tuōsè 使脱色

bleak countryside huāngliáng 荒凉; future àndàn 暗淡

bleed v/i liúxuè 流血

blend n & v/i hùnhé 混合

bless zhùfú 祝福

blind 1 adj máng 盲 **2** n: the

~ mángrén 盲人

blind spot mángdiǎn 盲点；
fig wúzhī 无知

blink *v/i* (of person) zhǎyǎn
眨眼；(of light) shǎnshuò
闪烁

blister *n* shuǐpào 水泡

blizzard bàofēngxuě 暴
风雪

bloc POL jítuán 集团

block 1 *n* kuài 块；(in town)
jiēqū 街区 2 *v/t* dǔsè 堵塞

blockage dǔjinfa 金发

blond dùsài 堵塞

blonde *n* (woman) jīnfa
nǚláng 金发女郎

blood xuèyè 血液

blood pressure xuèyā 血压

bloom *v/i* kāihuā 开花

blossom 1 *n* huā 花 2 *v/i* kāihuā 开花；*fig* fāzhǎn 发展

blouse chènshān 衬衫

blow¹ *n* jī 击；(setback) zǔ'ài
阻碍

blow² 1 *v/t* (of wind) chuī 吹；
whistle chuīshào 吹哨；
one's nose xǐng bítì 擤鼻
涕 2 *v/i* (of wind) guāfēng
刮风；(of fuse) shāoduàn
烧断；(of tire) bàozhà 爆炸

◆ **blow up** *v/t* (with

explosive) zhà zhà 炸炸；*balloon*
chōngqì 充气；PHOT fàngdà
放大

blow-dry *v/t* chuīgān 吹干

blue *adj* lánsè 蓝色

blues MUS bólùsī yīnyuè 勃
鲁斯音乐

bluff *v/i* xiàhu 吓唬

blunt *adj* dùn 钝；*person*
zhíshuài 直率

bluntly *speak* tǎnbái 坦白

blush *v/i* liǎnhóng 脸红

blusher (cosmetic) yānzhī
胭脂

BO (body odor) tǐxiù 体臭

board 1 *n* bǎn 板；(for game)
qípán 棋盘；(for notices)
pái pái 牌；(for directors)
dǒngshì huì 董事会；**on** ~
(plane) zài fēijī shàng 在
飞机上；(train) zài huǒchē
shàng 在火车上；(boat)
zài chuán shàng 在船上
2 *v/t* airplane etc shàng 上

board game qípán yóuxì 棋
盘游戏

boarding card dēngjīkǎ 登
机卡

board meeting dǒngshìhuì
huìyì 董事会会议

boast *n* & *v/i* chuīniú 吹牛

boat 202

boat chuán 船

body shēntǐ 身体; (dead) shītǐ 尸体

bodyguard bǎobiāo 保镖

boil v/t zhǔ 煮

boiled rice báifàn 白饭

boiled water kāishuǐ 开水

boiler guōlú 锅炉

bold 1 adj dàdǎn 大胆 2 n (print) cūtǐ 粗体

bolt 1 n luóshuān 螺栓; (on door) chāxiāo 插销 2 v/t (fix with bolts) shuānzhù 栓住; (close) shuān 闩

bomb 1 n zhàdàn 炸弹 2 v/t hōngzhà 轰炸

bomber (airplane) hōngzhàjī 轰炸机; (terrorist) tóudàn shǒu 投弹手

bond n (tie) liánjié 联结; FIN zhàiquàn 债券

bone n gǔtou 骨头

bonus (money) jiǎngjīn 奖金; (extra) éwài pǐn 额外品

boo 1 v/t speaker hè dàocǎi 喝倒彩 2 v/i fāchū xūxu shēng 发出嘘嘘声

book 1 n shū 书 2 v/t (reserve) yùdìng 预定; (of policeman) dēngjì 登记

bookcase shūjià 书架

booklet xiǎo cèzi 小册子

Book of Changes Yìjīng 易经

bookstore shūdiàn 书店

boom n & v/i (in business) fánróng 繁荣

boost 1 n (to sales, confidence) jīlì 激励; (to economy) cùjìn 促进 2 v/t sales zēngjiā 增加; confidence zēngqiáng 增强

boot n xuēzi 靴子

booth (at market) huòtān 货摊; (at exhibition) tānzi 摊子; (in restaurant) cānzuò 餐座

border n (of country) biānjiè 边界; (edge) biānyuán 边缘

bore¹ v/t hole zuānkǒng 钻孔

bore² 1 n (person) wúqùderén 无趣的人 2 v/t shǐ yànfán 使厌烦

bored: be ~ mèn 闷

boredom wúliáo 无聊

boring fáwèir 乏味儿

born: be ~ chūshēng 出生

borrow jiè 借

boss shàngjí 上级

botanical zhíwù 植物

both 1 *adj & pron* liǎnggè 两个; **~ of them** *(things)* nà liǎnggè 那两个; *(people)* nà liǎngrén 那两人 **2** *adv*: **~ ... and ...** yòu ... yòu ... 又 ... 又 ...

bother 1 *n* máfán 麻烦; **it's no ~** méi wèntí 没问题 **2** *v/t (disturb)* máfán 麻烦; *person working* dǎjiǎo 打 扰; *(worry)* shǐdānxīn 使 担心 **3** *v/i*: **don't ~** *(you needn't do it)* búyòng 不用了

bottle *n* píngzi 瓶子; *(for baby)* nǎipíng 奶瓶

bottled water píngzhuāng shuǐ 瓶装水

bottleneck *(in road, work)* zǔsāi diǎn 阻塞点

bottle-opener kāipíngqì 开瓶器

bottom 1 *adj* zuìdī 最低 **2** *n (underside)* dǐmiàn 底面; *(on the inside)* dǐbù 底部; *(of hill)* jiǎo 脚; *(of pile)* zuìdī 最底; *(of street)* zuìdīchù 最低处; *(buttocks)* pìgu 屁股

♦ **bottom out** dá zuìdī diǎn 达最低点

bottom line *fig (financial)* lìrùn 利润; *(real issue)* zhēnzhèng wèntí 真正 问题

bounce *v/i (of ball)* tánqǐ 弹 起; *(on sofa etc)* tàntiào 弹跳; *(of check)* bèi jù fù tuìhuí 被拒付退回

bouncer bǎménrén 把门人

bound: **be ~ to do** *(sure)* kěndìng zuò 肯定做; *(obliged)* bìxū zuò 必须做

boundary biānjiè 边界

bouquet *(flowers)* huāshù 花束; *(of wine)* fāngxiāng 芳香

bourbon bōpáng wēishìjì jiǔ 波旁威士忌酒

bout MED fāzuò 发作; *(in boxing)* jiàoliàng 较量

bow¹ *n & v/i (as greeting)* jūgōng 鞠躬

bow² *(knot)* húdié jié 蝴蝶 结; MUS gōng 弓

bowels jiécháng 结肠

bowl *(large)* pén 盆; *(small container for rice)* wǎn 碗

bowling bǎolíng qiú 保龄球

bow tie jiédài 领结

box *n* hézi 盒子; *(on form)* fānggé 方格

boxer quánjīshǒu 拳击手

boxing quánjī 拳击

boxing match quánjī bǐsài 拳击比赛

box office shòupiàochù 售票处

boy nánháir 男孩儿; (son) érzi 儿子

boycott n & v/i dǐzhì 抵制

boyfriend nán péngyou 男朋友

bracelet shǒuzhuó 手镯

bracket (for shelf) tuōjià 托架; (in text) kuòhào 括号

brag v/i chuīniú 吹牛

braid n (in hair) biànzi 辫子; (trimming) suìdài 穗带

brain nǎo 脑

brains (intelligence) nǎozi 脑子

brake n & v/i shāchē 刹车

branch n shùzhī 树枝; (of bank) fēnháng 分行; (of company) fēn gōngsī 分公司; (of chain store) fēndiàn 分店

brand n páizi 牌子

brand name shāngbiāo 商标; (famous) míngpái shāngpǐn 名牌商品

brand-new zhǎnxīn 崭新

brandy báilándì 白兰地

brassière xiōngzhào 胸罩

brat pej táoqìbāo 淘气包

brave adj yǒnggǎn 勇敢

bravery yǒnggǎn 勇敢

breach (violation) wéifàn 违犯; (in party) fēnliè 分裂

breach of contract LAW wéifàn hétóng 违反合同

bread miànbāo 面包

breadth kuāndù 宽度; (of knowledge) guǎngdù 广度

break 1 n (in bone) gǔzhé 骨折; (rest) xiūxi 休息; (in relations) fēnkāi 分开 2 v/t & v/i device, toy sǔnhuài 损坏; stick, leg zhéduàn 折断; glass, egg pòsuì 破碎; law, promise wéifàn 违反; record dǎpò 打破

♦ **break down** 1 v/i (of vehicle) chū máobìng 出毛病; (of talks) pòliè 破裂; (in tears) kòngzhì bùzhù 控制不住 2 v/t door dǎlàn 打烂; figures fēnlèi 分类

♦ **break even** COM shōuzhī pínghéng 收支平衡

♦ **break up** (of couple) fēnshǒu 分手; (of band, meeting) jiěsàn 解散

breakdown (of vehicle, machine) gùzhàng 故障; (of talks) pòliè 破裂; (nervous ~) bēngkuì 崩溃; (of figures) fēnlèi 分类

breakfast n zǎocān 早餐

break-in dàoqiè 盗窃

breakthrough tūpò 突破

breakup (of marriage etc) fēnshǒu 分手

breast (of woman) rǔfáng 乳房

breastfeed v/t bǔrǔ 哺乳

breath hūxī 呼吸

Breathalyzer® hūqì yànzuìqì 呼气验醉器

breathe v/i hūxī 呼吸

breathtaking jīngrén 惊人

breed 1 n pǐnzhǒng 品种 **2** v/t & v/i (of animals) fánzhí 繁殖

breeze wēifēng 微风

brew 1 v/t beer niàngzào 酿造; tea pào 泡 **2** v/i (of storm, trouble) yùnniàng 酝酿

bribe n & v/t huìlù 贿赂

bribery huìlù 贿赂

brick zhuāntóu 砖头

bride xīnniáng 新娘

bridegroom xīnláng 新郎

bridesmaid bànniáng 伴娘

bridge n qiáo 桥; (of ship) jiàshìtái 驾驶台

brief adj jiǎnduǎn 简短

briefcase gōngwén bāo 公文包

briefing jiǎnbào 简报

briefly (for short period) yīhuìr 一会儿; (in a few words) jiǎndān 简单; (to sum up) zǒngzhī 总之

briefs (for women) duǎn nèikù 短内裤; (for men) sānjiǎo kù 三角裤

bright color xiānyàn 鲜艳; light qiángliè 强烈; future guāngmíng 光明; room míngliàng 明亮; (intelligent) cōngmíng 聪明

♦ **brighten up** v/i (of weather) zhuǎnqíng 转晴; (of person) gāoxìng qǐlái 高兴起来

brilliant sunshine etc míngliàng 明亮; (very good) jiéchū 杰出; (very intelligent) yǒu cáihuá 有才华; idea yīngmíng 英明

bring dàilái 带来; sth close by nálái 拿来; person dài 带

♦ **bring back** (return) huán
还; (re-introduce) huīfù 恢
复; memories shǐ huíyì qǐ
使回忆起

♦ **bring down** government
shǐ kuǎtái 使垮台;
airplane shèluò 射落; price
shǐ jiàngdī 使降低

♦ **bring out** (produce: book)
chūbǎn 出版; video, CD,
new product tuīchū 推出

♦ **bring up** child yǎngyù 养
育; subject tíchū 提出;
(vomit) ǒutù 呕吐

Britain Yīngguó 英国;
(formal use) Dà Bùlièdiān
大不列颠

British 1 adj Yīngguó 英
国 **2** n: the ~ Yīngguórén
英国人

broad adj street, shoulders
kuān 宽; smile kuānróng
宽容; (general) gàikuòxìng
概括性

broadcast n & v/t guǎngbō
广播

broadcasting bōyīn 播音

broadminded xīnxiōng
kuānkuò 心胸宽阔

brochure xiǎo cèzi 小册子

broil v/t kǎo 烤

broiler n (on stove) kǎopán
烤盘; (chicken) nènjī 嫩鸡

broke F (temporarily)
méiyǒu yīgè zǐr 没有一个
子儿; (long term) bùmíng
yīwén 不明一文

broken adj chū máobìng 出
毛病; glass, window pòsuì
破碎; neck, arm gǔzhé 骨
折; home pòliè 破裂

broken-hearted xīnsuì 心碎

bronchitis qìguǎn yán 气
管炎

brooch xiōngzhēn 胸针

broth (soup) tāng 汤; (stock)
liàotāng 料汤

brothel jìyuàn 妓院

brother (own, elder) gēge 哥
哥; (own, younger) dìdi 弟
弟; (somebody else's, elder
or younger) xiōngdì 兄弟;
~s and sisters xiōngdì jiě
mèi 兄弟姐妹

brother-in-law (elder sister's
husband) jiěfu 姐夫;
(younger sister's husband)
mèifu 妹夫; (husband's
younger brother) xiǎoshūzi
小叔子; (husband's older
brother) dàbózi 大伯
子; (wife's older brother)

nèixiōng 内兄; (*wife's younger brother*) **nèidì** 内弟

brown *adj* zōngsè 棕色; (*tanned*) shàihēile 晒黑了

browse (*in store*) suíbiàn kànkan 随便看看

bruise *n* cuòshāng 挫伤

brunette zōngfà nǚzǐ 棕发女子

brush *n & v/t* shuā 刷

brutal cánrěn 残忍

brutality bàoxíng 暴行

bubble *n* qìpào 气泡

buck F (*dollar*) kuài 块

bucket shuǐtǒng 水桶

buckle¹ *n* dàgōu 搭钩

buckle² *v/i* (*of wood, metal*) biànxíng 变形

Buddha Fó 佛

Buddhism Fójiào 佛教

Buddhist 1 *n* Fójiàotú 佛教徒; **he's a ~** tā xìn Fó 他信佛 **2** *adj* Fójiào 佛教

Buddhist temple sì 寺

buddy F huǒbàn 伙伴; (*form of address*) gērmen 哥儿们

budget *n* yùsuàn 预算; (*of family*) kāizhī 开支

buffalo yěniú 野牛; **water ~**

shuǐniú 水牛

bug 1 *n* (*insect*) kūnchóng 昆虫; (*virus*) bìngdú 病毒; (*spying device*) qiètīngqì 窃听器; COMPUT gùzhàng 故障 **2** *v/t* F (*annoy*) shǐ nǎonù 使恼怒

buggy (*for baby*) yīng'ér chē 婴儿车

build *v/t* jiànzào 建造

♦ **build up 1** *v/t strength* zēngqiáng 增强; *relationship* fāzhǎn 发展 **2** *v/i* zhújiàn jījù 逐渐积聚

builder jiànzhù gōngrén 建筑工人; (*company*) jiànzhù gōngsī 建筑公司

building jiànzhù 建筑; (*activity*) jiànzào 建造

building site jiànzhù gōngdì 建筑工地

build-up jījù 积聚; (*publicity*) yúlùn zhǔnbèi 舆论准备

built-up area jiànzhù qū 建筑区

bulb BOT qiújīng 球茎; (*light ~*) diàndēng pào 电灯泡

bulge *v/i* (*of pocket*) gǔgu nāngnang 鼓鼓囊囊; (*of wall, eyes*) péngzhàng 膨胀

bulk dà duōshù 大多数; *in ~* zhěngpī 整批

bulky *parcel* tǐjī dà 体积大; *sweater* féidà 肥大

bulldozer tuītǔjī 推土机

bullet zǐdàn 子弹

bulletin bùgào 布告

bulletin board *(on wall)* bùgào bǎn 布告板

bullet-proof fángdàn 防弹

bull's-eye bǎxīn 靶心

bully *n* èbà 恶霸; *(child)* xiǎo táoqì 小淘气

bum *n* F *(worthless person)* lǎnhàn 懒汉; *(worthless person)* méiyòng de dōngxi 没用的东西

bump 1 *n (swelling)* zhǒngkuàir 肿块儿; *(in road)* tūkuàir 凸块儿 **2** *v/t* zhuàng 撞

bunch *n (of people)* huǒ huǒ伙; *(of keys)* chuàn 串; *a ~ of flowers* yīshù huā 一束花

bundle *n (of clothes)* bāo 包

bungle *v/t* gǎozāo 搞糟

bunk *n* chuángpù 床铺

burden *n* fùzhòng 负重; *fig* fùdān 负担

bureau *(furniture)* dǒuchú 斗橱; *(office)* bànshìchù

bureaucracy *(red tape)* guānliáo zhǔyì 官僚主义; *(system)* xíngzhèng xìtǒng 行政系统

bureaucrat guānliáo 官僚

bureaucratic guānliáo 官僚

burger hànbǎobāo 汉堡包

burglar xiǎotōu 小偷

burglar alarm fángqiè jǐngbàoqì 防窃警报器

burglarize dàoqiè 盗窃

burglary dàoqiè 盗窃

burial zànglǐ 葬礼

burn 1 *n* shāoshāng 烧伤 **2** *v/t* shāo 烧; *toast, meat* shāojiāo 烧焦; *(of sun)* shàishāng 晒伤

◆ **burn down** *v/t & v/i* shāohuǐ 烧毁

burp *n & v/i* dǎgé 打嗝

burst 1 *n (in pipe)* lièkǒu 裂口 **2** *v/i (of balloon, tire)* bàoliè 爆裂; *~ out laughing* tūrán dàxiào 突然大笑

bury máizàng 埋葬

bus *n* gōnggòng qìchē 公共汽车; *(long distance)* chángtú qìchē 长途汽车

bush *(plant)* guànmù 灌木

(*land*) huāngyě 荒野

business (*trade*) shēngyì 生
意; (*company*) gōngsī 公
司; (*work*) gōngzuò 工作;
(*affair, matter*) shìjiàn 事件

businessman shāngrén
商人

business studies shāngyè
xué 商业学

business trip chūchāi 出差

businesswoman nǚshāng-
rén 女商人

bus station gōnggòng qìchē
zǒngzhàn 公共汽车总站

bus stop chēzhàn 车站

bust *n* (*of woman*) xiōng 胸

busy *adj* máng 忙; *street* yǒu
shēngqì 有生气, *store,
restaurant: (making money)*
shēngyì xīnglóng 生意兴
隆; (*full of people*) xīxi
rǎngrang 熙熙攘攘; TELEC
zhànxiàn 占线

but dànshì 但是; *not me ~
...* būshì wǒ ér shì ... 不是

butcher màiròu de 卖肉的

butter *n* huángyóu 黄油

butterfly (*insect*) húdié 蝴蝶

buttocks túnbù 臀部

button *n* kòuzi 扣子; (*on
machine*) ànniǔ 按钮;
(*badge*) huīzhāng 徽章

buy *v/t* mǎi 买

buyer mǎijiā 买家

buzzer fēngmíngqì 蜂鸣器

by *prep* (*agency*) bèi 被;
(*near, next to*) kàojìn 靠
近; (*no later than*) bù chíyú
不迟于; (*past*) jīngguò
经过; (*with mode of
transportation*) chéng 乘;
~ day / night zài báitiān /
wǎnshàng 在白天/晚上;
a play ~ ... yóu ...xiěde
jùzuò 由...写的剧作; *~
oneself* zìjǐ 自己

bye (-**bye**) zàijiàn 再见

by-product fù chǎnpǐn 副
产品

C

cab (*taxi*) chūzū qìchē 出租
汽车; (*van-type*) miàndī

面的; (*of truck*) jiàshǐ shì
驾驶室

cabin (of plane) zuòcāng 座舱; (of ship) chuáncāng 船舱

cabin crew jīzǔ rényuán 机组人员

cabinet (cupboard) guìzi 柜子; (display ~) chénlièguì 陈列柜; POL nèigé 内阁

cable (electrical) diànxiàn 电线; ~ (TV) yǒuxiàn diànshì 有线电视

cab stand chūzūchē zhàn 出租车站

café fànguǎnr 小饭馆

cafeteria shítáng 食堂

caffeine kāfēiyīn 咖啡因

cage lóng 笼

cake xiǎo n dàngāo 蛋糕

calculate (work out) gūjì 估计; (in math) jìsuàn 计算

calculation jìsuàn jiéguǒ 计算结果

calculator jìsuànqì 计算器

calendar rìlì 日历

calf (young cow) xiǎoniú 小牛

call 1 n TELEC diànhuà 电话; (shout) hǎnjiào 喊叫 **2** v/t TELEC dǎ diànhuà gěi 打电话给; (summon) jiào 叫; meeting zhàojí 召集;

(describe as) shuōchéng shì 说成是; (shout) dàhǎn 大喊 **3** v/i TELEC dǎ diànhuà 打电话; (shout) hūhǎn 呼喊

♦ **call back 1** v/t TELEC huí diànhuà 回电话 **2** v/i TELEC zài dǎ diànhuà 再打电话; (visit again) zàilái 再来

♦ **call for** person jiē 接; goods qùná 去拿; (require) bìxū yào 必须要

♦ **call in** v/t expert qǐng 请

♦ **call on** (urge) dūncù 敦促; (visit) bàifǎng 拜访

caller TELEC dǎ diànhuàzhě 打电话者; (visitor) tànfǎngzhě 探访者

calligraphy shūfǎ 书法

calm adj weather píngjìng 平静; person lěngjìng 冷静

♦ **calm down** v/i píngjìng xiàlái 平静下来

calorie kǎlùlǐ 卡路里

Cambodia Jiǎnpǔzhài 柬埔寨

Cambodian 1 adj Jiǎnpǔzhài 柬埔寨 **2** n (person) Jiǎnpǔzhài rén 柬埔寨人

camcorder shèxiànjī 摄像机

camera zhàoxiàngjī 照像机

camouflage n wěizhuāng 伪装

camp 1 n yíng yíng 营 **2** v/i lùyíng 露营

campaign n yùndòng 运动

camper yěyíngzhě 野营者; (vehicle) yěyíng chē 野营车

campsite yíngdì 营地

campus xiàoyuán 校园

can¹ ~ I wǒ bùnéng 我不能; as fast as you ~ yuèkuài yuèhǎo 越快越好 ◊ (with skills) huì 会; ~ you speak French? nǐ huì shuō Fǎyǔma? 你会说法语吗? ◊ (permission) kěyǐ 可以; ~ I take this one? wǒ kěyǐ ná zhèige ma? 我可以拿这个吗? ◊ ~ I have a coffee? qǐng lái bēi kāfēi? 请来杯咖啡?

can² n (for drinks etc) guàntóu 罐头

Canada Jiānádà 加拿大

Canadian 1 adj Jiānádà 加拿大 **2** n Jiānádà rén 加拿大人

canal (waterway) yùnhé 运河

cancel qǔxiāo 取消

cancellation qǔxiāo 取消

cancer áizhèng 癌症

candid tǎnshuài 坦率

candidacy hòuxuǎn 候选

candidate (for position) hòuxuǎnrén 候选人; (in exam) kǎokǎorén 考卷人

candle làzhú 蜡烛

candor tǎnshuài 坦率

candy táng 糖

canned fruit etc guànzhuāng 罐装

cannot → **can¹**

can opener kāiguànqì 开罐器

canteen (in factory) shítáng 食堂

Canton Guǎngdōng 广东

Cantonese 1 adj Guǎngdōng 广东 **2** n Guǎngdōngrén 广东人; (language) Guǎngdōnghuà 广东话

cap (hat) màozi 帽子; (of bottle, lens) gàizi 盖子

capability nénglì 能力

capable nénggàn 能干; be ~ of yǒu nénglì 有能力

capacity (of container) róngliàng 容量; (of

engine) róngliàng 容量; (*of factory*) chǎnliàng 产量

capital n (*of country*) shǒudū 首都; (*letter*) dàxiě zìmǔ 大写字母; (*money*) zījīn 资金

capitalism zīběn zhǔyì 资本主义

capitalist 1 adj zīběn zhǔyì 资本主义 **2** n (*believer*) zīběn zhǔyìzhě 资本主义者; (*businessman*) zīběn jiā 资本家

capital punishment sǐxíng 死刑

capsize v/i fānchuán 翻船

capsule MED jiāonáng 胶囊; (*space*) tàikōng cāng 太空舱

captain n (*of ship*) chuánzhǎng 船长; (*of aircraft*) jīzhǎng 机长; (*of team*) duìzhǎng 队长

caption n shuōmíng 说明

captivate zháomí 着迷

captivity bèi guān 被关

capture v/t person zhuōdào 捉到; animal bǔhuò 捕获; city gōngxià 攻下; mood miáohuì 描绘

car chē 车; (*of train*) chē-

xiāng 车厢

carbohydrate tànshuǐ huàhéwù 碳水化合物

carbon monoxide yīyǎng huàtàn 一氧化碳

carbureter qìhuàqì 汽化器

card (*to mark special occasion*) kǎpiàn 卡片; (*post-*) míngxìnpiàn 明信片; (*business*) míngpiàn 名片; (*playing* ~) zhǐpái 纸牌

cardboard yìng zhǐbǎn 硬纸板

care 1 n (*of baby, elderly, sick*) zhàogù 照顾; (*medical*) yīliáo 医疗; (*worry*) yōulǜ 忧虑; *take* ~ (*be cautious*) xiǎoxīn 小心 **2** v/i guānxīn 关心; *I don't* ~! wǒbú zàihu! 我不在乎!

♦ **care about** guānxīn 关心

career (*profession*) shìyè 事业; (*path through life*) jīnglì 经历

careful (*cautious*) jǐnshèn 谨慎; (*thorough*) zǐxì 仔细; person xìxīn 细心

careless person cūxīn 粗心; work cǎoshuài 草率

cargo huòwù 货物

caricature n (picture) fěngcì huà 讽刺画

caring adj yǒu àixīn 有爱心

carousel (at fairground) xuánzhuǎn mùmǎ 旋转木马

carp (fish) lǐyú 鲤鱼

carpet dìtǎn 地毯

car rental qìchē chūzū gōngsī 汽车出租公司

carrier (company) yùnshū gōngsī 运输公司; (of disease) dàijùnzhě 带菌者

carrot húluóbo 胡萝卜

carry v/t (in hand) ná 拿; (on back) bēi 背; (hold in front) bàozhe 抱; (move: goods) bānyùn 搬运; (have on one's person) dàizhe 带着; (of ship, plane, bus etc) zàiyǒu 载有

◆ **carry out** survey etc jìnxíng 进行; orders etc zhíxíng 执行

cart (horsedrawn) mǎchē 马车; (for baggage) xínglǐ chē 行李车

cartel liánhé qǐyè 联合企业

carton (for milk, eggs etc) zhǐhé 纸盒; **a ~ of**

cigarettes yìtiáo xiāngyān 一条香烟

cartoon (in newspaper) fěngcì huà 讽刺画; (on TV, film) kǎtōng piān 卡通片

cartridge (for gun) zǐdàn 子弹

carve meat qiē 切; wood kè 刻

case¹ (container) hé 盒; (of Scotch, wine) xiāng 箱

case² n (instance) lìzi 例子; (argument) gēnjù 根据; (for police, attorney) ànjiàn 案件; MED bìnglì 病例; **in ~ ...** wànyī 万一...; **in any ~** zǒngzhī 总之

cash 1 n xiànjīn 现金 **2** v/t check duìxiàn 兑现

cash desk fùkuǎntái 付款台

cash flow xiànjīn liú 现金流

cashier n (in store etc) chūnàyuán 出纳员

cash machine qǔkuǎnjī 取款机

cash register xiànjīn chūnàjī 现金出纳机

casino dǔchǎng 赌场

casket (coffin) guāncai 棺材

cassette cídài 磁带

cassette player lùyīnjī 录

音机

cast 1 *n (of play)* yǎnyuán
biǎo 演员表

casual suíbiàn 随便; *(not
permanent)* línshí 临时

casualty shāngwáng rénshì
伤亡人士

cat māo 猫

catalog *n* mùlù 目录

catastrophe zāinàn 灾难

catch 1 *n* jiē 接; *(of fish)*
bǔhuò wù 捕获物;
(locking device) shuān 闩;
(problem) wèntí 问题 **2** *v/t
ball* jiēzhù 接住; *prisoner*
zhuōzhù 捉住; *(get on: bus,
train)* zuò 坐; *(not miss:
bus, train)* gǎnshàng 赶
上; *fish with rod* diàodào
钓到; *fish with net* bǔdào
捕到; *(in order to speak
to)* zhǎodào 找到; *illness*
rǎnshàng 染上; **~ (a) cold**
dé gǎnmào 得感冒

♦ **catch up** *v/i* gǎnshàng
赶上

♦ **catch up on** míbǔ 弥补

catcher *(in baseball)* jiēshǒu
接手

catching *disease*
chuánrǎnxìng 传染性

category fànchóu 范畴

Catholic 1 *adj* Tiānzhǔjiào
天主教 **2** *n* Tiānzhǔjiào tú
天主教徒

cattle niú 牛

cause 1 *n* yuányīn 原因;
(grounds) lǐyóu 理由; *(aim
of movement, charity etc)*
zhǔzhāng 主张 **2** *v/t* yǐnqǐ
引起

caution *n (carefulness)*
jǐnshèn 谨慎

cautious jǐnshèn 谨慎

cave dòng 洞

cavity *(in tooth)* zhùdòng
蛀洞

CD guāngpán 光盘

cease *v/t & v/i* zhōngzhǐ
中止

cease-fire tínghuǒ 停火

ceiling tiānhuābǎn 天花板;
(limit) zuìgāo xiàngdù 最
高限度

celebrate qìngzhù 庆祝

celebration qìngzhù huì
庆祝会

celebrity míngrén 名人

cell *(for prisoner)* láofáng 牢
房; BIO xìbāo 细胞

cellar dìjiào 地窖

cell(ular) phone shǒujī 手机

cemetery mùdì 墓地

censor v/t shěnchá 审查

censorship shěnchá zhìdù 审查制度

cent fēn 分

centenary, centennial yìbǎi zhōunián 一百周年

center n zhōngxīn 中心; POL zhōngjiān pài 中间派

central zhōngbù 中部; apartment zhōngyāng 中央; (main) zhǔyào 主要

central heating zhōngyāng nuǎnqì 中央暖气

centralize jízhōng 集中

century shìjì 世纪

CEO (= Chief Executive Officer) zǒng jīnglǐ 总经理

cereal (grain) gǔlèi 谷类

ceremony (event) diǎnlǐ 典礼; (ritual) yíshì 仪式

certain (sure) kěndìng 肯定; (particular) mǒuzhǒng 某种

certainly (definitely) yídìng 一定; (of course) méi wèntí 没问题

certainty (confidence) quèxìn 确信; (inevitability) bìránxìng 必然性

certificate (qualification) zhèngshū 证书; (official paper) zhèngmíng 证明

certify zhèngmíng 证明

Cesarean n pōufù 剖腹

CFC (= chlorofluorocarbon) fúlǜ huàtàn 氟氯化碳

chain n liàntiáo 链条; COM liánsuǒdiàn 连锁店

chair n 1 yǐzi 椅子; (armchair) fúshǒu yǐ 扶手椅 2 v/t meeting zhǔchí 主持

chairman zhǔxí 主席

Chairman Mao Máo Zhǔxí 毛主席

chairperson, chairwoman zhǔxí 主席

challenge 1 n tiǎozhàn 挑战 2 v/t (defy) fǎnduì 反对; (call into question) zhìyí 质疑; ~ X to Y tiǎozhàn X zuò Y 挑战X做Y

challenging job yǒu tiǎozhànxìng 有挑战性

champagne xiāngbīn jiǔ 香槟酒

champion n SP guànjūn 冠军; (of cause) hànwèizhě 捍卫者

championship (event) jǐnbiāosài 锦标赛; (title)

guànjūn 冠军

chance (*possibility*) kěnéng 可能; (*opportunity*) jīhuì 机会; (*risk*) fēngxiǎn 风险

change 1 *n* gǎibiàn 改变; (*small coins*) língqián 零钱; (*from purchase*) zhǎoqián 找钱; *for a ~* huàn kǒuwèi 换口味 **2** *v/t* (*alter*) gǎibiàn 改变; *bankbill, trains, clothes*, (*replace*) huàn 换 **3** *v/i* biàn 变; (*put on different clothes*) huàn yīfu 换衣服; (*in traveling*) huàn 换

channel (*on TV*) píndào 频道; (*waterway*) hǎixiá 海峡

chant *v/t* gāohū 高呼

chaos hùnluàn 混乱

chaotic hùnluàn 混乱

chapter zhāng 章

character (*nature*) běnxìng 本性; (*person*) rén 人; (*in book, play*) rénwù 人物; (*personality*) xìnggé 性格; (*for writing Chinese etc*) zì 字

characteristic 1 *n* tèdiǎn 特点 **2** *adj* diǎnxíng 典型

charbroiled kǎo 烤

charge 1 *n* (*fee*) fèiyòng 费

用; LAW kònggào 告诉; *be in ~* fùzé 负责; *take ~* jiēguǎn 接管 **2** *v/t sum of money* shōufèi 收费; (*put on account*) jìzhàng 记账; LAW zhǐkòng 指控; *battery* chōngdiàn 充电

charge account shēgòuzhì 赊购制

charge card jìzhàngkǎ 记账卡

charitable císhàn 慈善

charity (*organization*) císhàng jīgòu 慈善机构

charm *n* měilì 魅力; (*on bracelet*) xiǎo zhuāngshì pǐn 小装饰品

charming mírén 迷人

chart túbiǎo 图表; (*for ship*) hánghǎi tú 航海图; (*for airplane*) hángkōng tú 航空图

charter *v/t* bāozū 包租

chase 1 *n* zhuīzhú 追逐 **2** *v/t* zhuī 追

chat 1 *n* liáotiān 聊天 **2** *v/i* liáo 聊

chatter *v/i* (*talk*) xiánliáo 闲聊; (*of teeth*) dǎzhàn 打颤

chatterbox ráoshézhě 饶舌者

chemist

chauffeur *n* sījī 司机

chauvinist (male ~) dà nánrén zhǔyìzhě 大男人主义者

cheap *adj* piányi 便宜; (mean) xiǎoqì 小气

cheat 1 *n* (person) piànzi 骗子 2 *v/t* piàn 骗 3 *v/i* (in exam) zuòbì 作弊; (at cards etc) gǎoguǐ 搞鬼

check¹ *n & adj* (in pattern) fānggé 方格

check² FIN zhīpiào 支票; (in restaurant etc) zhàngdān 账单

check³ 1 *n* (to verify) jiǎnchá 检查 2 *v/t* (to verify) chá 查; (with ~mark) dǎgōu 打勾; coat, package etc cúnfàng 存放 3 *v/i* chá 查

◆ check in (at airport) lǐng dēngjīkǎ 领登机卡; (at hotel) dēngjì 登记

◆ check out *v/i* (of hotel) jiézhàng 结账

checkbook zhīpiào běn 支票本

check-in (counter) lǐng dēngjīkǎ guìtái 领登机卡柜台

checking account zhīpiào zhànghù 支票帐户

check-in time lǐng dēngjī kǎ shíjiān 领登机卡时间

checklist héduìbiǎo 核对表

check mark gōuhào 勾号

checkout (in store) guìtái 柜台

checkpoint guānqiǎ 关卡

checkroom (for coats) yīmào jiān 衣帽间; (for bags) xínglǐ cúnfàngchù 行李存放处

checkup medical jiànkāng jiǎnchá 健康检查

cheek miànjiá 面颊

cheer 1 *n* huānhū 欢呼; ~s! (toast) gānbēi! 干杯! 2 *v/t* shòu huānyíng 受欢迎 3 *v/i* hècǎi 喝采

◆ cheer up 1 *v/i* gāoxìng qǐlái 高兴起来; ~! gǔqǐ jìnr lái! 鼓起劲儿来! 2 *v/t* gǔ qǐ jìnr 鼓起劲儿

cheerful kuàihuó 快活

cheerleader lālāduì yuán 啦啦队员

cheese nǎilào 奶酪

chef chúshī 厨师

chemical 1 *adj* huàxué 化学 2 *n* huàxué zhìpǐn 化学制品

chemist huàxué jiā 化学家

chemistry huàxué 化学; *fig* mòqì 默契

chemotherapy huàxué liáofǎ 化学疗法

chess xiàngqí 象棋

chessboard qípán 棋盘

chest xiōng 胸; (*box*) xiāngzi 箱子

chew v/t jiáo 嚼; (*of dog, rats*) kěn 啃

chewing gum kǒuxiāng táng 口香糖

chicken n jī 鸡; (*food*) jīròu 鸡肉

chief 1 n tóunǎo 头脑 **2** adj zhǔyào 主要

chiefly zhǔyào 主要

child háizi 孩子

childhood tóngnián 童年

childish pej yòuzhì 幼稚

chill n (*in air*) lěngqì 冷气; (*illness*) gǎnmào 感冒

chilly *weather* hánlěng 寒冷

chimney yāncōng 烟囱

chin xiàba 下巴

China Zhōngguó 中国

Chinese 1 adj Zhōngguó 中国; (*in Chinese*) Zhōngwén 中文 **2** n (*written language*) Zhōngwén 中文; (*spoken language*) Zhōngguó

huà 中国话; (*person*) Zhōngguórén 中国人

Chinese character hànzì 汉字

chip n (*fragment*) suìxiè 碎屑; (*damage*) liè kǒu 裂口; (*in gambling*) chóumǎ 筹码; COMPUT xīnpiàn 芯片; *potato* ~s shǔpiàn 薯片

chocolate qiǎokèlì 巧克力

choice n xuǎnzé 选择; (*selection*) gèsè gèyàng 各色各样; (*preference*) xuǎnzé 选择

choir héchàngtuán 合唱团

choke 1 n MOT zǔfēngmén 阻风门 **2** v/i qiǎ 卡

cholesterol dǎngùchún 胆固醇

choose 1 v/t xuǎnzé 选择 **2** v/i tiāoxuǎn 挑选

chop 1 n (*meat*) páigǔ 排骨; (*seal*) túzhāng 图章 **2** v/t wood kǎn 砍; *food* duò 踩

chopsticks kuàizi 筷子

chore (*household*) jiāwù 家务

chorus héchàng 合唱; (*singers*) héchàng tuán 合唱团

christen xǐlǐ 洗礼

Christian 1 n Jīdūtú 基督徒 2 adj Jīdūjiào 基督教

Christmas Shèngdànjié 圣诞节; *Merry ~!* Shèngdàn kuàilè! 圣诞快乐!

Christmas card Shèngdànkǎ 圣诞卡

Christmas Day Shèngdànjié 圣诞节

Christmas Eve Shèngdàn yè 圣诞夜

Christmas present Shèngdàn lǐwù 圣诞礼物

Christmas tree Shèngdàn shù 圣诞树

chrome, chromium gè 铬

chronic mànxìng 慢性

chronological shíjiān shùnxù 时间顺序

church jiàotáng 教堂

CIA (= *Central Intelligence Agency*) Zhōngyāng Qíngbào Jú 中央情报局

cigar xuějiā 雪茄

cigarette xiāngyān 香烟

cinema diànyǐng 电影; (*Br: building*) diànyǐng yuàn 电影院

circle 1 n yuánquān 圆圈; (*group*) quānzi 圈子 2 v/i

(*of plane, bird*) pánxuán 盘旋

circular adj yuánxíng 圆形

circulate v/t memo etc chuányuè 传阅

circulation BIO xúnhuán 循环; (*of newspaper*) xiāolù 销路

circumstances qíngkuàng 情况

circus mǎxìtuán 马戏团

citizen gōngmín 公民

citizenship guójí 国籍

city chéngshì 城市

civil (*not military*) mínjiān 民间; (*polite*) yǒu lǐmào 有礼貌

civil engineer tǔmù gōngchéngshī 土木工程师

civilian n píngmín 平民

civilization wénmíng 文明

civil servant gōngwùyuán 公务员

civil war nèizhàn 内战

claim 1 n (*request*) suǒpéi 索赔; (*assertion*) zhǔzhāng 主张 2 v/t (*as a right*) suǒqǔ 索取; (*assert*) shēngchēng 声称; lost and found lǐng 领

clamp n (*fastener*) jiāzi 夹子

clandestine mìmì 秘密

clap 1 v/i (applaud) pāishǒu 拍手 **2** v/t pāi 拍

clarify chéngqīng 澄清

clarity qīngxīdù 清晰度

clash 1 n chōngtū 冲突; (of personalities) bù xiétiáo 不协调 **2** v/i fāshēng chōngtū 发生冲突

clasp 1 n jiázi 夹子 **2** v/t (in hand) jǐnwò 紧握

class n (lesson) kè 课; (group of people) bān 班; (category) děngjí 等级; (social) jiēcéng 阶层

classic 1 adj (typical) diǎnxíng 典型; (definitive) quánwēixìng 权威性 **2** n jīngdiǎn zuòpǐn 经典作品

classical music gǔdiǎn 古典

classified information jīmì 机密

classified ad fēnlèi guǎnggào 分类广告

classify fēnlèi 分类

classroom jiàoshì 教室

clause (in contract) tiáokuǎn 条款

claustrophobia yōubì kǒngbù zhèng 幽闭恐怖症

claw n (of lobster, crab) qiánzi 钳子; (of cat) zhuǎzi 爪子

clean 1 adj gānjìng 干净 **2** v/t teeth, shoes shuā 刷; room dǎsǎo 打扫; car, hands, clothes xǐ 洗

cleaning woman qīngjié nǚgōng 清洁女工

cleanser (for skin) qīngjiéjì 清洁剂

clear 1 adj explanation, voice qīngchu 清楚; (obvious) míngxiǎn 明显; weather, sky qínglǎng 晴朗; water qīngchè 清澈; conscience qīngbái 清白 **2** v/t roads qīngchú 清除; (acquit) chéngqīng 澄清; (authorize) yǔnxǔ 允许 **3** v/i (of mist) qíngle sànle

♦ **clear up** v/i (tidy up) shōushi 收拾; (of weather) zhuǎnqíng 转晴; (of illness, rash) xiāoshī 消失

clearance (authorization) xǔkě 许可

clearly (with clarity) qīngchu 清楚; (evidently) míngxiǎn 明显

clench teeth yǎojǐn 咬紧; fist

wòjǐn 握紧

clerk (administrative)
zhíyuán 职员; (in store)
fúwùyuán 服务员

clever cōngmíng 聪明;
gadget qiǎomiào 巧妙

client gùkè 顾客

climate qìhòu 气候

climax n gāocháo 高潮

climb 1 n (up hill) pāndēng
攀登 2 v/t & v/i pá 爬

climber dēngshānzhě 登
山者

clinic zhěnsuǒ 诊所

clip¹ n (fastener) jiāzi 夹子

clip² 1 n (extract) jiǎnjí 剪辑
2 v/t hair, hedge jiǎn 剪

clipping (from newspaper)
jiǎnbào 剪报

clock zhōng 钟

clock radio shōuyīnjī
nàozhōng 收音机闹钟

clockwise shùn shízhēn 顺
时针

close¹ adj friend qīnmì 亲
密; resemblance xiāngjìn 相
近; it's ~ to the stores lí
shāngdiàn jìn 离商店近

close² v/t & v/i guān 关

closed store guānmén 关门;
eyes bìshàng 闭上

closely listen, watch zǐxì 仔
细; cooperate mìqiè 密切

closet yīguì 衣柜

closing time guānmén
shíjiān 关门时间

closure guānbì 关闭

clot n (of blood) xuèkuài
血块

cloth (fabric) bùliào 布料;
(for cleaning) mābù 抹布

clothes yīfu 衣服

cloud n yún 云

cloudy yīntiān 阴天

club n jùlèbù 俱乐部; (golf
iron) qiúgān 球杆

clue xiànsuǒ 线索

clumsy person bènshǒu
bènjiǎo 笨手笨脚

clutch 1 n MOT líhéqì 离合
器 2 v/t jǐnwò 紧握

coach 1 n (trainer) jiàoliàn
教练 2 v/t zhǐdǎo 指导

coarse fabric cūcāo 粗糙;
(vulgar) cūsú 粗俗

coast n hǎibiān 海边

coastal línhǎi 临海

coastguard hǎi'àn jǐngwèi
duì 海岸警卫队

coat 1 n wàiyī 外衣; (over~)
dàyī 大衣; (of paint etc)
céng 层 2 v/t (cover) jiā

shàng yīcéng 加上一层

coating céng 层

coax hǒng 哄

cocaine kěkǎyīn 可卡因

cock n (chicken) gōngjī 公鸡

cockpit (of plane) zuòcāng 座舱

cockroach zhāngláng 蟑螂

code n mìmǎ 密码

co-educational nánnǚ héxiào 男女合校

coexistence gòngchǔ 共处

coffee kāfēi 咖啡

coffee break xiǎoxī 小息

coffee shop kāfēi diàn 咖啡店

coffin guāncai 棺材

cog lúnchǐ 轮齿

coherent liánguàn 连贯

coin n yìngbì 硬币

coincide qiǎohé 巧合

coincidence qiǎohé 巧合

Coke® kěkǒu kělè 可口可乐

cold 1 adj lěng 冷; it's ~ tiān lěng 天冷 2 n hánlěng 寒冷; I have a ~ wǒ gǎnmàole 我感冒了

collaborate hézuò 合作; (with enemy) gōujié 勾结

collaboration hézuò 合作;

(with enemy) gōujié 勾结

collapse dǎotā 倒塌; (of person) bēngkuì 崩溃

collar lǐngzi 领子; (for dog, cat) xiàngquān 项圈

colleague tóngshì 同事

collect 1 v/t person jiē接; tickets, cleaning etc ná拿; (gather, as hobby) shōují 收集 2 adv: call ~ shòuhuàrén fùfèi 受话人付费

collection (of art) shōucángpǐn 收藏品; (fashion) shízhuāng zhǎnlǎn 时装展览

collective n POL jítǐ 集体

collector shōucáng jiā 收藏家

college xuéyuàn 学院

collision xiāngzhuàng 相撞

colonial adj zhímíndì 殖民地

colony zhímíndì 殖民地

color n yánsè 颜色; (in cheeks) liǎnsè 脸色

colorful xiānyàn 鲜艳; account jīngcǎi 精彩

color photograph cǎisè zhàopiàn 彩色照片

column liè 列; (architectural) yuánzhù 圆柱; (text) lán

栏; (*in newspaper*) zhuānlán 专栏

columnist zhuānlán zuòjiā 专栏作家

coma hūnmí 昏迷

comb 1 *n* shūzi 梳子 **2** *v/t* shū 梳; *area* sōuxún 搜寻

combat 1 *n* zhàndòu 战斗 **2** *v/t* yǔ ... zuò dòuzhēng 与 ... 做斗争

combination zǔhé 组合; (*of safe*) mìmǎ 密码

combine *v/t* hùnhé 混合

come (*toward speaker*) lái 来; (*toward listener*) qù 去; (*of train, bus*) láile 来了

◆**come back** huílái 回来

◆**come down** xià lái 下来; (*in price etc*) xiàjiàng 下降

◆**come in** zǒu jìnlái 走进来; (*of tide*) zhǎngcháo zhǎng 涨潮; ~! qǐngjìn! 请进!

◆**come off** (*of handle etc*) tuōluò 脱落

◆**come on** (*progress*) jìnzhǎn 进展; ~! kuàidiǎnr! 快点儿!; (*in disbelief*) bùkěnéng 不可能

◆**come out** (*of person*) chū lái 出来; (*of sun, results, product*) chūlái 出来; (*of*

stain) xiāoshī 消失; (*of book, record*) fāxíng 发行

comedian xǐjù yǎnyuán 喜剧演员; *pej* chǒujiǎo 丑角

comedy xǐjù 喜剧

comfort 1 *n* xiǎngshòu 享受; (*consolation*) ānwèi 安慰 **2** *v/t* ānwèi 安慰

comfortable shūfu 舒服

comic 1 *n* (*to read*) mànhuà 漫画 **2** *adj* yǒuqù 有趣

comma dòuhào 逗号

command *n* & *v/t* mìnglìng 命令

commander zhīhuīguān 指挥官

commemorate jìniàn 纪念

comment 1 *n* yìjiàn 意见 **2** *v/i* fābiǎo yìjiàn 发表意见

commentary pínglùn 评论

commentator pínglùn jiā 评论家

commercial 1 *adj* shāngyè 商业 **2** *n* (*ad*) guǎnggào 广告

commission 1 *n* (*payment*) yòngjīn 佣金; (*job*) chéngbāo 承包; (*committee*) wěiyuánhuì 委员会 **2** *v/t* (*for a job*) wěituō 委托

commit ~ *a crime* fànzuì 犯罪; ~ *oneself* tóurù 投入

commitment zérèn 责任

committee wěiyuánhuì 委员会

commodity shāngpǐn 商品

common (*not rare*) píngcháng 平常; (*shared*) gòngtóng 共同

common sense chángshí 常识

communicate v/i (*make self understood*) gōutōng 沟通

communications tōngxùn yè 通讯业

communicative ài shuōhuà 爱说话

Communism Gòngchǎnzhǔyì 共产主义

Communist 1 *adj* Gòngchǎnzhǔyì 共产主义 **2** *n* Gòngchǎndǎngyuán 共产党员

Communist China Zhōnggòng 中共

Communist Party Gòngchǎndǎng 共产党

community shèqū 社区

commute v/i (*to work*) tōngqín 通勤

compact disc MUS jīguāng chàngpiān 激光唱片; COMPUT guāngpán 光盘

companion bànlǚ 伴侣

company COM gōngsī 公司; (*companionship*) péibàn 陪伴; (*guests*) kèrén 客人

comparatively xiāngduì éryán 相对而言

compare v/t bǐjiào 比较; ~ *X with Y* jiāng X yǔ Y xiāng bǐjiào 将X与Y相比较

comparison bǐjiào 比较

compassion tóngqíng 同情

compatible *people* hédelái 合得来; *blood, life styles* fúhé 符合; COMPUT jiānróng 兼容

compel (*force*) qiǎngpò 强迫

compensate v/t (*with money*) péicháng 赔偿

compensation (*money*) péicháng 赔偿; (*comfort*) ānwèi 安慰

compete jìngzhēng 竞争; (*take part*) cānjiā 参加; ~ *for* zhēngduó 争夺

competent *person* chèngzhí 称职; *work* hégé 合格

competition jìngzhēng 竞争;

SP bǐsài 比赛; *(competitors)* duìshǒu 对手

competitive *price* yǒu jìngzhēng lì 有竞争力; *person* hào jìngzhēng 好竞争

competitor *(in contest)* bǐsàizhě 比赛者; COM jìngzhēng duìshǒu 竞争对手

complain v/i bàoyuàn 抱怨; *(to store, manager)* tóusù 投诉

complaint tóusù 投诉; MED jíbìng 疾病

complete 1 *adj (total)* shízú 十足; *(full)* wánzhěng 完整; *(finished)* wángōng 完工 **2** v/t *course, task etc* wánchéng 完成; *form* tiánxiě 填写

completely wánquán 完全

completion wánchéng 完成

complex 1 *adj* fùzá 复杂 **2** n PSYCH qíngjié 情节; *(of buildings)* zhōngxīn 中心

complicated fùzá 复杂

compliment n & v/t zànměi 赞美

complimentary zànměi 赞美; *(free)* miǎnfèi 免费; *(in*

restaurant, hotel) zèngsòng 赠送

comply fúcóng 服从; **~ with ...** zūnshǒu ... 遵守...

component bùfen 部分

compose v/t zǔchéng 组成; MUS chuàngzuò 创作

composer MUS zuòqǔjiā 作曲家

composure zhènjìng 镇静

comprise *(consist of)* bāohán 包含; *(make up)* gòuchéng 构成; **be ~d of ...** yóu ... zǔchéng 由...组成

compromise n tuǒxié 妥协

compulsory yìwù 义务; *class* bìxiū 必修

computer diànnǎo 电脑

computer game diànzǐ yóuxì 电子游戏

conceal *fact, truth* yǐnmán 隐瞒; *object* yǐncáng 隐藏

conceited zìgāo zìdà 自高自大

concentrate v/i *(on task)* jízhōng jīnglì 集中精力

concentration zhuānxīn 专心

concept gàiniàn 概念

concern 1 n *(anxiety)* dānyōu 担忧; *(care)* guānxīn

关心; (company) gōngsī 公司 2 v/t (involve) shèjí 涉及; (worry) dānyōu 担忧

concerned (anxious) gǎndào bù ān 感到不安; (caring) guānxīn 关心; (involved) yǒuguān 有关

concert yīnyuè huì 音乐会

conclude 1 v/t (deduce) tuīduàn chū 推断出 2 v/i jiéshù 结束

conclusion (deduction) jiélùn 结论; (end) jiéwěi 结尾

concrete n hùnníngtǔ 混凝土

concussion zhèndàng 震荡

condition n (state, of health) zhuàngtài 状态; (requirement, term) tiáojiàn 条件; ~**s** (circumstances) tiáojiàn 条件

conditioner (for hair) hùfà sù 护发素

condolences diàoyàn 吊唁

condom bìyùn tào 避孕套

conduct 1 n (behavior) jǔzhǐ 举止 2 v/t (carry out) shíshī 实施; ELEC chuándǎo 传导; MUS zhǐhuī 指挥

conductor MUS zhǐhuī jiā

指挥家; RAIL lièchēzhǎng 列车长

conference tǎolùn huì 讨论会

confess v/t & v/i chéngrèn 承认; (to police) tǎnbái 坦白

confession gòngrèn 供认; (to police) rènzuì shū 认罪书; REL chànhuǐ 忏悔

confidence (assurance) xìnxīn 信心; (trust, secret) xìnrèn 信任

confident (assured) zìxìn 自信; (convinced) kěndìng 肯定

confidential jīmì 机密

confirm v/t quèdìng 确定; theory, fears zhèngshí 证实

confirmation zhèngmíng 证明; (of theory, fears) zhèngshí 证实

confiscate mòshōu 没收

conflict 1 n (disagreement) zhēngyì 争议; (clash) chōngtū 冲突; (war) zhànzhēng 战争 2 v/i (clash) chōngtū 冲突

conform zūnshǒu 遵守; (of product) fúhé 符合

confront (face) miànduì 面

对; (*tackle*) shǐ duìzhì 使
对质

confrontation chōngtū 冲突

confuse hùnxiáo 混淆: ~ **X
with Y** bǎ X dāngchéng Y
把 X 当成 Y

confusing lìngrén hútú 令
人糊涂

confusion hùnxiáo 混淆

congestion MOT dǔsè 堵塞;
(*in chest*) chōngxuè 充血

congratulate zhùhè 祝贺

congratulations zhùhè 祝贺

congress dàibiǎo dàhuì 代
表大会; *Congress* (*of US*)
Guóhuì 国会

Congressional Guóhuì 国会

Congressman Guóhuì
yìyuán 国会议员

conjunctivitis jiémó yán
结膜炎

connect (*join*) liánjiē 连
接; TELEC jiētōng 接通;
(*link*) yǒu guānxì 有关系;
(*to power supply*) jiētōng
diànlù 接通电路

connecting flight liányùn
fēijī 联运飞机

connection (*in wiring*)
liánjiē 连接; (*link, personal
contact*) guānxì 关系; (*when*

traveling) liányùn 联运; ~
to the Internet yīntèwǎng
jiēkǒu 因特网接口

conquer zhēngfú 征服; *fear
etc* zhànshèng 战胜

conscience liángxīn 良心

conscious *adj* (*aware*) zìjué
自觉; MED qīngxǐng 清醒

consciousness yìshí 意识;
MED zhījué 知觉

consecutive liánxù 连续

consent 1 *n* zànxǔ 赞许 **2** *v/i*
tóngyì 同意

consequence hòuguǒ 后果

consequently suǒyǐ 所以

conservative *adj* bǎoshǒu 保
守; *clothes* lǎoqì 老气

consider (*regard*) rènwéi 认
为; (*show regard for, think
about*) kǎolù 考虑

considerable xiāngdāng dà
相当大

considerate tǐtiē 体贴

consideration
(*thought*) kǎolù 考虑;
(*thoughtfulness, concern*)
guānxīn 关心; *take X into
~* kǎolù X 考虑 X

consignment COM huòwù
货物

♦ **consist of** bāokuò 包括

consistent yīguàn 一贯

consolation ānwèi 安慰

console v/t ānwèi 安慰

conspicuous xiǎnyǎn 显眼

conspiracy yīnmóu 阴谋

constant bùduàn 不断

constipation biànmì 便秘

constitution POL xiànfǎ 宪法

construction jiànzào 建造

construction industry jiànzhù yè 建筑业

construction worker jiànzhù gōngrén 建筑工人

constructive yǒu jiànshèxìng 有建设性

consul lǐngshì 领事

consulate lǐngshì guǎn 领事馆

consult (seek the advice of) hé …shāngliàng 和…商量

consultancy (company) zīxún gōngsī 咨询公司; (advice) zīxún 咨询

consultant gùwèn 顾问

consumer gùkè 顾客

consumption (of energy etc) xiāohào 消耗

contact 1 n (person) shóurén 熟人; (communication, physical) jiēchù 接触 2 v/t liánluò 联络

contact lens yǐnxíng yǎnjìng 隐形眼镜

contagious chuánrǎn 传染; fig mànyán 蔓延

contain tears, laughter kòngzhì 控制; *it ~ed my camera* wǒde zhàoxiàngjī zài lǐmiàn 我的照像机 在里面

container róngqì 容器; COM jízhuāng xiāng 集装箱

contemporary 1 adj dāngdài 当代 2 n tóngdàirén 同代人; (at school) tóngjiè 同届

contempt qīngmiè 轻蔑

contender jìngzhēngzhě 竞争者; (against champion) zhēngduózhě 争夺者; POL jìngxuǎnrén 竞选人

content[1] n nèiróng 内容

content[2] adj mǎnzú 满足

contentment mǎnzú 满足

contents nèiróng 内容

contest[1] (competition) bǐsài 比赛; (for power) zhēngduó 争夺

contest[2] v/t leadership etc jìngzhēng 竞争

contestant cānsàizhě 参赛者

context shàngxià wén 上下

文: *look at X in* ~ gēnjù jùtǐ huánjìng lái kǎolǜ X 根据具体环境来考虑X

continent *n* dàlù 大陆

continual bùduàn 不断

continue *v/t & v/i* jìxù 继续

continuous bùtíng 不停

contraception bìyùn 避孕

contraceptive *n* bìyùnqì 避孕器; *(pill)* bìyùn yào 避孕药

contract *n* hétong 合同

contractor chéngbāorén 承包人

contradict *statement* yǔ ... yǒu máodùn 与...有矛盾; *person* fǎnbó 反驳

contrary[1] *adj* duìlì 对立; ~ **to** ... yǔ ... xiāngfǎn 与...相反 **2** *n:* **on the** ~ zhèng xiāngfǎn 正相反

contrast *n & v/t* duìzhào 对照

contribute *v/t money* juānxiàn 捐献

control 1 *n (of country, emotion etc)* kòngzhì 控制 **2** *v/t (govern)* kòngzhì 控制; *(restrict)* xiànzhì 限制; *(regulate)* guǎnlǐ 管理

control panel kòngzhì pán 控制盘

control tower zhǐhuī diàodùtái 指挥调度台

controversial yǒu zhēngyì 有争议

convalescence liáoyǎng qī 疗养期

convenience fāngbiàn 方便

convenience store fāngbiàn xiǎo shāngdiàn 方便小商店

convenient *location* fāngbiàn 方便; *time, arrangement* héshì 合适

convention *(tradition)* shèhuì xísú 社会习俗; *(conference)* dàhuì 大会

convention center huìyì zhōngxīn 会议中心

conventional píngcháng 平常

conversation jiāotán 交谈

conversion *(of figures, money)* zhésuàn 折算

convert 1 *n* guīfùzhě 归附者 **2** *v/t house, room etc* gǎijiàn 改建; *unit of measurement* zhéhé 折合; *energy* zhuǎnhuà 转化

convertible *n (car)* zhépéng chē 折蓬车

convict 1 *n* qiúfàn 囚犯
2 *v/t* LAW xuānpàn yǒuzuì
宣判有罪

conviction LAW dìngzuì 定
罪; (*belief*) quèxìn 确信

convince shuōfú 说服

convincing lìngrén xìnfú 令
人信服

cook 1 *n* chúshī 厨师 **2** *v/t*
& *v/i* zuò 做; (*roast, bake*)
kǎo 烤; (*steam*) zhēng 蒸;
(*stir fry*) chǎo 炒 **3** *v/i* (*of
person*) zuòfàn 做饭

cookbook pēngrèn shū 烹
饪书

cookie qūqí 曲奇

cooking (*food*) fàncài 饭菜

cool 1 *adj* weather
liángshuǎng 凉爽; *drink*
liáng 凉; (*calm*) lěngjìng 冷
静; (*unfriendly*) lěngmò 冷
漠; F (*great*) kù 酷 **2** *v/i* (*of
food*) lěngquè 冷却; (*of
tempers*) píngxī 平息

cooperate hézuò 合作

cooperative 1 *n* hézuò
shè 合作社 **2** *adj* COM
hézuò 合作; (*helpful*) lèyì
pèihé 乐意配合

coordinate *activities* xiétiáo
协调

coordination xiétiáo 协调

cop F jǐngchá 警察

cope yìngfu 应付; ~ *with* ...
yìngfu ... 应付

copier (*machine*) fùyìnjī
复印机

copy 1 *n* (*imitation*) fùzhì
复制品; (*duplicate*) fùběn
副本; (*photocopy*) fùyìn
jiàn 复印件; (*of book*) běn
本; (*of record, CD*) pán 盘
2 *v/t* (*imitate*) fǎngzào 仿
造; (*duplicate*) fùxiě 复写;
(*photocopy*) fùyìn 复印;
COMPUT: *file* fùzhì 复制; (*in
writing*) chāoxiě 抄写; (*in
order to cheat*) chāoxí 抄袭

cord (*string*) shéng 绳;
(*cable*) xiàn 线

core 1 *n* (*of fruit*) hé 核;
(*of problem*) yàodiǎn 要
点; (*of organization, party*)
héxīn 核心 **2** *adj* issue zuì
zhòngyào 最重要

cork (*in bottle*) píngsāi 瓶塞;
(*material*) ruǎnmù 软木

corkscrew luósī qǐzi 螺丝
起子

corner *n* (*of room*) jiǎoluò
角落; (*of table*) zhuōjiǎo
桌角; (*bend: on road*)

zhuǎnwān 转弯; *(in soccer)* jiǎoqiú 角球

corporate COM jítuán 集团

corpse shīshǐ 死尸

correct 1 *adj* zhèngquè 正确; **2** *v/t* jiūzhèng 纠正; *proofs, homework* xiūgǎi 修改

correspondence *(letters)* xìnjiàn 信件; *(exchange of letters)* tōngxìn 通信

correspondent *(reporter)* tōngxùnyuán 通讯员

corridor zǒuláng 走廊

corroborate zhèngshí 证实

corrosion fǔshí 腐蚀

corrupt *adj* fǔbài 腐败; COMPUT pòhuài 破坏

corruption shòuhuì 受贿

cosmetics huàzhuāng pǐn 化妆品

cosmetic surgery zhěngróng wàikē 整容外科

cost 1 *n (price)* jiàgé 价格; *(in finance)* chéngběn 成本; *fig* dàijià 代价; **~s** COM fèiyòng 费用 **2** *v/t $50 etc* xūyào 需要

cost of living shēnghuó fèiyòng 生活费用

cot *(camp-bed)* xíngjūn chuáng 行军床

cotton 1 *n* miánhua 棉花 **2** *adj* miánbù 棉布

couch *n* cháng shāfā 长沙发

cough *n & v/i* késou 咳嗽

could: **~ I ...?** wǒ kěyǐ ... ma? 我可以 ... 吗？; **~ you ...?** qǐng nǐ ...? 请你 ...?; **you ~ be right** méizhǔn nǐshì duìde 没准儿你是对的

council *(assembly)* yìhuì 议会; *(authority)* zhèngfǔ 政府

councilor yìyuán 议员

counselor LAW lùshī 律师

count 1 *v/i (to ten etc)* shǔ shù 数; *(calculate)* jìsuàn 计算; *(be important)* yǒu zhòngyào yìyì 有重要意义; *(qualify)* suàn 算 **2** *v/t (~ up)* shǔ shù 数; *(calculate)* jìsuàn 计算; *(include)* bāokuò 包括

◆**count on** yīkào 依靠

countdown dào shǔshù 倒数数

counter¹ *(in store, café)* guìtái 柜台; *(in game)* chóumǎ 筹码

counter² *v/t* fǎnjī 反击

counteract zhōnghé 中和

counterbalance pínghéng lì

平衡力

counterfeit *v/t & adj* wěizào 伪造

counterpart *(person)* duìfāng 对方

counterproductive qǐ fǎn zuòyòng 起反作用

countless shǔbu jìn 数不尽

country *(nation)* guójiā 国家; *(not town)* xiāngxià 乡下

countryside nóngcūn 农村

coup POL zhèngbiàn 政变

couple *(married)* fūqī 夫妻; *(man & woman)* qínglǚ 情侣; *just a ~* zhǐyǒu jǐgè 只有几个; *a ~ of* jǐgè 几个

courage yǒngqì 勇气

courier xìnshǐ 信使; *(with tourists)* dǎoyóu 导游

course *n (lessons)* kèchéng 课程; *(of meal)* dào 道; *(of ship, plane)* hángxiàng 航向; *(for horse race, golf)* chǎng 场; *(for cross-country running, skiing)* dào 道; *of ~ (certainly)* dāngrán 当然; *(naturally)* zìrán 自然

court *n* LAW fǎtíng 法庭; SP chǎng 场

courthouse fǎyuàn 法院

courtroom shěnpàn shì 审判室

cousin *(older male on father's side)* tángxiōng 堂兄; *(younger male on father's side)* tángdì 堂弟; *(older female on father's side)* tángjiě堂姐; *(younger female on father's side)* tángmèi 堂妹; *(older male on mother's side)* biǎoxiōng 表兄; *(younger male on mother's side)* biǎodì 表弟; *(older female on mother's side)* biǎojiě 表姐; *(younger female on mother's side)* biǎomèi 表妹

cover 1 *n (protective)* zhào 罩; *(of book, magazine)* fēngmiàn 封面; *(for bed)* bèizi 被子; *(shelter)* yǎnbì 掩蔽 **2** *v/t (hide)* fùgài 覆盖; *(hide)* yǎngài 掩盖; *distance* xíngshǐ 行驶

◆ **cover up 1** *v/t* gàizhù 盖住; *fig* yǎngài 掩盖 **2** *v/i fig* yǐnmán 隐瞒

coverage *(by media)* bàodào 报道

covert mìmì 秘密

coverup yǎnshì 掩饰

cow n mǔniú 母牛

coward dǎnxiǎo guǐ 胆小鬼

cozy shūshì 舒适

crack 1 n lièfèng 裂缝; (joke) xiàohua 笑话 **2** v/t cup shǐ chǎnshēng lièfèng 使产生裂缝; nut zá 砸; code pòyì 破译

♦ crack down on zhìcái 制裁

cracker (to eat) bócuì bǐng-gān 薄脆饼干

craft (skill) gōngyì 工艺; (trade) zhíyè 职业

craftsman shǒuyìrén 手艺人

cramped (room) zhǎixiǎo 窄小

cramps chōujīn 抽筋

crane n (machine) qǐzhòngjī 起重机

crash 1 n (noise) huālā shēng 哗啦声; (accident), COMPUT sǐjī 死机; (plane) fēijī shīshì 飞机失事; COM dǎobì 倒闭 **2** v/i (of car) zhuàng 撞; (of airplane) zhuìhuǐ 坠毁; (of market) bàodiē 暴跌; COMPUT sǐjī 死机

crash helmet fángzhuàng tóukuī 防撞头盔

crawl v/i (on floor) pá 爬; (move slowly) huǎnmàn xíngjìn 缓慢行进

crazy adj fāfēng 发疯; be ~ about … duì …zháomí 对 …着迷

cream n (for skin, coffee) rǔshuāng 乳霜

crease n (deliberate) zhòuwén 皱纹; (deliberate) kùxiàn 裤线

create v/t chuàngzào 创造; (lead to) yǐnqǐ 引起

creative yǒu chuàngzào lì 有创造力

credible (believable) kě xiāngxìn 可相信; candidate etc kě xìnrèn 可信任

credit n FIN shēqiàn 赊欠; (use of ~ cards) xìnyòng 信用; (honor) zànyáng 赞扬; (payment received) dàifāng 贷方

credit card xìnyòngkǎ 信用卡

creditor zhàizhǔ 债主

creek xiǎohé 小河

creep 1 n pej tǎoyàn guǐ 讨厌鬼 **2** v/i nièshǒu nièjiǎo de zǒu 蹑手蹑脚地走

cremation huǒhuà 火化

crew n (of ship, airplane) quántǐ gōngzuò rényuán 全体工作人员

crime zuìxíng 罪行

criminal 1 n zuìfàn 罪犯 **2** adj xíngshì 刑事; (shameful) lìngrén yíhàn 令人遗憾

crisis wēijī 危机

crisp adj lettuce, apple xīnxiān ér cuìshēng 新鲜而脆生; shirt, bill tǐngkuò 挺括

criterion biāozhǔn 标准

critic pínglùn jiā 评论家

critical (making criticisms) tiāocìr 挑刺儿; (serious) wēijī de 危急; moment etc jǐnyào 紧要; MED yánzhòng 严重

criticism pīpíng 批评

criticize v/t pīpíng 批评

crook n (dishonest) piànzi 骗子

crooked (not straight) wānqū 弯曲; (dishonest) bù lǎoshí 不老实

crop 1 n shōucheng 收成 **2** v/t hair, photo xiūjiǎn 修剪

cross 1 adj (angry) shēngqì 生气

生气 n (X) chāzi 叉子; (Christian) shízìjià 十字架 **3** v/t (go across) chuānguò 穿过 **4** v/i (go across the road) guò mǎlù 过马路; (of lines) jiāochā 交叉

♦ **cross out** qǔxiāo 取消

cross-examine LAW pánjié 盘诘

crosswalk rénxíng héngdào 人行横道

crossword (puzzle) zònghéng zì mí 纵横字迷

crouch v/i dūn 蹲

crowd n rénqún 人群; (at sports event) guānzhòng 观众

crowded yōngjǐ 拥挤

crucial guānjiàn 关键

crude adj (vulgar) cūlǔ 粗鲁; (unsophisticated) jiǎnlòu 简陋

cruel cánrěn 残忍

cruelty cánrěn 残忍

crumb zházi 渣子

crumble v/i suìliè 碎裂; fig (of opposition) bēngkuì 崩溃

crush v/t yā 压; (crease) nòngzhòu 弄皱

cry v/i (weep) kū 哭

cube (*shape*) lìfāng xíng 立方形

cuddle n & v/t yǒngbào 拥抱

cue n (*for actor etc*) tíshì 提示; (*for pool*) qiúgān 球杆

cuff n (*of shirt*) xiùkǒu 袖口; (*of pants*) kùjiǎo fānbiān 裤角翻边

culinary pēngtiáo 烹调

culprit zuìfàn 罪犯

cult zōngpài 宗派

cultivate *land* gēngzuò 耕作

cultivated *person* yǒu xiūyǎng 有修养

cultural (*of arts*) yǒu xiūyǎng 有修养; (*of a country's identity*) wénhuà 文化

Cultural Revolution Wénhuà Dàgémìng 文化大革命

culture n (*artistic*) wénmíng 文明; (*of a country*) wénhuà 文化

cunning n & adj jiǎohuá 狡猾

cup n bēi 杯

cupboard guìzi 柜子

curb 1 n (*of street*) lùyuán biānyuán 路缘边缘 **2** v/t kòngzhì 控制

cure MED **1** n liáofǎ 疗法 **2** v/t zhìhǎo 治好

curiosity (*inquisitiveness*)

hàoqí xīn 好奇心

curious (*inquisitive*) hàoqí 好奇; (*strange*) qítè 奇特

currency (*money*) huòbì 货币; *foreign* ~ wàihuì 外汇

current 1 n (*in sea*) jīliú 激流; ELEC diànliú 电流 **2** adj (*present*) mùqián 目前

currently n mùqián 目前

curse 1 n (*spell*) zǔzhòu 诅咒 **2** v/i (*swear*) màrén 骂人

curtain chuānglián 窗帘; THEA wéimù 帷幕

curve 1 n qūxiàn 曲线 **2** v/i (*bend*) wānqū 弯曲

cushion n kàodiàn 靠垫

custody (*of children*) fúyǎng quán 抚养权; *in ~* LAW bèi jūliú 被拘留

custom (*tradition*) xíguàn 习惯; COM huìgù 惠顾

customer gùkè 顾客

customs hǎiguān 海关

customs officer hǎiguān guānyuán 海关官员

cut 1 n (*with knife, scissors*) qiēkǒu 切口; (*injury*) shāngkǒu 伤口 **2** v/t qiē 切; (*reduce*) xiāojiǎn 削减; COMPUT: *text* jiǎnqiē 剪切; *get one's hair* ~ jiǎn tóufa 剪头发

剪头发

♦ **cut back** *v/i (in costs)*
suōjiǎn 缩减
♦ **cut down 1** *v/t tree* kǎndǎo
砍倒 **2** *v/i (in smoking etc)*
jiǎnshǎo 减少
♦ **cut off** *(with scissors etc)*
jiǎndiào 剪掉; *(isolate)*
géjué 隔绝; TELEC
duànxiàn 断线
cute *(pretty)* kě'ài 可爱;
(sexually, male) yīngjùn
英俊; *(sexually, female)*

piàoliang 漂亮
cutting *adj remark* shāngrén
gǎnqíng 伤人感情
cycle 1 *n (bicycle)* zìxíngchē
自行车 **2** *v/i* qí zìxíngchē
骑自行车
cyclist qí zìxíngchē de rén 骑
自行车的人
cylinder MOT qìgāng 汽缸
cynic fēnshì jísúzhě 愤世
嫉俗者
cynical fēnshì jísú 愤世嫉
俗

D

DA (= *district attorney*)
dìfāng jiǎnchá guān 地方
检查官
dad bà 爸
daily 1 *n (paper)* rìbào 日报
2 *adj* měirì 每日
dairy products rǔzhì pǐn
乳制品
dam 1 *n (for water)* shuǐbà
水坝
damage 1 *n* sǔnshī 损失; *fig*
(to reputation etc) sǔnhài 损
害 **2** *v/t* sǔnhuài 损坏
damages LAW péicháng

赔偿
damn *interj & adj* gāisǐ 该死
damp shī 湿
dance 1 *n* tiàowǔ 跳舞;
(event) wǔhuì 舞会 **2** *v/i*
tiàowǔ 跳舞
dancer wǔdǎo jiā 舞蹈
家; *(performer)* wǔdǎo
yǎnyuán 舞蹈演员
dancing wǔdǎo 舞蹈
danger wēixiǎn 危险
dangerous wēixiǎn 危险
dare *v/i* gǎn 敢
daring *adj* dàdǎn 大胆

dark 1 n hēi'àn 黑暗 **2** adj room, night hēi 黑; hair, eyes shēn yánsè 深颜色

dash 1 n (in text) pòzhéhào 破折号 **2** v/i jíchōng 急冲

data shùjù 数据

database shùjù kù 数据库

date n rìqī 日期; (meeting) yuēhuì 约会; **what's the today?** jīntiān jǐhào? 今天几号？; **out of ~** clothes guòshí 过时; passport guòqī 过期

daughter nǚ'ér 女儿

daughter-in-law érxífu 儿媳妇

dawn n pòxiǎo 破晓

day tiān 天; **~ by ~** yī tiāntiān de 一天天地; **the other ~** (recently) zuìjìn 最近

daylight rìguāng 日光

dazed (by blow) fāhūn 发昏

dazzle v/t (of light) huǎng 晃

dead 1 adj sǐ 死; battery, phone shīlíng 失灵; F (place) sǐqì chénchén 死气沉沉 **2** n: **the ~** sǐrén 死人

dead end (street) sǐ hútòng 死胡同

deadline qīxiàn 期限

deadlock n jiāngjú 僵局

deaf lóng 聋

deafening jí dàshēng 极大声

deal n (deal) jiāoyì 交易; **a good ~** (bargain) hǎo jiàqián 好价钱; **a great ~** (a lot) hěnduō 很多

dealer shāngrén 商人; (drug ~) fàndúzhě 贩毒者

dealings (business) jiāowǎng 交往

dear adj qīn'ài 亲爱; **Dear Sir** zūnjìngde xiānsheng 尊敬的先生; **Dear Wang Li** qīn'àide Wáng Lì 亲爱的王丽

death sǐwáng 死亡

debate n (between opposing sides) biànlùn 辩论; (discussion) tǎolùn 讨论

debit n & v/t jièfāng 借方

debris cánjì 残迹

debt zhài 债

debtor jièfāng 借方

decade shínián 十年

decaffeinated wú kāfēiyīn 无咖啡因

decay n fǔlàn 腐烂

deceased: **the ~** sǐzhě 死者

deceitful bù lǎoshí 不老实

deceive qīpiàn 欺骗

December shí'èryuè 十二月

decency zhèngpài 正派

decent *person* zhèngpài 正派; *salary* kě jìshòu 可接受

deception qīpiàn 欺骗

deceptive kàobuzhù 靠不住

decide *v/t* juédìng 决定; *(settle)* pànjué 判决

decipher jiě mìmǎ 解密码

decision juédìng 决定

decision-maker dāngquánzhě 当权者

decisive guǒduàn 果断; *(crucial)* juédìngxìng 决定性

deck *(of ship)* jiǎbǎn 甲板; *(of cards)* yīfù zhǐpái 一副纸牌

declare shēngmíng 声明; *independence* xuānbù 宣布; *(at customs)* chéngbào 呈报

decline 1 *n* xiàjiàng 下降 2 *v/t invitation* xièjué 谢绝 3 *v/i (refuse)* xièjué 谢绝; *(decrease)* jiǎnshǎo 减少; *(of health)* shuāituì 衰退

decode yìmǎ 译码

décor zhuānghuáng 装潢

decorate zhuāngxiū 装修; *soldier* shòuxūn 授勋

decoy *n* yòu'ěr 诱饵

decrease 1 *n* xiàjiàng 下降 2 *v/t* suōjiǎn 缩减 3 *v/i* xiàjiàng 下降

dedicate *book etc* tíxiàn 题献

dedication *(to cause, work)* zhìlì 致力

deduce tuīlǐ 推理

deduct: ~ X from Y cóng Y zhōng jiǎnqù X 从 Y 中减去 X

deduction *(from salary)* kòuchú 扣除; *(conclusion)* tuīlùn 推论

deed *n (act)* xíngwéi 行为; LAW qìyuē 契约

deep shēn 深; *voice* shēnchén 深沉; *thinker* shēnrù 深入

deep freeze *n* bīngxiāng 冰箱

deep-fry yóuzhá 油炸

deface sǔnhuài biǎomiàn 损坏表面

defamation fěibàng 诽谤

defeat 1 *n (conquering)* jībài 击败; *(losing)* shībài 失败 2 *v/t* jībài 击败

defect n quēxiàn 缺陷

defective yǒu quēxiàn 有缺陷

defend bǎowèi 保卫; (justify) biànhù 辩护

defendant bèigào 被告

defense n bǎowèi 保卫; SP fángshǒu 防守; LAW bèigào 被告; (justification) biànhù 辩护

defiance duìkàng 对抗

defiant tiǎozhàn 挑战

deficit kuīsǔn 亏损

define word xià dìngyì 下定义; objective míngquè 明确

definite date, reply míngquè 明确; (certain) kěndìng 肯定

definitely kěndìng 肯定

definition dìngyì 定义; (of objective) chǎnshù 阐述

deformity jīxíng 畸形

defraud piànqǔ 骗取

defrost v/t food jiědòng 解冻; icebox huàbīng 化冰

defuse chāichú yǐnxìn 拆除引信; situation tiáojiě 调解

defy wéikàng 违抗

degrading dījí 低级

degree dù 度; (from university) xuéwèi 学位

dehydrated tuōshuǐ 脱水

dejected jǔsàng 沮丧

delay 1 n yánchí 延迟 **2** v/t tuīchí 推迟

delegate 1 n dàibiǎo 代表 **2** v/t shòuquán 授权

delegation shòuquán 授权

delete shānchú 删除

deli shóushí diàn 熟食店

deliberate 1 adj gùyì 故意 **2** v/i zīxì kǎolǜ 仔细考虑

deliberately gùyì 故意

delicate fabric jīngzhì 精致; problem mǐngǎn 敏感; health xūruò 虚弱

delicious hǎochī 好吃

delight n xīngfèn 兴奋

delighted gāoxìng 高兴

delightful yúkuài 愉快

deliver sòng 送; message dìjiāo 递交; baby shēng 生

delivery sònghuò 送货; (of baby) fēnmiǎn 分娩

delusion wàngxiǎng 妄想

demand 1 n yāoqiú 要求; COM xūqiú 需求 **2** v/t yāoqiú 要求

demanding job gāo yāoqiú 高要求; person kèkè 苛刻

democracy mínzhǔ 民主

democrat mínzhǔzhǔyìzhě
民主主义者; *Democrat*
POL Mínzhǔdǎngrén 民
主党人

democratic mínzhǔ 民主

demolish chāihuǐ 拆毁

demonstrate 1 v/t
zhèngmíng 证明;
machine shìfàn 示范 **2** v/i
(*politically*) shìwēi 示威

demonstration xiǎnshì 显
示; (*protest*) shìwēi 示威;
(*of machine*) shìfàn 示范

demonstrator (*protester*)
shìwēizhě 示威者

demoralized qìněi 气馁

denial (*of accusation*) fǒurèn
否认; (*of request*) jùjué
拒绝

denomination FIN miàn'é 面
额; REL jiàopài 教派

dense nónghòu 浓厚;
foliage chóumì 稠密;
crowd mìjí 密集; (*stupid*)
chídùn 迟钝

dent 1 n āochù 凹处 **2** v/t shǐ
āoxià 使凹下

dental *treatment* yáchǐ 牙齿;
hospital yákē 牙科

dentist yáyī 牙医

dentures jiǎyá 假牙

deny *charge, rumor* fǒurèn
否认; *right, request* jùjué
拒绝

deodorant chúxiùjì 除臭剂

department (*of company,
store*) bùmén 部门; (*at
university*) xì 系; POL bù 部

department store bǎihuò
shāngchǎng 百货商场

departure (*of
person from job*) líkāi 离开

depend: *that ~s* shì qíngxíng
ér dìng 视情形而定; *it ~s
on the weather* kàn tiānqì
ba 看天气吧

dependence yīlài 依赖

dependent n yīkàozhě 依
靠者

deplorable lìngrén yíhàn 令
人遗憾

deport qūchú chūjìng 驱
除出境

deposit 1 n (*in bank*) cúnchǔ
存储; (*on purchase*) dìngjīn
定金 **2** v/t cash cúnchǔ
存储

depressed *person* yōuyù
忧郁

depressing lìngrén shāngxīn
令人伤心

depression MED yōuyù

zhèng 忧郁症; (economic) xiāotiáo 萧条; (in weather) dīyāqū 低压区

deprive: ~ X of Y cóng X nàlǐ názǒu Y 从 X 那里拿走 Y

deprived pínkùn 贫困

depth shēndù 深度

deputy dàilǐ 代理

derelict adj shīxiū 失修

derive v/t dédào 得到

derogatory biǎnyì 贬义

descend v/i (of airplane) xiàjiàng 下降; (of road) xiàxié 下斜

descendant hòuyì 后裔

descent (from mountain) xiàlái 下来; (of airplane) xiàjiàng 下降; (ancestry) zǔxiān 祖先

describe miáoshù 描述

description miáoshù 描述

desert[1] n also fig shāmò 沙漠

desert[2] v/t pāoqì 抛弃

deserted huāngliáng 荒凉

deserter MIL táobīng 逃兵

deserve yīngdé 应得

design 1 n shèjì 设计; (pattern) tú'àn 图案 **2** v/t shèjì 设计

designer shèjì shī 设计师

desire n (wish) yuànwàng 愿望; (sexual) xìngyù 性欲

desk shūzhuō 书桌; (in hotel) wènxùntái 问讯台

desktop publishing zhuōmiàn páibǎn 桌面排版

despair n & v/i juéwàng 绝望

desperate person zǒutóu wúlù 走投无路; action gūzhù yīzhì 孤注一掷

despise kànbùqǐ 看不起

despite jǐnguǎn 尽管

dessert tiánpǐn 甜品

destination mùdìdì 目的地

destitute pínkùn 贫困

destroy cuīhuǐ 摧毁

destruction pòhuài 破坏

detach fēnkāi 分开

detached (objective) wú piānjiàn 无偏见

detail n zhījié 枝节; (piece of information) xìjié 细节

detailed xiángxì 详细

detain (hold back) dānge 耽搁; (as prisoner) jūliú 拘留

detainee: **political** ~ zhèngzhì fàn 政治犯

detect chájué 察觉; (of device) jiǎncè 检测

detective zhēntàn 侦探

detention (*prison*) jūliú 拘留

deter (*frighten*) wēishè 危慑；
(*stop*) zhìzhǐ 制止

detergent xǐdíjì 洗涤剂

deteriorate èhuà 恶化

determination juéxīn 决心

determined xià juéxīn 下决
心；*effort* jiānjué 坚决

deterrent *n* wēishè yīnsù 危
慑因素

detest tǎoyàn 讨厌

devaluation FIN biǎnzhí
贬值

develop 1 *v/t film* chōngxǐ
冲洗；*site* jiànshè 建设；
business kuòdà 扩大；
(*originate*) fāmíng 发明；
(*improve on*) gǎijìn 改进；
illness kāishǐ 开始 **2** *v/i*
(*grow*) fāzhǎn 发展

development (*of film*)
chōngxǐ 冲洗；(*of site*)
jiànshè 建设；(*of business,
country*) fāzhǎn 发展；
(*event*) shìjiàn 事件；
(*origination*) fāmíng 发明；
(*improving*) gǎijìn 改进

device (*tool*) qìjù 器具

devise fāmíng 发明

devote gòngxiàn 贡献

devotion zhuānxīn 专心

devour lángtūn hǔyàn 狼
吞虎咽

diagonal *adj* xié 斜

diagram tú 图

dial 1 *n* (*of meter*) yíbiǎo
yíbiǎo 仪表 **2** *v/t* TELEC: *number*
bō 拨

dialog duìhuà 对话

diameter zhíjìng 直径

diamond zuànshí 钻石；
(*shape*) língxíng 菱形

diaper niàobù 尿布

diarrhea lādùzi 拉肚子

diary rìjì 日记

dictator dúcáizhě 独裁者

dictionary zìdiǎn 字典

die sǐ 死

diet 1 *n* shíwù 食物；(*for
losing weight*) jiǎnféi shípǐn
减肥食品 **2** *v/i* (*to lose
weight*) jiǎnféi 减肥

differ (*be different*) bùtóng
不同

difference chābié 差别

different bùtóng 不同

difficult bù róngyì 不容易

difficulty kùnnan 困难

dig *v/t* wā 挖

digest *v/t* xiāohuà 消化

digestion xiāohuà 消化

digital shùzì 数字

digital camera shùmǎ zhàoxiàngjī 数码照相机

dignified yǒu zūnyán 有尊严

dignity zūnyán 尊严

dilapidated tānhuǐ 坍毁

dilemma jìntuì liǎngnán 进退两难

dilute v/t xīshì 稀释

dim adj light hūn'àn 昏暗; outline bù xiǎnzhù 不显著

dimension (measurement) chǐcùn 尺寸

diminish v/i biànshǎo 变少

dim sum diǎnxīn 点心

dine yòngcān 用餐

diner (person) yòngcānzhě 用餐者; (restaurant) xiǎo cānguǎn 小餐馆

dining car cānchē 餐车

dining room cānshì 餐室

dinner (evening) wǎncān 晚餐; (midday) wǔcān 午餐

dinner party yànhuì 宴会

dip n (for food) zhānliào 沾料; (in road) āoxiàn 凹陷

diploma wénpíng 文凭

diplomat wàijiāo guān 外交官

diplomatic wàijiāo 外交;

(tactful) lǎoliàn 老练

direct 1 adj zhíjiē 直接; flight, train zhídá 直达; person zhíshuǎng 直爽 **2** v/t (to a place) zhǐyǐn 指引; play, movie dǎoyǎn 导演

direction fāngxiàng 方向; ~s (instructions) zhǐshì 指示; (to a place) fāngwèi 方位; (for use) zhǐdǎo 指导; (for medicine) yòngfǎ 用法

director (of company) zhǔguǎn 主管; (of play, movie) dǎoyǎn 导演

directory zhídǎo 指导; TELEC diànhuà bù 电话簿

dirt zāng dōngxi 脏东西

dirty adj zāng zāng 脏脏; (pornographic) huángsè 黄色

disabled adj cánjí 残疾

disadvantage n bùlì zhīchù 不利之处

disagree (of person) bù tóngyì 不同意

disagreement bùtóng yìjiàn 不同意见; (argument) zhēngzhí 争执

disappear xiāoshì 消失; (run away) pǎodiào 跑掉

disappearance (of item)

xiāoshī 消失; (of person) shīzōng 失踪

disappoint shǐ shīwàng 使失望

disappointment shīwàng 失望

disapproval zhǐzé 指责

disapprove bù zànchéng 不赞成

disaster zāinàn 灾难

disastrous sǔnshī cǎnzhòng 损失惨重

discharge v/t (from hospital) yǔnxǔ chūyuàn 允许出院; (from army) qiǎnsàn 遣散

discipline n jìlǜ 纪律

disc jockey DJ DJ

disco (place) dītīng 迪厅

disconnect appliance shǐ bù jiētōng 使不接通; supply, telephone qiēduàn 切断

discount n zhékòu 折扣

discourage (dissuade) quànzǔ 劝阻; (dishearten) shǐ jǔsàng 使沮丧

discover fāxiàn 发现

discovery fāxiàn 发现

discreet jǐnshèn 谨慎; restaurant kǎolǜ zhōudào 考虑周到

discrepancy chācuò 差错

discretion pànduàn nénglì 判断能力

discrimination qíshì 歧视

discuss tǎolùn 讨论

discussion tǎolùn 讨论

disease jíbìng 疾病

disembark v/i (from plane) xià fēijī 下飞机; (from ship) xià chuán 下船

disgrace n xiūchǐ 羞耻

disgraceful yǒushī tǐmiàn 有失体面

disguise n wěizhuāng 伪装; (costume, make-up) jiǎ miànjù 假面具

disgust 1 n jíwéi fǎngǎn 极为反感 2 v/t shǐ fǎngǎn 使反感

disgusting lìngrén zuò'ǒu 令人作呕

dish diézi 碟子; (part of meal) cài cài 菜菜

dishonest bù chéngshí 不诚实

dishonesty bù chéngshí 不诚实

dishonor n chǐrǔ 耻辱

disinfectant xiāodújì 消毒剂

disintegrate lièkāi 裂开; (of marriage, wall) wǎjiě 瓦解

disjointed tuōjié 脱节

disk *(shape)* yuánpán 圆盘; COMPUT cípán 磁盘

diskette ruǎn cípán 软磁盘

dislike *v/t* bù xǐhuān 不喜欢

dislocate tuōwèi 脱位

disloyal bù zhōngchéng 不忠诚

dismal *weather* zāogāo 糟糕; *news* lìngrén jǔsàng 令人沮丧; *person (sad)* yōuxīn chōngchōng 忧心忡忡

dismantle chāi kāi 拆开; *company* shǐ jiětǐ 使解体

dismay 1 *n (alarm)* jīng'è 惊愕; *(disappointment)* shīwàng 失望 **2** *v/t* shǐ huīxīn 使灰心

dismiss *employee* jiěgù 解雇; *idea* bù kǎolǜ 不考虑

disobedience bù fúcóng 不服从

disobedient juéjiàng 倔强

disobey wéibèi 违背

disorder *(unrest)* bàoluàn 暴乱; MED shītiáo 失调

disorganized wú zǔzhī 无组织

disoriented míhuò 迷惑

display 1 *n* zhǎnlǎn 展览; *(of emotion)* biǎoshì 表示; COMPUT xiǎnshì 显示 **2** *v/t emotion* xiǎnshì 显示; *(at exhibition)* zhǎnlǎn 展览; *(for sale)* chénliè 陈列; COMPUT xiǎnshì 显示

displeasure bùmǎn 不满

disposable yīcìxìng 一次性

disposal rēngdiào 扔掉; *(of waste)* chǔlǐ 处理; **put X at Y's ~** ràng Y zìyóu zhīpèi X 让 Y 自由支配 X

dispose: ~ of rēngdiào 扔掉

disprove fǎnzhèng 反证

dispute *n* zhēnglùn 争论

disqualify qǔxiāo zīgé 取消资格

disrupt *trains* shǐ tíngdùn 使停顿; *meeting* pòhuài 破坏

disruptive pòhuàixìng 破坏性

dissatisfaction bùmǎn 不满

dissatisfied bù mǎnyì 不满意

dissent *n* chí yìyì 持异议

dissident *n* chí bùtóng zhèngjiànzhě 持不同政见者

dissolve *v/t & v/i* róngjiě 溶解

dissuade quànzhǐ 劝止

distance *n* jùlí 距离

distant yuǎn 远; *fig (aloof)*
bǎochí yīdìngde jùlí 保持
一定的距离

distinct *(clear)* míngxiǎn 明
显; *(different)* bùtóng 不同

distinctive tèyǒu 特有

distinctly qīngchǔ 清楚;
(decidedly) míngxiǎn 明显

distinguish *(see)* biànbié
辨别; *~ between X and Y*
qūfēn X hé Y 区分 X 和 Y

distinguished *(famous)*
zhùmíng 著名; *(dignified)*
yǔzhòng bùtóng 与众不同

distort wāiqū 歪曲

distract *person* shǐ fēnxīn
使分心; *attention* fēnsàn
zhùyì lì 分散注意力

distraught xīnshén búdìng
心神不定

distress *n (mental)* kǔnǎo 苦
恼; *(physical)* tòngkǔ 痛苦

distribute fēngěi 分给;
leaflets sànfā 散发; *wealth*
fēnpèi 分配; COM jīngxiāo
经销

distribution *(handing out)*
fēnfā 分发; *(of wealth)*
fēnpèi 分配; COM jīngxiāo
经销

distributor COM jīngxiāo

shāng 经销商

district qū 区

district attorney dìfāng
jiǎnchá guān 地方检查官

distrust *n & v/t* huáiyí 怀疑

disturb *(interrupt)* dǎjiǎo 打
搅; *(upset)* dānyōu 担忧

disturbance *(interruption)*
gānrǎo 干扰; *~s* sāoluàn
骚乱

disturbed *(worried)* dānxīn
担心

disturbing lìngrén shāngxīn
令人伤心

ditch *n* kēng 坑

dive *n & v/i* tiàoshuǐ 跳水;
(underwater) qiánshuǐ 潜
水; *(of plane)* fǔchōng
俯冲

diver *(off board)* tiàoshuǐzhě
跳水者; *(underwater)*
qiánshuǐzhě 潜水者

diverge chàkāi 岔开

diversify *v/i* COM duōzhǒng
jīngyíng 多种经营

diversion MOT gǎixiàn 改线;
(to distract) qiānzhì 牵制

divert *traffic* gǎixiàn 改线; *~
attention* fēnsàn zhùyì lì 分
散注意力

divide fēn 分; *fig: country,*

family fēnliè 分裂

dividend FIN gǔxí 股息

division MATH chúfǎ 除法;
(in party etc) fēnliè 分裂;
(splitting into parts) fēngē
分割; *(of company)* bùmén
部门

divorce *n, v/t & v/i* líhūn
离婚

divorced líhūn 离婚

dizzy: *feel ~* tóuyūn 头晕

do 1 *v/t* zuò 做; *what are
you ~ing tonight?* nǐ
jīnwǎn gànshénme? 你今
晚干什么？; *I don't know
what to ~* wǒ bùzhī gāi
zěnme bàn 我不知该怎么
办 **2** *v/i: well done!* gōngxǐ!
恭喜！; *how ~ you ~?* nǐ
hǎoma? 你好吗?

dock¹ *n* NAUT chuánwù 船
坞; *(of ship)* kào mǎtóu
靠码头

dock² LAW bèigào xí 被告席

doctor *n* MED yīshēng 医生

document *n* wénjiàn 文件

documentary *(program)* jìlù
piān 纪录片

documentation wénjiàn
文件

dodge *v/t blow* shǎnkāi 闪

开; *question* bìkāi 避开

dog *n* gǒu 狗

dogma jiàotiáo 教条

do-it-yourself zìjǐ dòngshǒu
自己动手

doll *(toy)* wáwa 娃娃

dollar měiyuán 美元

domestic *adj chore* jiātíng 家
庭; *news, policy* guónèi 国
内; *(in agriculture)* jiāchù
家畜

domestic flight guónèi
hángbān 国内航班

dominant *adj* zhǔyào 主要;
member zhǔdǎo 主导

dominate kòngzhì 控制;
landscape gāosǒng yú 高
耸于

donate juān 捐

donor juānxiànzhě 捐献者

donut zhá miànbǐngquān 炸
面饼圈

door mén 门

doorbell ménlíng 门铃

doorman shǒuménrén 守
门人

dose *n* yòngliàng 用量

dot *n* *(also in e-mail)* diǎn 点

double 1 *n* *(amount)*
shuāngbèi 双倍; *(person)*
chóngyǐng 重影; *(of movie*

star) tìdài yǎnyuán 替代
演员 **2** *adj (twice as much)*
liǎngbèi 两倍; *whiskey* jiā
bèi 加倍 **3** *v/t* jiābèi 加倍

double bed shuāngrén
chuáng 双人床

doublecheck *v/t & v/i* fùchá
复查

doublecross *v/t* qīpiàn 欺骗

double room shuāngrén fáng
双人房

doubt 1 *n* yíwèn 疑问;
(uncertainty) yóuyù 犹豫
2 *v/t* huáiyí 怀疑

doubtful *remark, look* zhídé
huáiyí 值得怀疑; *be ~ (of
person)* ná bùzhǔn 拿不准

doubtless wúyí 无疑

dough shēngmiàn tuán 生
面团

down 1 *adv* xià 下; *~ there*
zài xiàbiān 在下边; *$200
~ (deposit)* xiànfù èrbǎi
měiyuán 现付二百美元;
be ~ (of price, rate) xiàjiàng
下降; *(not working)* shīlíng
失灵 **2** *prep* xiàngxià 向下;
(along) yánzhe 沿着

downfall *n* kuǎitái 垮台; *(of
politician)* xiàtái 下台

download COMPUT xiàzǎi

下载

downmarket *adj* dījí 低级

down payment dìngjīn 定金

downpour qīngpén dàyǔ 倾
盆大雨

downstairs *adj & adv* lóuxià
楼下

down-town *adj & adv* shì
zhōngxīn 市中心

downturn *(in economy)*
xiàjiàng qūshì 下降趋势

doze *n & v/i* dǎdùn 打盹

dozen shí'èr 十二

draft *n (of air)* guòtáng fēng
过堂风; *(of document)*
cǎogǎo 草稿; MIL
zhēngbīng 征兵; *beer on ~*
shēng píjiǔ 生啤酒

drag 1 *v/t (pull)* lā 拉;
COMPUT tuōdòng 拖动
2 *(of show, movie)* méijìn
没劲儿

dragon lóng 龙

drain 1 *n (pipe)* xiàshuǐ
guǎndào 下水管道;
(under water) xiàshuǐ dào
下水道 **2** *v/t water* lǜ 滤;
oil páigān 排干; *land* shǐ
gānhé 使干涸; *glass, tank*
dàoguāng 倒光

drama xìjù 戏剧; *(play on*

TV) jiémù 节目；(dramatic event) xìjùxìng shìjiàn 戏剧性事件；(excitement) xīngfèn 兴奋

dramatic xìjù 戏剧；(exciting) xìjùxìng 戏剧性

drapes chuānglián 窗帘

drastic yánzhòng 严重；measure jíduān 极端；change jídà 极大

draw 1 n (in competition) píngjú 平局，(in lottery) kāijiǎng 开奖；(attraction) xīyǐn 吸引 **2** v/t picture huà 画；cart, curtain lā 拉；knife chōuchū 抽出；(attract) xīyǐn 吸引

drawback bìduān 弊端

drawer (in desk) chōuti 抽屉

drawing (picture) huà 画；(skill) huìtú 绘画

dread v/t hàipà 害怕

dreadful zāogāo 糟糕

dream 1 n mèng 梦 **2** v/t & v/i zuòmèng 做梦；(day~) mèngxiǎng 梦想

dreary chénmèn 沉闷

dress 1 n (for woman) liányīqún 连衣裙；(clothing) fúzhuāng 服装 **2** v/i chuān yīfu 穿衣

服，(well, in black etc) chuānzhe 穿著

dresser (dressing table) shūzhuāngtái 梳妆台；(in kitchen) wǎndié guì 碗碟柜

dressing (for salad) tiáowèi zhī 调味汁；MED fūliào 敷料

dress rehearsal cǎipái 彩排

dried fruit etc gān 干

drier shuǎigānjī 甩干机

drift v/i (of ship) piāofú 漂浮，(go off course) piāobó 漂泊；(of person) liúdàng 流荡

drill 1 n (tool) zuàn 钻；MIL cāoliàn 操练 **2** v/t hole zuàn 钻 **3** v/i (for oil) zuàn 钻

drink 1 n yǐnliào 饮料；(alcohol) jiǔ 酒 **2** v/t & v/i hē 喝

drinking water yǐnyòng shuǐ 饮用水

drip v/i dī 滴

drive 1 n lùtú 旅途；(outing) dōufēng 兜风；(energy) jīnglì 精力；COMPUT qūdòngqì 驱动器 **2** v/t vehicle jiàshǐ 驾驶；(take

in car) yòng chē sòng 用车
送; TECH qūdòng 驱动 3 *v/i*
jiàshǐ 驾驶
driver sījī 司机
driver's license jiàshǐ
zhízhào 驾驶执照
driving *n* jiàshǐ 驾驶
drizzle *n* máomáo yǔ 毛毛雨
droop *v/i* xiàchuí 下垂; (*of
plant*) kūwěi 枯萎
drop 1 *n* (*of rain*) dī 滴;
(*small amount*) yìdiǎn 一
点; (*in price, temperature*)
diē 跌; (*in number*) xiàjiàng
下降 2 *v/t* rēng 扔; (*and
lose*) diūshī 丢失; *person
from car* ràng ... xiàchē
让 ... 下车; *person from
team* chúqù 除去; *charges,
demand* qǔxiāo 取消
3 *v/i* diēluò 跌落; (*decline*)
xiàjiàng 下降; (*of wind*)
jiǎnhuǎn 减缓
drought gānhàn 干旱
drown *v/i* yānsǐ 淹死
drug *n* MED yào 药; (*illegal*)
dúpǐn 毒品
drug addict xīdú
chéngyǐnzhě 吸毒成瘾者
drug dealer fàndúzhě 贩
毒者

druggist yàojì 药剂师
drugstore yàofáng 药房
drug trafficking fàndú 贩毒
drum *n* MUS gǔ 鼓;
(*container*) tǒng 桶
drunk 1 *n* zuìguǐ 醉鬼 2 *adj*
hēzuìle 喝醉了
drunk driving jiǔhòu kāichē
酒后开车
dry 1 *adj* gān 干 2 *v/t dishes*
cāgān 擦干 3 *v/i* liànggān
晾干
dry cleaner gānxǐ diàn 干
洗店
dry cleaning (*clothes*) gānxǐ
yīwù 干洗衣物
due 1 (*owed*) qiàn 欠; (*proper*)
shìdàng 适当; *is there a
train ~?* huǒchē shìbùshì
gāiláile? 火车是不是该来
了？; ~ *to* yóuyú 由于
dull *weather* yīn chénchén
阴沉沉; *sound* bù qīngcuì
不清脆; *pain* dùn 钝;
(*boring*) dāndiào 单调
duly (*as expected*) zhǔnshí
准时; (*properly*) shìdàng
适当
dump 1 *n* (*for garbage*) lā
jīzhàn 垃圾站; (*unpleasant
place*) guǐdìfang 鬼地方

2 v/t (deposit) qīngdào 倾倒; (dispose of) rēng 扔; waste diūqì 丢弃

dumpling tuánzi 团子

duration qījiān 期间

during: ~ X zài X qījiān 在X期间

dusk huánghūn 黄昏

dust n chéntǔ 尘土

duty zérèn 责任; (task) rènwù 任务; (on goods) shuì 税; **be on ~** zhíbān 值班; **be off ~** xiàbān 下班

duty-free adj miǎnshuì 免税

DVD shùzì shìpín guāngpán 数字视频光盘

dye v/t rǎnsè 染色

dying chuísǐ 垂死; (tradition etc) jíjiāng mièjué 即将灭绝

dynamic person jīnglì chōngpèi 精力充沛

E

each adj & pron měigè 每个; **~ other** bǐcǐ 彼此

eager kěwàng 渴望

ear ěrduo 耳朵

early adj & adv (not late) zǎo 早; (ahead of time) tíqián 提前; (farther back in time) zǎoqī 早期; (in the near future) xùnsù 迅速

earn zhèng 挣; respect yíngdé 赢得

earnings zhuànde qián 赚的钱

earphones ěrjī 耳机

earring ěrhuán 耳环

earth tǔ 土; (world, planet) dìqiú 地球

earthquake dìzhèn 地震

east 1 n dōngfāng 东方 **2** adj dōng 东 **3** adv travel xiàng dōngfāng 向东方

East China Sea Dōnghǎi 东海

Easter Fùhuójié 复活节

eastern dōngbù 东部; (Oriental) Dōngfāng 东方

eastward xiàngdōng 向东

easy róngyì 容易; (relaxed) fàngsōng 放松

eat v/t & v/i chī 吃

eccentric adj gǔguài 古怪

echo 1 n huíshēng 回声 **2** v/i

huídàng 回荡

eclipse n (of sun) rìshí 日食；(of moon) yuèshí 月食

ecofriendly lǜsè 绿色

ecological shēngtài 生态

ecology shēngtàixué 生态学

economic jīngjì 经济

economical (cheap) jīngjì 经济；(thrifty) jiéshěng 节省

economics jīngjìxué 经济学；(financial aspects) jīngjì qíngkuàng 经济情况

economist jīngjìxuéjiā 经济学家

♦ **economize on** jiéshěng 节省

economy jīngjì 经济；(saving) jiéshěng 节省

economy class jīngjìcāng 经济舱

edge n (of knife) fēng fēng 锋；(of table, road) biānyuán 边缘

edible kě shíyòng 可食用

edit text biānjí 编辑；TV program jiǎnjí 剪辑

edition bǎnběn 版本

editor biānjí 编辑

educate jiàoyù 教育

education jiàoyù 教育

effect n xiàoguǒ 效果；(negative) hòuguǒ 后果；

come into ~ shíshī 实施

effective (efficient) yǒuxiào 有效

efficiency xiàolǜ 效率

efficient yǒu xiàolǜ 有效率

effort (struggle) fèilì 费力；(attempt) nǔlì 努力

egg (of hen) jīdàn 鸡蛋；(of bird) dàn 蛋

eggcup jīdànbēi 鸡蛋杯

eggplant qiézi 茄子

ego PSYCH zìwǒ 自我；(self-esteem) zìzūn 自尊

either 1 adj rèn yígè 任一个；(both) liǎng 两 **2** pron nǎge dōuxíng 哪个都行 **3** adv: I won't go ~ wǒ yě bú qù wǒ yě bú qù 我也不去 **4** conj: ~ ... or huòzhě ...huòzhě ...或者

eject v/t zhúchū 逐出

elaborate adj jīngxīn zhìzuò 精心制作

elastic n sōngjǐndài 松紧带

elbow n zhǒu 肘

elder adj niánzhǎng 年长

elderly shàng niánjì 上年纪

eldest adj: ~ brother dàgē 大哥；~ sister dàjiě 大姐

elect v/t xuǎn 选

election xuǎnjǔ 选举

election campaign jìngxuǎn huódòng 竞选活动

electric diàn 电

electrician diàngōng 电工

electricity diàn 电

electrocute diànsǐ 电死

electronic diànzǐ 电子

electronics diànzǐxué 电子学

elegant gāoyǎ 高雅

elementary (*rudimentary*) chūjí 初级

elementary school xiǎoxué 小学

elevator diàntī 电梯

eligible hégé 合格

eliminate (*get rid of*) chúdiào 除掉; (*rule out*) páichú 排除; *be ~d (from competition*) bèi táotài 被淘汰

elite 1 *n* jīngyīng 精英 **2** *adj* gāoděng 高等

eloquent xióngbiàn 雄辩

else: *anything ~?* hái yào biéde ma? 还要别的吗？; *no one ~* méiyǒu biérén 没有别人; *something ~* biéde dōngxi 别的东西; *or ~ fǒuzé* 否则

elsewhere biéchù 别处

e-mail *n* diànzǐ yóujiàn 电子邮件

e-mail address diànzǐ xìnxiāng 电子信箱

embargo *n* jìnyùn 禁运

embark *v/i* shàngchuán 上船
♦ **embark on** kāishǐ 开始

embarrass shǐ gāngà 使尴尬

embarrassed gāngà 尴尬

embarrassing lìngrén gāngà 令人尴尬

embarrassment gāngà 尴尬

embassy dàshǐguǎn 大使馆

embrace *v/t* yōngbào 拥抱

emerge (*appear*) chūxiàn 出现

emergency jǐnjí qíngkuàng 紧急情况

emergency exit jǐnjí chūkǒu 紧急出口

emergency landing jǐnjí zhuólù 紧急着陆

emigrate yíjū guówài 移居国外

eminent jiéchū 杰出

emotion qínggǎn 情感

emotional qínggǎn 情感; (*full of emotion*) fùyú qínggǎn 富于情感

emperor huángdì 皇帝

emphasis qiángdiào 强调

emphasize qiángdiào 强调

empire dìguó 帝国

employ gùyōng 雇佣; (use) shǐyòng 使用

employee gùyuán 雇员

employer gùzhǔ 雇主

employment gōngzuò 工作

empress huánghòu 皇后

empty 1 adj kōng 空 2 v/t glass, bottle dào kōng 倒空

enable shǐ nénggòu 使能够

enclose (in letter) fùrù 附入; area wéizhù 围住

enclosure (in letter) fùjiàn 附件

encore n zàilái yīgè 再来一个

encounter v/t problem yùdào 遇到

encourage gǔlì 鼓励

encouragement gǔlì 鼓励

end 1 n (extremity) jìntóu 尽头; (conclusion) jiéwěi 结尾; in the ~ zuìhòu 最后; at the ~ of July qīyuèmò 七月末 2 v/t & v/i jiéshù 结束

endless wúzhǐjìng 无止境

endorse check bèishū 背书; candidacy zhīchí 支持; product cùxiāo 促销

end product zhōngduān chǎnpǐn 终端产品

endurance rěnnàilì 忍耐力

endure 1 v/t rěnnài 忍耐 2 v/i (last) chíxù 持续

end-user zhōngduān yònghù 终端用户

enemy dírén 敌人

energetic yǒu jīngshen 有精神

energy jīnglì 精力; (gas, electricity etc) néngyuán 能源

enforce shíshī 实施

engaged (to be married) dìnghūn 订婚

engagement (appointment) yuēhuì 约会; (to be married) dìnghūn 订婚

engagement ring dìnghūn jièzhǐ 订婚戒指

engine yǐnqíng 引擎

engineer n gōngchéngshī 工程师; NAUT lúnjīzhǎng 轮机长

engineering gōngchéng 工程

England Yīngguó 英国

English 1 adj Yīngguó 英国 2 n (language) Yīngyǔ 英语

enjoy xǐhuan 喜欢; ~

oneself guòde kuàilè 过得很乐;~! (said to s.o. eating) chīhǎo! 吃好!

enjoyable lìngrén yúkuài 令人愉快

enjoyment lèqù 乐趣

enlarge kuòdà 扩大

enlist v/i MIL bàomíng cānjūn 报名参军

enormous jùdà 巨大; satisfaction etc jídà 极大

enough adj & pron zúgòu 足够; will $50 be ~? wǔshí měiyuán gòu le ma? 五十美元够了吗? I've had ~! wǒshòugòu le 我受够了!

enroll v/i zhùcè 注册

ensure bǎozhèng 保证

enter 1 v/t room jìnrù 进入; competition cānjiā 参加; COMPUT jiànrù 键入 **2** v/i jìnrù 进入; (in competition) bàomíng 报名 **3** n COMPUT huíchējiàn 回车键

enterprise v/i jìnqǔxīn 进取心; (venture) qǐyè 企业

entertain 1 v/t (amuse) shǐrén kuàilè 使人快乐 **2** v/i (have guests) zhāodài 招待

entertaining adj yǒuqù 有趣

entertainment yúlè 娱乐

enthusiasm rèqíng 热情

enthusiast rèzhōngzhě 热中者

enthusiastic rèxīn 热心

entire zhěnggè 整个

entirely wánquán 完全

entitle fùyǔ quánlì 赋予权利

entitled book dìngmíng 定名

entrance n (doorway) rùkǒu 入口; (entering) jìnrù 进入

entrance fee rùchǎngfèi 入场费

entrust: ~ X with Y bǎ Y wěituōgěi X 把 Y 委托给 X

entry (way in) rùkǒu 入口; (admission) jìnrù 进入; (for competition) cānjiā zhě 参加者; (in diary, accounts) xiàngmù 项目

entry form cānsàibiǎo 参赛表

envelope xìnfēng 信封

envious (way in) jídù 嫉妒; be ~ of X xiànmù X 羡慕 X

environment huánjìng 环境

environmentalist n huánjìng bǎohùlùn zhě 环境保护论者

environmentally friendly
lǜsè 绿色

envisage xiǎngxiàng 想象

envy 1 n jìdù 嫉妒 **2** v/t
dùxiàn 妒羡

epidemic liúxíngxìng 流
行性

episode (of story) yījí 一集;
(happening) shìjiàn 事件

equal 1 adj xiāngtóng 相同
2 n děngtóng 等同

equality píngděng 平等

equally tóngděng 同等; ~, ...
cǐwài, ... 此外...

equate: ~ X with Y děngtóng
X hé Y 等同X和Y

equator chìdào 赤道

equip zhuāngbèi 装备

equipment zhuāngbèi 装备

equivalent adj xiāngtóng 相
同; be ~ to xiāngdāngyú
相当于

era jìyuán 纪元

eradicate gēnchú 根除

erase (with eraser) cādiào
擦掉; tape xǐdiào 洗掉;
COMPUT shānchú 删除

erosion qīnshí 侵蚀; fig
qīnfàn 侵犯

erotic sèqíng 色情

errand chāishǐ 差使

erratic wúcháng 无常

error cuòwù 错误

erupt (of volcano) bàofā
爆发; (of violence) tūrán
fāshēng 突然发生

escalate zhúbù shēngjí 逐
步升级

escalator zìdòngfútī 自动
扶梯

escape n & v/i táotuō 逃脱;
(of gas) lòuchū 漏出

escort n péitóng 陪同;
(guard) hùwèi 护卫

especially yóuqí 尤其

espionage jiàndié huódòng
间谍活动

essential adj bìyào 必要

establish (create) chuàngzào
创造; (determine) quèdìng
确定; company chénglì
成立

establishment (firm, store
etc) jīgòu 机构

estimate n & v/t gūjì 估计

eternal yǒnghéng 永恒

ethical dàodé dàodé 道德

ethnic zhǒngzú 种族

ethnic minority shǎoshù
mínzú 少数民族

Europe Ōuzhōu 欧洲

European 1 adj Ōuzhōu 欧

洲 **2** *n* Ōuzhōurén 欧洲人

evacuate (clear people from) chèkōng 撤空; (leave) chèlí 撤离

evade bìkāi 避开

evasive bùtǎnshuài 不坦率

even 1 *adj* (regular) jūnyún 均匀; (level) píng 平; (number) ǒushù 偶数 **2** *adv* shènzhì 甚至; ~ *bigger / better* gèngdà /hǎo 更大/好; *not* ~ lián ... yěbù 连 ... 也不; ~ *if* jíshǐ 即使

evening wǎnshang 晚上; *this* ~ jīntiān wǎnshang 今天晚上; *good* ~ wǎnshang hǎo 晚上好

evening class yèxiào 夜校

evenly (regularly) jūnyún 均匀

event shìjiàn 事件; SP bǐsài xiàngmù 比赛项目

eventually zhōngyú 终于

ever *adv* (with past or perfect tense questions) céngjīng 曾经; (with past or perfect tense negative) cónglái 从来; (with conditionals) yídàn 一旦; *for* ~ yǒngyuǎn 永远; ~ *since* cóng nà yǐhòu 从那以后

Everest: *Mount* ~ Zhūmùlǎngmǎfēng 珠穆朗玛峰

every měiyī 每一

everybody měigèrén 每个人

everyday měitiān 每天

everyone měigèrén 每个人

everything yíqiè 一切

everywhere gèchù 各处; (wherever) dàochù 到处

evidence hénjì 痕迹; LAW zhèngjù 证据

evidently (clearly) míngxiǎn 明显; (apparently) xiǎnrán 显然

evil 1 *adj* xié'è 邪恶 **2** *n* è 恶

evolution jìnhuà 进化

evolve *v/i* (develop) zhújiàn xíngchéng 逐渐形成

ex *n* F (wife) qiánqī 前妻; (husband) qiánfū 前夫

exact *adj* quèqiè 确切

exactly qiàqià 恰恰

exaggerate 1 *v/t* kuādà 夸大 **2** *v/i* kuāzhāng 夸张

exam kǎoshì 考试

examine diàochá 调查; MED jiǎnchá 检查; EDU kǎo 考

example lìzi 例子; *for* ~ bǐrú 比如

exceed (be more than)

chāoguò 超过 ; (*go beyond*)
chāochū 超出

exceedingly jíduān 极端

excellence yōuxiù 优秀

excellent hěn hǎo 很好

except chúle 除了 ; **~ *that ...***
zhǐshì ... 只是 ...

exception lìwài 例外

exceptional (*very good*)
jiéchū 杰出 ; (*special*) tèshū
特殊

excess 1 *n* guòdù 过度 **2** *adj*
duōyú 多余

excess baggage chāo-
zhòngde xíngli 超重的
行李

exchange 1 *n* (*of*
information) jiāohuàn
交换 ; (*between schools*)
jiāoliú 交流 ; **in ~** zuòwéi
jiāohuàn 作为交换 ; **in ~**
for yònglái huànqǔ 用来换
取 **2** *v/t* addresses hùhuàn
互换 ; **X for Y** yòng X
huàn Y 用 X 换 Y

exchange rate FIN duìhuànlǜ
兑换率

excited xīngfèn 兴奋

exciting lìngrén xīngfèn 令
人兴奋

exclude páichú 排除

exclusive *hotel* dútè 独特 ;
rights dúyǒu 独有

excuse 1 *n* jièkǒu 借口
2 *v/t* (*forgive*) yuánliàng 原
谅 ; **~ me** (*to get attention*)
qǐngwèn 请问 ; (*to get past*)
láojià 劳驾 ; (*interrupting*)
hěn bàoqiàn 很抱歉

execute *criminal* chǔjué 处
决 ; *plan* shíshī 实施

execution (*of criminal*)
sǐxíng 死刑 ; (*of plan*)
shíshī 实施

executive *n* zhǔguǎn
rényuán 主管人员

exempt: **be ~ from** miǎnchú
免除

exercise 1 *n* (*physical*)
duànliàn 锻炼 ; EDU liànxí
练习 **2** *v/t* muscle duànliàn
锻炼 ; *dog* liù 遛

exert *authority* xíngshǐ 行
使 ; **~ oneself** yònglì 用力

exertion fèilì 费力

exhale hūchū 呼出

exhaust 1 *n* (*fumes*) fèiqì 废
气 ; (*pipe*) páiqìguǎn 排气
管 **2** *v/t* (*use up*) yòngjìn
用尽

exhausted (*tired*) jīnpílìjìn
筋疲力尽

exhausting lìngrén píjuàn 令
人疲倦

exhaustion láolèi guòdù 劳
累过度

exhibition zhǎnlǎnhuì 展
览会

exile n liúwáng 流亡;
(person) liúfàngzhě 流
放者

exist cúnzài 存在

existence cúnzài 存在; (life)
shēngcún 生存

existing xiàncún 现存

exit 1 n chūkǒu 出口; THEA
tuìchǎng 退场 2 v/i COMPUT
tuìchū 退出

exorbitant guògāo 过高

exotic fùyǒu yìguó qíngdiào
富有异国情调

expand 1 v/t kuòdà 扩大
2 v/i zēngzhǎng 增长; (of
metal) péngzhàng 膨胀

expansion zēngzhǎng 增长;
(of metal) péngzhàng 膨胀

expect 1 v/t qīdài 期待;
baby huáiyùn 怀孕;
(suppose) rènwéi 认为;
(demand) yāoqiú 要求
2 v/i: I ~ so wǒ xiǎng huì de
我想会的

expectation qīwàng 期望;

~s (demands) zhīwàng
指望

expedition tànxiǎn 探险

expel person kāichú 开除

expenditure huāfèi 花费

expense xiāofèi 消费

expenses kāizhī 开支

expensive ángguì 昂贵

experience 1 n (event) jīnglì
经历; (in life) tǐyàn 体验;
(in particular field) jīngyàn
经验 2 v/t pain, pleasure
gǎnjué 感觉; difficulty
yùdào 遇到

experienced yǒujīngyàn
有经验

experiment n & v/i shíyàn
实验

expert 1 adj shúliàn 熟练
2 n zhuānjiā 专家

expertise zhuānmén zhīshi
专门知识

expiration qīmǎn 期满

expiration date zhōngzhǐ
rìqī 终止日期

expire dàoqī 到期

explain 1 v/t shuōmíng 说明
2 v/i jiěshì 解释

explanation jiěshì 解释

explode v/i & v/t bomb
bàozhà 爆炸

exploit v/t person bōxuē 剥削; resources lìyòng 利用

exploration tànsuǒ 探索

explore country kǎochá 考察; possibility tàntǎo 探讨

explosion bàozhà 爆炸; (in population) jīzēng 激增

export n & v/t chūkǒu 出口

exporter chūkǒushāng 出口商

expose scandal jiēlù 揭露; person jiēchuān 揭穿

express 1 adj (fast) xùnsù 迅速; (explicit) míngquè 明确 2 n (train) tèkuài 特快; (bus) kuàisù 快速 3 v/t (speak of) biǎoshì 表示; feelings biǎodá 表达

expression (voiced) biǎoshì 表示; (on face) biǎoqíng 表情; (phrase) biǎodá 表达

expressway gāosù gōnglù 高速公路

expulsion (from school) kāichú 开除; (of diplomat) qūzhú 驱逐

extend v/t kuòdà 扩大; runway yáncháng 延长; contract, visa yánqī 延期

extension (to house) kuòjiàn 扩建; (of contract, visa)

yánqī 延期; TELEC fēnjī 分机

extensive guǎngfàn 广泛

extent chéngdù 程度

exterior 1 adj wàibù 外部 2 n (of building) wàiguān 外观; (of person) wàibiǎo 外表

external wàimiàn 外面

extinct species juézhǒng 绝种

extinguish fire pūmiè 扑灭; cigarette xīmiè 熄灭

extortion lèsuǒ 勒索

extra 1 n (sth ~) éwàide shìwù 额外的事物 2 adj éwài 额外; be ~ (cost more) lìngwài shōufèi 另外收费

extract 1 n xuǎnlù 选录 2 v/t qǔchū 取出; oil, juice zhàchū 榨出; tooth báchū 拔出; information huòqǔ 获取

extradition yǐndù 引渡

extraordinary bùpíngcháng 不平常

extravagant (with money) huīhuò 挥霍

extreme 1 n jíduān 极端 2 adj jídù 极度; views

piānjī 偏激
extremely jíqí 极其
extremist n jíduānzhǔyì zhě 极端主义者
eye n yǎnjīng 眼睛
eyebrow méimao 眉毛

eyelid yǎnjiǎn 眼睑
eyeliner yǎnxiànyè 眼线液
eyeshadow yǎnyǐnggāo 眼影膏
eyesight shìlì 视力
eyesore bú shùnyǎn 不顺眼

F

fabric bùliào 布料
fabulous jíhǎo 极好
face 1 n liǎn 脸 **2** v/t person, the sea miànduì 面对
facilitate shǐ … biànlì 使 …便利
facilities shèshī 设施
fact shìshí 事实; in ~ shíjì shang 实际上
factor yīnsù 因素
fade v/i (of colors) xiāotuì 消褪
fail v/i shībài 失败
failure shībài 失败
faint 1 adj bù míngxiǎn 不明显 **2** v/i hūndǎo 昏倒
fair¹ n COM jiāoyìhuì 交易会
fair² adj hair qiǎnsè 浅色; (just) gōngzhèng 公正
fairly treat gōngzhèng 公正; (quite) xiāngdāng 相当

faith xìnxīn 信心; REL xìnyǎng 信仰
faithful zhōngchéng 忠诚
fake 1 n yànpǐn 赝品 **2** adj fǎngzhì 仿制
fall¹ (autumn) qiūtiān 秋天
fall² v/i (of person) shuāidǎo 摔倒; (of government) kuǎtái 垮台; (of prices, temperature) xiàjiàng 下降; (of night) láilín 来临 **2** n (of person) shuāidǎo 摔倒; (of government, minister) dǎotái 倒台; (in price, temperature) xiàjiàng 下降
♦ **fall out** (of hair) diàoluò 掉落; (argue) nào bièniu 闹别扭
false cuòwù 错误
fame míngyù 名誉
familiar adj (intimate) qīnjìn

亲近

family jiātíng 家庭

family planning jìhuá shēngyù 计划生育

famine jīhuāng 饥荒

famous zhùmíng 著名

fan¹ n (supporter) mí 迷

fan² n (electric) diànshàn 电扇; (handheld) shànzi 扇子

fanatic kuángrèzhě 狂热者

fanatical kuángrè 狂热

fantastic (very good) bàngjíle 棒极了; (very big) jùdà 巨大

far adv yuǎn 远; (much) fēicháng 非常; ~ **away** yáoyuǎn 遥远; **how ~ is it to ...?** dào ...qù yǒu duōyuǎn? 到...去有多远?; **as ~ as I know** jùwǒsuǒzhī 据我所知

fare n (for travel) piàojià 票价

Far East Yuǎndōng 远东

farm n nóngchǎng 农场

farmer nóngfū 农夫

farsighted yǒu yuǎnjiàn 有远见; (optically) yuǎnshì 远视

farther adv gèngyuǎn 更远

farthest zuìyuǎn 最远

fascinate v/t shǐ zháomí 使着迷

fascinating mírén 迷人

fascination (with subject) chīmí 痴迷

fashion n (style) shíshàng 时尚; (manner) fāngshì 方式

fashionable shímáo 时髦

fashion designer shízhuāng shèjìshī 时装设计师

fast adj & adv kuài 快; ~ **asleep** shúshuì 熟睡

fasten v/t shǐ gùdìng 使固定

fast food kuàicān 快餐

fat 1 adj pàng 胖 **2** n (on meat) zhīfáng 脂肪

fatal zhìmìng 致命; error wúkě wǎnjiù 无可挽救

fatality sǐwáng 死亡

fate mìngyùn 命运

father n fùqīn 父亲

father-in-law (woman's) gōnggong 公公; (man's) yuèfù 岳父

fatigue n píjuàn 疲倦

faucet lóngtóu 龙头

fault n (defect) máobìng 毛病; **it's your / my ~** shì nǐde / wǒde cuò 是你的/我的错

favor n xǐ'ài 喜爱; **be in ~ of**

... zhīchí ... 支持...

favorable *reply etc* zànchéng 赞成

favorite *adj* zuì xǐhuān 最喜欢

fax 1 *n* chuánzhēn 传真 2 *v/t* yòng chuánzhēn chuán 用传真传

FBI (= *Federal Bureau of Investigation*) Liánbāng Diàochájú 联邦调查局

fear 1 *n* kǒngjù 恐惧 2 *v/t* hàipà 害怕

feasible qièshí kěxíng 切实可行

feature 1 *n* tèsè 特色; (*in paper*) zhuāntí 专题; (*movie*) zhèngpiān 正片 2 *v/t* (*of movie*) yóu ... zhǔyǎn 由... 主演

February èryuè 二月

federal liánbāngzhì 联邦制

fed up *adj* F yànfán 厌烦

fee fèi 费

feed *v/t* gōngyǎng 供养; *animal* wèi 喂

feedback fǎnkuì 反馈

feel 1 *v/t* (*touch*) chùmō 触摸; (*sense*) gǎndào 感到; *pain, pleasure* gǎnzhī 感知; (*think*) rènwéi 认为 2 *v/i:*

I ~ tired wǒ gǎnjué lèi le 我感觉累了

feeling (*of happiness*) gǎnjué 感觉; (*emotion*) gǎnqíng 感情; (*sensation*) zhījué 知觉

felony zhòngzuì 重罪

female 1 *adj* cíxíng 雌性; (*referring to people*) nǚxìng 女性 2 *n* (*of animals, plants*) cíxíng dòngzhíwù 雌性动植物; (*person*) nǚxìng 女性

feminine *adj qualities* yǒu nǚxìng qìzhí 有女性气质

feminism nǚquán zhǔyì 女权主义

feminist 1 *n* nǚquán zhǔyìzhě 女权主义者 2 *adj* nǚquán 女权

fen (*Chinese money*) fēn 分

fence *n* zhàlán 栅栏

fender MOT yìzǐbǎn 翼子板

fertile néng shēngyù 能生育; *soil* féiwò 肥沃

fertility fányù 繁育; (*of soil*) féiwò 肥沃

fertilizer (*for soil*) féiliào 肥料

festival jiérì 节日

festivities huānqìng 欢庆

fetch *person* jiē 接；*thing* ná 拿；*price* màidé 卖得

fetus tāi'ér 胎儿

feud *n* shìchóu 世仇

few 1 *adj (not many)* hěn- shǎo 很少；**a ~** *(things)* jǐge 几个；*quite* **a ~** xiāngdāng- duō 相当多 **2** *pron (not many)* shǎoshù jǐge 少数几 个；**a ~** *(some)* yìxiē 一些；*quite* **a ~** xǔduō 许多

fewer *adj* gèngshǎo 更少

fiancé wèihūnfū 未婚夫

fiancée wèihūnqī 未婚妻

fiber xiānwéi 纤维

fiction *(novels)* xiǎoshuō 小说

fictitious xūgòu 虚构

fidget *v/i* fánzào bù'ān 烦躁不安

field *n* tiándì 田地；*(for sport)* chǎng 场；*(competitors in race)* cānsàizhě 参赛者；*(of knowledge etc)* lǐngyù 领域

fierce *animal* xiōngměng 凶猛；*wind, storm* qiángliè 强烈

fifty-fifty *adv* duìbàn 对半

fight 1 *n* zhàndòu 战斗；*(for survival, championship)* zhēngdòu 争斗；*(in boxing)* quánjī 拳击 **2** *v/t enemy* yǔ…dǎzhàng 与… 打仗；*disease, injustice* yǔ …zuò dòuzhēng 与…作斗争 **3** *v/i* dǎjià 打架

♦ **fight for** zhēngqǔ 争取

figure *n (digit)* shùzì 数字；*(of person)* xíngtǐ 形体；*(form, shape)* túxíng 图形

file¹ *n (of documents)* dàng'àn 档案；COMPUT wénjiàn 文件

file² *n (tool)* cuòdāo 锉刀

file cabinet dàng'ànxiāng 档案箱

fill *v/t* zhùmǎn 注满

♦ **fill in** *hole* tiánmǎn 填满

♦ **fill out** *form* tiánxiě 填写

filling 1 *n (in sandwich)* xiàn 馅；*(in tooth)* bǔyá 补牙 **2** *adj food* róngyì bǎorén 容易饱人

film 1 *n (for camera)* jiāojuǎn 胶卷；*(movie)* diànyǐng 电影 **2** *v/t* pāishè 拍摄

film star diànyǐng míngxīng 电影明星

filter 1 *n* guòlùqì 过滤器 **2** *v/t* guòlù 过滤

filthy āngzāng 肮脏

final 1 adj (last) zuìhòu 最后; decision quèdìng 确定 **2** n SP juésài 决赛

finalist cānjiā juésài zhě 参加决赛者

finalize quèdìng 确定

finally zuìhòu 最后; (at last) zhōngyú 终于

finance 1 n jīnróng 金融 **2** v/t tígōng zījīn 提供资金

financial jīnróng 金融

find v/t zhǎodào 找到

◆**find out 1** v/t huòzhī 获知 **2** v/i (inquire) cháxún 查询; (discover) liǎojiědào 了解到

fine¹ adj weather qínglǎng 晴朗; wine, performance hǎo 好; distinction xìwēi 细微; *that's ~* hǎo 好

fine² n (penalty) fájīn 罚金 **2** v/t fákuǎn 罚款

finger n shǒuzhǐ 手指

fingernail shǒuzhǐjiǎ 手指甲

finish 1 v/t & v/i jiéshù 结束 **2** n (of product) bùfen 最后部分; (of race) zhōngdiǎn 终点

fire 1 n huǒ 火; (electric, gas) nuǎnlú 暖炉; (blaze) shīhuǒ 失火; *be on ~*

zháohuǒ 着火 **2** v/i (shoot) shèjī 射击 **3** v/t F (dismiss) jiěgù 解雇

fire alarm huǒjǐng 火警

fire department xiāofángduì 消防队

fire escape ānquán chūkǒu 安全出口

fire extinguisher mièhuǒqì 灭火器

firefighter xiāofángduìyuán 消防队员

fireplace bìlú 壁炉

fireworks yànhuǒ 焰火; (display) yànhuǒ biǎoyǎn 焰火表演

firm¹ adj grip wěn ér yǒulì 稳而有力; muscles jiēshí 结实; voice jiāndìng 坚定

firm² n COM gōngsī 公司

first 1 adj dìyī 第一 **2** n dìyīgè 第一个 **3** adv arrive, finish dìyī 第一; (beforehand) xiān 先; *at ~* qǐchū 起初

first aid jíjiù 急救

first class adj tóuděng 头等; (very good) yīliú 一流

first floor yīlóu 一楼

firstly shǒuxiān 首先

first name míngzi 名字

fish n yú 鱼

fisherman yúfū 渔夫

fishing bǔyú 捕鱼

fist quán 拳

fit¹ n MED hūnjué 昏厥

fit² adj (physically) jiànkāng 健康; (morally) qiàdàng 恰当

fit³ v/t (of clothes) héshì 合适; (of furniture) róngdexià 容得下

fitness jiànkāng 健康

fix v/t (attach) dīngláo 钉牢; (repair) xiūlǐ 修理; meeting, lunch zhǔnbèi 准备; (dishonestly) zuòbì 作弊

flabby muscles sōngchí 松弛

flag n qí 旗

flame n huǒyàn 火焰

flash 1 n (of light) shǎnshuò 闪烁, PHOT shǎnguāngdēng 闪光灯 **2** v/i (of light) shǎnliàng 闪亮

flashlight shǒudiàntǒng 手电筒

flat adj píngtǎn 平坦; battery yòngwán diàn 用完电; tire qì bùzú 气不足; shoes píngdǐ 平底

flatter v/t fèngcheng 奉承

flattery fèngcheng 奉承

flavor n wèidao 味道

flee v/i táopǎo 逃跑

fleet n NAUT jiànduì 舰队; (of taxis, trucks) chēduì 车队

flesh ròutǐ 肉体; (of fruit) guǒròu 果肉

flexible línghuó 灵活

flicker v/i shǎndòng 闪动

flight (in airplane) hángbān 航班; (flying) fēixíng 飞行

flight path fēixíng lùxiàn 飞行路线

flimsy furniture bù jiēshi 不结实; material qīng'érbó 轻而薄; excuse bù zúxìn 不足信

fling v/t rēng 扔

flirt v/i tiáoqíng 调情

float v/i piāofú 漂浮

flood 1 n hóngshuǐ 洪水 **2** v/t (of river) yānmò 淹没

floor n dìbǎn 地板; (story) lóucéng 楼层

floppy (disk) ruǎnpán 软盘

flour miànfěn 面粉

flourish v/i fánróng 繁荣

flow 1 v/i (of river, traffic) liúdòng 流动 **2** n (of information) jiāoliú 交流

flower *n* huā 花

flu liúgǎn 流感

fluctuate *v/i* bōdòng 波动

fluent *adj* liúlì 流利

fluid *n* liútǐ 流体

flush *v/t & v/i* toilet chōngxǐ 冲洗

fly[1] *n* (*insect*) cāngying 苍蝇

fly[2] (*on pants*) lāliànr 拉链儿

fly[3] *v/i* fēixíng 飞行; (*in airplane*) chéngjī 乘机

flying *n* fēixíng 飞行

foam *n* (*on liquid*) pàomò 泡沫

focus *n* (*of attention*) jízhōng 集中; PHOT jiāojù 焦距

fog wù 雾

foggy duōwù 多雾

fold *v/t* paper etc zhédié 折叠; ~ one's arms hébào shuāngbì 合抱双臂

folder also COMPUT wénjiànjiā 文件夹

folk (*people*) rénmen 人们

follow 1 *v/t* person gēnsuí 跟随; road yánzhe 沿着; ~ qiánjìn 前进; instructions zūnxún 遵循; TV series, news liánxù kàn 连续看 **2** *v/i* (*logically*) bìrán fāshēng 必然发生

♦ **follow up** *v/t* letter, inquiry hòuxù 后续

following *adj* day, night jìzhe 接着; points xiàshù 下述

fond (*loving*) xǐ'ài 喜爱; **be ~ of** xǐhuan 喜欢

food shíwù 食物

fool *n* chǔnrén 蠢人; **make a ~ of oneself** shǐ zìjǐ chūchǒu 使自己出丑

foolish yúchǔn 愚蠢

foot jiǎo 脚; (*length*) yīngchǐ 英尺; **on ~** bùxíng 步行

football měishì zúqiú 美式足球; (*ball*) gǎnlǎnqiú 橄榄球 (soccer, ball) zúqiú 足球

for ◊ (*purpose, destination etc*) wèile 为了; **a train ~ X** qù X de huǒchē 去X的火车; **this is ~ you** zhè shì gěi nǐ de 这是给你的; ~ **three days** sān tiān 三天 ◊ (*instead of, in behalf of*): **let me do that ~ you** ràng wǒ gěi nǐ zuò ba 让我给你做吧

forbid jìnzhǐ 禁止

Forbidden City Zǐjìnchéng 紫禁城

force 1 *n* (*violence*) wǔlì 武

力; (*of explosion, punch*)
lìliang 力量; **the ~s** MIL
bùduì 部队 **2** *v/t*: **X to do**
Y qiángpò X zuò Y 强迫
X 做 Y

forecast *n* yùcè 预测; (*of
weather*) yùbào 预报
foreground qiánjǐng 前景
forehead é 额
foreign wàiguó 外国
foreign currency wàibì 外币
foreigner wàiguórén 外国人
foreign policy wàijiāo
zhèngcè 外交政策
foresee yùjiàn 预见
forest sēnlín 森林
foretell yùbào 预料
forever *adv* yǒngyuǎn 永远
forfeit *v/t right* sàngshī 丧失
forge *v/t* (*counterfeit*) wěizào
伪造
forgery wěizàopǐn 伪造品
forget wàngjì 忘记
forgetful jiànwàng 健忘
forgive 1 *v/t* yuánliàng 原谅
2 *v/i* liàngjiě 谅解
forgiveness yuánliàng 原谅
fork *n* chāzi 叉子; (*in road*)
chàkǒu 岔口
form 1 *n* (*shape*) xíngzhuàng
形状; (*document*) biǎogé

表格 **2** *v/t* xíngchéng 形成
3 *v/i* (*take shape*) xíngchéng
形成
formal zhèngshì 正式;
recognition guānfāng 官方
format 1 *v/t disk* shǐ
géshìhuà 使格式化;
document ānpái ... bǎnshì
安排...版式 **2** *n* kāiběn
开本
former yǐqián 以前; **the ~**
qiánzhě 前者
formidable kěpà 可怕
formula MATH gōngshì 公式;
CHEM fēnzǐshì 分子式
forth: **back and ~** láihuí 来
回; **and so ~** děngděng
等等
fortnight Br liǎngzhōu 两周
fortunate xìngyùn 幸运
fortune yùnqì 运气; (*money*)
dàbǐde qián 大笔的钱
forward 1 *adv* xiàngqián 向
前 **2** SP qiánfēng 前锋
3 *v/t letter* zhuǎndì 转递
foul 1 *n* SP fànguī 犯规 **2** *adj
smell, taste* nánwén 难闻;
weather èliè 恶劣
found *v/t* chuàngbàn 创办
foundation (*of organization etc*) chénglì 成立;

(organization) jījīnhuì 基金会

foundations dìjī 地基

founder n chuàngjiànrén 创建人

four-star sìxīngjí 四星级

fracture 1 n gǔzhé 骨折 2 v/t zhéduàn 折断

fragile yìsuì 易碎

fragment n yībùfen 一部分

frail xūruò 虚弱

frame n kuàng 框

frank tǎnshuài 坦率

frantic fāfēng 发疯

fraud qīpiàn 欺骗; *(person)* piànzi 骗子

freak 1 n *(event)* fǎncháng xiànxiàng 反常现象; F *(strange person)* guàirén 怪人 2 adj wind, storm etc yìcháng qiángliè 异常强烈

freckle quèbān 雀斑

free 1 adj *(at liberty)* zìyóu 自由; *(no cost)* miǎnfèi 免费; room, table kòngyú 空余 2 v/t prisoners shìfàng 释放

freedom zìyóu 自由

freelance adj zìyóu zhíyè 自由职业

free speech zìyóu yánlùn 自由言论

freeway gāosù gōnglù 高速公路

freeze 1 v/t lěngdòng 冷冻; bank account dòngjié 冻结; video zàntíng 暂停 2 v/i *(of water)* nínggù 凝固

freezer lěngdòngshì 冷冻室

freight n huòwù 货物; *(costs)* yùnfèi 运费

frequency pínlǜ 频率; *(of radiowave)* bōduàn 波段

frequent adj jīngcháng 经常

frequently shícháng 时常

fresh fruit, meat xīnxiān 新鲜; *(cold)* liángshuǎng 凉爽; *(new)* xīn 新; *(impertinent)* cūlǔ 粗鲁

friction PHYS mócā 摩擦; *(in group)* chōngtú 冲突

Friday xīngqīwǔ 星期五

fridge bīngxiāng 冰箱

fried egg jiāndàn 煎蛋

friend péngyou 朋友

friendly adj yǒuhǎo 友好

friendship yǒuyì 友谊

fries shǔtiáo 薯条

fright jīngxià 惊吓

frighten v/t jīngxià 惊吓; be ~ed hàipà 害怕

frill (*on dress etc*) shìbiān 饰
边; (*extra*) fùjiāwù 附加物
from ◊ (*in space, time*) cóng
从 ◊ (*origin*): *a letter ~ Jo*
Qiáo de láixìn 乔的来信;
I'm ~ New Jersey wǒ láizì
Xīn Zéxī zhōu 我来自新
泽西州
front 1 *n* zhèngmiàn 正面;
(*of weather*) fēng fēng 锋; *in ~*
zài qiánmian 在前面; (*in
race*) lǐngxiān 领先; *in ~
of X* zài X de qiánmian 在
X 的前面 **2** *adj wheel, seat*
qiánmian 前面
front door qiánmén 前门
frontier biānjiāng 边疆; *fig
(of science etc)* qiányán
前沿
front page tóubǎn 头版
frost *n* shuāng shuāng 霜
frosting tángshuāng 糖霜
frown *n & v/i* zhòuméi 皱眉
frozen *feet etc* bīngliáng 冰
凉; *food* lěngdòng 冷冻
fruit shuǐguǒ 水果
fruit juice guǒzhī 果汁
frustrated jǔsàng 沮丧
frustrating shǐrén xīnfán 使
人心烦
fry *v/t* (*stir-~*) chǎo 炒; (*deep-*

~) yóuzhá 油炸
fuel *n* ránliào 燃料
fulfill *v/t* shíxiàn 实现
full mǎn 满; *report* xiángxì
详细
full moon mǎnyuè 满月
full-time *adv* quánrì 全日
fully wánquán 完全
fumes fèiqì 废气
fun kāixīn 开心; *have ~!*
jìnqíng wánr ba! 尽情玩儿
吧！; *make ~ of X* qǔxiào
X 取笑X
function 1 *n* zuòyòng 作用;
(*reception etc*) jíhuì 集会
fund 1 *n* jījīn 基金 **2** *v/t
project etc* bōkuǎn 拨款
fundamental jīběn 基本
funeral zànglǐ 葬礼
funny (*comical*) kěxiào 可
笑; (*odd*) gǔguài 古怪
fur máopí 毛皮
furious (*angry*) fènnù 愤怒
furnish *room* zhuāngbèi
装备
furniture jiājù 家具
further 1 *adj* (*additional*)
jìnyíbù 进一步; (*more
distant*) gèngyuǎn 更远
2 *adv* walk, drive gèngyuǎn
更远; *2 miles ~* (*on*) zài

zǒu liǎng yīnglǐ 再走两英里

furthest *adj & adv* zuìyuǎn 最远

fury (*anger*) bàonù 暴怒

fuse ELEC **1** *n* bǎoxiǎnsī 保险丝 **2** *v/i* bǎoxiǎnsī

shǎoduàn 保险丝烧断

fuss *n* dàjīng xiǎoguài 大惊小怪

fussy *person* tiāotī 挑剔

futile wúxiào 无效

future *n* wèilái 未来; *in* ~ jīnhòu 今后

G

gadget xiǎozhuāngzhì 小装置

gain *v/t* (*acquire*) yíngdé 赢得

gallery (*for art*) huàláng 画廊

gallon jiālún 加仑

gamble dǔbó 赌博

gambler dǔtú 赌徒

gambling dǔbó 赌博

game *n* (*match*) bǐsài 比赛; (*sport*) yùndòng 运动; (*children's*) yóuxì 游戏; (*in tennis*) yìjú 一局

gang yìbāng 一帮

Gang of Four Sìrénbāng 四人帮

gangway tiàobǎn 跳板

gap (*in wall*) lièfèng 裂缝; (*in time*) jiànxì 间隙

gape *v/i* (*of person*) zhāngkǒu 张口

garage *for parking* chēkù 车库; *for gas* jiāyóuzhàn 加油站; *for repairs* qìchē xiūlǐzhàn 汽车修理站

garbage lājī 垃圾; *fig* (*nonsense*) fèihuà 废话

garbage can lājīxiāng 垃圾箱

garden huāyuán 花园

garlic dàsuàn 大蒜

gas *n* qìtǐ 气体; (*gasoline*) qìyóu 汽油

gasp *v/i* qìchuǎn 气喘

gas station jiāyóuzhàn 加油站

gate dàmén 大门; (*at airport*) dēngjīkǒu 登机口

gather *v/t facts* sōují 搜集

gay n & adj tóngxìngliàn 同性恋

♦ **gaze at** níngshì 凝视

gear n (equipment) yòngjù 用具; мот chǐlún 齿轮

gear shift biànsùgǎn 变速杆

gender xìngbié 性别

gene jīyīn 基因

general 1 n (in army) jiāng-jūn 将军 **2** adj (overall, miscellaneous) zǒngde 总的; (widespread) pǔbiàn 普遍

generalize gàikuò 概括

generally yìbānde 一般地

generate chǎnshēng 产生, ~ **electricity** fādiàn 发电

generation dài 代

generator fādiànjī 发电机

generosity dàfang 大方

generous dàfang 大方; (not too critical) kuānhóng dàliàng 宽宏大量

genetic yíchuán 遗传

genetics yíchuánxué 遗传学

genitals shēngzhíqì 生殖器

genius tiāncái 天才

gentle wēnróu 温柔

genuine zhēnpǐn 真品; (sincere) zhēnchéng 真诚

geographical dìlǐ 地理

geography dìlǐxué 地理学

geological dìzhì 地质

geology dìzhìxué 地质学

geometry jǐhé 几何

germ bìngjūn 病菌

gesture n (with hand) shǒushì 手势; fig (of friendship) biǎoshì 表示

get n (obtain) dédào 得到; (fetch) gěi ...ná 给 ... 拿; (receive: letter) shōudào 收到; (catch: bus, train etc) zuò 坐; (understand) míngbai 明白◊; (become, grow): **~ tired** / **~ old** lèi le /lǎo le 累了 /老了◊ (causative) bǎ ... bǎ ...;: **one's hair cut** bǎ tóufa jiǎn le 把头发剪了; **~ X to do Y** jiào X zuò Y 叫X 做Y ◊: **have got** yǒu 有◊: **have got to** bìxū 必须

♦ **get on** v/i (be friendly) chǔdelái 处得来; (make progress) jìnzhǎn 进展; ~ **the train** / **bus** / **one's bike** shàng chē 上车

♦ **get out** v/i (of car etc) chūlái 出来; ~! gǔnchūqù! 滚出去! **2** v/t nail etc nòngchū 弄出

◆**get up 1** *v/i (in morning)* qǐchuáng 起床; *(from chair)* zhànqǐlái 站起来 **2** *v/t hill* pá 爬

ghost guǐ 鬼

giant *n* jùrén 巨人

gift lǐwù 礼物

gigantic jùdà 巨大

giggle *v/i* gēgē de xiào 咯咯地笑

gin dùsōngzǐjiǔ 杜松子酒

ginseng rénshēn 人参

girl nǚhái 女孩

girlfriend *(of boy)* nǚ péngyou 女朋友; *(of girl)* nǚxìng péngyou 女性朋友

gist yàozhǐ 要旨

give gěi 给; **~ a talk** zuò jiǎngzuò 作讲座

◆**give away** *(as present)* sòng 送; *(betray)* xièlù 泄露

◆**give in 1** *v/i (surrender)* qūfú 屈服 **2** *v/t (hand in)* jiāochū 交出

◆**give up 1** *v/t smoking etc* jiè 戒 **2** *v/i (cease habit)* jiè 戒; *(stop trying)* fàngqì 放弃

glad gāoxìng 高兴

gladly yúkuài 愉快

glamor mèilì 魅力

glamorous yǒu mèilì 有魅力

glance *n* yìpiē 一瞥

◆**glance at** sǎoshì 扫视

glare *v/i (of light)* shǎnyào 闪耀

◆**glare at** nùmù ér shì 怒目而视

glass *(material)* bōli 玻璃; *(for drink)* bōlibēi 玻璃杯

glasses *(eye~)* yǎnjìng 眼镜

glimpse *v/t* piējiàn 瞥见

gloat *v/i* zhānzhānzìxǐ 沾沾自喜

global quánqiú 全球; *(without exceptions)* pǔbiàn 普遍

global warming quánqiú biànnuǎn 全球变暖

globe *(earth)* dìqiú 地球; *(model)* dìqiúyí 地球仪

gloomy *room* yīn'àn 阴暗; *mood, person* yōuchóu 忧愁

glorious *weather* qínglǎng 晴朗; *victory* guāngróng 光荣

glove shǒutào 手套

glow *n* guānghuī 光辉

glue 1 *n* jiāo 胶 **2** *v/t:* **~ X zhānzài Y shàng 把

X 粘在 Y 上

glutinous rice nuòmǐ 糯米

go v/i qù去; (*leave*) líkāi
离开; (*work, function*)
yùnzhuǎn 运转; (*become*)
biànde 变得; (*cease: of
pain etc*) méile 没了;
(*match: of colors etc*) pèi
配; *I must be ~ing* wǒ děi
zǒule 我得走了; *let's ~*
zǒuba 走吧; *hamburger
to ~* hànbǎobāo, dàizǒu 汉
堡包带走; *be all gone*
(*finished*) yòngwánle 用完
了; *be ~ing to do X* yàozuò
X 要做 X

◆ **go back** (*return*) huíqù 回
去; (*date back*) zhuīsù 追溯

◆ **go down** xiàqù 下去; (*of
sun, ship*) luòxià 落下; (*of
swelling*) xiāoqù 消去

◆ **go in** (*to room, house*)
jìnqù 进去; (*fit: of part
etc*) ān 安

◆ **go off** v/i (*leave*) líkāi 离
开; (*of bomb*) bàozhà 爆
炸; (*of gun*) zǒuhuǒ 走火;
(*of alarm*) xiǎngqǐ 响起

◆ **go on** (*continue*) jìxù 继
续; (*happen*) fāshēng 发生

◆ **go out** (*of person*) chūqù

出去; (*of light, fire*) xīmiè
熄灭

goal mùbiāo 目标; (*sport:
point*) bǐfēn 比分

goalkeeper shǒuményuán
守门员

go-between zhōngjiānrén
中间人

Gobi Desert Gēbìtān 戈
壁滩

god shén 神

gold 1 n huángjīn 黄金
2 adj jīn 金

golf gāo'ěrfū 高尔夫

gong luó 锣; (*in wrestling*)
mínglúo lìng 鸣锣令

good hǎo 好; *food* hǎochī
好吃; *be ~ at ...* shànyú ...
善于 ...; *be ~ for X* duì X
yǒuyòng 对X有用

goodbye zàijiàn 再见

good-looking hǎokàn 好看

good-natured píqí hǎo 脾
气好

goods COM shāngpǐn 商品

gorgeous *day* fēnghé rìlì
风和日丽; *dress, woman*
piàoliang 漂亮

gossip 1 n liúyán fēiyǔ 流言
蜚语; (*person*) ràoshézhě
饶舌者 2 v/i xiánliáo 闲聊

government zhèngfǔ 政府

governor zhōuzhǎng 州长

grab v/t zhuāzhù 抓住

grade n (quality) děngjí 等级; EDU year niánjí 年级

gradual zhújiàn 逐渐

graduate n bìyèshēng 毕业生

grain lì 粒; (in wood) mùwén 木纹

grand adj zhuàngguān 壮观

granddaughter (son's daughter) sūnnǚ 孙女; (daughter's daughter) wàisūnnǚ 外孙女

grandfather (paternal) zǔfù 祖父; (maternal) wàizǔfù 外祖父

grandmother (paternal) zǔmǔ 祖母; (maternal) wàizǔmǔ 外祖母

grandparents (paternal) zǔfùmǔ 祖父母; (maternal) wàizǔfùmǔ 外祖父母

grandson (son's son) sūnzi 孙子; (daughter's son) wàisūnzi 外孙子

grant n money bōkuǎn 拨款; (for school) zhùxuéjīn 助学金

grape pútao 葡萄

grapefruit pútaoyòu 葡萄柚

graph túbiǎo 图表

graphics COMPUT túxíngxué 图形学

grasp 1 n (physical) zhuā 抓; (mental) zhǎngwò 掌握 **2** v/t (physically) zhuāzhù 抓住

grass cǎo 草

grate v/i (of sounds) cāxiǎng 擦响

grateful gǎnjī 感激

gratitude gǎn'ēn 感恩

grave n fénmù 坟墓

gray adj huīsè 灰色

graze 1 v/t arm etc cāshāng 擦伤 **2** v/i mùcǎo 牧草

greasy food yóunì 油腻; hair, plate duō yóuzhī 多油脂

great hěndà 很大; quantity dàliàng 大量; composer, writer wěidà 伟大; (very good) hěnbàng 很棒

Great Leap Forward Dàyuèjìn 大跃进

greatly fēicháng 非常

Great Wall (of China) (Wànlǐ) Chángchéng (万里)长城

greed tānxīn 贪心

greedy tānlán 贪婪

green lǜsè 绿色

greet yíngjiē 迎接

greeting wènhòu 问候

grief bēishāng 悲伤

grieve bēitòng 悲痛

grim kěbù 可怖

grin 1 n liězuǐ xiào 咧嘴笑 **2** v/i lòuchǐ'ěrxiào 露齿而笑

grind v/t coffee, meat niǎnsuì 碾碎

grip 1 n (on rope etc) jǐnwò 紧握 **2** v/t zhuāzhù 抓住

groan v/i shēnyín 呻吟

gross adj (coarse) cúsú 粗俗; FIN zǒng 总

ground 1 n dìmiàn 地面; (reason) lǐyóu 理由; ELEC dìxiàn 地线 **2** v/t ELEC shǐjiēdì 使接地

group n zǔ 组

grow 1 v/i shēngzhǎng 生长; (of number, amount) zēngzhǎng 增长; (of business) fāzhǎn 发展; ~ tired lèi le 累了 **2** v/t rice, crop zhòngzhí 种植

♦ **grow up** zhǎngdà 长大; (of city etc) kuòdà 扩大

growl v/i páoxiào 咆哮

grown-up n chéngrén 成人

growth chéngzhǎng 成长; (of company) fāzhǎn 发展; (increase) zēngzhǎng 增长; MED liú 瘤

grumble n & v/i bàoyuàn 抱怨

grunt n hūlūshēng 呼噜声

guarantee 1 n dānbǎo bǎozhèng 担保保证 **2** v/t dānbǎo 担保

guard 1 n (security ~) jǐngwèi 警卫; MIL wèibīng 卫兵; (in prison) kānshǒu 看守 **2** v/t shǒuwèi 守卫

guerrilla yóujīduì 游击队

guess 1 n cāicè 猜测 **2** v/t answer cāixiǎng 猜想 **3** v/i cāi 猜

guest kèrén 客人

guidance zhǐdǎo 指导

guide 1 n (person) dǎoyóu 导游; (book) zhǐnán 指南 **2** v/t xiàngdǎo 向导

guilt yǒukuì 有愧; (guilty feeling) nèijiù 内疚

guilty LAW yǒuzuì 有罪; (responsible) nèijiù 内疚

guitar jítā 吉他

gulf hǎiwān 海湾

gum (in mouth) chǐyín 齿龈; (glue) shùjiāo 树胶;

(to chew) kǒuxiāngtáng
口香糖
gun qiāng 枪
gutter yáncáo 檐槽; *(on roof)* tiāngōu 天沟

guy F jiāhuo 家伙
gym tǐyùguǎn 体育馆; *(in school)* yùndòngshì 运动室
gynecologist fùkē yīshēng
妇科医生

H

habit xíguàn 习惯
hacker COMPUT hēikè 黑客
hair tóufa 头发; *(on body, animal)* máo 毛
hairbrush shūzi 梳子
haircut lǐfà 理发
hairdresser lǐfàshī 理发师
hairdrier chuīfēngqì 吹风器
hairstyle fàxíng 发型
half n yíbàn 一半; **~ past ten** shídiǎnbàn 十点半; **~ an hour** bàngè xiǎoshí 半个小时
half time n SP bànchǎng 半场
halfway 1 adj stage bàntú 半途 **2** adv zhōngjiān 中间
hall tīng 厅; *(hallway in house)* zǒuláng 走廊
halt 1 v/i tíngzhǐ 停止 **2** v/t zhìzhǐ 止住
halve v/t fēnchéng liǎngbàn 分成两半

hamburger hànbǎobāo 汉堡包
hammer n chuízi 锤子
hamper v/t zǔ'ài 阻碍
hand 1 n shǒu 手; *(of clock)* zhēn 针; *(worker)* gōngrén 工人; **on the one ~ ..., on the other ~ ...** yìfāngmiàn ...lìngyìfāngmiàn ... 一方面...另一方面...
♦ **hand over** yíjiāo 移交; *to authorities* shàngjiāo 上交
hand baggage shǒutí xíngli 手提行李
handcuffs shǒukào 手铐
handicap n zhàng'ài 障碍
handicapped *(physically)* cánjí 残疾
handkerchief shǒujuàn 手绢
handle 1 n bǎshou 把手 **2** v/t goods bānyùn 搬运; *case, deal* chǔlǐ 处理

handmade shǒugōng zhìzuò 手工制作

handsome shuài 帅

handwriting bǐjì 笔迹

handwritten shǒuxiě 手写

handy *device* fāngbiàn 方便

hang 1 *v/t picture* guà 挂; *person* diàosǐ 吊死 **2** *v/i* *(of dress, hair)* chuíxià 垂下

♦ **hang up** TELEC guàduàn 挂断

hanger yīfújià 衣服架

hangover (jiǔhòu) tóutòng (酒后)头痛

haphazard ǒuránxìng 偶然性

happen fāshēng 发生; *what has ~ed to you?* nǐ zěnme le? 你怎么了？

happily gāoxìng 高兴; *(luckily)* xìngyùn 幸运

happiness xìngfú 幸福

happy kuàilè 快乐

harass sāorǎo 骚扰

harassment sāorǎo 骚扰

harbor *n* gǎngwān 港湾

hard yìng 硬; *(difficult)* nán 难; *facts, evidence* bùrónghuáiyí 不容怀疑

hardback yìngpíshū 硬皮书

hard-boiled *egg* zhǔ de lǎo 煮得老

hard currency yìngtōnghuò 硬通货

hardliner qiángyìng lùxiànzhě 强硬路线者

hardly jīhūbù 几乎不

hard seat RAIL yìngzuò 硬座

hardship jiānnán 艰难

hardware jīnshǔ qìjù 金属器具; COMPUT yìngjiàn 硬件

hard-working qínmiǎn 勤勉

harm *n & v/t* sǔnhài 损害

harmful yǒuhài 有害

harmless wúhài 无害

harsh jiānkè 尖刻

harvest *n* shōuhuò 收获

hasty cǎoshuài 草率

hat màozi 帽子

hate *n & v/t* zēnghèn 憎恨

have 1 *(possess)* yǒu 有; *do you ...?* nǐ yǒu ... ma? 你有 ... 吗？◊ *breakfast, lunch* chī 吃◊: *can I ~ a ...?* qǐng gěiwǒ ... 请给我 ...◊ *(must)*: *(got to)* bìxū 必须 ◊ *(causative)* bǎ 把; *I had my hair cut* wǒ bǎ tóufa jiǎnle 我把头发剪了

♦ **have on** *(wear)* chuān

穿; (have planned) yǒu
shì 有事

hay fever huāfěnrè 花粉热

hazy view wùméngméng
雾蒙蒙; memories móhu
模糊

he tā 他

head 1 n tóu 头; (boss,
leader) lǐngdǎo 领导; (of
line) qiánmiàn 前面 **2** v/t
(lead) lǐngdǎo 领导

headache tóutòng 头痛

heading (in list) biāotí 标题

headlight qiándēng 前灯

headline dàzì biāotí 大字
标题

head office zǒngbù 总部

headphones ěrjī 耳机

headquarters zǒng zhǐhuībù
总指挥部

heal v/t & v/i yùhé 愈合

health jiànkāng 健康

healthy jiànkāng 健康

heap n duī 堆

hear tīngjiàn 听见

hearing tīnglì 听力

hearing aid zhùtīngqì 助
听器

heart xīn 心; (of city etc)
zhōngxīn 中心; know X by
~ shóujì X 熟记X

heart attack xīnzàngbìng
心脏病

heat rè 热

heated pool jiā le rè 加了热;
discussion rèliè 热烈

heater fārèqì 发热器

heating nuǎnqì 暖气

heatwave rèlàng 热浪

heaven tiāntáng 天堂

heavy zhòng 重; rain dà 大;
traffic yōngjǐ 拥挤; food
yóunì 油腻; financial loss
chénzhòng 沉重

hectic fánmáng 繁忙

heel (of foot) jiǎohòugēn
脚后跟; (of shoe) xiégēn
鞋跟

height gāodù 高度; (of
season) shèng 盛

heir jìchéngrén 继承人

helicopter zhíshēngfēijī 直
升飞机

hell dìyù 地狱

hello nǐ hǎo 你好; TELEC
wèi 喂

helmet tóukuī 头盔

help n & v/t bāngzhù 帮
助; ~! jiùmìng! 救命！；
can you ~ me? jiègè shǒu,
xíngma? 借个手行吗？；
~ oneself (to food) suíbiàn

chī 随便吃; **I can't ~ it** wǒ
rěnbúzhù 我忍不住

helpful yǒu bāngzhù 有帮助

helpless wúzhù 无助

hemisphere bànqiú 半球

hemorrhage n & v/i chūxuè
出血

her 1 adj tāde 她的 **2** pron
tā 她

herb yàocǎo 药草

herb(al) tea yàocǎochá 药
草茶

herbal medicine cǎoyào
草药

here zhèr 这儿; **~ you are**
(giving sth) gěi nǐ 给你;
~ we are! (finding sth) zài
zhèr! 在这儿！

hereditary yíchuán 遗传

heritage yíchǎn 遗产

hero yīngxióng 英雄

heroin hǎiluòyīn 海洛因

heroine nǚyīngxióng 女英雄

herpes MED pàozhěn 疱疹

hers tāde 她的

herself tā zìjǐ 她自己

hesitate yóuyù 犹豫

hesitation yóuyù 犹豫

heterosexual adj yìxìng'ài
异性爱

hiccup n dǎgérdǎ 嗝儿打

hide v/t & v/i cáng 藏

high 1 adj gāo 高 **2** n MOT
gāo 高; (in statistics)
gāofēng 高峰

high jump tiàogāo 跳高

high-level gāo jiēcéng 高
阶层

highlight 1 n (main event)
zuìjīngcǎi chǎngmiàn 最精
采场面; (in hair) rǎnsè 染
色 **2** v/t (with pen) tūchū
突出; COMPUT xuǎn 选

highly likely fēicháng 非常;
~ paid xīnshuǐ gāo 薪水高

high point dǐngfēng 顶峰

high school zhōngxué 中学

high tech n & adj gāoxīn
jìshù 高新技术

highway gōnglù 公路

hijack v/t: **~ a plane** jiéjī 劫
机; **~ a bus** jiéchē 劫车

hijacker (of plane) jiéjīzhě
劫机者; (of bus) jiéchēzhě
劫车者

hike 1 n yuǎnzú 远足 **2** v/i
bùxíng 步行

hilarious fēicháng huáijī 非
常滑稽

hill xiǎoshānpō 小山坡;
(slope) shānpō 山坡

him tā 他

Himalayas Xǐmǎlāyǎshān 喜玛拉雅山

himself tā zìjǐ 他自己

hinder zǔzhǐ 阻止

hint tíshì 提示

hip túnbù 臀部

his adj & pron tāde 他的

historian lìshǐxuéjiā 历史学家

historic yǒu lìshǐ yìyì 有历史意义

historical yǒuguān lìshǐ 有关历史

history lìshǐ 历史

hit 1 v/t dǎ 打; (collide with) zhuàng 撞 **2** n (blow) dǎjī 打击; MUS liúxíng chàngpiàn 流行唱片; (success) jùdà chénggōng 巨大成功

hitchhike miǎnfèi dāchē 免费搭车

HIV rénlèi sàngshī miǎnyìlì bìngdú 人类丧失免疫力病毒

hoarse sīyǎ 嘶哑

hoax n qīpiàn 欺骗

hobby shìhào 嗜好

hog n (pig) zhū 猪

hold 1 v/t (in hands) ná 拿; (support, keep in place)

zhīchí 支持; (passport, license) chíyǒu 持有; (prisoner) guānyā 关押; (contain) chéngyǒu 盛有; **~ the line** TELEC qǐng bié guàduàn 请别挂断 **2** n (in ship, plane) huòcāng 货舱; **take ~ of** zhuāzhù 抓住

holdup (robbery) qiǎngjié 抢劫; (delay) yánwù 延误

hole dòng dòng 洞洞

holiday (single day) xiūxírì 休息日; Br (period) jiàqī 假期

hollow zhōngkōng 中空

holy shénshèng 神圣

home 1 n jiā 家; (native country) zǔguó 祖国; (town, part of country) jiāxiāng 家乡; (for old people) lǎorényuàn 老人院; **at ~** (in my house) zài jiā 在家; (in my country) zài guónèi 在国内 **2** adv jiā 家; **go ~** huíjiā 回家; (to own country) huíguó 回国

homeless adj wújiā 无家

homesick be ~ xiǎngjiā 想家

home town jiāxiāng 家乡

homework EDU zuòyè 作业

homicide (*crime*) móushā 谋杀; (*police department*) míng'ànbù 命案部

homosexual *n & adj* tóngxìngliàn 同性恋

honest chéngshí 诚实

honesty chéngshí 诚实

honeymoon *n* mìyuè 蜜月

Hong Kong Xiānggǎng 香港

honor 1 *n* róngyù 荣誉 **2** *v/t* gěiyǐ róngyù 给以荣誉

honorable guāngróng 光荣

hood (*on head*) dōumào 兜帽

hook (*for clothes*) guàgōu 挂钩; (*for fishing*) yúgōu 鱼钩

hookey: play ~ táoxué 逃学

hope *n & v/t* xīwàng 希望

hopeful (*optimistic*) lèguān 乐观; (*promising*) yǒu xīwàng yǒu 有希望

hopefully *say* bàoyǒu xīwàng 抱有希望; (*I / we hope*) dànyuàn 但愿

hopeless *position etc* méiyǒu xīwàng 没有希望; (*useless: person etc*) méi qiántú 没前途

horizon dìpíngxiàn 地平线

horizontal shuǐpíng 水平

horoscope zhānxīngshù 占星术

horrible zāogāo 糟糕

horrify: I was horrified wǒ bèi xiàhuàile 我被吓坏了

horrifying kěpà 可怕

horror kǒngbù 恐怖

horse mǎ 马

hose ruǎnguǎn 软管

hospitable hàokè 好客

hospital yīyuàn 医院

hospitality rèqíng zhāodài 热情招待

host *n* (*at party*) zhǔrén 主人; (*of TV show*) zhǔchírén 主持人

hostage rénzhì 人质

hostel (*for students*) xiàowài jìsùshè 校外寄宿舍

hostess (*at party*) nǚzhǔrén 女主人; (*air ~*) kōngjiě 空姐

hostility díyì 敌意

hot rè 热; (*spicy*) là 辣

hotel bīnguǎn 宾馆

hour xiǎoshí 小时

house *n* fángzi 房子; **at your ~** zài nǐjiā 在你家

House of Representatives Zhòngyìyuàn 众议院

housework jiāwù 家务

how zěnme 怎么；~ *are you?* nǐ hǎo ma? 你好吗？；~ *about … ?* …zěnmeyàng? …怎么样？；~ *many?* jǐge? 几个？；~ *much?* duōshao? 多少？；~ *much is it?* duōshao qián? 多少钱？；~ *funny!* duō huájī! 多滑稽！

however bùguò 不过；~ *rich they are* bùguǎn tāmen duō fù 不管他们多富

howl v/i háojiào 嚎叫

hug v/t yōngbào 拥抱

huge jùdà 巨大

human 1 n rén 人 **2** adj rénlèi 人类

human being rén 人

humane réndào 人道

humanitarian réndàozhǔyǐ zhě 人道主义者

human resources (*department*) rénlì zīyuán 人力资源

humble qiānbēi 谦卑； *origins* dīwēi 低微；*house* jiǎnlòu 简陋

humid shīrè 湿热

humidity shīdù 湿度

humiliate xiūrǔ 羞辱

humor (*comical*) yōumò 幽

默；(*mood*) qíngxù 情绪

hunch (*idea*) yùgǎn 预感

hundred bǎi 百

hunger jīrè 饥饿

hungry jīrè 饥饿；*I'm ~* wǒ è le 我饿了

hunt n (*for animals*) shòuliè 狩猎；(*for criminal, missing child*) xúnzhǎo 寻找

hurry 1 n cōngmáng 匆忙；*be in a ~* jímáng 急忙 **2** v/i kuàidiǎnr 快点儿

◆**hurry up** v/i kuàidiǎnr 快点儿；~! gǎnjǐn! 赶紧!

hurt 1 v/i tòng 痛 **2** v/t shāng 伤

husband zhàngfu 丈夫

◆**hush up** zhēyǎn 遮掩

hut péngwū 棚屋

hydraulic yèyā 液压

hydroelectric shuǐlì fādiàn 水力发电

hygiene wèishēng 卫生

hygienic wèishēng 卫生

hyphen liánzìhào 连字号

hypnotize ~ **X** shǐ X jìnrù cuīmián zhuàngtài 使X进入催眠状态

hypocrite wěijūnzi 伪君子

hysterical xièsīdǐlǐ 歇斯底里

I

I wǒ 我

ice bīng 冰

icebox bīngxiāng 冰箱

ice cream bīngqílín 冰淇淋

I-Ching Yìjīng 易经

icon (cultural) shèngxiàng 圣
像; COMPUT túbiāo 图标

icy road huá 滑

idea zhǔyì 主意

ideal (perfect) lǐxiǎng 理想

identical yìmúyíyàng 一
模一样

identification yànzhèng 验
证; (papers etc) shēnfēn
zhèngmíng 身分证明

identify jiànbié 鉴别

identity shēnfēn 身分; ~
card shēnfenzhèng 身分证

idiot báichī 白痴

idle adj person lǎnduò 懒惰

idolize chóngbài 崇拜

if rúguǒ 如果

ignition MOT fādòng zhuāngzhì 发动装置; ~ key
dǎhuǒ yàoshi 打火钥匙

ignorance wúzhī 无知

ignore hūlüè 忽略

ill yǒubìng 有病; be taken ~
shēngbìng 生病

illegal fēifǎ 非法

illegible biànrèn bùqīng 辨
认不清

illiterate wénmáng 文盲

illness jíbìng 疾病

illogical bù hé luójí 不合
逻辑

illusion huànxiàng 幻象

illustration chātú 插图

image (of politician,
company) xíngxiàng 形象

imaginary jiǎxiǎng 假想

imagination xiǎngxiàng
想象

imaginative jùyǒu
xiǎngxiànglì 具有想象力

imagine xiǎngxiàng 想象

imitate mófǎng 模仿

imitation (copying) mófǎng
模仿; (something copied)
fǎngzào 仿造

immature bù chéngshú 不
成熟

immediate jíkè 即刻

immediately lìjí 立即

immigrant n yímín 移民

immigration yímín 移民

immoral bú dàodé 不道德

immunity (to infection)
miǎnyì 免疫; **diplomatic**
~ wàijiāo huòmiǎnquán 外
交豁免权

impact n (of missile, vehicle)
zhuàngjī 撞击; (effect)
yǐngxiǎng 影响

impartial gōngzhèng 公正

impassable bùtōng 不通

impatient bú nàixīn 不耐心

imperial huángdì 皇帝

impersonal bú jù réngéxìng
不具人格性

impetuous qīngshuài 轻率

implement n gōngjù 工
具 2 v/t measures etc shíshí
实施

implicate: ~ **X in Y** shǐ X
qiānshè dào Y zhōng 使
X牵涉到Y中

implication ànshì 暗示

imply ànzhǐ 暗指

import n & v/t jìnkǒu 进口

importance zhòngyàoxìng
重要性

important zhòngyào 重要

impossible bù kěnéng 不
可能

impression yìnxiàng 印象;
(impersonation) huájī de
mófǎng 滑稽的模仿

impressive gěi rén yǐ
shēnkè yìnxiàng 给人以深
刻印象

imprison jiānjìn 监禁

improve 1 v/t gǎijìn 改进
2 v/i (of health) hǎozhuǎn
好转; (of Chinese, skills)
tígāo 提高

improvement gǎijìn 改进

improvize v/i jíxìng 即兴

impulsive yì chōngdòng
易冲动

in 1 prep ◊ zài 在 ◊: ~ **1999**
yījiǔjiǔjiǔnián 1999 年;
~ **two hours** (from now)
liǎng ge xiǎoshí yǐhòu 两个
小时以后; (over period of)
liǎng ge xiǎoshí yǐnèi 两个
小时以内; (of Chinese, skills)
~ **August** bāyuè 八月 ◊:
~ **English** / **Chinese** yòng
Yīngyǔ/Hànyǔ shuō 用英语/汉
语◊: **one** ~ **ten** shífēnzhīyī
十分之一 2 adv (at home,
in building etc) zài lǐmian
在里面 3 adj (fashionable)
liúxíng 流行

inability wúnéng 无能

inaccessible nán jiējìn 难

接近

inadequate bú shìdàng 不
适当

inappropriate bú shì dàng
不适当

inaugural *speech* jiùzhí 就职

incentive dònglì 动力

incessant liánxù 连续

inch n yīngcùn 英寸

incident shìjiàn 事件

incidentally shùnbiàn shuō
yíxià 顺便说一下

incite shāndòng 煽动

incline: *be ~d to do X* yǒu
zuò X de qīngxiàng 有做
X 的倾向

include bāokuò 包括

including *prep* bāokuò 包括

inclusive *adj* & *prep* bāokuò
zàinèi 包括在内

incoherent bù liánguàn 不
连贯

income shōurù 收入

income tax suǒdéshuì 所
得税

incoming *flight* jídá 即达;
president xīnrèn 新任

incompatible bù xiāngfú
不相符

incompetent bú chènzhí 不
称职

incomprehensible bùkě lǐjiě
不可理解

inconsiderate kǎolǜ bùzhōu
考虑不周

inconsistent bù yízhì 不
一致

inconvenient bù fāngbiàn
不方便

increase 1 *v/t* & *n* zēngjiā 增
加 **2** *v/i* tígāo 提高

incredible (*very good*) nányí
zhìxìn 难以置信

incurable bùkě zhìyù 不
可治愈

indeed (*in fact*) shìshí shàng
事实上; (*yes, agreeing*)
díquèshì 的确是; *very
much* ~ fēicháng 非常

indefinitely wú xiànqī 无
限期

independence dúlì 独立

Independence Day Dúlìrì
独立日

independent dúlì 独立

indicate *v/t* biǎomíng 表明

indifferent mò bù guānxīn
漠不关心

indigestion xiāohuà bùliáng
消化不良

indignant fènkǎi 愤慨

indirect jiànjiē 间接

indiscriminate rènyì ér wéi 任意而为

indispensable bùkě quēshǎo 不可缺少

individual 1 *n* gèrén 个人 **2** *adj* (*separate*) dāndú 单独; (*personal*) gèrén 个人

individually gèzì 各自

indoor shìnèi 室内

indoors zài shìnèi 在室内

industrial gōngyè 工业

industry gōngyè 工业

inefficient wúxiàolǜ 无效率

inequality bùpíngděng 不平等

inevitable bùkě bìmiǎn 不可避免

inexpensive piányi 便宜

inexperienced méi jīngyàn 没经验

infant yīng'ér 婴儿

infantry bùbīng 步兵

infatuated: be ~ with X míliàn X 迷恋 X

infect (*of person*) yǐngxiǎng 影响; *food, water* wūrǎn 污染

infection chuánrǎn 传染

infectious chuánrǎn 传染; *fig: laughter* gǎnrǎn 感染

inferior *quality* lièzhì 劣质

inferiority complex zìběigǎn 自卑感

infidelity bùzhōng 不忠

infiltrate *v/t* dǎrù 打入

infinite wúxiàn 无限

infinity wúqióng 无穷

inflammable yìrán 易燃

inflammation MED fāyán 发炎

inflation tōnghuò péngzhàng 通货膨胀

inflexible gùzhí 固执

influence *n* & *v/t* yǐngxiǎng 影响

influential yǒu yǐngxiǎng 有影响

inform *v/t* tōngzhī 通知

informal fēi zhèngshì 非正式

informant tígōng xiāoxirén 提供消息人

information xìnxī 信息

informer gàofārén 告发人

infuriating lìngrén shēngqì 令人生气

ingenious jīngmíng 精明

ingredient yuánliào 原料; *fig* (*for success*) yīnsù 因素

inhabit jūzhù 居住

inhabitant jūmín 居民

inhale 1 *v/t* xīrù 吸入 **2** *v/i*

(*when smoking*) xīqì 吸气

inherit jìchéng 继承

inhibition yāyì 压抑

in-house *adj & adv* zài gōngsī nèi 在公司内

initial 1 *adj* zuìchū 最初 **2** *n* xìngmíng shǒu zìmǔ 姓名 首字母

initiative zhǔdòngxìng 主动性

inject MED zhùshè 注射; *capital* tóurù 投入

injured 1 *adj leg* shòushāng 受伤; *feelings* shòushāng-hài 受伤害 **2** *n: the ~* shòushāngzhě 受伤者

injury shānghài 伤害

in-laws yīnqīn 姻亲

inner nèibù 内部

inner city jiùchéngqū 旧城区

Inner Mongolia Nèi Měnggǔ 内蒙古

innocence (*of child*) tiānzhēn 天真; LAW wúzuì 无罪

innocent *child* tiānzhēn 天真; LAW wúzuì 无罪

innovative géxīn 革新

input *n & v/t* (*to project*) tóurù 投入; COMPUT shūrù 输入

inquest shěnxùn 审讯

inquire xúnwèn 询问

inquiry xúnwèn 询问

inquisitive hàoqí 好奇

insane fēngkuáng 疯狂

insanity fēngkuáng 疯狂

inscription míngwén 铭文

insect kūnchóng 昆虫

insert *v/t* chārù 插入

inside 1 *n* (*of house, box*) nèibù 内部; *~ out* lǐmiàn fāndào wàimiàn 里面翻到外面 **2** *prep* zài … lǐ 在 … 里; *~ of 2 hours* bú dào liǎng xiǎoshí 不到两小时 **3** *adv* stay zài lǐmiàn 在里面; *go, carry* lǐmiàn 里面 **4** *adj* nèibù 内部; *~ information* nèibù xiāoxi 内部消息; *~ lane* (*on road*) lǐdào 里道

insider nèibùrén 内部人

insides lǐmiàn 里面

insight dòngchá 洞察

insist jiānchí 坚持

insistent jiānchí 坚持

insomnia shīmián 失眠

inspect *work, tickets, baggage* jiǎnchá 检查; *factory, school* shìchá 视察

inspiration línggǎn 灵感

inspire respect etc yǐnqǐ 引起; **be ~d by X** cóng X dédào línggǎn 从 X 得到灵感

install ānzhuāng 安装

installment (of story) jí集; FIN yīqī fùkuǎn 一期付款

instant 1 adj lìjí 立即 2 n chànà 刹那

instant coffee sùróng kāfēi 速溶咖啡

instantly jíkè 即刻

instant noodles fāngbiànmiàn 方便面

instead dàitì 代替; **would you like coffee ~?** nǐ hē kāfēi xíng ma? 你喝咖啡行吗？**; ~ of** ér bùshì 而不是

instinct běnnéng 本能

instinctive běnnéng 本能

institute n xiéhuì 协会; (special home) yuàn 院

institution (governmental) jīgòu 机构; (sth traditional) fēngsú xíguàn 风俗习惯

instruct (order) zhǐshì 指示; (teach) zhǐdǎo 指导

instruction shuōmíng 说明

instrument MUS yuèqì 乐器;

(tool) qìjù 器具

insulation ELEC juéyuán cáiliào 绝缘材料; (against cold) géré 隔热

insult n & v/t wǔrǔ 侮辱

insurance bǎoxiǎn 保险

insurance company bǎoxiǎn gōngsī 保险公司

insurance policy bǎoxiǎndān 保险单

insure v/t gěi … bǎoxiǎn 给 … 保险

intact (not damaged) wèishòusǔn 未受损

integrity (of person) chéngshí 诚实

intellectual 1 adj zhìlì 智力 2 n zhīshifènzǐ 知识分子

intelligence zhìlì 智力; (news) qíngbào 情报

intelligent cōngmíng 聪明

intend (plan) dǎsuàn 打算; **~ to do X** (do on purpose) zhìzài zuò X 旨在做X

intense jùliè 剧烈

intensive qiánghuà 强化

intention yìtú 意图

intentional yǒuyì 有意

interactive jiāohùshì 交互式

intercept ball lánjié 拦截; message jiéchá 截查

missile jiéjī 截击

intercom duìjiǎngjī 对讲机

intercourse (*sexual*) xìngjiāo 性交

interest 1 *n* xìngqù 兴趣; FIN lìxī 利息 **2** *v/t*: ~ **X** yǐnqǐ X de xìngqù 引起X的兴趣

interesting yǒuqù 有趣

interfere gānshè 干涉

♦ **interfere with** *controls* nònghuài 弄坏; *plans* gānrǎo 干扰

interference gānshè 干涉; (*on radio*) gānrǎo 干扰

interior *adj & n* nèibù 内部

intermediary *n* zhōngjiānrén 中间人

intermediate *adj* zhōngjí 中级

internal nèibù 内部; *trade* guónèi 国内

international *adj* guójì 国际

Internet yīntèwǎng 因特网

interpret 1 *v/t* kǒuyì 口译; *music, comment etc* jiěshì 解释 **2** *v/i* zuò kǒuyì 作口译

interpretation kǒuyì 口译; (*of music, meaning*) lǐjiě 理解

interpreter kǒuyìzhě 口

译者

interrogate xúnwèn 询问

interrupt 1 *v/t* dǎduàn 打断 **2** *v/i* chāhuà 插话

interruption zhōngduàn 中断

intersection shízì lùkǒu 十字路口

interstate *n* zhōujìjiān 州际间

interval jiàngé 间隔; (*in theater*) jiànxiē 间歇

intervene (*of police etc*) jièrù 介入

interview *n & v/t* (*on TV, for paper*) cǎifǎng 采访; (*for job*) miànshì 面试

intimacy (*sexual*) qīnnì 亲昵

intimidate wēixié 威胁

into dào …lǐ 到…里; *translate ~ English* fānyì chéng Yīngyǔ 翻译成英语; *be ~ X* F (*like*) xǐhuan X 喜欢X; (*be involved with*) chīmí X 痴迷X

intolerable bùnéng rěnshòu 不能忍受

intolerant bù róngrěn 不容忍

introduce jièshào 介绍; *new technique etc* yǐnjìn 引进

introduction (*to person, new food, sport etc*) jièshào 介绍; (*in book*) xùyán 序言; (*of new techniques etc*) yǐnjìn 引进

intruder qīnfànzhě 侵犯者

invade qīnlüè 侵略

invalid *n* MED bìngruò 病弱

invaluable *help* wújià 无价

invasion qīnlüè 侵略

invent fāmíng 发明

invest *v/t & v/i* tóuzī 投资

investigate diàochá 调查

investigation diàochá 调查

investment tóuzī 投资

invitation yāoqǐng 邀请

invite yāoqǐng 邀请

invoice 1 *n* zhàngdān 帐单 **2** *v/t* kāi zhàngdān 开帐单

involve *work, expense* xūyào 需要; (*concern*) shèjí 涉及

inwardly nèixīn 内心

IQ (= *intelligence quotient*) zhìshāng 智商

iron 1 *n* tiě 铁; (*for clothes*) yùndǒu 熨斗 **2** *v/t* yùn 熨

ironic(al) fěngcì 讽刺

irony fěngcì 讽刺

irrelevant bùxiānggān 不

相干

irrespective: *~ of X* búgù X 不顾X

irritable fánzào 烦躁

irritate rěnù 惹怒

irritating fánrén 烦人

irritation fánzào 烦燥

Islam Yīsīlánjiào 伊斯兰教

island dǎo 岛

isolate (*separate*) gélí 隔离; (*cut off*) gūlì 孤立

isolated *house* gūlì 孤立; *occurrence* dānyī 单一

issue 1 *n* (*matter*) shìqíng 事情; (*of magazine*) qīqī 期 **2** *v/t* fāxíng 发行

it tā 它◊ (*not translated*): *~'s me* shì wǒ 是我; *~'s yellow* shì huángde 是黄的; *that's ~!* (*that's right*) duìle! 对了！; (*finished*) wánle! 完了！

itch 1 *n* yǎng 痒 **2** *v/i* fāyǎng 发痒

item tiáo 条

itemize lièxiàng lièjǔ 分项列举

its tāde 它的

itself tāzìjǐ 它自己

J

jacket jiākè 茄克; (of book) hùfēng 护封

jade n yù 玉

jail n jiānyù 监狱

January yīyuè 一月

Japan Rìběn 日本

Japanese 1 adj Rìběn 日本 2 n (person) Rìběnrén 日本人; (language) Rìyǔ 日语

jar n (container) guàn 罐

jasmine tea mòlìhuāchá 茉莉花茶

jaw n hé 颌

jazz juéshìyuè 爵士乐

jealous dùjì 妒忌

jeans niúzǎikù 牛仔裤

jeopardize shǐ xiànyú kùnjìng 使陷于困境

jerk n měngrán yídòng 猛然一动 2 v/t měnglā 猛拉

jet 1 n pēnqìshì 喷气式; (nozzle) guǎnzuǐ 管嘴

jetlag shíchā fǎnyìng 时差反应

jeweler zhūbǎoshāng 珠宝商

jewelry zhūbǎo 珠宝

jiao (Chinese money) jiǎo 角

job gōngzuò 工作; (task) rènwù 任务

jog v/i mànpǎo 慢跑

join 1 v/i (of roads, rivers) huìhé 汇合; (become a member) cānjiā 参加 2 v/t (connect) liánjiē 连接; person yǔ ... huìmiàn 与 ... 会面; club cānjiā 参加

joint 1 n ANAT guānjié 关节; (in woodwork) liánjiēchù 连接处 2 adj gòngtóng 共同

joint account liánhé zhànghù 联合帐户

joint venture hézī qǐyè 合资企业

joke n gùshì 故事; (practical ~) xiàohuà 笑话

jolt 1 n diānbǒ 颠簸 2 v/t (push) tuī 推

jostle v/t tuījǐ 推挤

journalism (writing) xīnwén xiězuò 新闻写作; (trade) xīnwényè 新闻业

journalist xīnwén gōngzuòzhě 新闻工作者

journey n lǚxíng 旅行

joy kuàilè 快乐

judge 1 n LAW fǎguān 法官; (in competition) píngwěi 评委 **2** v/t pànduàn 判断

judgment LAW cáijué 裁决; (opinion) kànfǎ 看法; (good sense) juéduànlì 决断力

judo róudào 柔道

juice zhī 汁

July qīyuè 七月

jumble n yìtuán 一团

jump 1 n tiào 跳; (increase) tūzēng 突增 **2** v/i tiào 跳; (in surprise) jīngtiào 惊跳

jumpy jǐnzhāng 紧张

June liùyuè 六月

junior adj (subordinate) dìwèi dī dìwèi dī 地位低; (younger) xiǎo 小

junk[1] fèipǐn 废品

junk[2] (boat) fānchuán 帆船

junk food lājī shípǐn 垃圾食品

junkie yǒu dúyǐnzhě 有毒瘾者

junk mail lājī yóujiàn 垃圾邮件

juror péishěnyuán 陪审员

jury péishěntuán 陪审团

just adv (barely) gānggāng 刚刚; (exactly) qiàhǎo 恰好; (only) zhǐshì 只是: I've ~ seen her wǒ gānggāng kàndào tā wǒ gānggāng kàndào tā gānggāng kàndào tā 我刚刚看到她; ~ about (almost) jīhū 几乎; ~ now (a few moments ago) gāngcái 刚才; (at the moment) xiànzài 现在; ~ you wait! nǐ děngzhe ba! 你等着吧！

justice gōngpíng 公平; (of cause) zhèngyì 正义

justify zhèngmíng ...shì zhèngdàng 证明...是正当

K

karate kōngshǒudào 空手道

keep 1 v/t bǎoliú 保留; (not give back) yōngyǒu 拥有;

(in specific place) cúnfàng 存放; family gōngyǎng 供养; animals yǎng 养;

~ *a promise* bǎoshǒu chéngnuò 保守承诺; ~ ... *to oneself* (*not tell*) bǎ ... bǎozhù mìmì 把...保住秘密; ~ *X from Y* búràng Y zhīdào X 不让Y知道X; ~ *on trying* jìxù chángshì 继续尝试 **2** v/i (*remain*) bǎochí 保持; (*of food, milk*) bǎochí 保质

♦ **keep down** v/t *voice* yādī 压低; *costs* bǎochí dīshuǐpíng 保持低水平; *food* tūnxià 吞下

♦ **keep up 1** v/i (*when running etc*) gēnshàng 跟上 **2** v/t *pace, payments* gēnshàng 跟上; *bridge* zhīchēng 支撑; *pants* tí 提

ketchup fānqiéjiàng 番茄酱

kettle hú 壶

key 1 n yàoshi 钥匙; COMPUT, MUS jiàn 键 **2** adj (*vital*) guānjiàn 关键 **3** v/t COMPUT jiànrù 键入

keyboard COMPUT, MUS jiànpán 键盘

keyring yàoshiquān 钥匙圈

kick n, v/t & v/i tī 踢

kid F **1** n (*child*) xiǎoháir 小孩儿 **2** v/t & v/i kāi wánxiào 开玩笑

kidnap n & v/t bǎngjià 绑架

kill v/t shāsǐ 杀死

kind[1] adj yǒuhǎo 友好

kind[2] n zhǒnglèi 种类; (*make*) pǐnpái 品牌; *what of ...* ? shénmeyàngde ...? 什么样的...？; ~ *of sad* F yǒudiǎnr nánguò 有点儿难过

kindness hǎoyì 好意

kiss 1 n & v/t wěn 吻 **2** v/i qīnwěn 亲吻

kit chéngtào yòngpǐn 成套用品; (*to assemble*) zǔzhuāngjiàn 组装件

kitchen chúfáng 厨房

kitten xiǎomāo 小猫

knack juéqiào 诀窍

knee n xī 膝

kneel guìxià 跪下

knife n dāo 刀

knock 1 n (*at door*) qiāo 敲; (*blow*) zhuàngjī 撞击 **2** v/t (*hit*) jī 击 **3** v/i (*at door*) qiāo 敲

♦ **knock down** (*of car*) zhuàngdǎo 撞倒; *object, building etc* chāichú 拆除

♦ **knock out** *boxer etc* shǐ hūnmí 使昏迷

landlady

knot n jié 结

know 1 v/t zhīdào 知道; *person* rènshi 认识; *place* shúxī 熟悉; *language* dǒng 懂; (*recognize*) rènchū 认 出 2 v/i: **I don't ~** wǒ bù zhīdào 我不知道

knowhow jìnéng 技能

knowledge zhīshi 知识

Korea (*South*) Nán Hán 南 韩; (*North*) Běi Cháoxiǎn

北朝鲜

Korean 1 adj (*South*) Nán Hán 南韩; (*North*) Běi Cháoxiǎn 北朝鲜 2 n (*South*) Nán Hánrén 南韩人; (*North*) Běi Cháoxiǎnrén 北朝鲜人; (*language*) Cháoxiǎn yǔ 朝鲜语

Kowloon Jiǔlóng 九龙

kung-fu gōngfu 功夫

L

label n biāoqiān 标签

labor n (*work*) láodòng 劳 动; (*workers*) gōngrén 工 人; (*in pregnancy*) fēnmiǎn 分娩

laboratory shíyàn shì 实 验室

Labor Day Láodòngjié 劳 动节

lace n (*material*) huābiān 花 边; (*for shoe*) xiédài 鞋带

lack 1 n quēshǎo 缺少 2 v/t & v/i quēfá 缺乏

lacquerware qīqì 漆器

ladder tīzi 梯子

ladies' room nǚcè 女厕

lady nǚshì 女士

♦ lag behind luòhòu 落后

lake hú 湖

lamb gāoyáng 羔羊; (*meat*) gāoyáng ròu 羔羊肉

lame *person* qué 瘸

lamp dēng 灯

land 1 n tǔdì 土地; (*shore*) lùdì 陆地; (*country*) guójiā 国家 2 v/i (*of airplane*) zhuólù 着陆; (*of ball, stone*) luò 落

landing (*top of staircase*) (lóutī) píngtái (楼梯) 平台

landlady (*of apartment etc*) fángdōng 房东

landlord (*of apartment etc*) fángdōng 房东

landmark lùbiāo 路标; *fig* lǐchéng bēi 里程碑

landscape n fēngjǐng 风景

lane (*in country*) xiǎoxiàng 小巷; (*alley*) hútong 胡同; (*on freeway*) hángdào 行道

language yǔyán 语言

Lantern Festival Yuánxiāo-jié 元宵节

Lao Lǎowō yǔ 老挝语

Laos Lǎowō 老挝

Laotian 1 adj Lǎowō 老挝 **2** n (*person*) Lǎowōrén 老挝人

lap¹ n (*of track*) quān 圈

lap² n (*of person*) dàtuǐ 大腿

laptop COMPUT xiédài shì diànnǎo 携带式电脑

large dà 大; *sum* duō 多

largely (*mainly*) zhǔyào 主要

laryngitis hóuyán 喉炎

laser jīguāng 激光

last¹ adj (*in series*) zuìhòu 最后; (*preceding*) shàng yícì 上一次; ~ *but one* dàoshǔ dì'èrge 倒数第二个; ~ *night* zuówǎn 昨晚; *at* ~ zhōngyú 终于

last² v/i chíxù 持续

lastly zuìhòu 最后

late (*behind time*) chídào 迟到; (*in day*) wǎn 晚

lately zuìjìn 最近

later adv hòulái 后来

latest *news etc* zuìxīn 最新

latter hòuzhě 后者

laugh 1 n xiàoshēng 笑声 **2** v/i xiào 笑

♦ **laugh at** cháoxiào 嘲笑

laughter xiàoshēng 笑声

launch 1 n (*boat*) xiǎotǐng 小艇; (*of rocket*) fāshè 发射; (*of ship*) xiàshuǐ 下水; (*of product*) fāxíng 发行 **2** v/t rocket fāshè 发射; *new product* fāxíng 发行

launch pad fāshètái 发射台

laundromat zìzhù xǐyī diàn 自助洗衣店

laundry (*place*) xǐyī diàn 洗衣店; (*clothes*) yīwù 衣物

lavatory (*place*) cèsuǒ 厕所

law fǎlìng 法令; (*as subject*) fǎlǜ 法律

lawn cǎopíng 草坪

lawsuit sùsòng 诉讼

lawyer lǜshī 律师

lay v/t (*put down*) fàngxià 放下; *eggs* xià 下

layer n céng 层

layout n bùjú 布局; COMPUT géshì 格式

lazy lǎn 懒; *day* lìngrén lǎnsǎn 令人懒散

lead[1] **1** v/t *party etc*, *(take)* dàilíng 带领; *race* lǐngxiān 领先 **2** v/i *(in race, competition)* lǐngxiān 领先

lead[2] n *(for dog)* jiāngsheng 缰绳

lead[3] n *(substance)* qiān 铅

leader lǐngxiù 领袖

leadership *(of party etc)* lǐngdǎo dìwèi 领导地位

leading-edge adj *technology* lǐngxiān 领先

leaf yèzi 叶子

leaflet chuándān 传单

leak 1 n lòu 漏; *(to press etc)* xièlòu 泄漏 **2** v/i lòu 漏

lean[1] v/i *(at an angle)* wāi zhe 歪着; **~ against** kàozhe 靠着

lean[2] adj *meat* shòu 瘦

leap 1 n **& v/i** tiào 跳

learn xuéxí 学习

learning n *(knowledge)* zhīshi 知识; *(act)* xuéxí 学习

lease 1 n zūqī 租契 **2** v/t zū 租

least 1 adv *likely etc* zuìbù 最不 **2** n zuìshǎo 最少; **at ~** zhìshǎo 至少

leather n **& adj** pí 皮

leave 1 n *(vacation)* jiàqī 假期; **on ~** fàngjià 放假 **2** v/t *place* líkāi 离开; *person* yǔ...fēnshǒu 与...分手; *husband, wife* pāoqì 抛弃; *(forget, leave behind)* wàngjì 忘记; **~ X alone** *(not touch)* biépèng X 别碰 X; *(not interfere with)* bù dǎjiǎo 不打搅; **be left** shèngxia 剩下 **2** v/i líkāi 离开

lecture 1 n jiǎngzuò 讲座 **2** v/i *(at university)* jiāo 教

lecturer jiǎngshī 讲师

ledge *(of window)* chuāngtái 窗台

left 1 adj zuǒ 左 **2** n zuǒbiān 左边; POL zuǒpài 左派; **on the ~** zài zuǒbiān 在左边 **3** adv *turn etc* zài zuǒcè 在左侧

left-handed guànyòng zuǒshǒu 惯用左手

left-wing POL zuǒyì 左翼

leg tuǐ 腿

legacy yíchǎn 遗产

legal (*allowed*) héfǎ 合法；(*relating to the law*) fǎlǜ 法律

legality héfǎxìng 合法性

legalize shǐhéfǎ 使合法

legend chuánshuō 传说

legible yìbiànrèn 易辨认

legitimate héfǎ 合法

leisure kòngxián 空闲

lemon níngméng 柠檬

lend：◆ *X to Y* jiègěi Y X 借给 Y X

length chángdù 长度；*at ~ describe* xiángxì de 详细地；(*eventually*) zuìzhōng 最终

lengthen shǐ biàncháng 使变长

lenient kuāndà 宽大

lens yǎnjìng 眼镜；(*of camera*) jìngtóu 镜头

less：*eat / talk* ~ shǎo chī / shuō 少吃/说；~ *interesting* méi nàme yǒuqù 没那么有趣；~ *than $200* shǎoyú liǎngbǎi měiyuán 少于两百美元

lesson kè 课

let *v/t* (*allow*) ràng 让；~ *me go!* ràng wǒzǒu! 让我走！；~ *'s go* wǒmen zǒu

ba 我们走吧；◆ *go of* (*rope, handle*) fàngkāi 放开

lethal zhìmìng 致命

letter (*of alphabet*) zìmǔ 字母；(*in mail*) xìnjiàn 信件

lettuce shēngcài yè 生菜叶

leukemia báixuè bìng 白血病

level **1** *adj surface* píngtǎn 平坦；(*in score*) bìngjìn 并进 **2** *n* (*on scale*) shuǐpíng 水平；(*in hierarchy*) jíbié 级别；(*amount, quantity*) liángxì 量

lever *n* gànggǎn 杠杆

liable (*answerable*) fùzé 负责；*be ~ to* (*likely*) yǒu kěnéng huì 有可能

◆ liaise with yǔ … jiànlì liánxì 与…建立联系

liar shuōhuǎngzhě 说谎者

liberal *adj* (*broad-minded*) dàfāng 大方；POL zìyóu 自由

liberate jiěfàng 解放

liberty zìyóu 自由

library túshūguǎn 图书馆

license **1** *n* zhízhào 执照 **2** *v/t* xǔkě 许可

license number zhízhào hàomǎ 执照号码

license plate chēpái 车牌

lick v/t tiǎn 舔

lid gàizi 盖子

lie¹ **1** n (untruth) huǎnghuà 谎话 **2** v/i shuō huǎnghuà 说谎话

lie² v/i (of person: on back) tǎng 躺; (on stomach) pā 趴; (of object) píng fàngzhe 平放着; (be situated) wèiyú 位于

♦ lie down tǎngxià 躺下

life shēngmìng 生命

life insurance rénshòu bǎoxiǎn 人寿保险

life jacket jiùshēng yī 救生衣

lift **1** v/t jǔqǐ 举起 **2** v/i (of fog) xiāosàn 消散 **3** n (in car) dā biànchē 搭便车

light¹ **1** n guāngxiàn 光线; (lamp) dēng 灯; cigarette diǎnhuǒ 点火; (illuminate) zhàomíng 照明 **3** adj (not dark) míngliàng 明亮

light² adj (not heavy) qīng 轻

light bulb diàndēng pào 电灯泡

lighter (for cigarettes) dǎhuǒjī 打火机

lighting zhàomíng 照明

lightning shǎndiàn 闪电

like¹ prep xiàng 象

like² v/t xǐhuan 喜欢; **I ~ it** wǒxǐhuan 我喜欢; **I would ~ ...** wǒxiǎngyào ... 我想要...; **I would ~ to ...** wǒxīwàng ... 我希望...; **would you ~ ... ?** nǐyào ... ma? 你要...吗？; **~ to do X** xǐhào X 喜好X; **if you ~** suíbiàn nǐ 随便你

likeable kě'ài 可爱

likelihood kěnéngxìng 可能性

likely (probable) kěnéng 可能

limit **1** n xiàndù 限度 **2** v/t xiànzhì 限制

limp n bǒxíng 跛行

line¹ n (on paper, road) xiàntiáo 线条; diànhuà xiàn 电话线; TELEC (of people, trees) páiré 排; (of text) háng 行; (of business) zhíyè 职业

line² v/t (with material) ānchènlǐ 安衬里

♦ line up v/i páiduì 排队

linger (of person) dòuliú 逗留; (of pain) áizhe 挨着

lining (of clothes) chènlǐ 衬里

衬里

link 1 *n* liánjiē 连接; (*in chain*) yìjié 一节 **2** *v/t* liánjiē 连接

lip zuǐchún 嘴唇

lipstick kǒuhóng 口红

liqueur lìkǒu jiǔ 利口酒

liquid 1 *n* yètǐ 液体 **2** *adj* yèzhuàng 液状

liquor jiǔjīng yǐnliào 酒精 饮料

liquor store mài jiǔdiàn 卖 酒店

list *n* yīlán biǎo 一览表

listen tīng 听

♦ **listen to** tīng 听

literature wénxué 文学

litter lājī 垃圾

little 1 *adj* xiǎo 小 **2** *n*: a ~ yīdiǎn 一点; a ~ wine yīdiǎn jiǔ 一点酒 **3** *adv* shāoxǔ 稍许; ~ by ~ zhújiànde 逐渐地; a ~ better hǎo yīdiǎn 好一点

live¹ *v/i* (*reside*) zhùzài 住在; (*be alive*) shēnghuó 生活

live² *adj* broadcast shíkuàng 实况

livelihood shēngjì 生计

lively huópō 活泼

liver MED gānzàng 肝藏

(*food*) gān 肝

livestock shēngchù 牲畜

living 1 *adj* huóde 活的 **2** *n* móushēng 谋生

living room kètīng 客厅

load 1 *n* fùdàn 负担 **2** *v/t* zhuāng 装

loaf miànbāo 面包

loan 1 *n* dàikuǎn 贷款; on ~ jièyòng 借用 **2** *v/t* jiè 借

local 1 *adj* dìfang 地方 **2** *n* (*person*) běndìrén 本地人

local call TELEC qūnèi diànhuà 区内电话

locally zài dāngdì 在当地

local time dāngdì shíjiān 当地时间

locate factory etc shèzhì 设置; (*identify position of*) zhǎochū 找出

lock *n* & *v/t* door suǒ 锁

locker yǒusuǒguì 有锁柜

log (*wood*) yuánmù 圆木; (*written record*) jìlù 记录

logic luójí 逻辑

logical yǒu luójí 有逻辑

logo biāozhì 标志

London Lúndūn 伦敦

lonely person gūdú 孤独; place jìmò 寂寞

long¹ 1 *adj* cháng 长;

journey yuǎn 远；*it's a ~ way* hěnyuǎn a 很远啊 **2** adv chángjiǔ 长久；*~ before* lǎozǎo 老早；*before ~* bùjiǔ 不久；*so ~ as (provided)* zhǐyào 只要；*so ~!* mànzǒu! 慢走!

long² v/i: *~ for X* pànwàng X 盼望 X；*be ~ing to do X* kě wàng zuò X 渴望做 X

long-distance adj phonecall chángtú 长途；race, flight yuǎn jùlí 远距离

long jump tiàoyuǎn 跳远

long-range missile yuǎnchéng 远程；forecast chángyuǎn 长远

long-term adj chángqī 长期

look 1 n (appearance) wàiguān 外观；(glance) kàn看；*have a ~ at* (examine) kànyíkàn kàn yīkàn 看一看；*can I have a ~?* wǒ néng kàn yíxià ma? 我能看一下吗？**2** v/i kàn 看；(search) xúnzhǎo 寻找；(seem) sìhū 似乎；*you ~ tired* nǐ kànqǐlái hěn lèi 你看起来很累

♦ **look after** zhàogù 照顾

♦ **look at** kàn 看；(examine) jiǎnchá 检查

♦ **look for** zhǎo 找

♦ **look out** v/i (of window) cháowàikàn 朝外看；*~!* xiǎoxīn! 小心!

♦ **look up to** (respect) zūnjìng 尊敬

loose wire, button sōng 松；clothes kuānsōng 宽松；morals fàngdàng 放荡

loosen jiěkāi 解开

lorry Br huòchē 货车

lose 1 v/t object diūshī 丢失；game shū 输；*I'm lost* wǒ mílù le 我迷路了 **2** v/i sp shūdiào 输掉；(of clock) zǒumàn 走慢

loser sp shūzhě 输者

loss (of object) sǔnshī 损失；(of loved one) sàngshī 丧失；(in business) kuīsǔn 亏损

lost shīqù 失去

lot: *a ~/a ~ of* hěnduō 很多；*a ~ better* hǎo de duō 好得多

lotion xǐjì 洗剂

loud xiǎng 响

loudspeaker yángshēngqì 扬声器

lousy bù zěnme yàng 不怎

么样; *thing to do* tǎoyàn
讨厌

love 1 *n* ài 爱; *(in tennis)*
língfēn 零分; *be in ~* zài
liàn'ài zhīzhōng 在恋爱之
中; *fall in ~ with* àishàng 爱
上 2 *v/t* ài 爱

love affair fēngliú yùnshì 风
流韵事

lovely *face, hair* měilì 美丽;
color piàoliang 漂亮; *tune*
yōuměi 优美; *person, meal*
hěn hǎo 很好; *vacation,
day* lìngrén yúkuài 令人
愉快

lover qíngrén 情人

low 1 *adj wall* ǎi 矮; *salary,
price, voice* dī 低; *quality*
chà 差 2 *n (in statistics)* zuì
dīdiǎn 最低点

loyal zhōngxīn 忠心

luck yùnqì 运气; *bad ~* èyùn
恶运; *good ~* xìngyùn 幸

运; *good ~!* zhùnǐ zǒuyùn!
祝你走运！

luckily xìngyùnde 幸运地

lucky *person* xìngyùn 幸运;
day, number jíxiáng 吉祥;
you were ~ nǐ zhēn zǒuyùn
你真走运

luggage xíngli 行李

lukewarm wēiwēn 微温;
reception bú rèqíng 不热情

lull *n* zànshí píngxī 暂时
平息

lump *(of sugar)* kuài 块;
(swelling) zhǒngkuài 肿块

lump sum zǒng'é 总额

lunar yuèliang 月亮

lunatic *n* fēngzi 疯子

lunch wǔcān 午餐

lung fèi 肺

lung cancer fèi'ái 肺癌

lust *n* xìngyù 性欲

luxury *n & adj* háohuá 豪华

lychee lìzhī 荔枝

M

Macao Àomén 澳门

machine *n* jīqì 机器

macho dànánzǐ qì 大男
子气

mad fēng 疯

made-to-measure dìngzuò
定做

madness jīngshén shīcháng

精神失常

magazine (*printed*) zázhì
杂志

magic 1 *n* mófǎ 魔法;
(*tricks*) móshù 魔术 **2** *adj*
jiémiào 绝妙

magnetic yǒucíxìng 有磁性

magnificent zhuàngguān
壮观

magnify fàngdà 放大

mah-jong májiàng 麻将

maid nǔpú 女仆; (*in hotel*)
nǔ qīnglǐgōng 女清理工

mail 1 *n* yóuzhèng 邮政 **2** *v/t*
letter yóujì 邮寄

mailbox (*in street*) yóutǒng
邮筒; (*for house, e-mail*)
xìnxiāng 信箱

mailman yóudìyuán 邮递员

main *adj* zhǔyào 主要

mainland dàlù 大陆

mainland China Zhōngguó
dàlù 中国大陆

mainly zhǔyào 主要

main street zhǔjiē 主街

maintain *law and order*
wéichí 维持; *speed* bǎochí
保持; *machine* bǎoyǎng 保
养; *innocence* jiānchí 坚持

major 1 *adj* zhǔyào 主要 **2** *n*
MIL shàoxiào 少校

majority dàduōshù 大多数;
POL duōdéde piàoshù 多得
的票数

make 1 *n* (*brand*) páizi 牌
子 **2** *v/t* zuò 做; ~ **X do Y**
(*force to*) bī X zuò Y 逼
使X做Y; (*cause to*) cùshǐ
X zuò Y 促使X做Y; ~ **X**
happy shǐ X gāoxìng 使
X高兴; **made in China**
Zhōngguó zhìzào 中国
制造

♦ **make out** *check* kāichū 开
出; (*see*) biànrèn 辨认;
(*imply*) ànshì 暗示

♦ **make up 1** *v/i* (*after
quarrel*) héjiě 和解
2 *v/t story* biānzào 编
造; (*constitute*) zhàn 占;
be made up of X yóu X
zǔchéng 由X组成

♦ **make up for** bǔbù 弥补

maker zhìzàozhě 制造者

make-up (*cosmetics*)
huàzhuāngpǐn 化妆品

Malay Mǎláixīyà rén 马来西
亚人; (*language*) Mǎlái yǔ
马来语

Malaysia Mǎláixīyà 马来
西亚

Malaysian Mǎláixīyà 马

来西亚

male 1 *adj* nánxìng 男性; *animal* xióng 雄 **2** *n* nánrén 男人; *(animal)* xióngxìng 雄性

male chauvinist dànánzǐ zhǔyìzhě 大男子主义者

malfunction 1 *n* shīlíng 失灵 **2** *v/i* fāshēng gùzhàng 发生故障

mall *(shopping ~)* gòuwù zhōngxīn 购物中心

malnutrition yíngyǎng bùliáng 营养不良

man *n* nánrén 男人; *(human being)* rén 人; *(humanity)* rénlèi 人类

manage 1 *v/t business* jīngyíng 经营; *money* guǎn 管; *suitcase etc* nádòng 拿动; **to ...** zuòchéng ... 做成... **2** *v/i (cope)* yìngfu 应付

management guǎnlǐ 管理; *(managers)* zhǔguǎn rényuán 主管人员

manager jīnglǐ 经理

managing director zǒngjīnglǐ 总经理

Mandarin Pǔtōnghuà 普通话

mandatory qiángzhì 强制

maneuver 1 *n* xíngdòng 行动 **2** *v/t* shèfǎyídòng 设法移动

maniac kuángrén 狂人

manipulate *person* bǎibù 摆布

manner *(of doing sth)* fāngshì 方式; *(attitude)* tàidu 态度

manners: good / bad ~ yǒu / méiyǒu lǐmào 有 / 没有礼貌; **have no ~** méilǐmào 没礼貌

manpower láodònglì 劳动力

manual 1 *adj* shǒugōng 手工 **2** *n book* zhǐnán 指南

manufacture *n & v/t* zhìzào 制造

manufacturer zhìzàoshāng 制造商

many *adj & pron* xǔduō 许多; **too ~ ...** tàiduō... 太多 ...; **how ~ do you need?** nǐ xūyào duōshao? 你需要多少?

mao *(money)* máo 毛

Mao Tse-tung Máo Zédōng 毛泽东

map *n* dìtú 地图

March sānyuè 三月

march 1 n xíngjūn 行军；(demo) yóuxíng 游行 **2** v/i (in protest) yóuxíng 游行

margin (of page) kòngbái 空白，com yínglì 盈利

marine 1 adj hǎiyáng 海洋 **2** n MIL hǎilùbīng 海陆兵

mark 1 n (stain) wūdiǎn 污点，(sign, token) biāozhì 标志，(trace) jìxiàng 迹象，EDU fēnshù 分数 **2** v/t (stain) liú hénjì yú 留痕迹于，(indicate) biāomíng 标明

market 1 n jíshì 集市，(for particular commodity) shìchǎng 市场 **2** v/t xiā oshòu 销售

market economy shìchǎng jīngjì 市场经济

marketing tuīxiāo 推销

market research shìchǎng diàochá 市场调查

mark-up jiàgé tígāo 价格提高

marriage (institution) hūnyīnzhì 婚姻制，(being married) hūnyīn 婚姻，(event) hūnlǐ 婚礼

marriage certificate jiéhūn zhèngshū 结婚证书

married yǐhūn 已婚；**be ~ to X** yǔ X jiéhūn 与X 结婚

marry jiéhūn 结婚；**get married** jiéhūn 结婚

martial arts wǔshù 武术

marvelous jíhǎo 极好

Marxism Mǎkèsīzhǔyì 马克思主义

mascara jiémáogāo 睫毛膏

masculine nánzǐqì 男子气

mass (great amount) zhòngduō 众多

massacre n dàtúshā 大屠杀

massage n ànmó 按摩

massive jùdà 巨大

master 1 n (of dog) zhǔrén 主人，(of ship) chuánzhǎng 船长 **2** v/t skill jīngtōng 精通

masterpiece jiézuò 杰作

mastery jīngtōng 精通

match[1] (for light) huǒchái 火柴

match[2] **1** n (competition) bǐsài 比赛 **2** v/t (be the same as) yǔ … yíyàng 与 … 一样 **3** v/i (of colors etc) xiāngpèi 相配

matching adj xiétiáo 协调

mate 1 n (of animal) ǒu 偶 **2** v/i jiāopèi 交配

material *n* (*fabric*) bùliào
布料; (*substance*) cáiliào
材料

materials yuánliào 原料

maternal mǔqīn fāngmiàn 母
亲方面

maternity mǔxìng 母性

math shùxué 数学

mathematical shùxué 数学

matter (*affair*) shìqing 事
情; PHYS wùzhì 物质

what's the ~? zěnmele?
怎么了? *it ~s* yàojǐn 要
紧; *it doesn't ~* méiguānxi
没关系

mattress chuángdiàn 床垫

mature *adj* chéngshú 成熟

maturity chéngshú 成熟

maximum 1 *adj* (*highest*)
zuìgāo 最高; (*biggest*)
zuìdà 最大 **2** *n* zuìduō
最多

May wǔyuè 五月

may ◇ (*possibility*) yěxǔ
也许; *it ~ rain* kěnéng
huì xiàyǔ 可能会下雨 ◇
(*permission*) kěyǐ 可以

maybe kěnéng 可能

May Day Wǔyī Jié 五一节

mayonnaise dànhuángjiàng
蛋黄酱

me wǒ 我

meal cān 餐

mean¹ (*with money*) lìnsè 吝
啬; (*nasty*) bēibǐ 卑鄙

mean² (*intend*) yìzhǐ 意
指; (*signify*) biǎoshì 表示

meaning hányì 含义

means (*financial*) cáiyuán 财
源; (*way*) fāngfǎ 方法

meantime: *in the ~* tóngshí
同时

measure 1 *n* (*step*) cuòshī
措施 **2** *v/t* cèliáng 测量

measurement chǐcun 尺寸;
(*action*) cèliáng 测量

meat ròu 肉

mechanic jìgōng 技工

mechanism jīxiè zhuāngzhì
机械装置

medal jiǎngzhāng 奖章

media: *the ~* dàzhòng
chuánméi 大众传媒

median strip zhōngyāng
fēnchēdài 中央分车带

mediator tiáojiěrén 调解人

medical 1 *adj* yīliáo 医疗
2 *n* tǐgé jiǎnchá 体格检查

medicine (*science*) yīxué 医
学; (*medication*) yào 药

mediocre píngyōng 平庸

meditate míngxiǎng 冥想

medium 1 adj zhōngděng 中
等 **2** n (in size) zhōnghào
中号

meet 1 v/t jiàn 见; (collect)
jiē 接; (satisfy) dádào 达
到 **2** v/i jiànmiàn 见面; (in
competition) bǐsài 比赛; (of
committee etc) jùhé 聚合
    3 n SP yùndònghuì 运动会

meeting huìyì 会议

melon guā 瓜

melt v/t & v/i rónghuà 融化

member chéngyuán 成员

memo bèiwànglù 备忘录

memoirs huíyìlù 回忆录

memorable zhídé jìniàn 值
得纪念

memorial n jìniànbēi 纪念碑

memorize jìzhù 记住

memory jìyì 记忆; (power of
recollection) jìyìlì 记忆力

mend v/t xiūlǐ 修理

men's room náncè 男厕

mental jīngshén 精神

mentality xīnlǐ zhuàngtài 心
理状态

mention v/t tídào 提到;
don't ~ it búyòng kèqì 不
用客气

menu also COMPUT càidān
菜单

merchandise huòpǐn 货品

mercy réncí 仁慈

merger COM hébìng 合并

merit n (worth) jiàzhí 价值;
(advantage) yōudiǎn 优点

merry yúkuài 愉快

mess n zānggluàn 脏乱;
(trouble) kùnjìng 困境

message qǐshì 启示; **can I
leave a ~?** wǒkěyǐ liúyán
ma? 我可以留言吗？

messy room língluàn 凌乱;
person lāta 邋遢

metal n & adj jīnshǔ 金属

meter¹ (for measuring) biǎo
表; (parking ~) tíngchē jìshí
qì 停车计时器

meter² (unit of length) mǐ 米

method fāngfǎ 方法

methodical yǒutiáolǐ 有
条理

metropolitan adj dà dūshì
大都市

microphone màikèfēng 麦
克风

microwave wēibōlú 微波炉

midday zhōngwǔ 中午

middle 1 adj zhōngjiān 中间
    2 n zhōngyāng 中央

middle-aged zhōngnián
中年

middle-class adj zhōngchǎn jiējí 中产阶级

Middle East Zhōngdōng 中东

midnight wǔyè 午夜

Midwest Zhōngxībù 中西部

might yěxǔ 也许; *I ~ be late* wǒyěxǔ chídào 我也许迟到

mild wēnhé 温和

mile yīnglǐ 英里

militant n jījí fènzǐ 积极分子

military 1 adj jūnshì 军事 **2** n: *the ~* jūnduì 军队

milk n nǎi 奶

millionaire bǎiwànfùwēng 百万富翁

mimic v/t mófǎng 模仿

mind 1 n tóunǎo 头脑; *change one's ~* gǎibiàn zhǔyì 改变主意 **2** v/t (*look after*) zhàokàn 照看; (*object to*) jièyì 介意; (*heed*) liúxīn 留心; *~ your own business!* bùguān nǐ de shì! 不关你的事! **3** v/i: *~!* (*be careful*) dāngxīn 当心; *never ~!* méiguānxì! 没关系! *I don't ~* wǒwúsuǒwèi 我无所谓

mine[1] pron wǒde 我的

mine[2] n (*for coal etc*) kuàng 矿

mine[3] n (*explosive*) dìléi 地雷

mineral n kuàngwù 矿物

mineral water kuàngquánshuǐ 矿泉水

miniature adj xiùzhēnxíng 袖珍型

minimal zuìxiǎo 最小

minimum 1 adj zuìshǎo 最少 **2** n zuìdīxiàndù 最低限度

minor 1 adj cìyào 次要 **2** n LAW wèichéngniánrén 未成年人

minority shǎoshù 少数

minute[1] n (*of time*) fēnzhōng 分钟

minute[2] adj (*tiny*) wēixiǎo 微小; (*detailed*) xiángxì 详细

minutes (*of meeting*) jìlù 记录

miracle qíjì 奇迹

mirror n jìngzi 镜子

miscarriage MED liúchǎn 流产

miserable nánguò 难过; *day* lìngrén bùkuài 令人不快

misfortune búxìng 不幸

misjudge cuòwù gūjì 错

误估计

misleading shǐ rén wùjiě 使人误解

misprint n cuòyìn 错印

miss¹: **Miss Wang** Wáng xiǎojiě 王小姐

miss² v/t (not hit) wèijīzhòng 未击中; (emotionally) xiǎngniàn 想念; bus méigǎnshàng 没赶上; (not notice, fail to take) cuòguò 错过; (not be present at) bùchūxí 不出席

missile (guided) dǎodàn 导弹

missing diūshī 丢失; be ~ xiàluòbùmíng 下落不明

mist bówù 薄雾

mistake 1 n cuòwù 错误; **make a ~** fàn cuòwù 犯错误 2 v/t wùjiāng X rènzuò Y 误将X认作Y

mistress (lover) qíngfù 情妇; (of dog) nǚzhǔrén 女主人

mistrust 1 n búxìnrèn 不信任 2 v/t huáiyí 怀疑

misty bówù lǒngzhào 薄雾笼罩

misunderstand wùjiě 误解

misunderstanding wùjiě 误解

mitt (in baseball) bàngqiú shǒutào 棒球手套

mix 1 n (mixture) hùnhé 混合; (in cooking) hùnhéwù 混合物 2 v/t hùnhé 混合 3 v/i (socially) xiāngchǔ 相处

mixed feelings fùzá 复杂

mixture hùnhéwù 混合物; MED fùfāngyào 复方药

moan v/i (in pain) shēnyín 呻吟

mob n bàomín 暴民

mobile 1 adj kěyídòng 可移动 2 n (for decoration) fēngdòng shìwù 风动饰物; Br (phone) shǒujī 手机

mock v/t qǔxiào 取笑

mockery (derision) cháonòng 嘲弄

model 1 n boat, plane móxíng 模型 2 n (miniature) chúxíng 雏型; (pattern) móshì 模式; (fashion) mótèr 模特儿

modem tiáozhì jiětiáoqì 调制解调器

moderate 1 adj shìdù 适度; POL wēnhé 温和 2 n POL wēnhépài 温和派

modern xiàndài 现代

modernize 1 *v/t* shǐ xiàndàihuà 使现代化 **2** *v/i* xiàndàihuà 现代化

modest *house* pǔsù 朴素; (*not conceited*) qiānxùn 谦逊

modify xiūgǎi 修改

moist cháoshī潮湿

moisturizer (*for skin*) rùnfūshuāng 润肤霜

mold¹ *n* (*on food*) méi 霉

mold²1 *n* múzi 模子 **2** *v/t* clay etc jiāozhù 浇铸

mom mā 妈

moment piànkè 片刻; **at the ~** xiànzài 现在; **for the ~** zànshí 暂时

Monday xīngqīyī 星期一

monetary huòbì 货币

money qián 钱

Mongolia Měnggǔ 蒙古

Mongolian 1 *adj* Měnggǔ 蒙古 **2** *n* (*person*) Měnggǔrén 蒙古人

monitor 1 *n* COMPUT jiānshìqì 监视器 **2** *v/t* jiānkòng 监控

monopolize lǒngduàn 垄断

monopoly dúzhàn 独占

monosodium glutamate wèijīng 味精

monotonous dāndiào fáwèi 单调乏味

month yuè 月

monthly *adj* měiyuè 每月

monument jìniànbēi 纪念碑

mood xīnqíng 心情; (*bad ~*) huàiqíngxù 坏情绪; *be in a good* / *bad ~* qíngxù hǎo / huài 情绪好 / 坏

moon yuèliang 月亮

moral 1 *adj* dàodé 道德 **2** *n* (*of story*) yùyì 寓意; ~*s* xíngwéi biāozhǔn 行为标准

morale shìqì 士气

morality měidé 美德

more 1 *adj* gèngduō 更多; *some ~ tea?* zài láidiǎnr chá ma? 再来点儿茶吗？ **2** *adv* gèng (duō) 更(多); *~ important* gèng zhòngyào 更重要; *once ~* zàiyícì 再一次; *~ than* duōyú 多于; *I don't live there any more* wǒbúzài zhù nàrle 我不再住那了了 **3** *pron: do you want some ~?* nǐ hái yàodiǎnr ma? 你还要点儿吗？

moreover érqiě 而且

morning shàngwǔ 上 午;
(early) zǎochén 早 晨;
good ~ shàngwǔ hǎo 上 午
好; zǎochén hǎo 早晨好

morphine mǎfēi 吗啡

Moscow Mòsīkē 莫斯科

mosquito wénzi 蚊子

most 1 adj duōshù 多数
2 adv (very) hěn 很; **the ~
interesting** zuì yǒuqù 最
有趣; **~ of all** zuì zhòngyào
最重要 **3** pron dàduōshù
大多数; **at ~** zhìduō至多

mostly zhǔyào 主要

mother mǔqīn 母亲

mother-in-law (of man)
yuèmǔ岳母; (of woman)
pópo 婆婆

mother tongue mǔyǔ 母语

motivation dònglì 动力

motive dòngjī 动机

motor fādòngjī 发动机

motorbike mótuōchē 摩
托车

motorcyclist qí mótuōchēde
rén 骑摩托车的人

motor rickshaw bèngbèng-
chē 蹦蹦车

mountain shān 山

mountaineering dēngshān
yùndòng 登山运动

mourn v/t dàoniàn 悼念

mouse shǔ 鼠; COMPUT
shǔbiāo 鼠标

mouth zuǐ 嘴; (of river)
hékǒu 河口

move 1 n (in chess) yíbù
一步; (step, action)
jǔcuò 举措; (change
of house) bānjiā 搬家
2 v/t object yídòng 移动;
(transfer) zhuǎnyí 转移;
(emotionally) gǎndòng 感
动 **3** v/i yídòng 移 动; (transfer)
zhuǎn 转

movement dòngzuò 动作;
(organization) yùndòng 运
动; MUS yuèzhāng 乐章

movie diànyǐng 电影

movie theater diànyǐngyuàn
电影院

moving (emotionally) gǎnrén
感人

mph (= miles per hour)
yīnglǐshísù 英里时速

Mr xiānsheng 先生; **~ Wang**
Wáng xiānsheng 王先生

Mrs tàitai 太太; **~ Wang**
Wáng tàitai 王太太

Ms nǚshì 女士; **~ Wang**
Wáng nǚshì 王女士

much 1 adj xǔduō 许多

***there's not ~ ...** méiyǒu
duōshao ... 没有多少...
2 *adv* hěn 很; **I don't like
him ~** wǒ bútài xǐhuan
tā 我不太喜欢他; ~
better hǎo de duō 好得
多; **very ~** fēicháng 非常;
too ~ guòduō 过多 **3** *pron*
duōshǎo 多少; **nothing ~**
méi shénme 没什么
mud ní 泥
mug¹ *n* (for drink) dàbēi
大杯
mug² *v/t* (attack) xíngxiōng
qiǎngjié 行凶抢劫
multinational *n* COM duōguó
多国
multiple *adj* duōgè 多个
multiply *v/t* chéng 乘
murder *n & v/t* móushā

谋杀
murderer xiōngshǒu 凶手
muscle jīròu 肌肉
museum bówùguǎn 博物馆
mushroom *n* mógu 蘑菇
music yīnyuè 音乐; (written)
yuèpǔ 乐谱
musician yīnyuèjiā 音乐家
must bìxū 必须; **I ~n't be
late** wǒbùnéng chídào 我
不能迟到
mustache bāzi hú 八字胡
mustard jièmò 芥末
mutter 1 *v/i* gūnong 咕哝
2 *v/t* dīshēng shuō 低声说
mutual xiānghù 相互
my wǒde 我的
myself wǒzìjǐ 我自己
mysterious shénmì 神秘
mystery mí 谜

N

nag *v/i* (of person) láodao
bùtíng 唠叨不停
nail (for wood) dīng 钉; (on
finger, toe) zhǐjia 指甲
nail file zhǐjia cuò 指甲锉
nail polish zhǐjia yóu 指
甲油

naive tiānzhēn 天真
naked luǒtǐ 裸体
name *n* míngzi 名字; **what's
your ~?** nǐ jiào shénme
míngzi? 你叫什么名字？
nap *n* xiǎoshuì 小睡
narrow street, bed etc xiázhǎi

狭窄; *views* xiá'ài 狭隘;
victory miǎnqiǎng 勉强
narrow-minded xīnxiōng
xiázhǎi 心胸狭窄
nasty *person, remark* bēibí
卑鄙; *smell, weather* èliè
劣; *cut, disease* yánzhòng
严重
nation guójiā 国家
national 1 *adj* guólì 国立;
newspaper, security guójiā
国家; *pride* àiguó 爱国 **2** *n*
guómín 国民
Nationalist Party (*KMT*)
Guómíndǎng 国民党
nationality guójí 国籍
nationalize shǐguóyǒu huà
使国有化
National People's Congress
Quánguó Rénmín Dàibiǎo
Dàhuì 全国人民代表
大会
native *adj* (*of country*)
běnguó 本国; (*of place*)
běndì 本地
natural zìrán 自然; *flavor*
tiānrán 天然
natural gas tiānrán qì 天
然气
naturally (*of course*) dāngrán
当然; *behave* zìrán 自然;

(*by nature*) tiānshēng 天生
nature zìrán 自然; (*of
person*) xìnggé 性格; (*of
problem*) běnzhì 本质
naughty táoqì 淘气
nausea ěxin 恶心
nauseous: feel ~ juéde ěxin
得恶心
nautical hánghǎi 航海
naval hǎijūn 海军
navigate *v/i* cèháng 测航
navigator (*on ship*) hánghǎi
jiā 航海家; (*in airplane*)
jiàshǐyuán 驾驶员
navy hǎijūn 海军
navy blue *n* & *adj* hǎijūn lán
海军蓝
near 1 *adj* & *adv* jìn 近
2 *prep* jiējìn 接近; **~ the
bank** kàojìn yínháng 靠
近银行
nearby *adv* zài fùjìn 在附近
nearly jīhū 几乎
neat zhěngjié 整洁; *whiskey*
chún 纯; *solution* qiǎomiào
巧妙; F (*terrific*) tǐnghǎo
挺好
necessary bìbù kěshǎo 必不
可少; **it is ~ to** yǒu bìyào
zuò 有必要做
necessity bìyàoxìng 必要

性; (*sth necessary*) bìxūpǐn
必需品

neck bózi 脖子

necklace xiàngliàn 项链

necktie lǐngdài 领带

need 1 *n* xūyào 需要; *in ~*
yǒu kùnnán 有困难 **2** *v/t*
xūyào 需要; *you don't ~*
to wait nǐ búbì děngzhe 你
不必等着

needle (*for sewing*) zhēn 针;
(*for injection*) zhēntóu 针
头; (*on dial*) zhǐzhēn 指针

negative *adj* GRAM fǒudìng
否定; *attitude, person* xiāojí
消极; ELEC fùdiàn 负电

neglect 1 *n* hūlüè 忽略 **2** *v/t*
zhàogù bùzhōu 照顾不周

negligence wánhū zhíshǒu
玩忽职守

negotiate *v/t & v/i* xiéshāng
协商

neighbor línjū 邻居

neighborhood jiēqū 街区

neither 1 *adj* liǎngzhě dōu
bù 两者都不 **2** *pron*
něige dōu bù 哪个都不;
~ of them recognized
me tāmenliǎ shéi dōu méi
rènchūwǒ lai 他们俩谁
都没认出我来 **3** *adv*: *~*

... nor ... jìbù ... yěbù ...
既不... 也不...**4** *conj* yě
bù 也不; *~ do I* wǒ yěbù
我也不

Nepal Níbó'ěr 尼泊尔

Nepalese 1 *adj* Níbó'ěr 尼
泊尔 **2** *n* Níbó'ěrrén 尼泊
尔人; (*language*) Níbó'ěr
yǔ尼泊尔语

nephew (*brother's son*)
zhízi 侄子; (*sister's son*)
wàisheng 外甥

nerve shénjīng 神经

nervous jǐnzhāng 紧张

net *adj price* chún 纯; *weight*
jìng 净

net profit jìnglì 净利

network liánluò wǎng 联络
网; COMPUT wǎngluò 网络

neurotic *adj* shénjīng zhì
神经质

neutral 1 *adj country* zhōnglì
中立; *color* fēi cǎisè 非彩
色 **2** *n* (*gear*) kōngdǎng
空档

neutrality zhōnglì dìwèi 中
立地位

never (*past*) cónglái méi 从
来没; (*present*) cónglái bù
从来不; (*future*) juébúhuì
绝不会

nevertheless dànshì 但是

new xīn 新

news xīnwén 新闻; (TV, radio) xīnwén bàodǎo 新闻报道

newspaper bàozhǐ 报纸

New Territories (in Hong Kong) Xīnjiè 新界

New Year Xīnnián 新年; (Chinese) Chūnjié 春节; **Happy ~!** Xīnnián kuàilè! 新年快乐!

New Year's Day (Jan 1) Yuándàn 元旦; (Chinese) Chūyī 初一

New Year's Eve (Dec 31) Yuándàn Qiányè 元旦前夜; (Chinese) Chúxī 除夕

New York Niǔyuē 纽约

next 1 adj (in time, space) xià yíge 下一个 **2** adv xià yíbù 下一步; **to X** (beside) zài X de pángbiān 在X的旁边; (in comparison with) yǔ X xiāngbǐ 与X相比

next door adj & adv gébì 隔壁

next of kin zuìjìnde qīnshǔ 最近的亲属

nice hǎo 好

nickname n wàihào 外号

niece (brother's daughter) zhínǚ 侄女; (sister's daughter) wài shengnǚ 外甥女

night yè 夜; **11 o'clock at ~** wǎnshàng shíyídiǎn 晚上十一点; **good ~** wǎn'ān 晚安

nightclub yèzǒnghuì 夜总会

nightdress shuìyī 睡衣

nightmare èmèng 恶梦; fig kěpàde jīnglì 可怕的经历

night school yèxiào 夜校

no 1 adv bù 不; **do you understand? –** ~ nǐ dǒng ma? – bùdǒng 你懂吗？– 不懂 **2** adj méiyǒu 没有; **I have ~ money** wǒ méiyǒu qián 我没有钱; ~ **parking** jìnzhǐ tíngchē 禁止停车

nobody méirén 没人

nod n & v/i diàntóu 点头

noise shēngyīn 声音; (loud, unpleasant) zàoyīn 噪音

noisy xuānhuá 喧哗

nominate (appoint) tímíng 提名; ~ **X for a post** (propose) tuījiàn X rèn mǒuge zhíwèi 推荐X任某个职位

nonalcoholic bù hán jiǔjīng 不含酒精

noncommittal bù mínglǎng 不明朗

none méiyǒu yígè 没有一个

nonetheless rán'ér 然而

nonpayment wèifù 未付

nonsense húshuō hú shuō 胡说

nonsmoker bù xīyānzhě 不吸烟者

nonstop adj & adv zhídá 直达; chatter bùtíng 不停

noodles miàntiáo 面条

noon zhōngwǔ 中午

nor yòubù 又不; ~ do I wǒ yěbù 我也不

normal zhèngcháng 正常

normally (usually) yìbān de 一般地; (in a normal way) zhèngcháng de 正常地

north 1 n miàntiáo 北部 2 adj běibù 北部 3 adv travel xiàngběi 向北

North America Běiměi 北美

North American 1 adj Běiměizhōu 北美洲 2 n Běiměizhōu rén 北美洲人

northern běifāng 北方

nose bízi 鼻子

nosebleed liú bíxuè 流鼻血

nostalgia huáijiù 怀旧

nosy hàoguǎn xiánshì 好管闲事

not ◊ (present and future) bù 不; ~ there nàr bùxíng 那儿不行; ~ like that bùnéng nàyàng 不能那样; ~ a lot yìdiǎndian 一点点 ◊ (past tense, and with yǒu) méi 没; we don't have a car wǒmen méiyǒu chē 我们没有车

note n (short letter) biàntiáo 便条; MUS yīndiào 音调; (comment on text) zhùshì 注释; take ~s jì bǐjì 记笔记

notebook also COMPUT bǐjìběn 笔记本

notepaper biàntiáo zhǐ 便条纸

nothing méiyǒu shénme 没有什么; ~ for me thanks wǒ shénme yě búyào xièxie 我什么也不要谢谢; ~ but zhǐ 只

notice 1 n (on bulletin board, in newspaper) tōnggào 通告; (advance warning) yùxiān tōngzhī 预先通知; (to leave job) cízhí tōngzhī 辞职通知; (to leave house)

zūlìn tōngzhī 租赁通知;
at short ~ tūrán 突然;
take ~ *of X* zhùyì X 注意
X; *take no* ~ *of X* búyào
guǎn X 不要管 X **2** *v/t*
zhùyì 注意
notify tōngzhī 通知
notorious shēngmíng lángjí
声名狼籍
nourishing yǒu yíngyǎng
有营养
novel *n* xiǎoshuō 小说
novelist xiǎoshuōjiā 小说家
November shíyīyuè 十一月
novice xuétú 学徒
now xiànzài 现在; ~ *and
again* yǒushí yǒu shí; *by* ~
zhèshí 这时; *from* ~ *on*
cóng xiànzài kāishǐ 从现
在开始; *right* ~ cǐkè 此刻

nowadays xiànjīn 现今
nowhere wúchù 无处
nuclear yuánzhě 原子核
nuclear energy hénéng 核能
nuclear power station
hénéngzhàn 核能站
nuclear weapons hé wǔqì
核武器
nude *adj* luǒtǐ 裸体
nuisance fánrén 烦人
number *n* (*figure*) shùmù 数
目; (*quantity*) ruògān 若
干; (*of room, phone etc*)
shùzì 数字
numerous xǔduō 许多
nurse hùshì 护士
nut jiānguǒ 坚果; (*for bolt*)
luómǔ 螺母
nutritious yǒu yíngyǎng
有营养

O

oath LAW shìyán 誓言
obedience fúcóng 服从
obedient fúcóng 服从
obey fúcóng 服从
obituary fúgào 讣告
object¹ *n* wùtǐ 物体; (*aim*)
mùdì 目的; GRAM bīnyǔ

宾语
object² *v/i* fǎnduì 反对
objection fǎnduì 反对
objective **1** *adj* kèguān 客观
2 *n* mùbiāo 目标
obligation yìwù 义务
obliterate *city* huǐmiè 毁灭;

memory chúqú 除去

obnoxious yǐnrén fǎngǎn 引人反感

obscene yínhuì 淫秽

observant liúxīn 留心

observation (*of nature*) guānchá 观察; (*comment*) yìjiàn 意见

observe *behavior* zhùyì 注意; *people* kàndào 看到; *nature* guāncè 观测

obsession pǐ 癖; (*with a person, hobby*) zháomí 着迷

obsolete yīfèiqì 已废弃

obstacle zhàng'ài 障碍

obstinate wángù 顽固

obstruct *road* zǔsè 阻塞; *investigation* zǔdǎng 阻挡

obtain dédào 得到

obvious míngxiǎn 明显

occasion jīhuì 机会

occasional ǒu'ěr 偶尔

occasionally ǒurán 偶然

occupant (*of vehicle*) chéngkè 乘客; (*of house*) jūzhùzhě居住者

occupation (*job*) zhíyè 职业; (*of country*) zhànlǐng 占领

occupy *time, mind* zhànyòng

占用; *job* chōngrèn 充任; *country* zhànlǐng 占领

occur (*happen*) fāshēng 发生

ocean hǎiyáng 海洋

o'clock: *at five* wǔ diǎnzhōng 五点钟

October shíyuè 十月

odd (*strange*) qíguài 奇怪; (*not even*) jīshù 奇数

odor qìwèi 气味

of: *the name ~ the street* jiē de míngzi 街 的名字; *five / ten minutes ~ twelve* shí'èr diǎn chà wǔ / shí fēn 十二点差五/十分; *die ~ cancer* sǐ yú áizhèng 死于癌症

off *adv*: *be ~* (*of light*) méi kāidēng 没开灯; (*of machine*) méikāi 没开; (*of lid, top*) méi gàizhe gàir 没盖着盖儿; (*canceled*) qǔxiāo 取消; *it's 3 miles ~* sān yīnglǐ yuǎn 三英里远; *drive / walk ~* kāizǒu / zǒukāi 开走/走开 3 *adj*: *~ switch* guānbì jiàn 关闭键

offend *v/t* màofàn 冒犯

offense LAW zuìxíng 罪行

offensive 1 *adj* tǎoyàn 讨

厌 **2** *n* MIL (attack) gōngjī
攻击; **go onto the ~**
cǎiqǔgōngshì 采取攻势

offer 1 *n* tígōng 提供 **2** *v/t*
tígōng 提供; **~ X Y gěi X**
Y 给 X Y

office (building) bàngōnglóu
办公楼; (room)
bàngōngshì 办公室

office block bàngōng dàlóu
办公大楼

office hours bàngōng shíjiān
办公时间

officer MIL jūnguān 军官; (in
police) jǐngguān 警官

official 1 *adj* guānfāng 官方;
(confirmed) zhèngshì 正式
2 *n* guānyuán 官员

often jīngcháng 经常

oil *n* yóu 油

oil company shíyóu gōngsī
石油公司

oil tanker yóuchuán 油船

oil well yóujǐng 油井

ointment ruǎngāo 软膏

ok kěyǐ 可以; **are you ~?**
(well, not hurt) nǐ méishìr
ba? 你没事儿吧？

old lǎo 老; (previous) jiù 旧;
how ~ are you? nǐ duōdà
niánjì le? 你多大年纪

了？

old age lǎonián 老年

old-fashioned guòshí 过时

omit yílòu 遗漏

on 1 *prep*: **~ the table** zài
zhuō shang 在桌上; **~
the bus / train** gōnggòng
qìchē / huǒchēlǐ 公共汽车
/ 火车里; **~ TV** diànshì
shang / guǎngbōlǐ
电视上 / 广播里 **2** *adv*:
be ~ (of light) kāidēng 开
灯; (of TV, computer etc)
kāi 开; (of lid, top) gàizhe
gàir 盖着盖儿; **what's
~ tonight?** (on TV etc)
jīnwǎn yǒu shénme jiémù?
今晚有什么节目？;
(what's planned?) jīnwǎn
gàn shénme? 今晚干什
么？ **3** *adj*: **~ switch** kāiqǐ
jiàn 开启键

once *adv* (one time) yícì 一
次; (formerly) céngjīng 曾
经; (immediately) lìjí
立即; **all at ~** (suddenly)
tūrán 突然; (together)
yìqǐ 一起

one 1 *n* (number) yī 一;
(in phone numbers) yāo
幺 **2** *adj* yígè 一个; **~ day**

yìtiān 一天 **3** *pron* yígè 一个; *which ~?* nǎyígè? 哪一个？; *the little ~s* xiǎo péngyǒumen 小朋友们

one child policy jìhuà shēngyù 计划生育

onion yángcōng 洋葱

on-line *adj* shàngwǎng 上网

only 1 *adv* zhǐ 只; *not ~ X but also Y* bù jǐnjǐn X, Y yěshì 不仅仅X, Y也是; *~ just* gānggang 刚刚 **2** *adj* wéiyī 唯一; *~ son / daughter* dúzǐ / nǚ 独子/女

onto: *put X ~ Y* bǎ X fàngdào Y shang 把X放到Y上

open 1 *adj* kāizhe 开着; (*frank*) tǎnbái 坦白 **2** *v/t* kāi 开; *book* tānkāi 摊开; *file* dǎkāi 打开; *meeting* kāishǐ 开始 **3** *v/i* kāi 开

opera gējù 歌剧

operate 1 *v/i* MED dòng shǒushù 动手术 **2** *v/t* *machine* cāozuò 操作

operation MED shǒushù 手术

opinion kànfǎ 看法

opponent duìshǒu 对手

opportunity jīhuì 机会

oppose fǎnduì 反对

opposite 1 *adj* *side of road* duìmiàn 对面; *direction, meaning* xiāngfǎn 相反 **2** *n* fǎnmiàn 反面

oppressive *rule* bàonüè 暴虐; *weather* chénzhòng 沉重

optimist lèguānzhě 乐观者

optimistic lèguān 乐观

option xuǎnzé 选择

optional kě xuǎnzé 可选择

or huò 或

orange *n* (*fruit*) chéng 橙; (*color*) chéngsè 橙色

orange juice chéngzhīr 橙汁儿

orchestra guǎnxián yuèduì 管弦乐队

order 1 *n* (*command*) mìngling 命令; (*sequence*) cìxù 次序; (*being well arranged*) zhìxù 秩序; (*for goods*) dìnggòu 定购; (*in restaurant*) diǎn càidān 定菜单; *out of ~* (*not functioning*) shīling 失灵; (*not in sequence*) cìxù diāndǎo 次序颠倒 **2** *v/t* *goods* dìnghuò 定货; *meal* jiàocài 叫菜; *~ X to*

do Y mìnglìng X qù zuò Y 命令X去做Y 命令 Y v/i (*in restaurant*) diǎncài 点菜

ordinary pǔtōng 普通

organic *food* tiānrán 天然

organization jīgòu 机构; (*organizing*) zǔzhī 组织

organize zǔzhī 组织

Orient Dōngfāng 东方

origin qǐyuán 起源

original adj (*not copied*) yuánzuò 原作; (*first*) zuìchū 最初

originally yuánxiān 原先

other 1 adj qítā 其 他 **2** n: **the ~s** qítāde 其 他 的

otherwise bùrán dehuà 不然 的话; (*differently*) bùtóng 不同

ought yīnggāi 应该

our wǒmen 我们

ours wǒmende 我们的

ourselves wǒmen zìjǐ 我 们自己

out: be ~ (*of light*) guāndiào 关灭; (*of fire*) xīmiè 熄灭; (*of flower*) shèngkāi 盛开; (*of sun*) chūlái 出来; (*not at home, not in building*) búzài 不在; (*no longer in competition*) táotài 淘汰

(*get*) **~!** chūqù! 出去！

outbreak (*of violence, war*) bàofā 爆发

outcome jiéguǒ 结果

outdoor(s) shìwài 室外

outer *wall etc* wàibù 外部

outgoing *flight* chūháng 出 航; *personality* kāilǎng 开朗

outlet (*of pipe*) chūkǒu 出 口; (*for sales*) xiāoshòu diǎn 销售点; ELEC chāzuò 插座

outlook zhǎnwàng 展望

out of ◊ (*motion*): **run ~ the house** pǎochū wūwài 跑 出屋外◊ (*position*): **20 miles ~ Nanjing** Nánjīng yǐwài èrshí yīnglǐ 南京以 外二十英里◊ (*cause*): **~ jealousy** yóuyú jídù 由于 嫉妒◊ (*without*): **we're ~ gas** wǒmen chēméi yóu le 我们车没油了◊: **5 ~ 10** shífēn zhīwǔ 十分之五

output 1 n (*of factory*) chǎnliàng 产量 **2** v/t (*produce*) shēngchǎn 生产

outrage n (*feeling*) gōngfèn 公愤; (*act*) bàoxíng 暴行

outrageous *acts* wúchǐ 无

耻; prices guòfèn 过分

outside 1 adj wàibù 外部
2 adv wàimian 外面 3 prep
zài ... yǐwài 在 ... 以外

outsider júwàirén 局外人

outskirts jiāoqū 郊区

outstanding quality xiǎnzhù
显著; writer, athlete
jiéchū杰出; payment etc
wèifù 未付

oval adj tuǒyuán 椭圆

oven kǎoxiāng 烤箱

over 1 prep (across) guò 过;
(more than) chāoguò 超过;
(above) zài ... shàngfāng
在 ... 上方 2 adv: be ~
(finished) wánjié 完结;
(left) shèngyú 剩余;
here zài zhèlǐ 在这里; it
hurts all ~ wǒhúnshēn dōu
téng 我浑身都疼; do X
~ (again) zàicì zuò X 再
次做X

overcoat dàyī 大衣

overcome difficulty zhēngfú
征服

overdo kuāzhāng 夸张;
(cooking) zhǔ guòhuǒr 煮
过火儿

overdone meat guòhuǒ 过火

overdose n guòliàng 过量

overdraft chāozhī 超支

overestimate guògāo gūjì 过
高估计

overhead n FIN tōngcháng
kāizhī通常开支

overhear tōutīng 偷听

overlook (of tall building
etc) fǔshì 俯视; (not see)
hūlüè 忽略

overnight adv yèjiān 夜间

overrated guògāo gūjì 过
高估计

overseas adj & adv hǎiwài
海外

overseas Chinese Huáqiáo
华侨

oversight shūhū 疏忽

overtake chāoguò 超过;
Br MOT chāochē 超车

overtime work jiābān 加班

owe v/t qiàn 欠

owing to yóuyú 由于

own[1] v/t yōngyǒu 拥有

own[2] 1 adj zìjǐ 自己 2 pron:
on his ~ tā zìjǐ 他自己

owner yōngyǒuzhě 拥有者

oyster sauce háoyóu 蚝油

ozone layer chòuyǎng céng
臭氧层

P

pace n (step) bù 步; (speed)
sùdù 速度
Pacific: the ~ (Ocean)
Tàipíngyáng 太平洋
Pacific Rim: the ~
Tàipíngyáng quān 太平
洋圈
pack 1 n (back~) bēibāo 背
包; (of cereal, food) dài dài 袋;
(of cigarettes) bāo 包 2 v/t
bag jiāng dōngxi zhuāngrù
将东西装入; item of
clothing etc fàngrù xínglǐ
放入行李; goods bāo-
zhuāng 包装 3 v/i zhěnglǐ
xíngzhuāng 整理行装
package n bāoguǒ 包裹; (of
offers etc) zhěngtàa cáiliào
整套材料
package deal (for vacation)
bāobàn lǚxíng 包办旅行
packet n bāo 包
paddy dàozi 稻子
page¹ n (of book etc) yè 页
page² v/t (call) chuánhū 传呼
pager chuánhūjī 传呼机
pagoda bǎotǎ 宝塔

pail tǒng 桶
pain téngtòng 疼痛
painful téngtòng 疼痛;
(distressing) lìngrén
tòngkǔ 令人痛苦
painkiller zhǐtòngpiàn 止
痛片
paint 1 n túliào 涂料; (for
artist) yánliào 颜料 2 v/t
wall etc shàng túliào 上涂
料; picture yòng yánliào
huà 用颜料画 3 v/i (as art
form) huìhuà 绘画
painter (artist) huìjiā 画家
painting (activity) huìhuà 绘
画; (picture) túhuà 图画
pair duì 对; a ~ of
shoes / sandals yìshuāng
xié / liángxié 一双鞋/凉鞋
pajamas shuìyīkù 睡衣裤
pale person cāngbái 苍白
palm (of hand) shǒuzhǎng
手掌
pamphlet xiǎocèzi 小册子
pan n guō 锅
panic 1 n kǒnghuāng 恐慌
2 v/i shòujīng 受惊

pant v/i chuǎnxī 喘息

panties nèikù 内裤

pants kùzi 裤子

pantyhose liánkùwà 连裤袜

paper 1 n zhǐ 纸; (news~) bàozhǐ 报纸; (academic) lùnwén 论文; (examination ~) kǎoshìjuàn 考试卷; **~s** (documents) wénjiàn 文件; (identity ~) zhèngjiàn 证件

paperback píngzhuāngshū 平装书

parade n (procession) yuèbīng 阅兵

paradise lèyuán 乐园; fig tiāntáng 天堂

paragraph duànluò 段落

parallel n (line) píngxíngxiàn 平行线; fig xiāngsì zhīchù 相似之处

paralyze tānhuàn 瘫痪; fig bù zhīsuǒcuò 不知所措

paramedic hùlǐ rényuán 护理人员

paranoia wàngxiǎngkuáng 妄想狂

paranoid adj duōyí 多疑

parcel n bāoguǒ 包裹

pardon v/t yuánliàng 原谅; LAW shèmiǎn 赦免; **~ me?** nǐ shuō shénme? 你说

什么？

parent jiāzhǎng 家长

parental fùmǔ 父母

park[1] (area) gōngyuán 公园

park[2] MOT 1 v/t tíngfàng 停放 2 v/i tíngchē 停车

parking MOT tíngchē 停车

parking garage shìnèi tíngchēchǎng 室内停车场

parking lot tíngchēchǎng 停车场

parking meter tíngchējìshí shōufèiqì 停车计时收费器

parking ticket wéizhāng tíngchē fákuǎndān 违章停车罚款单

parliament yìhuì 议会

part n (section, area) bùfen 部分; (of machine) língjiàn 零件; (in play, movie) juésè 角色; (in hair) fèng 缝; **take ~ in** cānjiā 参加

participate cānjiā 参加

particular (specific) tèbié 特别; (special) tèshū 特殊; (fussy) tiāoti 挑剔

particularly tèbié 特别

partition n (screen) píngfēng 屏风; (of country) fēnliè 分裂

partly bùfen 部分

partner COM héhuǒrén 合伙人; (*in relationship*) tóngbàn 同伴; (*in activity*) dādàng 搭档

partnership COM héhuǒ jīngyíng 合伙经营; (*in activity*) dādàng guānxi 搭档关系

part-time *adj & adv* jiānzhí 兼职

party *n* qìngzhùhuì 庆祝会; POL dǎng 党; (*group*) zǔ组

party member dǎngyuán 党员

pass 1 *n* (*for entrance*) tōngxíngzhèng 通行证; SP chuánqiú 传球; (*in mountains*) guān'ài 关隘 **2** *v/t* (*hand*) dì 递; (*go past*) jīngguò 经过; *car, cyclist* yuèguò 越过; (*go beyond*) chāoguò 超过; (*approve*) biǎojué tōngguò 表决通过; SP chuánqiú 传球; *~ an exam* tōngguò kǎoshì 通过考试 **3** *v/i* (*of time*) tuīyí 推移; (*in exam*) jígé 及格

passage (*corridor*) tōngdào 通道; (*from book*) yíduàn 一段

passenger chéngkè 乘客

passer-by guòlùrén 过路人

passion (*fervor*) rèqíng 热情; (*sexual*) xìng'ài 性爱

passive *adj* bèidòng 被动

passport hùzhào 护照

password kǒulìng 口令

past 1 *adj* (*former*) yǐqián 以前; *the ~ few days* jìnjǐtiān 近几天 **2** *n* guòqù 过去; *in the ~* zài guòqù 在过去 **3** *prep* (*in time*) chíyú 迟于; (*in position*) jīngguò 经过; *it's half ~ two* xiànzài liǎngdiǎnbàn 现在两点半

pastime xiāoqiǎn 消遣

pastry (*for pie*) yóusū miàntuán 油酥面团

paternal *relative* fùxì 父系; *pride, love* fùqīnbān 父亲般

paternity fùqīn shēnfen 父亲身分

path xiǎolù 小路

pathetic zhāorén liánmǐn 招人怜悯; F (*bad*) kěbēi 可悲

patience nàixīn 耐心

patient 1 *n* bìngrén 病人 **2** *adj* yǒu nàixīn 有耐心

patriotic àiguó 爱国

patrol 1 n xúnluóduì 巡逻队
2 v/t xúnluó 巡逻

patrolman xúnjǐng 巡警

patronizing gāorén yìděng
高人一等

pattern n (on fabric) tú'àn 图
案; (for sewing) yàngshì 样
式; (model) móxíng 模型;
(in events) fāngshì 方式

pause 1 n & v/i tíngdùn 停
顿 **2** v/t tape zàntíng 暂停

pavement (roadway) lùmiàn
路面

paw n zhuǎzi 爪子

pay 1 n xīnjīn 薪金 **2** v/t
employee fùqián gěi fù
钱给; sum, bill fù 付
3 v/i fùzhàng 付帐; (be
profitable) yǒu lìrùn 有
利润

pay check xīnjīn zhīpiào 薪
金支票

payday fāxīnrì 发薪日

payment (of bill) fùkuǎn
付款; (money) fùchūde
kuǎnxiàng 付出的款项

pay phone gōngyòng
diànhuà 公用电话

PC (= *personal computer*)
gèrén diànnǎo 个人电
脑; (= *politically correct*)

détǐ 得体

peace hépíng 和平; (quiet)
níngjìng 宁静

peaceful píngjìng 平静

peak n (of mountain) shāndǐng 山顶; fig dǐngfēng
顶峰

peak hours gāofēng shíjiān
高峰时间

pear lí 梨

Pearl River Zhūjiāng 珠江

peck n & v/t (bite) zhuó 啄

peculiar (odd) qíguài 奇怪

pedal n (of bike) tàbǎn 踏板

pedal rickshaw dàoqílǘ倒
骑驴

pedestrian n xíngrén 行人

pediatrician érkēzhuān jiā儿
科专家

pedicab sānlúnchē三轮车

peel 1 n guǒpí 果皮 **2** v/t
fruit xiāopí 削皮 **3** v/i (of
skin) tuōluò 脱落

peer v/i níngshì 凝视; **~ at**
zǐxìkàn 仔细看

Peking Opera Jīngjù 京剧

pen n (ballpoint) yuánzhūbǐ
圆珠笔

penalize búlìyú 不利于

penalty chéngfá 惩罚; SP
fáqiú 罚球

penalty clause wéiyuē fákuǎn tiáokuǎn 违约罚款条款

pencil qiānbǐ 铅笔

penetrate chuāntòu 穿透; *market* dǎrù 打入

penicillin qīngméisù 青霉素

peninsula bàndǎo 半岛

penitentiary jiānyù 监狱

pension yǎnglǎojīn 养老金

Pentagon: the ～ Wǔjiǎo Dàlóu 五角大楼

penthouse dǐngcéng gōngyù 顶层公寓

people rén 人; *(race, tribe)* mínzú 民族

People's Commune Rénmín Gōngshè 人民公社

pepper hújiāofěn 胡椒粉; *(vegetable)* làjiāo 辣椒

percent bǎifēnzhī 百分之

perception *(with senses)* gǎnzhī nénglì 感知能力; *(of situation)* kànfǎ 看法

perfect 1 *adj* wánměi 完美 **2** *v/t* wánshàn 完善

perfection wánměi 完美

perfectly jíjiā 极佳; *(totally)* wánquán 完全

perform *v/t (carry out)* zuò 做; *(of actor)* biǎoyǎn 表演

performance *(by actor*

etc) biǎoyǎn 表演; *(of employee, machine etc)* biǎoxiàn 表现; *(of machine)* xìngnéng 性能

perfume xiāngshuǐ 香水; *(of flower)* xiāngwèi 香味

perhaps yěxǔ 也许

peril wēixiǎn 危险

perimeter zhōubiān 周边

period yíduàn 一段; *(menstruation)* yuèjīng 月经; *(punctuation)* jùhào 句号

perjury wěizhèng 伪证

permanent *adj* yǒngjiǔ 永久

permanently chángqī 长期

permission xǔkě 许可

permit 1 *n* xǔkèzhèng 许可证 **2** *v/t* róngxǔ 容许

perpetual chíxù 持续

persecute pòhài 迫害

persecution pòhài 迫害

persist chíxù 持续; **～ in** zhíyì zuò 执意做

persistent *person* gùzhí 固执; *questions, rain etc* chíxù búduàn 持续不断

person rén 人; **in ～** qīnzì 亲自

personal *(private)* sīrén 私人; *(of an individual)* gèrén

个人

personal computer gèrén diànnǎo 个人电脑

personality gèxìng 个性; (celebrity) míngrén 名人

personally (for my part) jiù wǒláishuō 就我来说; (in person) qīnzì 亲自

personnel zhíyuán 职员; (department) rénshì bùmén 人事部门

perspiration hànshuǐ 汗水

persuade shuōfú 说服

persuasion quànshuō 劝说

pessimist bēiguānzhě 悲观者

pessimistic bēiguān 悲观

pest (bird) hàiniǎo 害鸟; (insect) hàichóng 害虫; (animal) hàishòu 害兽

pester jiūchán 纠缠

pesticide shāchóngjì 杀虫剂

pet 1 n chǒngwù 宠物 **2** adj (favorite) zuì xǐhuān 最喜欢

petition n qǐngyuànshū 请愿书

petrochemical shíyóu huàxué chǎnpǐn 石油化学产品

petroleum shíyóu 石油

petty person xiǎoqì 小气; details, problem suǒsuì 琐碎

pharmaceuticals zhìyào gōngsī 制药公司

pharmacist yàoshāng 药商

pharmacy (store) yàofáng 药房

phase jiēduàn 阶段

philosopher zhéxuéjiā 哲学家

philosophical yǒu zhélǐ 有哲理

philosophy zhéxué 哲学

phobia kǒngbùzhèng 恐怖症

phone 1 n diànhuàjī 电话机 **2** v/t & v/i dǎ diànhuà 打电话

phone book diànhuàbù 电话簿

phone booth diànhuàtíng 电话亭

phonecall diànhuà 电话

phone number diànhuà hàomǎ 电话号码

phon(e)y adj wěizhuāng 伪装

photo n xiàngpiàn 相片

photocopier yǐngyìnjī 影印机

photocopy 1 *n* yǐngyìnběn 影印本 **2** *v/t* yǐngyìn 影印

photographer shèyǐngshī 摄影师

photography shèyǐng 摄影

phrase *n* piànyǔ 片语

physical *adj* (of the body) shēntǐ 身体

physician yīshēng 医生

physicist wùlǐ xuéjiā物理学家

physics wùlǐ 物理

physiotherapy lǐliáo 理疗

piano gāngqín 钢琴

pick *v/t* (choose) xuǎn 选; *flowers, fruit* cǎi 采

♦ **pick up** *v/t* náqǐ 拿起; (from ground) jiǎnqǐ 拣起; (collect) qǔhuí 取回; (from airport etc) jiē 接; (in car) ràngrén dābiànchē 让人搭便车; (in sexual sense) gōuyǐn 勾引; *skill* xuéhuì 学会

pick-up (truck) qīngxíng xiǎohuòchē 轻型小货车

picnic *n & v/i* yěcān 野餐

picture 1 *n* (photo) zhàopiàn 照片; (painting) huìhuà 绘画; (illustration) chātú 插图; (movie) diànyǐng 电影

picturesque rúhuà 如画

pie pài 派

piece (fragment) suìpiàn 碎片; (component) bùfen 部分; (in board game) zǐr 子儿; **a ~ of pie / bread** yíkuài pài / miànbāo 一块派 / 面包

pierce (penetrate) cìtòu 刺透; *ears* zhāyǎn 扎眼

pig zhū 猪; (unpleasant person) húndàn 混蛋

pigeon gēzi 鸽子

pile duī 堆

pill yào 药; **the ~** kǒufú bìyùnyào 口服避孕药

pillar zhùzi 柱子

pillow *n* zhěntou 枕头

pilot *n* (of airplane) fēixíngyuán 飞行员

pilot plant shìyàn qū 试验区

PIN (= *personal identification number*) mìmǎ 密码

pin *n* (for sewing) dàtóuzhēn 大头针; (in bowling) mùzhù 木柱; (badge) huīzhāng 徽章

pinch *n* niē 捏; (of salt etc) yìniē 一捏

pine n (*tree*) sōngshù 松树;
(*wood*) sōngmù 松木

pineapple bōluó 菠萝

pink fěnhóngsè 粉红色

pinyin pīnyīn 拼音

pioneering adj kāituò 开拓

pipe n guǎnzi 管子; (*to smoke*) yāndǒu 烟斗

pipeline guǎndào 管道

pirate v/t *software etc* dàobǎn 盗版

pistol shǒuqiāng 手枪

pitch 1 v/i (*in baseball*) tóuqiú 投球 2 v/t *tent* dā 搭; *ball* tóu 投

pitcher[1] (*in baseball*) tóushǒu 投手

pitcher[2] (*container*) guàn 罐

pitiful lìngrén liánmǐn 令人怜悯

pity n tóngqíng 同情; *it's a ~ that ...* yíhàn ... 遗憾...

pizza bǐsà 比萨

PLA (= *People's Liberation Army*) Jiěfàngjūn 解放军

place 1 n dìfang 地方; (*bar, restaurant*) cānyǐnchù 餐饮处; (*home*) jiā 家; (*seat*) zuòwèi 座位; *at my / his ~* zài wǒ / tānàr 在我 / 他那儿 2 v/t fàng 放

plain adj (*clear*) qīngchǔ 清楚; (*not patterned*) méiyǒu tú'àn 没有图案

plan 1 n jìhuà 计划; (*drawing*) shèjìtú 设计图 2 v/t (*prepare*) zhǔnbèi 准备; (*design*) shèjì 设计; *~ to do X* dǎsuàn zuò X 打算做X

plane n (*airplane*) fēijī 飞机

planet xíngxīng 行星

plank mùbǎn 木板

planning jìhuà 计划

plant[1] 1 n zhíwù 植物 2 v/t zhòng 种

plant[2] n (*factory*) chǎng 厂; (*equipment*) shèbèi 设备

plaque (*on wall*) shìbǎn 饰板

plaster n (*on wall*) huīní 灰泥

plastic n & adj sùliào 塑料

plastic surgery zhěngxíng wàikē 整形外科

plate n (*for food*) pánzi 盘子

platform wǔtái 舞台; (*at station*) zhàntái 站台

platinum n & adj bó 铂

play 1 n (*in theater, on TV*) jù 剧; (*of children*) yóuxì 游戏 2 v/i (*of children*) wánr 玩儿 ; (of musician) tánzòu 弹奏 ; (SP: perform) dǎ 打 ; (SP: take part) cānsài 参赛 3 v/t instrument tán 弹 ; music yǎnzòu 演奏 ; game wánr 玩儿 ; opponent yǔ... bǐsài 与... 比赛 ; role bànyǎn 扮演

player SP yùndòngyuán 运动员 ; (musician) yǎnzòuzhě 演奏者 ; (actor) yǎnyuán 演员

playing card zhǐpái 纸牌

playwright jùzuòjiā剧作家

plea n kěnqiú 恳求

plead v/i qǐngqiú 请求 ; ~ for kěnqiú 恳求 ; ~ guilty / not guilty fú / bùfú zuì 服 / 不服罪

pleasant lìngrén yúkuài 令人愉快

please 1 adv qǐng 请 ; more tea? – yes, ~ hái yào chá ma? – hǎode, xièxiè 还要茶吗？– 好的, 谢谢 ; ~ do méiwèntí 没问题 2 v/t shǐ gāoxìng 使高兴

pleased gāoxìng 高兴 ; ~ to meet you hěn gāoxìng rènshí nǐ 很高兴认识你

pleasure kuàilè 快乐 ; (as opposed to work) yúlè 娱乐 ; **plenty** fùzú 富足 ; ~ of xǔduō 许多

plot 1 n yīnmóu 阴谋 ; (of novel) qíngjié 情节 2 v/t & v/i móumóu 密谋

plow 1 n lí 犁 2 v/t & v/i gēngdì 耕地

plug 1 n (for bath) sāizi 塞子 ; ELEC chātóu 插头 ; (for new book etc) xuānchuán 宣传

plum n lǐzi 李子

plumber shuǐnuǎngōng 水暖工

plumbing (pipes) guǎndào zhuāngzhì 管道装置

plump adj fēngmǎn 丰满

plunge n/i tūrán diēluò 突然跌落 ; (of prices) xiàdiē 下跌

plus prep jiāshàng 加上

pneumonia fèiyán 肺炎

poach v/t & v/i salmon etc tōubǔ 偷捕

poached egg wò jīdàn 卧鸡蛋

P.O. Box yóuzhèng xìnxiāng 邮政信箱

pocket n kǒudài 口袋

pocketbook (woman's) xiǎo shǒutíbāo 小手提

包; (wallet) qiánbāo 钱
包; (book) píngzhuāngshū
平装书
poem shī 诗
poet shīrén 诗人
poetry shīgē 诗歌
point 1 n (of knife etc)
jiānduān 尖端; (in contest)
fēn 分; (purpose) yìyì 意
义; (in discussion) guān-
diǎn 观点; (in decimals)
diǎn 点 **2** v/i zhǐ 指
♦ **point at** zhǐxiàng 指向
♦ **point out** sights shǐ 指示
使注意; advantages etc
zhǐchū 指出
pointless wúyìyì 无意义
poison 1 n dúyào 毒药
poke v/t tǒng 捅; (stick)
shēnchū 伸出
pole (of wood, metal) gān 杆
police n jǐngfāng 警方
policeman jǐngchá 警察
police station jǐngchájú 警
察局
policy¹ zhèngcè 政策
policy²: *insurance ~*
bǎoxiǎndān 保险单
polish 1 n cāguāngjì 擦光剂
2 v/t cāliàng 擦亮
Politbureau Zhèngzhìjú

政治局
polite yǒu lǐmào 有礼貌
politeness lǐmào 礼貌
political zhèngzhì 政治
politician zhèngzhìjiā 政
治家
politics zhèngzhì 政治
poll n (survey) mínyì cèyàn
民意测验
pollute wūrǎn 污染
pollution wūrǎn 污染
pond chítáng 池塘
ponytail mǎwěifà 马尾发
pool¹ (swimming ~) chí 池;
(of water, blood) tān 摊
pool² (game) pǔ'ěrdànzǐ xì
普尔弹子戏
poor adj pínqióng 贫穷;
(not good) bùhǎo 不好;
(unfortunate) búxìng 不幸
pop¹ v/i (of balloon etc) fāchū
pēngde yīshēng 发出砰
的一声
pop² n MUS liúxíng yīnyuè 流
行音乐
Popsicle® bàngbàngbīng
棒棒冰
popular shòu huānyíng 受欢
迎; belief, support pǔbiàn
普遍
popularity (of person)

shēngwàng 声望

population rénkǒu 人口

porcelain n & adj cí 瓷

pork zhūròu 猪肉

pornographic huángsè 黄色

pornography sèqíng zuòpǐn 色情作品

port n (town) gǎngshì 港市; (area) gǎngkǒu 港口; COMPUT duānkǒu 端口

portable adj shǒutíshì 手提式 **~ TV** wēixíng diànshì 微型电视

porter (at railroad station) bānyùnggōng 搬运工; (doorman) ménwèi 门卫

portion n (of food) fèn 份

portrait n (of person) xiàoxiàng 肖像

pose v/i (for artist) bǎi zīshì 摆姿势

position 1 n (location) wèizhi 位置; (stance) zīshì 姿势; (in race, competition) wèi位; (point of view) lìchǎng 立场; (situation) chǔjìng 处境 **2** v/t ānfàng 安放

positive attitude lèguān 乐观; response biǎoshì tóngyì 表示同意; medical test yángxìng 阳性; GRAM kěndìng 肯定; ELEC zhèngjí 正极

possession chíyǒu 持有; (thing owned) cáichǎn 财产; **~s** suǒyǒuwù 所有物

possibility kěnéngxìng 可能性

possible kěnéng 可能; **the best ~ ...** jìn kěnéng zuìhǎo ... 尽可能最好...

possibly kěnéng 可能; (perhaps) yěxǔ 也许

post[1] 1 n (of wood, metal) gānzi 杆子 **2** v/t notice zhāngtiē 张贴

post[2] v/t guards bùzhì 布置

postage yóuzī 邮资

postcard míngxìnpiàn 明信片

postdate tiánwǎn rìqī 填晚日期

poster hǎibào 海报

posting (assignment) wěipài 委派

postmark yóuchuō 邮戳

post office yóujú 邮局

postpone tuīchí 推迟

pot (for cooking) guō 锅; (for coffee, tea) hú 壶; (for plant) pén 盆

potato tǔdòu 土豆

potato chips zháshǔpiàn

炸薯片

potential 1 adj kěnéng chūxiàn 可能出现 2 n qiánlì 潜力

pothole (in road) kēngwā 坑洼

poultry (birds) jiāqín 家禽; (meat) jiāqínròu 家禽肉

pound¹ n (weight) bàng 磅

pound² v/i (of heart) tiàodòng 剧烈跳动

pound sterling yīngbàng 英镑

pour v/t liquid dào 倒

poverty pínkùn 贫困

powder n fěnmò 粉末; (for face) fěn 粉

powder room nǚcèsuǒ 女厕所

power n (strength) lì 力; (authority) quánlì 权力; (energy) néngliàng 能量; (electricity) diàn 电

power cut tíngdiàn 停电

powerful qiángyǒulì 强有力

powerless wúlìliàng 无力量

power station fādiànzhàn 发电站

PR (= public relations) gōngguān 公关

practical experience shíjì 实

际; person xiànshí 现实; (functional) shíyòng 实用

practice 1 n liànxí 练习; (rehearsal) páiliàn 排练; (custom) chángguī 常规 2 v/i xùnliàn 训练 3 v/t liànxí 练习; law, medicine zhíyè 执业

praise 1 n zànyù 赞誉 2 v/t chēngzàn 称赞

precaution yùfáng cuòshī 预防措施

precede v/t xiānyú 先于

precious bǎoguì 宝贵

precise zhǔnquè 准确

precisely jīngquè 精确

predecessor (in job) qiánrènzhě 前任者

predict yùyán 预言

predominant zhàn yōushì 占优势

predominantly zhǔyào 主要

preface n qiányán 前言

prefer gèng xǐhuān 更喜欢

preferable gèng chènxīn 更称心

preference piān'ài 偏爱

preferential yōuxiān 优先

pregnancy yùnqī 孕期

pregnant huáiyùn 怀孕

prejudice n piānjiàn 偏见

preliminary adj yùbèixìng
预备性

premature: ~ birth zǎochǎn
早产

première n shǒucì gōngyǎn
首次公演

premises dìfang 地方

premium n (insurance)
bǎoxiǎnfèi 保险费

prepare v/t yùbèi 准备

prescription MED yàofāng
药方

presence zàichǎng 在场

present¹ adj (current)
mùqián 目前; **be ~**
zàichǎng 在场 **2** n: **the
~** xiànzài 现在; GRAM
xiànzàishí 现在时; **at ~**
cǐkè 此刻

present² 1 n (gift) lǐwù 礼物
2 v/t award shòuyǔ 授予;
program zhǔchí 主持

presentation (to audience)
bàogào 报告

presently (at the moment)
xiànzài 现在; (soon) bùjiǔ
不久

preserve v/t peace etc wéihù
维护; wood etc bǎohù 保
护; food bǎocún 保存

presidency zǒngtǒng zhíwèi
总统职位

president POL zǒngtǒng
总统; (of company)
dǒngshìzhǎng 董事长

presidential zǒngtǒng 总统

press 1 n: **the ~** xīnwénjiè
新闻界 **2** v/t button àn 按;
clothes yùn 熨

pressure 1 n yālì 压力 **2** v/t
qiǎngpò 强迫

prestige wēiwàng 威望

presumably dàgài 大概

pretend v/i jiǎzhuāng 假装

pretense xūjiǎ 虚假

pretext jièkǒu 借口

pretty 1 adj piàoliang 漂亮
2 adv (quite) xiāngdāng
相当

prevent fángzhǐ 防止; **~ X
(from) doing Y** zǔzhǐ X
zuò Y 阻止X做Y

preview n yùzhǎn 预展

previous qiányī 前一

prey n lièwù 猎物

price n jiàgé 价格

priceless wújià 无价

pride n zìháo 自豪; (self-
respect) zìzūn 自尊

priest mùshī 牧师

primary 1 adj zhǔyào 主要
2 n POL chūxuǎn 初选

prime minister shǒuxiàng
首相

primitive yuánshǐ 原始;
conditions jiǎnlòu 简陋

principal 1 *adj* zhǔyào 主要
2 *n* EDU xiàozhǎng 校长

principle *moral* zhǔnzé 准
则; *(rule)* yuánzé 原则

print 1 *n (in book)* yìnshuā
zìtǐ 印刷字体; *out of ~*
juébǎn 绝版 **2** *v/t* yìnshuā
印刷; COMPUT dǎyìn 打印

printer dǎyìnjī 打印机;
(person) yìnshuāshāng
印刷商

prior *adj* shìxiān 事先

prioritize *(order)* huàfēn
qīngzhònghuǎnjí 划分轻
重缓急; *(put first)* jǐyǔ
yōuxiān 给予优先

priority yàowèi 要位

prison jiānyù 监狱

prisoner qiúfàn 囚犯

privacy sīrén kōngjiān 私
人空间

private *adj* sīrén 私人

privately *(in private)* sīxià
私下; *owned* gèrén 个人;
(inwardly) nèixīn 内心

privilege *(special treatment)*
tèquán 特权; *(honor)*

róngxìng 荣幸

prize *n* jiǎngshǎng 奖赏

prizewinner huòjiǎngzhě
获奖者

probability kěnéngxìng 可
能性

probable hěn kěnéng 很
可能

probably yěxǔ 也许

probe *n (investigation)*
diàochá 调查

problem wèntí 问题

procedure bùzhòu 步骤

process 1 *n* guòchéng 过
程 **2** *v/t food, materials*
jiāgōng 加工; *data* chǔlǐ 处
理; *application etc* shěnchá
审查

produce 1 *n* chǎnpǐn 产品
2 *v/t commodity* shēngchǎn
生产; *(bring about)* yǐnqǐ
引起; *(bring out)* náchū 拿
出; *play, movie* zhìzuò
制作

producer zhìzào chǎngjiā 制
造厂家; *(of play, movie)*
zhìpiānrén 制片人

product chǎnpǐn 产品

production chǎnliàng 产量;
(play, movie) zuòpǐn 作品

productive duōchǎn 多

产; talks yǒu chéngxiào
有成效
productivity shēngchǎnlì
生产力
profession zhíyè 职业
professional 1 adj zhuānyè
专业; work yǒu jìqiǎo 有
技巧 **2** n zhuānyè rénshì
专业人士; (not amateur)
zhíyè rényuán 职业人员
professor jiàoshòu 教授
profit n lìrùn 利润
profitable kěhuò lìrùn 可
获利润
profit margin lìrùnlǜ 利
润率
program n jìhuà 计划;
(radio, TV) jiémù 节目;
COMPUT chéngxù 程序;
THEA jiémùdān 节目单
programmer COMPUT
chéngxùyuán 程序员
progress 1 n jìnbù 进步
2 v/i (in time) jìnzhǎn 进
展; (make ~) qǔdé jìnbù 取
得进步
project[1] n (plan) jìhuà 计
划; (undertaking) xiàngmù
项目; (houses) tǒngjiàn
zhùzháiqū 统建住宅区
project[2] **1** v/t figures jìhuà 计

划 **2** v/i (stick out) tūchū
突出
projection (forecast) yùcè
预测
projector (for slides)
fàngyìngjī 放映机
proletariat wúchǎn jiējí 无
产阶级
prolong yáncháng 延长
prom (dance) wǔhuì 舞会
promise 1 n chéngnuò 承诺
2 v/t xǔnuò 许诺
promote employee jìnshēng
晋升; COM xuānchuán
宣传
promotion (of employee)
jìnjí 晋级; COM cùxiāo
促销
prompt adj (on time) zhǔnshí
准时; (speedy) jíshí 及时
pronounce word fāyīn 发音
proof n zhèngjù 证据
propaganda xuānchuán
宣传
proper (real) zhēnzhèng 真
正; (correct) qiàdàng 恰当;
(fitting) shìdàng 适当
properly zhèngquè 正确
property cáichǎn 财产;
(land) fángdìchǎn 房地产
proportions miànjī 面积

proposal tíyì 提议; (of marriage) qiúhūn 求婚

propose 1 v/t (suggest) jiànyì 建议; (plan) jìhuà 计划 **2** v/i (to marry) qiúhūn 求婚

prosecute v/t LAW tíqǐ gōngsù 提起公诉

prosperous xīngwàng 兴旺

prostitute n jìnǚ 妓女

protect v/t bǎohù 保护

protection bǎohù 保护

protest 1 n kàngyì 抗议; (demonstration) shìwēi 示威 **2** v/i shēngbiàn 声辩; (demonstrate) shìwēi 示威

proud jiāo'ào 骄傲; be ~ of yǐ … wéi zìháo 以… 为自豪

prove zhèngmíng 证明

provide tígōng 提供; ~d (that) zhǐyào 只要

province shěng 省

provisional línshí 临时

provoke (cause) yǐnqǐ 引起; (annoy) jīnù 激怒

proximity línjìn 邻近

psychiatric jīngshénbìng 精神病

psychiatrist jīngshénkēyī shēng 精神科医生

psychiatry jīngshénbìngxué 精神病学

psychoanalysis jīngshén fēnxī 精神分析

psychoanalyst jīngshén fēnxīxuéjiā 精神分析学家

psychological xīnlǐ 心理

psychologist xīnlǐ xuéjiā 心理学家

psychology xīnlǐxué 心理学

public 1 adj gōngzhòng 公众 **2** n: the ~ mínzhòng 民众

publication (of book) chūbǎn 出版; (by newspaper) kānchū 刊出

publicity xuānchuán 宣传

publicly dāngzhòng 当众

public relations gōngguān 公关

publish chūbǎn 出版

publisher chūbǎnshè 出版社

pull 1 n (on rope) lā 拉 **2** v/t (drag) lā 拉; (tug) chě 扯; muscle lāshāng 拉伤 **3** v/i zhuāi 拽

♦ **pull out** v/i (of agreement, competition) tuìchū 退出

pulse màibó 脉搏

pump n bèng 泵

punch 1 n (blow) jīdǎ 击打
2 v/t (with fist) yòng quán
jī 用拳击

punctual zhǔnshí 准时

punish chéngfá 惩罚

punishment chéngfá 惩罚

pupil (student) xuésheng
学生

purchase n & v/t gòumǎi
购买

purchaser mǎizhǔ 买主

pure silk chún 纯; air, water
jiéjìng 洁净; (morally)
chúnjié 纯洁

purely wánquán 完全

purify water jìnghuà 净化

purpose (aim, object) mùdì
目的; on ~ gùyì 故意

purse n (pocketbook)
shǒudài 手袋

pursue v/t person zhuīzhú
追逐; course of action jìxù
jìnxíng 继续进行

pursuer zhuīgǎnzhě 追赶者

push v/t tuī 推; button àn 按;

(pressure) bīpò 逼迫
put fàng 放; question wèn 问

♦ put down fàngxià 放下;
deposit fù dìngjīn 付定金;
rebellion zhènyā 镇压

♦ put off light, TV guāndiào
关掉; (deter) shǐ rén búzuò
使人不做

♦ put on light, TV dǎkāi
打开; music fàng 放;
jacket chuān 穿; make-up
cháyòng 搽用

♦ put out hand shēnchū 伸
出; fire xīmiè 熄灭; light
guāndiào 关掉

♦ put up v/t hand jǔqǐ 举起;
(give a bed) gōngyìng shísù
供应宿舍; (erect) shùqǐ
竖起; price tígāo 提高;
poster zhāngtiē 张贴

♦ put up with rěnshòu 忍受

puzzle 1 n (mystery) mí
谜; (game) zhìlì yóuxì 智
力游戏 2 v/t shǐ kùnhuò
使困惑

Q

qualification wénpíng 文凭
qualified nurse etc hégé 合格

qualify v/i EDU qǔdé zīgé 取
得资格; (in contest) qǔdé

bísài zīgé 取得比赛资格
quality zhìliàng 质量；
(characteristic) tèxìng 特性
quantity liàng 量
quarrel *n & v/i* chǎozuǐ 吵嘴
quart kuātuō 夸脱
quarter *n* sìfēn zhīyī 四分之
一；*~ of an hour* yīkèzhōng
一刻钟；*a ~ of 5* wǔdiǎn
chà yīkè 五点差一刻；
~ after 5 wǔdiǎn yīkè 五
点一刻
quarterfinal sìfēn zhīyī
juésài 四分之一决赛
quarterly *adj & adv* jìdù
季度
query 1 *n* yíwèn 疑问 2 *v/t*
(doubt) duì ... biǎoshì
yíwèn 对 ... 表示疑问
question 1 *n* wèntí 问题
2 *v/t person* wèn 问；
(doubt) huáiyí 怀疑
question mark wènhào 问
号

questionnaire wènjuàn 问卷
quick kuài 快
quickly kuài 快
quiet xiǎoshēng 小声；*street*
ānjìng 安静；*town* píngjìng
平静
quit *v/t & v/i* cízhí 辞职
quite *(fairly)* xiāngdāng
相当；*(completely)*
wánquán 完全；*I didn't
~ understand* wǒbú tài
míngbai 我不太明白；*~!*
zhèngshì zhèyàng! 正是这
样！；*a lot* hěn duō 很多；
it was ~ a surprise zhēn
jīngrén 真惊人
quiz *n* wèndá bǐsài 问答
比赛
quota dìngliàng 定量
quote 1 *n (from author)*
yǐnwén 引文；*(price)* bàojià
报价；*(~ mark)* yǐnhào 引
号 2 *v/t text* yǐnyòng 引用；
price bàojià 报价

R

rabbit tùzi 兔子
race1 *n* SP jìngsài 竞赛；*the
~s (horse ~s)* pǎomǎ 跑马

2 *v/i (run fast)* jíxíng 疾行
racial zhǒngzú 种族
racism zhǒngzú qíshì 种

族歧视

racist n zhǒngzú qíshìzhě 种
族歧视者

rack n (for bikes)
zìxíngchējià 自行车架;
(for bags on train) xíngli
jià 行李架; (for CDs)
chàngpiān jià 唱片架

racket[1] sp qiúpāi 球拍

racket[2] (noise) xuānnào 喧
闹; criminal piànjú 骗局

radar léidá 雷达

radiator nuǎnqì 暖气; (in
car) qǔnuǎnqì 取暖器

radical 1 adj chèdǐ 彻底,
POL jìjìn 激进 **2** n POL jìjìn
zhǔyìzhě激进主义者

radio shōuyīnjī 收音机

radioactive fàngshèxìng
放射性

rag (for cleaning) mābù 抹布

rage n kuángnù 狂怒

raid 1 n (MIL, by police) tūxí
突袭; (by robbers) qiǎngjié
抢劫 **2** v/t (MIL, of police)
tūrán sōuchá 突然搜查;
(of robbers) tūrán xíjī 突
然袭击

rail (on track) tiěguǐ 铁轨;
(hand~) fúshǒu 扶手

railings lángān 栏杆

railroad tiělù 铁路

railroad station huǒchēzhàn
火车站

rain 1 n yǔ 雨; **the ~s** yǔjì
雨季 **2** v/i xiàyǔ 下雨;
it's ~ing xià zhe yǔne 下
着雨呢

raincoat yǔyī 雨衣

raise 1 n (in pay) zēngjiā
增加 **2** v/t children fǔyǎng
抚养

rally n (meeting) jíhuì 集会

ranch n dà mùchǎng 大牧场

rancher mùchǎng zhǔ 牧
场主

random 1 adj suíjī 随机 **2** n:
at ~ suíbiàn 随便

range n (of goods) xìliè 系
列; (of gun) shèchéng 射
程; (of airplane) zuìdà
xíngchéng 最大行程; (of
mountains) shānmài 山脉

rank n MIL jūnxián 军衔

ransack xǐjié 洗劫

ransom shújīn 赎金;
**hold
X to ~** bǎngjià X yǐ lèsuǒ
shújīn 绑架 X 以勒索赎金

rape n & v/t qiángjiān 强奸

rapid kuài 快

rapids jíliú 急流

rare hǎnjiàn 罕见

rarely hěnshǎo 很少

rash¹ MED pízhěn 皮疹

rash² adj action lǔmǎng 鲁莽

rat lǎoshǔ 老鼠

rate n (of exchange) bǐlǜ 比率; (speed) sùdù 速度

rather (fairly) xiāngdāng 相当

rational hélǐ 合理

rationalize v/t production etc shǐ hélǐhuà 使合理化

raw food shēng 生; sugar, iron wèijīng jiāgōng 未经加工

raw materials yuán cáiliào 原材料

ray guāngxiàn 光线

razor tìxūdāo 剃须刀

razor blade tìxūdāo dāopiàn 剃须刀刀片

reach v/t city etc dàodá 到达; (go as far as) dào 到; decision dédào 得到

react fǎnyìng 反应

reaction fǎnyìng 反应

reactionary n & adj POL fǎndòng pài 反动派

reactor (nuclear) fǎnyìng duī 反应堆

read 1 v/t dú 读; Chinese rènshi 认识 2 v/i yuèdú 阅读

reader (person) dúzhě 读者

readily admit xīnrán 欣然

reading yuèdú 阅读; (from meter etc) dúshù 读数

ready (prepared) zhǔnbèi hǎo 准备好; (willing) yuànyì 愿意

real adj zhēn 真

realistic xiànshí 现实

reality xiànshí 现实

realize v/t truth yìshí dào 意识到; ideal shíxiàn 实现

really zhēnzhèng 真正; (very) hěn 很; ~? zhēnde ma? 真的吗？

realtor búdòng chǎn zhōngjiān shāng 不动产中间商

rear adj legs hòu 后; seats, lights hòumian 后面

reason n (faculty) lǐzhì 理智; (cause) yuányīn 原因

reasonable person hélǐ 合理; price gōngpíng 公平

reassuring lìngrén yǒu xìnxīn 令人有信心

rebel n fǎnpànzhě 反叛者

rebellion fǎnpàn 反叛

recall v/t ambassador zhàohuí 召回; (remember) jìqǐ 记起

receipt shōujù 收据; *acknowledge ~ of* quèrèn shōudào 确认收

receive shōudào 收到

recent zuìjìn 最近

recently zuìjìn 最近

reception (*in hotel, company*) jiēdàichù 接待处; (*party*) zhāodài huì 招待会; (*welcome*) huānyíng 欢迎; (*for phone etc*) jiēshōu 接收

reception desk jiēdàichù 接待处

receptionist jiēdàiyuán 接待员

recession bù jǐngqì 不景气

recipe càipǔ 菜谱

recipient (*of parcel etc*) jiēshōurén 接收人; (*of money*) shōukuǎnrén 收款人

reciprocal hùhuì 互惠

recite *poem* bèisòng 背诵

reckless búgù hòuguǒ 不顾后果

reckon rènwéi 认为

recognition (*of state, achievements*) chéngrèn 承认

recognize *person, tune* rènde

认得; *symptoms* biànrèn chū 辨认出; POL chéngrèn 承认

recommend tuījiàn 推荐

recommendation tuījiàn 推荐

reconciliation tiáojiě 调解

recondition xiūfù 修复

reconnaissance MIL zhēnchá 侦察

reconsider *v/t & v/i* chóngxīn kǎolǜ 重新考虑

record 1 *n* MUS chàngpiàn 唱片; SP jìlù 纪录; (*written, in database*) jìlù 记录; *~s* dǎng'àn 档案 **2** *v/t* (*on tape etc*) lù 录

record-breaking dǎpò jìlù 打破纪录

record holder jìlù bǎochízhě 纪录保持者

recording lùyīn 录音

recover 1 *v/t sth lost* zhǎohuí 找回 **2** *v/i* MED huīfù 恢复

recovery (*of sth lost*) zhǎohuí 找回; MED huīfù 恢复

recreation yúlè 娱乐

recruit 1 *n* MIL xīnbīng 新兵; (*to company*) xīnlái de 新来的 **2** *v/t new staff* zhā opìn 招聘；MIL zhēngmù 征募

recruitment zhāopìn 招聘

rectangle chángfāng xíng 长方形

recurrent zàifā 再发

recycle huíshōu 回收

recycling huíshōu 回收

red hóng 红

Red Army Hóngjūn 红军

Red Cross Hóngshízì 红十字

redevelop *part of town* chóngxīn fāzhǎn 重新发展

red-handed: *catch X ~* dāngchǎng bǔhuò X 当场捕获X

redhead yǒu hóng tóufà de rén 有红头发的人

red light MOT hóngdēng 红灯

red tape guānliáo chéngxù 官僚程序

reduce jiàngdī 降低

reduction jiǎnshǎo 减少

reel *(of film, thread)* juǎn 卷

refer v/i: *~ to* tídào 提到

referee SP cáipàn 裁判；*(for job)* tuījiànrén 推荐人

reference shèjí 涉及；*(for job)* tuījiàn 推荐；*(~*

number) cānkǎo hàomǎ 参考号码

refinery tíliàn chǎng 提炼厂

reflect 1 v/t *light* fǎnshè 反射 **2** v/i *(think)* fǎnxíng 反省

reflection fǎnshè 反射；*(consideration)* fǎnxíng 反省

reflex fǎnyìng nénglì 反应能力

reform n & v/t gǎigé 改革

refreshing *drink* qīngshuǎng 清爽；*experience* qīngxīn yuèmù 清新悦目

refrigerate lěngcáng 冷藏

refrigerator bīngxiāng 冰箱

refuel v/t & v/i jiā ránliào 加燃料

refugee nànmín 难民

refund n & v/t tuìkuǎn 退款

refusal jùjué 拒绝

refuse: *~ to do X* jùjué zuò X 拒绝做X

regard 1 n: *(kind) ~s* wènhòu 问候 **2** v/t: *~ as Y* bǎ X kànzuò Y 把X看作Y

regardless: *~ of* bùgù 不顾

regime POL zhèngquán 政权

regiment n tuán 团

region dìqū 地区

regional dìqū 地区

register 1 n dēngjì bù 登记簿 **2** v/t birth, death dēngjì 登记; car shàngpái 上牌; letter guàhào 挂号 **3** v/i (for course, with police) dēngjì 登记

regret 1 v/t hòuhuǐ 后悔 **2** n yíhàn 遗憾

regular 1 adj flights dìngqī 定期; intervals yǒu guīlǜ 有规律; pattern, shape yúnchèn 匀称; (normal) pǔtōng 普通 **2** n (at bar etc) chángkè 常客

regulate kòngzhì 控制

regulation (rule) guīzhāng 规章

rehearsal páiyǎn 排演

rehearse v/t & v/i páiyǎn 排演

reimburse bǔcháng 补偿

reinforce structure xiūbǔ 修补; beliefs jiāqiáng 加强

reject v/t jùjué 拒绝

relapse MED jiùbìng fùfā 旧病复发

related (by family) yǒu qīnshǔ guānxì 有亲属关系; events, ideas xiāngguān 相关

relation (in family) qīnshǔ 亲属; (connection) guānxi 关系

relationship guānxi 关系

relative 1 n qīnqi 亲戚 **2** adj xiāngduì 相对

relatively xiāngduì 相对

relax v/i fàngsōng 放松

relaxation fàngsōng 放松

relay n: ~ (race) jiēlìsài 接力赛

release 1 n (from prison) shìfàng 释放; (of CD etc) fāxíng 发行 **2** v/t prisoner shìfàng 释放; parking brake sōngkāi 松开; information gōngbù 公布

relent ràngbù 让步

relentless (determined) búxiè 不懈; rain etc wúqíng 无情

relevant yǒuguān 有关

reliable kěkào 可靠

relief kuānwèi 宽慰

relieve pressure, pain jiǎnqīng 减轻; **be ~d** (at news etc) kuānwèi 宽慰

religion zōngjiào 宗教

relocate v/i bānqiān 搬迁

reluctance miǎnqiǎng 勉强

reluctant miǎnqiǎng 勉强

be ~ to do X bù qíngyuàn zuò X 不情愿做X

♦ **rely on** yīkào 依靠

remain (be left) shèngxia 剩下; (stay) dāizài 呆在

remark n huà 话

remarkable fēifán 非凡

remember v/t & v/i jìde 记得

remind: **~ X to do Y** tíxǐng X zuò Y 提醒X做Y; **~ of Y** (call to mind) shǐ X xiǎngqǐ Y 使X想起Y

reminder tíxǐng wù 提醒物; (to pay) cuīzhàng dān 催账单

reminisce huáijiù 怀旧

remnant cánjì 残迹

remorse àohuǐ 懊悔

remote village piānpì 偏僻; ancestor jiǔyuǎn 久远

remote control yáokòng 遥控

removal yídòng 移动; (from home) qiānjū 迁居

remove yídòng 移动; top, lid nákāi 拿开; tumor qùchú 去除; doubt jiěchú 解除

renew contract etc yánqī 延期; talks chóngxīn kāishǐ 重新开始

renounce v/t xuānbù fàngqì 宣布放弃

rent 1 n zūjīn 租金; **for ~** chūzū 出租 **2** v/t zū 租; (~ out) chūzū 出租

rental zūjīn 租金

rental car zūyòngde chē 租用的车

reopen v/t store chóngxīn kāizhāng 重新开张; negotiations zài jìnxíng 再进行

repair v/t & n xiūlǐ 修理

repay money chánghuán 偿还; person bàodá 报答

repeal v/t law fèichú 废除

repeat 1 v/t chóngfù 重复 **2** n (TV program) chóngbō 重播

repeated fǎnfù 反复

repel v/t attack jītuì 击退; insects qūgǎn 驱赶

repercussions yīngxiǎng 影响

repetitive chóngfù 重复

replace (put back) fànghuí fàngloù 放回; (take place of) tìdài 替代

replacement dàitìrén 代替人; (thing) dàitì wù 代替物

replica fùzhì pǐn 复制品

reply n, v/t & v/i huídá 回答

report 1 n (account) bàogào 报告; (by journalist) bàodào 报道 **2** v/t (to authorities) tōngzhī 通知

reporter jìzhě 记者

represent (act for) dàibiǎo 代表; (stand for) zhǔzhāng 主张

representative n dàibiǎorén 代表人; COM dàilǐshāng 代理商; POL zhòngyìyuán 众议员

repress revolt zhènyā 镇压; feelings yāyì 压抑; laugh rěnzhe 忍着

reprieve n & v/t huǎnxíng 缓刑

reprimand v/t shēnchì 申斥

reprisal bàofù xíngwéi 报复行为

reproach n zébèi 责备

reproduce 1 v/t zàixiàn 再现 **2** v/i BIO fánzhí 繁殖

republic gònghé guó 共和国

republican 1 n gònghé zhǔyìzhě 共和主义者; POL **Republican** Gònghé dǎngrén 共和党人 **2** adj gònghé zhǔyì 共和主义

Republic of China Zhōnghuá Mínguó 中华民国

repulsive lìngrén yànwù 令人厌恶

reputable yǒu míngshēng 有名声

reputation míngyù 名誉

request n & v/t yāoqiú 要求

require (need) xūyào 需要

requirement (need) xūyào 需要; (condition) tiáojiàn 条件

rescue n & v/t yuánjiù 援救

research n yánjiū 研究

research and development yánjiū yǔ fāzhǎn 研究与发展

resemble xiàng 像

resent bùmǎn 不满

reservation (of room, table) yùdìng 预定

reserve 1 n (store) chǔbèi 储备; SP yùbèi duìyuán 预备队员; ~ FIN chǔbèi jīn 储备金 **2** v/t room, table yùdìng 预定

residence (stay) jūzhù 居住

residence permit jūliúzhèng 居留证

resident n jūmín 居民

resign v/i cízhí 辞职

resignation cízhí 辞职

(mental) wúkěnàihé 无
可奈何
resist v/t dǐkàng 抵抗
resistance dǐkàng 抵抗
resolution (decision) juéyì
决议; (New Year) juédìng
决定
resort n (place) dùjià
shèngdì 度假胜地
resource zīyuán 资源
resourceful zúzhì duōmóu
足智多谋
respect 1 n for older
people zūnjìng 尊敬;
(consideration) zūnzhòng
尊重; **with ~ to** guānyú 关
于 2 v/t person, opinion,
privacy zūnzhòng 尊重;
law zūnshǒu 遵守
respectable person tǐmiàn
体面; bar xiàngyàng 象样
respond dáfù 答复; (react)
zuòchūfǎnyìng 做出反应
response dáfù 答复;
(reaction) fǎnyìng 反应
responsibility zérèn 责任
responsible fùzé 负责
rest[1] 1 n & v/i xiūxi 休息
2 v/i (lean etc) kào 靠
rest[2] n: **the ~** yúxià 余下
restaurant cānguǎn 餐馆

restore building xiūfù 修复
restrain yuēshù 约束; **~
oneself** kòngzhì zìjǐ 控
制自己
restraint (moderation) jiézhì
节制
restrict xiànzhì 限制
restricted area MIL jìndì
禁地
restriction xiànzhì 限制
rest room wèishēngjiān 卫
生间
result n jiéguǒ结果
resume v/t huīfù 恢复
résumé lǚlì 履历
retail adv yǐ língshòu fāngshì
以零售方式
retaliate bàofù 报复
retire v/i (from work) tuìxiū
退休
retirement tuìxiū 退休
retract v/t claws suōjìn 缩进;
statement shōuhuí 收回
retreat v/i MIL chètuì 撤退
retrieve wǎnjiù 挽救
retrospective huígù 回顾
return 1 n fǎnhuí 返回;
(giving back) tuìhuán 退
还; COMPUT fǎnhuí 返回;
(in tennis) huíqiú 回球 2 v/t
(give back) tuìhuán 退还

(put back) fànghuí 放回

favor, invitation huíbào 回
报 **3** v/i *(go back)* fǎnhuí 返
回; *(of old days, doubts)*
huīfù 回复

reunion tuánjù 团聚

reunite v/t tǒngyī 统一

reveal *(make visible)* xiǎnshì
显示; *secret* jiēlù 揭露

revealing *remark* tòulù
zhēnxiàng 透露真相

revenge n bàofù 报复

revenue shōurù 收入

reverse 1 n *(opposite)*
xiāngfǎn 相反; *(back)*
bèimiàn 背面; MOT
dàodǎng 倒档 **2** v/i MOT
dàochē 倒车

review 1 n *(of book, movie)*
pínglùn 评论 **2** v/t *book,
movie* pínglùn 评论;
situation shěnchá 审查;
EDU fùxí 复习

reviewer pínglùn jiā 评论家

revise v/t *opinion* xiūzhèng
修正; *text* jiàozhèng 校正

revision *(of text)* jiàozhèng
校正

revisionism POL xiūzhèng
zhǔyì 修正主义

revive 1 v/t *custom* fùxīng 复
兴; *patient* shǐ sūxǐng 使
苏醒 **2** v/i *(of business)* shǐ
shàngshēng 使上升

revolt 1 n fǎnkàng 反抗 **2** v/i
zàofǎn 造反

revolting *(awful)* èxīn 恶心

revolution POL *etc* gémìng 革
命; *(turn)* xuánzhuǎn 旋转

revolutionary 1 n POL
gémìng jiā 革命家 **2** adj
ideas chuàngxīn 创新

revolutionize chèdǐ biàngé
彻底变革

revulsion fǎngǎn 反感

reward n *(financial)* shǎngjīn
赏金; *(benefit)* bàochóu
报酬

rewarding zhíde zuò 值得做

rhyme n yùn 韵

rhythm jiézòu 节奏

rib lèigǔ 肋骨

ribbon sīdài 丝带

rice mǐ 米; *(food)* mǐfàn
米饭

rice bowl fànwǎn 饭碗

rich 1 adj yǒuqián 有钱;
food yóunì 油腻 **2** n: the ~
fùrén 富人

rickshaw rénlìchē 人力车

rid: get ~ of *waste* rēngdiào
扔掉; *accent etc* bǎituō

摆脱

ride 1 n (on horse) qímǎ 骑马; (in vehicle) chèngchējīhuì 乘车机会; (journey) lǚtú 旅途 **2** v/t horse, bike qí 骑 **3** v/i (on horse) qímǎ 骑马; (on bike) qí zìxíngchē 骑自行车; (in vehicle) chèngchē 乘车

ridicule 1 n xīluò 奚落 **2** v/t fēngcì 讽刺

ridiculous huāngmiù 荒谬

rifle n láifú qiāng 来复枪

right 1 adj (correct) zhèngquè 正确; (proper, just) zhèngdàng 正当; (suitable) héshì 合适; (not left) yòu 右; be ~ (of answer) zhèngquè 正确; (of person) zhèngzhí 正直; that's ~! duì a! 对啊! **2** adv (directly) jiù 就; (correctly) zhèngquè 正确; (not left) yòu 右; ~ now (immediately) mǎshàng 马上; (at the moment) xiànzài 现在 **3** n (civil, legal) quánlì 权利; (not left) yòu 右; POL yòupài 右派; on the ~ zài yòubiān 在右边; POL zài

yòuyì nàbiān 在右翼那边

rightful owner etc héfǎ 合法

right-handed yòu piězi 右撇子

right wing POL, SP yòuyì 右翼

rigid material jiānyìng 坚硬; attitude kèbǎn 刻板

rigorous discipline yángé 严格; tests jīngquè 精确

rim (of wheel) lúnyuán 轮缘

ring¹ (circle) yuánquān 圆圈; (on finger) jièzhi 戒指; (boxing) quánjīchǎng 拳击场

ring² **1** n (of bell) zhōngshēng 钟声 **2** v/t bell qiāozhōng 敲钟 **3** v/i (of bell) míng 鸣

ringleader tóumù 头目

rinse 1 n (for hair) rǎnsè 染色 **2** v/t piǎoxǐ 漂洗

riot 1 n bàoluàn 暴乱 **2** v/i nàoshì 闹事

rip n & v/t (in cloth) sīliè 撕裂

ripe fruit shóu 熟

rip-off n F bōxuē 剥削

rise n & v/i (in price, temperature) shàngzhǎng 上涨; (in water level) shàngshēng 上升; (of sun) shēngqǐ 升起

risk 1 n fēngxiǎn 风险 **2** v/t mào ... fēngxiǎn 冒 ... 风险

rival n duìshǒu 对手

rivalry jìngzhēng 竞争

river héliú 河流

road lù 路

roadblock lùzhàng 路障

road map xiànlù tú 线路图

roadsign lùbiāo 路标

roam mànyóu 漫游

roar v/i (of lion) páoxiào 咆哮; (of person) dàshēng chǎo 大声吵

roast v/t & v/i kǎo 烤

rob qiǎngjié 抢劫

robber qiǎngjiézhě 抢劫者

robbery qiǎngjié 抢劫

robot jīqìrén 机器人

robust health jiànzhuàng 健壮; material jiāngù 坚固

ROC (= **Republic of China**) Zhōnghuá Mínguó 中华民国

rock 1 n yánshí 岩石 **2** v/i (on chair) yáodòng 摇动; (of boat) yáohuàng 摇晃

rocket n huǒjiàn 火箭

rock'n'roll yáogǔn yuè 摇滚乐

role juésè 角色

role model bǎngyàng 榜样

roll 1 n (bread) xiǎo yuán miànbāo 小圆面包; (of film) juǎn 卷 **2** v/i (of ball) gǔn 滚

roller skate n hànbīng xié 旱冰鞋

romantic làngmàn 浪漫

roof wūdǐng 屋顶

room fángjiān 房间; (space) kōngjiān 空间

roommate shìyǒu 室友

room service fángjiān fúwù 房间服务

root gēn 根; **~s** (of person) gēnjī 根基

rope shéng 绳

rot n & v/i fǔlàn 腐烂

rotate v/i xuánzhuàn 旋转

rotten food, wood fǔlàn 腐烂

rough adj surface bùpíng 不平; voice shǎyǎ 沙哑; (violent) cūbào 粗暴; seas jiānnán 艰难; (approximate) dàgài 大概

roughly (approximately) dàyuē 大约

round 1 adj yuán 圆 **2** n (of competition) chǎng 场

round trip láihuí lǚxíng 来回旅行

rouse (*from sleep*) xǐng 醒;
interest shāndòng 煽动
route lùxiàn 路线
routine adj & n chángguī
常规
row (*line*) pái 排; (*in
spreadsheet etc*) háng 行
rowboat huátǐng 划艇
royal adj huángjiā 皇家
rub v/t cuō 搓
rubber 1 n xiàngpí 橡皮
2 adj xiàngjiāo 橡胶
rude cūlǔ 粗鲁
rudeness wúlǐ 无礼
rudimentary jīběn 基本
rug xiǎo dìtǎn 小地毯;
(*blanket*) tǎnzi 毯子
rugged scenery qíqū 崎岖;
face cūguǎng 粗犷
ruin 1 n: **~s** fèixū 废墟 **2** v/t
party, plans pòhuài 破坏;
reputation huǐhuài 毁坏;
~ed (*financially*) pòchǎn
破产
rule 1 n (*of club, game*) guīzé
规则; **as a ~** tōngcháng 通
常 **2** v/t & v/i (*of monarch*)
tǒngzhì 统治
ruler (*to measure*) chǐzi 尺
子; (*of state*) tǒngzhìzhě
统治者

ruling adj POL. dāngquán
当权
rumor n yáoyán 谣言
run 1 n (*on foot*) pǎobù 跑
步; (*in pantyhose*) chōusī
抽丝 **2** v/i pǎo 跑; (*of
river*) liú 流; (*of trains etc*)
xíngshǐ 行驶; (*of makeup*)
tǎngliú 淌流; (*of faucet*)
kāi 开; (*of play*) liánxù
yǎnchū 连续演出; (*of
engine, software*) yùnzhuǎn
运转; **~ for President**
jìngxuǎn zǒngtǒng 竞选总
统 **3** v/t race jìngsài 竞赛; 3
miles etc pǎo 跑; business
guǎnlǐ 管理
run-down person píjuàn
疲倦; area pòjiù 破旧;
building shīxiū 失修
runner sàipǎozhě 赛跑者
runner-up yàjūn 亚军
running dog pej zǒugǒu
走狗
running water (*from
faucet*) zìláishuǐ 自来水;
(*flowing*) liúshuǐ 流水
runway pǎodào 跑道
rural nóngcūn 农村
rush 1 n tūjī 突击 **2** v/t
person cuī 催 **3** v/i gǎn 赶

rush hour gāofēng shíjiān 高
峰时间

rust *n* xiù 锈

rusty shēngxiù 生锈; *French
etc* shēngshū 生疏

ruthless wúqíng 无情

S

sack *n* dà kǒudài 大口袋

sad bēishāng 悲伤; *state of
affairs* yíhàn 遗憾

sadist nüèdàikuáng 虐待狂

sadly yōuchóu 忧愁;
(*regrettably*) lìngrén yíhàn
令人遗憾

sadness yōuchóu 忧愁

safe 1 *adj* (*not dangerous*)
ānquán 安全; (*not in
danger*) wúwéixiǎn 无危
险 **2** *n* bǎoxiǎnguì 保险柜

safely *arrive* píng'ān 平安;
drive ānquán 安全

safety ānquán 安全

safety pin biézhēn 别针

sail 1 *n* fān 帆; (*trip*)
hángchéng hángxíng 航程 **2** *v/i*
jiàshǐchuán 驾驶船;
(*depart*) qǐháng 启航

sailboat fānchuán 帆船

sailing SP fānchuán yùndòng
帆船运动

sailor (*in navy*) hǎiyuán 海

员; SP shuǐshǒu 水手

saint shèngtú 圣徒

sake: *for my / your ~* wèile
wǒ / nǐ 为了我 / 你

salad sèlā 色拉

salary xīnshuǐ 薪水

sale xiāoshòu 销售;
(*reduced prices*) liánjià
chūshòu 廉价出售; *for ~*
dàishòu 待售

sales clerk shòuhuòyuán
售货员

salesman tuīxiāoyuán 推
销员

salt yán 盐

salty xián 咸

salute 1 *n* MIL jìnglǐ 敬礼
2 *v/t & v/i* zhìjìng 致敬

same 1 *adj* tóngyàng 同样
2 *pron*: *I'll have the ~ as
you* hé nǐ yíyàng 和你
一样 **3** *adv*: *look the ~*
kànqǐlái yíyàng 看起来
一样

sample n yàngběn 样本

sanction n (penalty) zhìcái 制裁

sand n shā 沙

sandal liángxié 凉鞋

sandwich n sānmíngzhì 三明治

sane shénzhì zhèngcháng 神志正常

sanitarium liáoyǎngyuàn 疗养院

sanitary wèishēng 卫生; installations qīngjié 清洁

sanitary napkin wèishēngjīn 卫生巾

sanitation (installations) wèishēng shèbèi 卫生设备; (waste removal) páiwū 排污

sanity shénzhì zhèngcháng 神志正常

sarcasm jīfèng 讥讽

sarcastic jīfèng 讥讽

SARS fēidiǎn 非典

satellite wèixīng 卫星

satire fěngcì 讽刺

satirical hán fěngcì yìwèi 含讽刺意味

satisfaction mǎnzú 满足

satisfactory lìngrén mǎnyì 令人满意; (just ok) fúhé yāoqiú 符合要求

satisfy customers shǐ mǎnyì 使满意; needs mǎnzú 满足; conditions fúhé 符合

Saturday xīngqīliù 星期六

sauce jiàng 酱

saucer chábēidié 茶杯碟

sauna sāngná 桑拿

sausage xiāngcháng 香肠

savage adj animal yěxìng 野性; attack cánkù 残酷; criticism èdú 恶毒

save 1 v/t (rescue) jiù 救; money chǔcún 储存; time jiéshěng 节省; COMPUT cúnpán 存盘 **2** v/i (put money aside) zǎnqián 攒钱 **3** n SP jiùqiú 救球

saving (amount) jiéshěng 节省; (activity) cúnqián 存钱

savings cúnkuǎn 存款

saw n (tool) jù 锯

say v/t shuō 说

saying yànyǔ 谚语

scaffolding jiǎoshǒujià 脚手架

scale n (size) guīmó 规模; (of map) bǐlì 比例; MUS yīnjiē 音阶

scales (to weigh) tiānpíng 天平

scan v/t horizon, page sǎoshì 扫视; MED sǎomiáo 扫描; COMPUT sōusuǒ 搜索

scandal liúyán fēiyǔ 流言 蜚语

scanner MED sǎomiáoqì 扫 描器; COMPUT sǎomiáoyí 扫描仪

scar n shāngbā 伤疤

scarce duǎnquē 短缺

scarcely jīhūbù 几乎不

scare 1 v/t jīngxià 惊吓; **be ~d of** hàipà 害怕 **2** n (panic, alarm) jīngkǒng 惊恐

scarf (for neck) wéijīn 围巾; (over head) tóujīn 头巾

scary hěn kǒngbù 很恐怖

scatter 1 v/t leaflets, seed sǎ 撒 **2** v/i (of crowd) sànkāi 散开

scenario qíngkuàng 情况

scene THEA chǎng 场; (view, sight) qíngjǐng 情景; (of accident etc) shìfā dìdiǎn 事发地点; (argument) chǎonào 吵闹

scenery jǐngsè 景色; THEA wǔtái bùjǐng 舞台布景

scent n xiāngwèi 香味

schedule n (of events)

chéngxùbiǎo 程序表; (of work) jìhuàbiǎo 计划 表; (for trains) shíkèbiǎo 时 刻表; **be on ~** àn yùdìng shíjiān 按预定时间; **be behind ~** luòhòuyú yùdìng jìhuà 落后于预定计划

scheduled flight dìngqī hángbān 定期航班

scheme n (plan) jìhuà 计划; (plot) yīnmóu 阴谋

schizophrenia jīngshén fēnlièzhèng 精神分裂症

scholarship xuéshù chéngjiù 学术成就; (financial award) jiǎngxuéjīn 奖学金

school xuéxiào 学校; (university) xuéyuàn 学院; **go to ~** shàngxué 上学

schoolchildren zhōngxiǎo-xué xuésheng 中小学 学生

schoolteacher zhōngxiǎoxué jiàoshī 中小学教师

science kēxué 科学

science fiction kēhuàn 科幻

scientific kēxué 科学

scientist kēxuéjiā 科学家

scissors jiǎnzi 剪子

scoff v/i jīxiào 讥笑

scold v/t zémà 责骂

scooter MOT xiǎoxíng mótuōchē 小型摩托车

scope fànwéi 范围; (opportunity) jīhuì 机会

scorch v/t tàngjiāo 烫焦

score 1 n SP bǐfēn 比分; (written music) yuèpǔ 乐谱 **2** v/t & v/i SP défēn 得分

scorn n bǐshì 鄙视

scornful qīngmiè 轻蔑

scowl n nùróng 怒容

scrap 1 n (metal) fèijīnshǔ 废金属; (little bit) shǎoliàng 少量 **2** v/t project etc fèidiào 废掉

scrape 1 n (on paint) guācā 刮擦 **2** v/t paint guādiào 刮掉; arm cāshāng 擦伤

scratch 1 n (mark) huáhén 划痕 **2** v/t guācā 刮擦; itch sāoyǎng 搔痒

scream 1 n jiānjiàoshēng 尖叫声 **2** v/i jiānjiào 尖叫

screen 1 n (in room, hospital) gélián 隔帘; (protective) yǎnbìwù 掩避物; (for movie) yínmù 银幕; COMPUT píngmù 屏幕 **2** v/t (protect, hide) zhēbì 遮蔽; (for security) shěnchá

审查

screw n luósīdīng 螺丝钉

screwdriver luósīdāo 螺丝刀

scribble n liáocǎode zìjì 潦草的字迹

script (for play) jiǎoběn 脚本; (writing) shūxiětǐ 书写体

scriptwriter zhuàngǎorén 撰稿人

scroll n (manuscript) zhǐjuǎn 纸卷

scrub v/t floor etc cāxǐ 擦洗

scruples gùlǜ 顾虑

scrutinize xìchá 细察

scuba diving dài shuǐfèi qiánshuǐ 戴水肺潜水

sculpture n (art) diāokè 雕刻; (object) diāosù 雕塑

sea dàhǎi 大海; **by the ~** zài hǎibiān 在海边

seafood hǎiwèi 海味

seal 1 n (on document) yìnzhāng 印章; TECH mìfēng 密封 **2** v/t container mìfēng 密封

sea level: above / below ~ gāoyú / dīyú hǎipíngmiàn 高于 / 低于海平面

seam n (on garment) fèng 缝

search 1 *n* sōuxún 搜寻
2 *v/t* sōuchá 搜查
◆ search for xúnzhǎo 寻找
searchlight tànzhàodēng
探照灯
search party sōusuǒduì 搜
索队
seasick yùnchuán 晕船
season *n* (of year) jìjié 季
节; (for tourism etc) wàngjì
旺季
seasoning zuóliào 作料
season ticket chángqīpiào
长期票
seat *n* zuòwèi 座位; (of
pants) túnbù 臀部
seat belt ānquándài 安全带
seaweed hǎidài 海带
secluded rénjìhǎnzhì 人
迹罕至
second 1 *n* (of time) yī
miǎozhōng 一秒钟 2 *adj*
dì'èr 第二 3 *adv* come yī
dì'èrwèi 以第二位
second best *adj* dì'èr hǎo
第二好
second class *adj* ticket
èrděng 二等
second-hand èrshǒu 二手
secondly qícì 其次
second-rate èrliú 二流

secrecy bǎomì 保密
secret *n* mìmì 秘密
secretary mìshū 秘书; POL
bùzhǎng 部长
Secretary of State
Guówùqīng 国务卿
secretive ài bǎomì 爱保密
sect pàibié 派别
section bùfen 部份
sector bùmén 部门
secure *adj* láogù 牢固;
feeling wú yōulǜ 无忧虑;
job yǒu bǎozhèng 有保证
security (in job) bǎozhàng
保障; (for investment)
bǎozhèng 保证; (at
airport etc) ānquán 安全;
(department) bǎo'ānbù
保安部
sedan xiǎo jiàochē 小轿车
sedative *n* zhènjìngyào 镇
静药
seduce gōuyǐn 勾引
see kànjiàn 看见;
(understand) míngbai 明
白; *can I ~ the manager?*
wǒ kěyǐ jiàn jīnglǐ ma? 我
可以见经理吗？; *~
you!* zàijiàn! 再见！
◆ see off (at airport etc)
sòngxíng 送行

♦**see to** (*handle*) chǔlǐ 处理

seed zhǒngzi 种子

seeing (*that*) jìrán 既然

seek v/t *job* xúnzhǎo 寻找

seem kànqǐlái 看起来

seemingly kànshangqu 看上去

segment bàn 瓣

segregate gélí 隔离

seize zhuāzhù 抓住;
opportunity bǎwò 把握;
(*of customs, police*) kòuyā 扣押

seldom hǎnjiàn 罕见

select 1 v/t xuǎnzé 选择
2 adj (*exclusive*) gāojí 高级

selection xuǎnzé 选择;
(*that chosen*) jīngxuǎn pǐn 精选品

selective tiāojiǎn 挑拣

self-confidence zìxìn 自信

self-conscious búzìrán 不自然

self-defense zìwèi 自卫

selfish zìsī 自私

self-respect zìzūn 自尊

self-service adj zìzhùshì 自助式

sell 1 v/t mài 卖 **2** v/i (*of products*) xiāoshòu 销售

semester xuéqī 学期

semi (*truck*) jiǎojiēchē 铰接车

semicircle bànyuánxíng 半圆形

semifinal bànjuésài 半决赛

seminar yántǎohuì 研讨会

senate cānyìyuàn 参议院

senator cānyìyuán 参议员

send v/t (*by mail*) yóujì 邮寄; (*by e-mail, fax etc*) fā 发

senile shuāilǎo 衰老

senior niánzhǎng 年长; (*in rank*) gāojí 高级

senior citizen lǎorén 老人

sensation (*feeling*) gǎnjué 感觉; (*surprise event*) hōngdòng 轰动

sensational hōngdòng 轰动; (*very good*) juémiào 绝妙

sense n (*meaning*) yìyì 意义; (*purpose, point*) yìsi 意思; (*common ~*) jiànshi 见识; (*of sight, smell etc*) guānnéng 官能; (*feeling*) gǎnjué 感觉

sensible míngzhì 明智; *advice* hélǐ 合理

sensitive skin jiāonèn 娇嫩; person mǐngǎn 敏感

sensuality ròuyù 肉欲

sentence n GRAM jùzi 句子; LAW túxíng 徒刑

sentimental shānggǎn 伤感

separate 1 adj dúlì 独立 2 v/t fēnkāi 分开 3 v/i (of couple) fēnjū 分居

separated couple fēnshǒu 分手

separation fēnlí 分离; (of couple) fēnshǒu 分手

September jiǔyuè 九月

sequel xùjí 续集

sequence n shùnxù 顺序

sergeant zhōngshì 中士

serial n liánxù gùshi 连续 故事

serial number biānhào 编号

series xìliè 系列

serious yánzhòng 严重; (person: earnest) rènzhēn 认真

seriously yánzhòng 严重

serve 1 n (in tennis) fāqiú 发球 2 v/t food duānshang 端上; customer zhāodài 招待; the people fúwù 服务 3 v/i (as politician etc) gòngzhí 供职; (in tennis) fāqiú 发球

service n fúwù 服务; (for machine) wéixiū 维修

service charge fúwùfèi 服务费

service industry fúwù hángyè 服务行业

service station jiāyóuzhàn 加油站

sesame oil xiāngyóu 香油

session (of Congress etc) huìyì 会议

set 1 n (of tools, books etc) tào 套; (of people) yìhuǒrén 一伙人; (for movie) pāishè chǎngdì 拍摄场地; (in tennis) pán 盘 2 v/t (place) fàng 放; date, time dìng 定; alarm clock tiáo 调; broken limb jiēhǎo 接好; ~ the table bǎifàng cānjù 摆放餐具 3 v/i (of sun) luò 落; (of glue) níngjié 凝结 4 adj views, ideas wángù 顽固; ~ meal dìngcān 定餐

setback zǔ'ài 阻碍

settle 1 v/i (of liquid) chéngqīng 澄清; (to live) dìngjū 定居 2 v/t dispute jiějué 解决; debts chánghuán 偿还

settlement (of claim, debt) qīngcháng 清偿; (of

dispute) jiějué 解决

sever *v/t* arm, cable qiēduàn 切断; *relations* zhōngduàn 中断

several *adj & pron* jǐgè 几个

severe *illness, penalty* yánzhòng 严重; *teacher, face* yánlì 严厉; *weather* èliè 恶劣

sew *v/i* féng 缝

sewer wūshuǐguǎn 污水管

sewing féngrèn 缝纫

sex (*act*) xìngjiāo 性交; (*gender*) xìngbié 性别

sexual xìng fāngmiàn 性方面

sexy xìnggǎn 性感

shabby *coat* hánsuān 寒酸

shade *n* (*for lamp*) dēngzhào 灯罩; (*of color*) sèdù 色度; (*on window*) liánzi 帘子

shadow *n* yǐngzi 影子

shady yīnliáng 阴凉; *dealings* kàobúzhù 靠不住

shake 1 *v/t* yáo 摇; **~ hands** wòshǒu 握手 **2** *v/i* (*of hands, voice*) chàndǒu 颤抖; (*of building*) huàngdòng 晃动

shallow qiǎn 浅; *person*

qiānbó 浅薄

shame 1 *n* xiūchǐ 羞耻; *what a ~!* zhēn yíhàn! 真遗憾! **2** *v/t* shǐ diūliǎn 使去脸

shampoo *n* xǐfàjīng 洗发精

Shanghai Shànghǎi 上海

shape *n* xíngzhuàng 形状

share 1 *n* yífèn 一份; FIN gǔfèn 股份 **2** *v/t* fēnxiǎng 分享; *opinion* gòngtóng jùyǒu 共同具有

sharp *adj knife* fēnglì 锋利; *mind* língmǐn 灵敏; *pain* jùliè 剧烈; *taste* xīnlà 辛辣

shatter *v/t glass* fěnsuì 粉碎; *illusions* pòmiè 破灭

shattering *news, experience* lìngrén zhènjīng 令人震惊

shave 1 *v/t* guā 刮 **2** *v/i* guāliǎn 刮脸

shaver (*electric*) tìdāo 剃刀

shawl pījiān 披肩

she tā 她

shed¹ *v/t blood, tears* liú 流

shed² *n* péng 棚

sheep miányáng 绵羊

sheer *adj madness, luxury* shízú 十足; *cliffs* jìnhū chuízhí 近乎垂直

sheet (for bed) chuángdān
床单; (of paper) zhāng 张;
(of metal, glass) bǎn 板

shelf jià 架

shell n ké 壳; MIL pàodàn
炮弹

shellfish bèilèi 贝类

shelter 1 n (refuge) bìhù 庇
护; yǎnbìwù
掩蔽物 2 v/i (from rain,
bombing etc) duǒbì 躲避
3 v/t (protect) bǎohù 保护

shift 1 n (in thinking)
gǎibiàn 改变; (switchover)
zhuǎnbiàn 转变; (period
of work) bān 班 2 v/t
(move) yídòng 移动 3 v/i
(move) nuódòng 挪动; (in
opinion) gǎibiàn 改变

shine 1 v/i zhàoyào 照耀;
(of polish) fāguāng 发光;
fig chūzhòng 出众 2 v/t
light zhàoyízhào 照一照

ship 1 n chuán 船 2 v/t
(send) yùnsòng 运送;
(send by sea) hǎiyùn 海运

shipment huòwù 货物

shipyard zàochuánchǎng
造船厂

shirt chènshān 衬衫

shiver v/i chàndǒu 颤抖

shock 1 n zhènjīng 震惊;
ELEC chùdiàn 触电 2 v/t
shǐrén zhènjīng 使人震惊

shocking lìngrén zhènjīng 令
人震惊; F (very bad) hěn
zāo 很糟

shoe xié 鞋

shoot v/t shèzhòng 射中;
(and kill) qiāngshā 枪毙;
movie pāishè 拍摄

shop 1 n shāngdiàn 商店
2 v/i mǎi dōngxi 买东西

shopper gòuwùrén 购物人

shopping (activity) gòuwù
购物; (items) mǎidào de
dōngxi 买到的东西

shore àn 岸

short adj (in height) ǎi 矮;
distance, time duǎn 短; be ~
of quēfá 缺乏

shortage quēfá 缺乏

shortcoming quēdiǎn 缺点

short cut jiéjìng 捷径

shorten v/t nòngduǎn 弄
短; text biànduǎn 变短;
vacation suōduǎn 缩短

shortfall chìzì 赤字

short-lived duǎnzàn 短暂

shortly (soon) bùjiǔ 不久

shorts duǎnkù 短裤;
(underwear) sānjiǎo kù

三角裤

shortsighted jìnshì 近视;
fig wú yuǎnjiàn 无远见

short-term duǎnqī 短期

shot shèjīshēng 射击声;
(photograph) jìngtóu 镜头

shotgun lièqiāng 猎枪

should yīnggāi 应该; *what ~
I do?* wǒ gāi zuò shénme?
我该做什么?; *you ~n't
do that* nǐ bù yīnggāi nàme
zuò 你不应该那么做

shoulder n jiānbǎng 肩膀

shout 1 n hǎnshēng 喊声
2 v/i jiàohǎn 叫喊 **3** v/t
mìnglìng 命令

shove 1 n zhuàng 撞 **2** v/t tuī
推 **3** v/i jǐ 挤

show 1 n THEA, TV jiémù 节
目; *(display)* biǎolù 表露
2 v/t *passport* chūshì 出示;
interest, emotion biǎodá 表
达; *movie* diànyǐng 电影
3 v/i *(be visible)* kàndéjiàn
看得见; *(of movie)*
shàngyìng 上映

shower 1 n *(of rain)* zhènyǔ
阵雨; *(to wash)* línyù 淋浴
2 v/i línyù 淋浴

show-off ài xuànyào de rén
爱炫耀的人

shred v/t *paper* sīchéng
suìpiàn 撕成碎片; *food*
qiēchéng xiǎotiáo 切成
小条

shrewd jīngmíng 精明

shrink v/i suōshuǐ 缩水; *(of
support etc)* jiǎnruò 减弱

shrug v/i sǒngjiān 耸肩

shudder v/i *(of person)*
fādǒu 发抖; *(of building)*
zhèndòng 震动

shun duǒbì 躲避

shut v/t & v/i guān 关
♦ **shut up** *(be quiet)*
ānjìng 安静; *~!* zhùzuǐ!
住嘴!

shy hàixiū 害羞

sick shēngbìng 生病; *I feel
~ (about to vomit)* wǒ gǎndào
ěxin 我感到恶心; *be
~ of* gǎndào yànwù 感到
厌恶

sick leave bìngjià 病假

side n *(of box, house)* cèmiàn
侧面; *(of room, field)* biān
边; *(of mountain)* miàn 面;
(of person) lèi bù 肋部; sp yìfāng
一方; *I'm on your ~* wǒ
zhīchí nǐ 我支持你; *~ by
~* bìngpái 并排

sideboard *(furniture)*

cānjùguì 餐具柜

sideburns liánbìn húzi 连鬓胡子

side effect fùzuòyòng 副作用

side street xiǎoxiàng 小巷

sidewalk rénxíngdào 人行道

sigh 1 *n* tànxí 叹息 2 *v/i* tànqì 叹气

sight *n* qíngjǐng 情景; (*power of seeing*) shìlì 视力; **~s** (*of city*) míngshèng 名胜

sightseeing guānguāng 观光

sign 1 *n* (*indication*) jìxiàng 迹象; (*road* ~) zhǐshìpái 指示牌; (*outside store*) zhāopai 招牌 2 *v/t & v/i* qiānzì 签字

signal 1 *n* xìnhào 信号 2 *v/i* (*of driver*) zhǐshì 指示

signature qiānmíng 签名

significance (*importance*) zhòngyàoxìng 重要性; (*meaning*) yìyì 意义

significant zhòngyào 重要; (*large*) dàliàng 大量

sign language shǒushì yǔ 手势语

silence 1 *n* chénmò 沉默 2 *v/t* yāzhì 压制

silent ānjìng 安静

silk 1 *n* sīchóu 丝绸 2 *adj shirt etc* sīzhì 丝制

silly shǎ 傻

silver 1 *n* yín 银 2 *adj* yínzhì 银制; *hair* huībái 灰白

similar xiāngsì 相似

similarity xiāngsì 相似

simple jiǎndān 简单; *person* tóunǎo jiǎndān 头脑简单

simplicity jiǎndān 简单

simplified characters jiǎntǐzì 简体字

simplify shǐ jiǎndān 使简单

simply (*absolutely*) juéduì 绝对

simultaneous tóngshí 同时

sin *n* zuì'è 罪恶

since 1 *prep* zìcóng 自从; **~** *last week* zìcóng shàngzhōu yǐlái 自从上周以来 2 *adv* zìnà yǐhòu 自那以后 3 *conj* (*time*) cóng … yǐlái 从 … 以来; (*seeing that*) jìrán 既然

sincere chéngzhì 诚挚

sincerity zhēnchéng 真诚

sing chàng 唱

Singapore Xīnjiāpō 新加坡

singer gēshǒu 歌手

single n (sole) wéiyī 唯一;
(not double) yígè 一个;
(not married) dúshēn 独身

single parent dānqīn 单亲

sinister xié'è 邪恶

sink 1 n xǐdícáo 洗涤槽
2 v/i chénmò 沉没; (of
sun) luòxia 落下

sip n yìxiǎokǒu 一小口

sir xiānsheng 先生

sister (older) jiějie 姐姐;
(younger) mèimei 妹妹

sister-in-law (wife's elder
sister) qīzǐ 妻姊; (wife's
younger sister) qīmèi
妻妹; (husband's elder
sister) dàgūjiě 大姑姐;
(husband's younger sister)
xiǎogū 小姑; (younger
brother's wife) dìmèi 弟
妹; (older brother's wife)
sǎozi 嫂子

sit v/i zuò 坐

♦ **sit down** zuòxia 坐下

sitcom qíngjǐng xǐjù 情景
喜剧

site n chǎngdì 场地

sitting room kètīng 客厅

situated: be ~ zuòluòzai
坐落在

situation xíngshì 形势; (of
building etc) wèizhi 位置

size dàxiǎo 大小; (of jacket,
shoes) hàomǎ 号码

skate v/i (on ice) huábīng
滑冰; (roller skating) huá
hànbīng 滑旱冰

skateboard n huábǎn 滑板

skeptic n huáiyílùn zhě 怀
疑论者

skeptical huáiyí 怀疑

skepticism huáiyí tàidu 怀
疑态度

sketch 1 n cǎotú 草图; THEA
huájī duǎnjù 滑稽短剧
2 v/t xièshēng 写生

ski n & v/i huáxuě 滑雪

skid n shāchē 刹车 2 v/i
dǎhuá 打滑

skiing huáxuě 滑雪

skill jìqiǎo 技巧

skilled yǒujìnéng 有技能

skillful shúliàn 熟练

skin 1 n pífū 皮肤 2 v/t qùpí
去皮

skinny píbāogǔ 皮包骨

skip 1 n (little jump) bèng 蹦
2 v/t (omit) lüèguò 略过

skipper NAUT chuánzhǎng
船长; (of team) duìzhǎng
队长

skirt *n* qúnzi 裙子

skull *n* tóulúgǔ 头颅骨

sky tiānkōng 天空

skyscraper mótiān dàlóu 摩天大楼

slack *rope* sōngchí 松驰; *discipline* xièdài 懈怠; *work* cūxīn 粗心; *period* qīngdàn 清淡

slacken *rope* sōngchí 松驰; *pace* fàngmàn 放慢

slam *v/t door* pēngde guān-shang 砰地关上

slander *n* & *v/t* fěibàng 诽谤

slant *v/i* qīngxié 倾斜

slap *n* & *v/t* zhǎngjī 掌击

slash *n* 1 (*cut*) kǎnhén 砍痕; (*punctuation*) xiéxiàn 斜线 2 *v/t cost* dà xuējiǎn 大削减

slaughter *n* & *v/t* túshā 屠杀; (*of people*) shālù 杀戮

slave *n* núlí 奴隶

sleazy xiàliú 下流

sleep 1 *n* shuìjiào 睡觉; *go to* ~ qù shuìjiào 去睡觉 **2** *v/i* shuì 睡

sleeping bag shuìdài 睡袋

sleeping pill ānmiányào 安眠药

sleepless *night* bùmián

不眠

sleepy *town* yōujìng 幽静; *I'm* ~ wǒ kùn le 我困了

sleeve xiùzi 袖子

slender *figure* xiānxì 纤细; *margin* wēibó 微薄

slice 1 *n* piàn 片 **2** *v/t loaf etc* qiēchéng báopiàn 切成薄片

slide 1 *n* (*for kids*) huátī 滑梯; PHOT huàndēngpiàn 幻灯片 **2** *v/i* huá 滑

slight *adj person* miáotiáo 苗条; (*small*) xiǎo 小

slightly shāowēi 稍微

slim 1 *adj* miáotiáo 苗条; *chance* wēixiǎo 微小 **2** *v/i* jiǎnféi 减肥

slip *v/i* (*on ice etc*) huá 滑; (*of quality etc*) xiàjiàng 下降

slipper tuōxié 拖鞋

slippery huá 滑

slit 1 *n* (*tear*) kǒuzi 口子; (*in skirt*) kāichà 开叉 **2** *v/t* sīkāi 撕开

slogan kǒuhào 口号

slope 1 *n* pō 坡 **2** *v/i* qīngxié 倾斜

sloppy *work* cǎoshuài 草率

slot *n* fèngxì 缝隙

slouch *v/i* lǎnsǎn 懒散

slow *adj* màn 慢

♦ **slow down 1** *v/t* jiǎnmàn 减慢 **2** *v/i* mànxiàlái 慢下来

slum *n* pínmínkū 贫民窟

slump *n* (*in trade*) xiāotiáoqī 萧条期

slurred *speech* hánhúbùqīng 含糊不清

slush bànróngxuě 半融雪

sly jiǎohuá 狡猾

small *adj* xiǎo 小

small hours língchén shífēn 凌晨时分

small talk liáotiān 聊天

smart *adj* piàoliang 漂亮; (*intelligent*) cōngmín 聪敏

smash 1 *n* MOT zhuàngsuì 撞碎 **2** *v/t* (*break*) dǎsuì 打碎; (*hit hard*) zhàngjī 撞击 **3** *v/i* (*break*) pòsuì suìliè

smear 1 *n* (*of ink etc*) wūjì 污迹; (*on character*) wūmiè 污蔑

smell 1 *n* qìwèi 气味 **2** *v/t* wénchū 闻出 **3** *v/i* (*bad*) yǒu chòuwèi 有臭味; (*sniff*) wén 闻

smile *n* & *v/i* wēixiào 微笑

smirk *n* & *v/i* shǎxiào 傻笑

smoke 1 *n* yān 烟 **2** *v/t* *cigarette* xī yān 吸 **3** *v/i* xīyān 吸烟

smoker (*person*) xīyānderén 吸烟的人

smoking xīyān 吸烟; *no ~* jìnzhǐ xīyān 禁止吸烟

smolder (*of fire*) huǎnmàn ránshāo 缓慢燃烧

smooth *adj* *surface* guānghuá 光滑; *ride* píngwěn 平稳; *transition* shùnlì 顺利

smother *flames* mēnzhù 闷住; *person* shǐ zhìxī 使窒息

smug zìmǎn 自满

smuggle *v/t* zǒusī 走私

smuggler zǒusīzhě 走私者

smuggling zǒusī 走私

snack *n* xiǎochī 小吃

snake *n* shé 蛇

snap 1 *n* (*break*) duànliè 断裂; (*say sharply*) lìshēng shuō 厉声说 **2** *v/i* (*break*) pāde zhéduàn 啪地折断

snarl *n* (*of dog*) nùhǒu 怒吼

snatch *v/t* duódé 夺得; (*steal*) tōuzǒu 偷走; (*kidnap*) bǎngjià 绑架

sneakers fānbùxié 帆布鞋

sneer *n* & *v/i* lěngxiào 冷笑

sneeze 1 n pēntì 喷嚏 2 v/i dǎ pēntì 打喷嚏

sniff 1 v/i (to clear nose) yòng bí xīqì 用鼻吸气; (of dog) xiù xiù 嗅嗅 2 v/t (smell) wén 闻

sniper jūjīshǒu 狙击手

snob shìlì xiǎorén 势利小人

snooty mùzhōngwúrén 目中无人

snore v/i dǎ hān 打鼾

snow 1 n xuě 雪 2 v/i xià xuě 下雪

snowball n xuěqiú 雪球

snowplow xuělí 雪犁

snowstorm bàofēngxuě 暴风雪

snub n & v/t dàimàn 怠慢

so 1 adv: ~ hot tài rè 太热; not ~ much búnàme 不那么; ~ much better hǎo róngyìle 好容易了; ~ am I / do I wǒ yě shì 我也是; and ~ on děng děng 等等 2 pron: I hope ~ wǒ xīwàng rúcǐ 我希望如此 3 conj (for that reason) yīncǐ 因此; (in order that) shǐde 使得; ~ what? nà yòu zěnmeyàng? 那又怎

么样？

soak v/t (steep) pào 泡; (of water, rain) jìnshī 浸湿

soaked shītòu 湿透

soap n féizào 肥皂

soap (opera) féizào jù 肥皂剧

soar (of rocket) shēngrù 升入; (of bird, plane) áoxiáng 翱翔

sob 1 n wūyān 呜咽 2 v/i chōuqì 抽泣

sober qīngxǐng 清醒

soccer zúqiú 足球

sociable héqún 合群

social adj shèhuì 社会; (recreational) shèjiāo 社交

socialism shèhuì zhǔyì 社会主义

socialist 1 adj shèhuì zhǔyì 社会主义 2 n shèhuì zhǔyì zhě 社会主义者

socialize shèjiāo 社交

social worker shègōng 社工

society shèhuì 社会; (organization) shètuán 社团

sock wàzi 袜子

socket ELEC chāzuò 插座; (of arm, eye) wō 窝

soda (~ water) sūdá 苏打

(*ice-cream ~*) bīngqílíng sūdá shuǐ 冰淇淋苏打水; (*soft drink*) ruǎnxìng yǐnliào 软性饮料

sofa shāfā 沙发

soft *pillow, chair* ruǎn 软; *voice* wēnróu 温柔; *music* yuè'ěr 悦耳; *light, color* róuhé 柔和; *skin* róuhuá 柔滑; (*lenient*) kuānhòu 宽厚

soft drink ruǎnxìng yǐnliào 软性饮料

soft seat RAIL ruǎnzuò 软座

soft sleeping car RAIL ruǎnwò 软卧

software ruǎnjiàn 软件

soil *n* (*earth*) tǔrǎng 土壤

solar energy tàiyáng néng 太阳能

soldier shìbīng 士兵

sole *n* (*of foot*) jiǎodǐ bǎn 脚底板; (*of shoe*) xiédǐ 鞋底

solemn (*serious*) yánsù 严肃; *promise* zhèngzhòng 郑重

solid *adj* (*hard*) yìng bāng-bāng 硬梆梆; (*without holes*) wú kòngxì 无空隙; *gold* chún 纯; (*sturdy*) láogù 牢固; *support* chèdǐ 彻底

solidarity tuánjié yízhì 团结一致

solitaire (*card game*) dānrén zhǐpái xì 单人纸牌戏

solitary *life* gūdú 孤独; (*single*) gū línglíng 孤零零一人

solitude dúzì yīrén 独自一人

solo 1 *n* dúzòu qǔ 独奏曲; (*of singer*) dúchàng qǔ 独唱曲 2 *adj* dānrén 单人

solution jiědá 解答; (*mixture*) róngyè 溶液

solve jiějué 解决

somber *dark* huī'àn 灰暗; (*serious*) yánjùn 严峻

some 1 *adj* yìxiē 一些; ~ **people say ...** yǒu rén shuō ... 有人说... 2 *pron* yìxiē 一些; **would you like ~?** nǐ yào diǎnr ma? 你要点儿吗?

somebody yǒurén 有人

someday yǒuzhāo yīrì 有朝一日

somehow xiǎng bànfa 想办法; (*for unknown reason*) bùzhī zěnde 不知怎的

someone yǒurén 有人

someplace → somewhere

something mǒu shìwù 某事

物; *is ~ wrong?* zěnme le?
怎么了？

sometimes yǒushí 有时

somewhere 1 *adv* mǒugè
dìfang 某个地方 2 *pron*
mǒuchù 某处

son érzi 儿子

song gēqǔ 歌曲

son-in-law nǚxù 女婿

soon kuài 快; *soon after*
bùjiǔ zhīhòu 不久之后;
as ~ as ... yī ... jiù 一
... 就; *as ~ as possible*
jínkuài 尽快

soothe *pain* jiǎnqīng 减轻

sophisticated *person*
jīngtōng shìgù 精通世故;
machine jīngmì 精密

sordid bēibǐ 卑鄙

sore 1 *adj* (*painful*) téng 疼
2 *n* chuāng 疮

sorghum gāoliáng 高粱

sorrow yōushāng 忧伤

sorry (*regretful*) hòuhuǐ 后
悔; (*sad*) nánguò 难过;
I'm ~ duìbuqǐ
... 对不起 ...; (*expressing
sympathy*) hěn yíhàn ... 很
遗憾 ...

sort 1 *n* zhǒng 种 2 *v/t* fēnlèi
分类; COMPUT páiliè 排列

sound 1 *n* shēngyīn 声音;
(*noise*) shēng 声 2 *v/i*: *that
~s interesting* tīngqǐlái hěn
yǒuqù 听起来很有趣

soundproof *adj* géyīn 隔音

soup tāng 汤

sour *adj* suān 酸; *milk* sōu
馊; *comment* jiānsuān kèbó
尖酸刻薄

source n láiyuán 来源; (*of
river*) yuántóu 源头

south 1 *adj* nán 南 2 *n*
nánbù 南部 3 *adv*
wǎngnán 往南

Southeast Asia Dōngnán
Yà 东南亚

southern nánfāng 南方

souvenir jìniàn pǐn 纪念品

sovereignty zhǔquán 主权

Soviet Union Sūlián 苏联

sow *v/t seeds* bōzhòng 播种

soy sauce jiàngyóu 酱油

space *n* (*beyond earth*)
tàikōng 太空; (*area*)
kòngbái 空白; (*room*)
kōngjiān 空间

spacecraft yǔzhòu fēichuán
宇宙飞船

space shuttle hángtiān fēijī
航天飞机

spacious kuānchang 宽敞

spade *(for digging)* qiāo qiū 锹

spare **1** *v/t time, money* yúnchū 匀出; *(do without)* shěngdiào 省掉 **2** *adj money* duōyú 多余; *(extra)* bèiyòng 备用 **3** *n (part)* língjiàn 零件

spare ribs páigǔ 排骨

spare room kèfáng 客房

spare time yèyú shíjiān 业余时间

spare tire MOT bèiyòng lúntāi 备用轮胎

spark *n* huǒxīng 火星

spark plug huǒhuāsāi 火花塞

sparse *vegetation* xīshū 稀疏

speak **1** *v/i* shuōhuà 说话; ～*ing* TELEC wǒshì 我是 **2** *v/t language* huìjiǎng 会讲

speaker *(at conference)* yǎnjiǎngzhě 演讲者; *(of sound system)* yīnxiāng 音箱

special tèshū 特殊; *(particular)* tèbié 特别

specialist zhuānjiā 专家

specialize zhuānmén cóngshì 专门从事

specially tèbié 特别

specialty zhuāncháng 专长; *(food)* tèsè cài 特色菜

species zhǒnglèi 种类

specific tèbié 特别

specify zhǐdìng 指定

specimen yàngpǐn 样品

spectacle *(impressive sight)* zhuàngguān 壮观

spectator guānzhòng 观众

speculate *v/i* cāicè 猜测; FIN zuò tóujī mǎimài 做投机买卖

speech *(address)* jiǎnghuà 讲话; *(in play)* táicí 台词

speed **1** *n* sùdù 速度 **2** *v/i (drive)* jíshǐ 疾驶; *(walk)* kuàizǒu 快走; *(drive too quickly)* chāosù 超速

speeding *n* MOT chāosù 超速

speed limit xiànsù 限速

spell¹ *v/t & v/i* pīn 拼

spell² *(period of time)* yīduàn shíjiān 一段时间

spelling pīnxiě 拼写

spend *money* huāqián 花钱; *time* dùguò 度过

spice *n* xiāngliào 香料

spider zhīzhū 蜘蛛

spill *v/t & v/i* sǎ 洒

spin *n, v/t & v/i (of wheel)*

xuánzhuǎn 旋转

spinach bōcài 菠菜

spinal jízhù 脊柱

spine jízhù 脊柱；(of book) shūjí 书脊

spin-off pàishēng chǎnpǐn 派生产品

spiral n luóxuán 螺旋

spirit n (not body) jīngshén 精神；(of dead) línghún 灵魂；(courage) yǒngqì 勇气；(attitude) tàidu 态度

spirits¹ (alcohol) lièjiǔ 烈酒

spirits² (morale) qíngxù 情绪

spiritual adj shén 神

spit v/i (of person) tǔtán 吐痰

spite n èyì 恶意

spiteful huáiyǒu èyì 怀有恶意

splash v/t person jiàn jiàn 溅；water, mud pō 泼

splendid jíhǎo 极好

splendor zhuàngguān 壮观

splinter 1 n cì 刺 刺 2 v/i fēnliè 分裂

split 1 n (tear) lièkǒu 裂口；(disagreement) fēnliè 分裂；(division, share) fēngē 分割 2 v/t & v/i (tear) lièkāi 裂开

spoil v/t child chǒnghuài 宠坏；party, fun pòhuài … de xìngzhì 破坏 … 的兴致；cooking, essay nòngzāo 弄糟

spoilsport F bàixìngzhě 败兴者

spoilt adj kid chǒnghuài 宠坏

spokesperson fāyánrén 发言人

sponsor 1 n dānbǎorén 担保人 2 v/t dānbǎo 担保

sponsorship dānbǎo 担保

spontaneous zìfā 自发；person zìrán 自然

spoon n sháo 勺

sporadic língsǎn 零散

sport n tǐyù yùndòng 体育运动

sportscar pǎochē 跑车

sportsman yùndòngyuán 运动员

sportswoman nǚyùndòngyuán 女运动员

spot¹ n (pimple) fěncì 粉刺；(from measles etc) qiūzhěn 丘疹；(in pattern) bāndiǎnr 斑点儿

spot² (place) dìdiǎn 地点

spot³ v/t (notice) zhǎodào 找到; (identify) biànrèn 辨认

spot check chōuyàng jiǎnchá 抽样检查

spotlight n jùguāng dēng 聚光灯

sprain n & v/t niǔshāng 扭伤

sprawl v/i shēnkāi sìzhī 伸开四肢; (of city) mànyán 蔓延

spray 1 n (of sea water) lànghuā 浪花; (paint) pēnqī 喷漆; (for hair) pēnfà jiāo 喷发胶 **2** v/t pēn 喷

spread 1 n (of disease, religion etc) mànyán 蔓延 **2** v/t butter mǒ 抹; news, disease chuánbō 传播 **3** v/i (of fire) mànyán 蔓延; (of news, disease) chuánbō 传播

spring¹ n (season) chūntiān 春天

spring² n (device) tánhuáng 弹簧

springboard tiàobǎn 跳板

sprinkle v/t sǎ 撒

sprint n & v/i bēnpǎo 奔跑

spurt 1 n (in race) chōngcì 冲刺 **2** v/i (of liquid) pēnshè 喷射

spy n jiàndié 间谍

♦ **spy on** ànzhōng jiānshì 暗中监视

squalid āngzāng 肮脏

squander huīhuò 挥霍

square 1 adj shape fāng 方; ~ mile píngfāng yīnglǐ 平方英里的 sìfāng xíng 四方形; (in town) guǎngchǎng 广场

squash¹ n (vegetable) nánguā 南瓜

squash² n (game) bìqiú 壁球

squash³ v/t yālàn 压烂

squat v/i dūn 蹲; (illegally) shànzì zhànyòng 擅自占用

squeak n (of mouse) zhīzhī shēng 吱吱声; (of hinge) zhīgā shēng 吱嘎声

squeeze v/t jǐ 挤; hand jǐnwò 紧握; orange etc zhà zhà 榨

squint n xiéyǎn 斜眼

stab v/t cì 刺

stability wěndìng 稳定

stable adj wěndìng 稳定

stadium tǐyùchǎng 体育场

staff n (employees) gùyuán 雇员; (teachers) jiàoyuán

教员

stage **1** n/i (in project) jiēduàn 阶段; (of journey) duàn lù 段路

stage² n THEA wǔtái 舞台

stagger **1** v/i diēdiē zhuàngzhuàng 跌跌撞撞 **2** v/t (in time) cuòkāi 错开

stain **1** n (mark) wūjì 污迹; (for wood) rǎnsèjì 染色剂 **2** v/t (dirty) zhānwū 沾污; wood rǎnsè 染色

stainless steel n bùxiùgāng 不锈钢

stair tījí 梯级; the ~s lóutī 楼梯

stake n (of wood) zhuāng 桩; (in gambling) dǔzhù 赌注; (investment) gǔfèn 股份

stale bread zǒuwèir 走味儿; air mèn 闷; news guòshí 过时

stall v/i (of engine) xīhuǒ 熄火; (of vehicle) pāomáo 抛锚; (for time) tuōyán 拖延

stamina nàilì 耐力

stammer n & v/i jiēba 结巴

stamp n (for letter) yóupiào 邮票; (on visa etc) yìn 印

stance (position) tàidu 态度

stand **1** n (at exhibition) tānzi 摊子 **2** v/i (not sit) zhànzhe 站着; (rise) qǐlì 起 立 **3** v/t (tolerate) rěnshòu 忍受

◆ stand by **1** v/i (be ready) zuò hǎo zhǔnbèi 作好准 备 **2** v/t person zhīchí 支 持; decision jiānchí 坚持

◆ stand for (represent) dàibiǎo 代表

◆ stand up v/i zhàn qǐlái 站起来

standard **1** adj (usual) chángguī 常规 **2** n (level) shuǐzhǔn 水准; TECH biāozhǔn 标准

standardize v/t shǐ biāo-zhǔnhuà 使标准化

standard of living shēnghuó shuǐzhǔn 生活水准

standby: ~ (for flight) hòubǔ 候补

standpoint guāndiǎn 观点

standstill: be at a ~ tíngdùn 停顿

staple diet zhǔshí 主

stapler dìngshūjī 订书机

star **1** n xīng 星; fig míngxīng 明星 **2** v/t & v/i (in movie) zhǔyǎn 主演

stare 1 *n* níngshì 凝视 **2** *v/i* mùbù zhuǎnjīng de kàn 目不转睛地看; **~ at** dīngzhe 盯着

Stars and Stripes Xīngtiáo qí 星条旗

start 1 *n* kāitóu 开头 **2** *v/i* kāishǐ 开始; *(of engine)* fādòng 发动 **3** *v/t* kāishǐ 开始; *engine* fādòng 发动; *business* chuàngbàn 创办

starter *(food)* tóupán 头盘; MOT qǐdòng zhuāngzhì 起动装置

starvation jī'è 饥饿

starve *v/i* ái'è 挨饿

state¹ 1 *n (condition)* zhuàngkuàng 状况; *(part of country)* zhōu 州; *(country)* guójiā 国家; **the States** Měiguó 美国 **2** *adj capital etc* zhōu 州; *banquet* guóyàn 国宴

state² *v/t* shēngmíng 声明

State Department Guówù Yuàn 国务院

statement *(announcement)* shēngmíng 声明; *(to police)* kǒugòng 口供; *(bank ~)* jiésuàn dān 结算单

state-of-the-art *adj* zuì yōuliáng 最优良

statesman zhèngzhìjiā 政治家

station *n* RAIL huǒchēzhàn 火车站; RAD, TV diàntái 电台

stationary jìngzhǐ 静止

statistics *(science)* tǒngjì xué 统计学; *(figures)* tǒngjì zīliào 统计资料

statue sùxiàng 塑像

status dìwèi 地位

status symbol shēnfènde xiàngzhēng 身份的象征

stay 1 *n* dòuliú 逗留 **2** *v/i* dòuliú 逗留; *(in a condition)* bǎochí 保持; **~ at home** dāi zài jiā lǐ 呆在家里; **~ in a hotel** dāi zài lǚguǎn 呆在旅馆

steady *adj (not shaking)* píngwěn 平稳; *(regular)* yǒu guīlǜ 有规律

steak niúpái 牛排

steal *v/t money etc* tōu 偷

steam 1 *n* zhēngqì 蒸汽 **2** *v/t food* zhēng 蒸

steamed bread mántou 馒头

steamer *(for cooking)*

zhēngguō 蒸锅

steel n & adj gāng 钢

steep adj hill etc dǒu 陡

steer v/t jiàshǐ 驾驶

steering wheel fāngxiàng
pán 方向盘

stem n (of plant) gàn 干

step n (pace) bù 步; (stair)
jiētī 阶梯; (measure)
cuòshī 措施

♦ **step down** (from post etc)
ràngwèi 让位

stereo n (sound system)
lìtǐshēng 立体声

stereotype n chéngjiàn 成见

sterilize jiézhá 结扎;
equipment xiāodú 消毒

stern adj yánsù 严肃

steroids jīsù 激素

stew n dùn shípǐn 炖食品

steward (on plane, ship)
chéngwùyuán 乘务员

stewardess (on plane, ship)
nǚ chéngwùyuán 女乘
务员

stick[1] n mùgùn 木棍; (of
policeman) jǐnggùn 警棍

stick[2] 1 v/t (with adhesive)
niánzhù 粘住 2 v/i niánzhù
粘住; (jam) qiǎ zhù le
卡住了

sticky nián hūhū 黏糊糊

stiff adj brush, leather
yìng bāngbāng 硬邦邦;
muscle jiāngyìng 僵硬;
(in manner) jūjǐn 拘谨;
competition jīliè 激烈

stifle v/t yawn rěnzhe 忍着;
debate èshā 扼杀

stifling lìngrén zhìxī 令人
窒息

stigma chǐrǔ 耻辱

still[1] 1 adj píngjìng 平静
2 adv keep ~! bié dònglái
dòngqù! 别动来动去！

still[2] 1 adv (yet) hái 还;
(nevertheless) wúlùn
rúhé 无论如何; ~ more
gèngduō 更多

stimulant xīngfènjì 兴奋剂

stimulate person cìjī 刺激;
demand cùjìn 促进

stimulation jīlì 激励

stimulus dònglì 动力

sting 1 v/t (of bee, jellyfish)
zhē 蜇 2 v/i (of eyes) fātòng
发痛; (of scratch) gǎndào
cìtòng 感到刺痛

stipulate guīdìng 规定

stir v/t jiǎobàn 搅拌

stir-fry v/t wànghuǒ biānchǎo
旺火煸炒

stitch 1 n (sewing) zhēnjiǎo 针脚; (knitting) yìzhēn 一针; **~es** MED féngzhēn 缝针 **2** v/t (sew) féng 缝

stock 1 n (reserves) chǔcún 储存; (COM: of store) huò huò 货; FIN gǔpiào 股票; **in ~ / out of ~** yǒu / wúhuò 有 / 无货 **2** v/t COM bèiyǒu 备有

stockbroker gǔpiào jīngjìrén 股票经纪人

stock exchange gǔpiào jiāoyìsuǒ 股票交易所

stockholder gǔdōng 股东

stock market gǔpiào shìchǎng 股票市场

stockpile n chǔbèi wùzī 储备物资

stomach n (insides) dùzi 肚子; (abdomen) fùbù 腹部

stomach-ache dùzi téng 肚子疼

stone n shítou 石头

stoop v/i (bend) wānyāo 弯腰; (have bent back) hāyāo 哈腰

stop 1 n (for train, bus) zhàn 站 **2** v/t (put an end to, cease) tíngzhǐ 停止; (prevent) zǔzhǐ 阻止;

car, bus, train etc tíng 停; **~ talking immediately!** mǎshàng zhùzuǐ! 马上住嘴! **3** v/i tíng 停

stopover dòuliú 逗留; (in air travel) zhōngtú tíngliú 中途停留

stop sign tíngchē biāozhì 停车标志

storage zhùcáng 贮藏

store 1 n shāngdiàn 商店; (stock) chǔbèi 储备; (storehouse) cāngkù 仓库 **2** v/t cúnfàng 存放; COMPUT chǔcún 储存

storm n bàofēngyǔ 暴风雨

stormy yǒu bàofēngyǔ 有暴风雨; relationship yìbō sānzhé 一波三折

story¹ gùshì 故事; (newspaper article) bàodào 报道

story² (of building) céng 层

stove (for cooking) lúzi 炉子; (for heating) jiārèqì 加热器

straight 1 adj line zhí 直; back bízhí 笔直; (honest, direct) tǎnshuài 坦率; whiskey chún 纯 **2** adv (in a straight line) jìngzhí 径

直; (directly, immediately)
zhíjiē 直接; **~ ahead** be
jiùzài qiánmiàn 就在前
面; walk, drive zhízhe zǒu
直着走; look xiàngqián
kàn 向前看; **~ away**
mǎshàng 马上

straighten v/t nòngzhí 弄直

straightforward (honest,
direct) zhíjié liǎodàng 直
截了当; (simple) jiǎndān
简单

strain n (on rope, engine)
zuòyòng lì 作用力; (on
person) zhòngfù 重负

strand v/t: **be ~ed** chǔyú
kùnjìng 处于困境

strange (odd) qíguài 奇怪;
(unknown) mòshēng 陌生

stranger mòshēngrén 陌
生人

strap n (of bag) shūbāo dài
书包带; (of dress) jiāndài
肩带; (of watch) biǎodài
表带

strategy zhànlüè 战略

straw (for drink) xīguǎn
吸管

strawberry cǎoméi 草莓

stray n (dog) zǒushī de gǒu
走失的狗; (cat) zǒushī de

māo 走失的猫

stream n fig (of people,
complaints) yìliánchuàn
一连串

street jiēdào 街道

streetcar yǒuguǐ diànchē 有
轨电车

strength (of person:
physical) lìqì 力气; fig
(strong point) yōudiǎn
优点; (of wind, current)
qiángdù 强度; (of emotion,
friendship) lìliàng 力量;
(of country, currency) shílì
实力

strengthen v/t jiāqiáng 加强

stress 1 n (emphasis)
zhòngdiǎn 重点; (tension)
yālì 压力; **be under ~**
shòudào yālì 受到压力
2 v/t urgency qiángdiào
强调

stressful jǐnzhāng 紧张

stretch 1 n (of land, water)
piàn 片 **2** v/t material
shēnzhǎn 伸展; income
jiéyuē 节约 **3** v/i (to relax)
shēn lǎnyāo 伸懒腰; (to
reach sth) shēnshǒu 伸手;
~ from X to Y (extend) cóng
X yánshēn zhì Y 从 X 延

伸至 Y

strict yángé 严格

stride n dàbù 大步

strike 1 n (of workers) bàgōng 罢 工; (in baseball) hǎoqiú 好球; (of oil) fāxiàn 发现; **be on ~** zài bàgōng 在罢工 **2** v/i (attack) xíjī 袭击; (of disaster) jiànglín 降临 **3** v/t (hit) zhuàng 撞; oil fāxiàn 发现

string n xìshéng 细绳; (of violin etc) xián 弦; (of tennis racket) bēngshéng 绷绳

strip 1 n chángtiáo 长条 **2** v/t (remove) chúqù 除 去; (undress) bōguāng yīfu 剥光衣服 **3** v/i (undress) tuōguāng yīfu 脱去衣服

stripe n tiáowén 条纹

strive 1 v/t: **~ to do** nǔlì zuò 努力做 **2** v/i: **~ for** lìzhēng 力争

stroke 1 n MED zhòngfēng 中风; (in writing) bǐhuà 笔 画; (in swimming) yóufǎ 游 法 **2** v/t fǔmō 抚摸

stroll 1 n sànbù 散步 **2** v/i xiánzǒu 闲走

stroller (for baby) yīng'érchē 婴儿车

strong person qiángzhuàng 强壮; structure jiāngù 坚 固; candidate qiáng 强; support jiāndìng 坚 定; wind qiángjìn 强劲; drink lièxìng 烈性; tea, coffee nóng 浓; taste, smell wèinóng 味浓; views jiānjué 坚决; currency jiāntǐng 坚挺

structural gòujià 构架

structure n (sth built) jiànzhùwù 建筑物; (way sth is built) jiégòu 结构

struggle 1 n (fight) zhēngdòu 争斗; (hard time) jiānnán 艰难 **2** v/i (with a person) gédòu 格 斗; (have a hard time) nǔlì 努力

stub n (of cigarette) yāndì 烟蒂; (of check, ticket) cúngēn 存根

stubborn gùzhí 固执; defense wánqiáng 顽强

stuck-up F bǎi jiàzi 摆架子

student xuésheng 学生; (at college, university) dàxuéshēng 大学生

studio (of artist) gōngzuòshì 工作室; (recording ~) lùyīnpéng 录音棚; (film ~) shèyǐngpéng 摄影棚; (TV ~) yǎnbōshì 演播室

study 1 n (room) shūfáng 书房; (learning) xuéxí 学习; (investigation) yánjiū 研究 2 v/t (at school) gōngdú 攻读; (examine) zǐxì chákàn 仔细观察看 3 v/i xuéxí 学习

stuff n dōngxi 东西; (belongings) suǒyǒuwù 所有物

stuffing (for turkey, in chair etc) tiánliào 填料

stuffy room mèn 闷, person gǔbǎn 古板

stumble v/i bànjiǎo 绊脚

stumbling block zhàng'ài 障碍

stun dǎhūn 打昏; (of news) dàchīyījīng 大吃一惊

stupid yúchǔn 愚蠢

stupidity yúchǔn 愚蠢

stutter v/i jiēba 结巴

style n fēnggé 风格; (fashion) liúxíng kuǎnshì 流行款式; (elegance) gédiào 格调

subconscious: the ~ qiányìshí qiánnéng 潜意识潜能

subcontract v/t fēnbāo hétóng 分包合同

subcontractor fēnbāorén 分包人

subdued lights róuhé 柔和; voice dīluò 低落

subject 1 n (topic) zhǔtí 主题; (of learning) kēmù 科目; GRAM zhǔyǔ 主语 2 adj: be ~ to X yǒu X de qīngxiàng 有 X 的倾向

subjective zhǔguān 主观

submarine qiántǐng 潜艇

submissive shùncóng 顺从

submit v/t plan chéngjiāo 呈交

subordinate n xiàshǔ 下属

♦ subscribe to magazine etc dìngyuè 订阅

subscription dìng dìng 订订

subside (of flood) tuìqù 退去; (of building) xiàxiàn 下陷

subsidiary n fùshǔ gōngsī 附属公司

subsidy bǔzhù 补助

substance (matter) wùzhì 物质

substantial xiāngdāng dà

相当大

substitute 1 *n* dàitìpǐn 代替品; SP tìhuànzhě 替换者 **2** *v/t*: **X for Y** yòng X qǔdài Y 用 X 取代 Y

subtitle *n* zìmù 字幕

subtle qiǎomiào 巧妙

subtract *v/t* jiǎnqù 减去

suburb jiāoqū 郊区; **the ~s** shìjiāo 市郊

subway dìtiě 地铁

succeed 1 *v/i* chénggōng 成功 **2** *v/t* (*come after*) jìrèn 继任

success chénggōng 成功

successful chénggōng 成功

successive jiēlián búduàn 接连不断

successor jìrènrén 继任人

such 1 *adj* (*of that kind*) zhèyàng 这样; **~ a** (*so much of a*) nàme 那么 **2** *adv* zhème 这么; **~ nice** ... zhème hǎode ... 这么好的...

suck shǔnxī 吮吸

sudden yìwài 意外

suddenly tūrán 突然

sue *v/t* kònggào 控告

suffer 1 *v/i* shòukǔ 受苦 **2** *v/t loss* zāoshòu 遭受

sufficient zúgòu 足够

suffocate *v/i* zhìxī ér sǐ 窒息而死

sugar *n* táng 糖

suggest *v/t* jiànyì 建议

suggestion jiànyì 建议

suicide zìshā 自杀

suit 1 *n* xīzhuāng 西装 **2** *v/t* (*of color etc*) shìhé 适合

suitable shìyí 适宜

suitcase shǒutí yīxiāng 手提衣箱

suite (*of rooms*) tàojiān 套间; (*furniture*) yītào jiājù 一套家具

sulk shēng mènqì 生闷气

sum (*total*) zǒngshù 总数; (*amount*) shùmù 数目; (*in arithmetic*) suànshù 算术

summarize *v/t* gàikuò 概括

summary *n* zǒngjié 总结

summer xiàtiān 夏天

summit shāndǐng 山顶; POL zuì gāojí huìyì 最高级会议

summon *staff* zhàojí 召集; *meeting* zhàokāi 召开

sun tàiyáng 太阳; **in the ~** zài yángguāng xià 在阳光下

sunbathe shài tàiyáng 晒

太阳

sunblock fángshàigāo 防
晒膏

sunburn shàibān 晒斑

Sunday xīngqīrì 星期日

sunglasses mòjìng 墨镜

sunrise rìchū 日出

sunset rìluò 日落

suntan shàihēi 晒黑

superb bàngjíle 棒极了

superficial fūqiǎn 肤浅;
person qiǎnbó 浅薄

superintendent (of
apartment block)
guǎnlǐyuán 管理员

superior 1 adj gènghǎo 更
好; *attitude* yǒu yōuyuègǎn
有优越感 2 n (in
organization) shàngjí 上级

supermarket chāojí shìchǎng
超级市场

superpower POL chāojí
dàguó 超级大国

superstitious *person* míxìn
迷信

supervise jiāndū 监督

supervisor (at work)
zhǐdǎozhě 指导者

supper wǎnfàn 晚饭

supplier COM gōngyìngshāng
供应商

supply 1 n gōngyìng 供应
2 v/t goods tígōng 提供

support 1 n (for structure)
zhīzhù 支柱; (backing)
zhīchí 支持 2 v/t
structure zhīchēng 支撑;
(financially) yuánzhù 援
助; (back) zhīchí 支持

supporter yōnghùzhě 拥护
者; SP zhīchízhě 支持者

supportive zhīchí 支持

suppose (imagine) liàoxiǎng
料想; (be meant to)
yīnggāi ... 应该
...; (be said to be) jùshuō ...
据说...; **you are not ~d to
...** (not allowed) nǐ bùgāi ...
你不该 ...

suppress *rebellion* zhènyā
镇压

Supreme Court Gāojí Fǎtíng
高级法庭

sure adj: **I'm ~** wǒ néng
quèdìng 我能确定; **make
~ that ...** cháming ... 查明
...; **~!** dāngrán! 当然!

surely yídìng 一定; (gladly)
dāngrán 当然

surf 1 n (on sea) jīlàng 激浪
2 v/t the Net sōuxún 搜寻

surface n biǎomiàn 表面;

(of water) shuǐmiàn 水面

surfing chōnglàng yùndòng 冲浪运动

surge n (growth) jīzēng 激增

surgeon n wàikē yīshī 外科 医师

surgery shǒushù 手术

surname xìng 姓

surplus 1 n guòshèng 过剩 **2** adj shèngyú 剩余

surprise 1 n jīngqí 惊奇 **2** v/t shǐ … chījīng 使 … 吃 惊; **be ~d** chīle yìjīng 吃 了一惊

surprising lìngrén jīngyà 令 人惊讶

surrender n & v/i MIL tóuxiáng 投降

surround v/t bāowéi 包围

surroundings huánjìng 环境

survival xìngcún 幸存

survive 1 v/i (of species) cúnhuó 存活; (of patient) yǒuxìng cúnhuó 有幸存 活 **2** v/t accident xìngcún 幸存

survivor xìngcúnzhě 幸 存者

suspect n xiányífàn 嫌疑

犯 **2** v/t person huáiyí 怀 疑; (suppose) juéde 觉得

suspend (from office) lèlìng tíngzhí 勒令停职

suspense jǐnzhānggǎn 紧 张感

suspicion huáiyí 怀疑

suspicious (causing suspicion) kěyí 可疑; (feeling suspicion) yǒu yíxīn 有疑心

swallow v/t yàn 咽

sway v/i yáobǎi 摇摆

swear v/i zhòumà 咒骂; LAW xuānshì 宣誓

swearword màrénhuà 骂 人话

sweat 1 n hànshuǐ 汗水 **2** v/i chūhàn 出汗

sweater máoyī 毛衣

sweatshirt wúlǐng chángxiùshān 无领长 袖衫

sweep v/t floor sǎo 扫

sweet adj taste tián 甜

sweet and sour adj tángcù 糖醋

swell 1 v/i (of limb etc) zhǒngzhàng 肿胀 **2** adj F (good) jíhǎo 极好

swelling n MED zhǒngkuài

肿块

swerve v/i tūrán zhuǎnxiàng
突然转向

swim n & v/i yóuyǒng 游泳

swimming pool yóuyǒngchí
游泳池

swimsuit yóuyǒngyī 游
泳衣

swindle n piànjì 骗计

swing n zhuǎnbiàn 转
变; (child's) qiūqiān 秋
千 **2** v/t huīdòng 挥动
3 v/i bǎidòng 摆动; (turn)
zhuàndòng 转动; (of
opinion) biàndòng 变动

switch n **1** (for light) kāiguān
开关 **2** v/t (change) huàn
换 **3** v/t (change) gǎihuàn
改换

♦ **switch off** v/t & v/i lights
etc guāndiào 关掉

♦ **switch on** v/t lights etc
kāi 开 **2** v/t lights etc
kāijī 开机

swollen zhǒngzhàng 肿胀

syllabus dàgāng 大纲

symbol (written) fúhào 符
号; (poetic etc) xiàngzhēng
象征

symbolic yǒu xiàngzhēng-
xìng 有象征性

symmetric(al) duìchèn 对称

sympathetic (showing pity)
biǎoshì tóngqíng 表示同
情; (understanding) lǐjiěrén
理解人

sympathizer POL yōnghùzhě
拥护者

sympathy (pity) tóngqíngxīn
同情心; (understanding)
lǐjiě 理解

symphony jiāoxiǎngyuè
交响乐

symptom MED zhèngzhuàng
症状; fig zhēngzhào 征
兆

synthetic rénzào 人造

syringe zhùshèqì 注射器

system (method) xìtǒng 系
统; (orderliness) chéngxù
程序

T

table n zhuōzi 桌子; (of
figures) biǎo 表

tablet yàopiànr 药片儿

table tennis pīngpāngqiú

兵乓球

tact jīzhì 机智

tactful détǐ 得体

tactics cèlüè 策略

tactless bù détǐ 不得体

tag (label) biāoqiān 标签

tai chi tàijíquán 太极拳

tail light wěidēng 尾灯

tailor cáifeng 裁缝

tailor-made dīngzuò 定做;
solution shìdàng 适当

Taiwan Táiwān 台湾

Taiwanese 1 adj Táiwān 台
湾 2 n Táiwānrén 台湾人;
(dialect) Táiyǔ 台语

take v/t (remove) ná 拿;
(transport) sòng 送;
(accompany) péi 陪;
(accept: credit cards)
jiēshòu 接受; photograph
zhàoxiàng 照相; exam,
degree kǎo 考; (endure)
rěnshòu 忍受; (require)
xūyào 需要; how long
does it ~? yào duōcháng
shíjiān? 要多长时间?
I'll ~ it (when shopping) wǒ
mǎi le 我买了

◆ take out (from bag) náchū
拿出; appendix shānchú
删除; (to dinner etc) dài

... chūqù 带 ... 出去;
insurance policy bànlǐ 办理

◆ take over 1 v/t company etc
jiānbìng 兼并 2 v/i (of new
management etc) jiēguǎn
接管

◆ take up carpet etc jiēqǐ 揭
起; (carry up) ná shàngqù
拿上去; judo, new
language kāishǐ xuéxí 开始
学习; space, time zhànqù
占去

takeoff (of plane) qǐfēi 起飞

takeover jiānbìng 兼并

talented yǒu tiānfù 有天赋

talk 1 v/i tánhuà 谈话 2 v/t
English etc shuō 说 3 n
(conversation) jiāotán 交
谈; (lecture) yǎnjiǎng 演讲

talk show tánhuà jiémù 谈
话节目

tall gāo 高

tame animal xùnfú 驯服

tampon yuèjīng shuān 月
经栓

tank chúshuǐ chí 储水池;
MOT xiāng 箱; MIL tǎnkè
坦克

tanker (ship) yóuchuán 油
船; (truck) guànchē 罐车

tanned shài hēi 晒黑

Tao Dào 道

tap 1 *n* lóngtóu 龙头 2 *v/t*
(knock) qīngqiāo 轻敲;
phone qiètīng 窃听

tape 1 *n* (for recording) cídài
磁带;(sticky) jiāodài 胶带
2 *v/t conversation etc* lùyīn
录音;(with sticky tape)
zhān zhān 粘

tape measure juǎnchǐ 卷尺

tape recorder lùyīnjī 录
音机

target 1 *n* mùbiāo 目标 2 *v/t
market* bǎ ... zuòwéi mù-
biāo 把 ... 作为目标

tart *n* guǒxiàn bǐng 果馅
儿饼

task rènwù 任务

taste 1 *n* wèidao 味道;(in
clothes, art etc) pǐnwèi 品
味 2 *v/t food* cháng 尝

taunt *n & v/t* cháoxiào 嘲笑

taut jǐn 紧

tax *n* shuì 税

tax-free miǎnshuì 免税

taxi chūzūchē 出租车

tax payer nàshuìrén 纳税人

tax return (form) nàshuì dān
纳税单

tea chá 茶; *black* ~ hóngchá
红茶; *green* ~ lǜchá 绿茶

teach 1 *v/t* jiāo 教 2 *v/i*
jiāoshū 教书

teacher lǎoshī 老师

teacup chábēi 茶杯

team zǔ 组

teamwork pèihé 配合

teapot cháhú 茶壶

tear[1] 1 *n* (in cloth etc) lièkǒu
裂口 / *paper, cloth* sī 撕
3 *v/i* (go fast) jí bēn 急奔

tear[2] (in eye) lèi 泪

tearful yǎnlèi wāngwāng 眼
泪汪汪

tear gas cuīlèi qì 催泪气

tease *v/t* dòunòng 逗弄

technical jìshù xìng 技术性

technician jìshùyuán 技
术员

technique fāngfǎ 方法

technological jìshù 技术

technology jìshù 技术

teenager qīngshàonián 青
少年

telecommunications diànxìn
电信

telephone 1 *n* diànhuà 电话
2 *v/t & v/i* dǎ diànhuà 打电
话 → *phone*

telephoto lens shèyuǎn
jìngtóu 摄远镜头

television diànshì 电视

(set) diànshìjī 电视机

television program diànshì jiémù 电视节目

tell v/t story, lie jiǎng 讲;~ difference qūfēn 区分;~ X Y gàosù X Y 告诉 X Y;~ X to do Y jiào X zuò Y 叫 X 做 Y

teller (in bank) chūnàyuán 出纳员

temp n (employee) línshígōng 临时工

temper (bad ~) píqì 脾气; keep one's ~ nàzhe xìngzi 捺着性子; lose one's ~ fā píqì 发脾气

temperamental (moody) yì jīdòng 易激动

temperature wēndù 温度; (fever) fāshāo 发烧

temple REL miàoyǔ 庙宇

temporary zànshí 暂时

tempting yǒu xīyǐnlì 有吸引力

tenant fángkè 房客; (of land) diànhù 佃户

tendency qīngxiàng 倾向

tender¹ adj (sore) xūruò 虚弱; (affectionate) wēnróu 温柔; steak ruǎn 软

tender² n COM tóubiāo 投标

tennis wǎngqiú 网球

tense adj muscle jǐn 紧; voice, moment jǐnzhāng 紧张

tension (of rope) lālì 拉力; (in atmosphere, voice) jǐnzhāng 紧张; (in movie) jǐnyào guāntóu 紧要关头

tent zhàngpeng 帐篷

tentative yóuyù 犹豫

term (time) shíqī 时期; EDU xuéqī 学期; (condition) tiáojiàn 条件; long / short ~ cháng / duǎnqī 长 / 短期

terminal 1 n (at airport) chūrùjìng kǒu 出入境口; (for buses) zhōngdiǎnzhàn 终点站 2 adj MED wǎnqī 晚期

terminate v/t contract zhōngzhǐ zhǐ 止; pregnancy liúchǎn 流产

terminus zhōngdiǎnzhàn 终点站

terracotta warriors bīngmǎyǒng 兵马俑

terrain dìshì 地势

terrible kěpà 可怕

terrific liǎobuqǐ 了不起

terrify kǒnghè 恐吓

terrifying kěpà 可怕

territory lǐngtǔ 领土; *fig* lǐngyù 领域

terrorism kǒngbù zhǔyì 恐怖主义

terrorist kǒngbù fènzi 恐怖分子

terrorize kǒnghè 恐吓

test **1** *n* (scientific) cèyàn 测验; (exam) kǎoyàn 考验 **2** *v/t machine, theory* cèyàn 测验; *student* kǎo 考

testify *v/i* LAW zuòzhèng 作证

text yuánwén 原文

textbook kèběn 课本

textile fǎngzhī 纺织

texture zhìdì 质地

than bǐ 比; *bigger ~ me* bǐ wǒ dà 比我大

thank *v/t* xiè 谢

thanks gǎnxiè 感谢; *~!* xièxie 谢谢

thankful gǎnjī 感激

Thanksgiving (Day) Gǎn'ēn jié 感恩节

that **1** *adj* nàge 那个; *~ one* nàge 那个 **2** *pron* nà 那; *what's ~?* nàshì shénme? 那是什么?; *I think ~ ...* wǒ xiǎng ... 我想 ...; *the person ~ you see* nǐ

kànjiàndè nàge rén 你看见的那个人

thaw *v/i* huà 化

the *no translation*

theater jùchǎng 剧场

theft tōuqiè 偷窃

their tāmende 他们的; (his or her) tā / tāde 他 / 她的

theirs tāmende 他们的

them tāmen 他们; (him or her) tā / tā 他 / 她

theme zhǔtí 主题

themselves tāmen zìjǐ 他们自己

then (at that time) nàshí 那时; (after that) érhòu 而后; (deducing) nàme 那么

theory lǐlùn 理论

therapist zhìliáo xuéjiā 治疗学家

therapy liáofǎ 疗法

there nàr 那儿; *~ is / are ...* yǒu ... 有 ...; *~ is / are not ...* méiyǒu ... 没有 ...; *~ you are* (giving) gěinǐ 给你

therefore yīncǐ 因此

thermometer wēndùjì 温度计

thermos flask bǎowēnpíng 保温瓶

these *adj & pron* zhèxie

这些

they tāmen 他们; (he or she) tā 他/她

thick hair mì 密; soup chóu 稠; fog duō 多; wall hòu 厚

thief xiǎotōu 小偷

thigh dàtuǐ 大腿

thin hair, soup xī 稀; coat báo 薄; line xì 细; person shòu 瘦

thing dōngxi 东西; ~s (belongings) suǒyǒuwù 所有物

think xiǎng 想; I ~ so wǒ rènwéi rúcǐ 我认为如此; what do you ~? nǐ shuō ne? 你说呢?

Third World Dìsān Shìjiè 第三世界

thirst kě 渴

thirsty: be ~ kě 渴

this 1 adj zhège 这个; ~ one zhège 这个 2 pron zhège 这个; ~ is ... (introducing) zhèshì ... 这是...; TELEC wǒshì ... 我是...

thorough search chèdǐ 彻底; person búyànfán 不厌其烦

those adj & pron nàxiē 那些

though 1 conj (although)

jǐnguǎn 尽管; as ~ hǎoxiàng 好象 2 adv (however) rán'ér 然而

thought xiǎngfa 想法; (collective) sīxiǎng 思想

thoughtful chénsī 沉思; (considerate) xìxīn 细心

thoughtless cūxīn 粗心

thousand qiān 千; ~s of wúshù 无数; ten ~ wàn 万

thread n xiàn 线

threat wēixié 威胁

threaten wēixié 威胁

thrill n xìngfèn 兴奋 2 v/t: be ~ed gāoxìng 高兴

thriller (movie) jīngxiǎn diànyǐng 惊险电影; (book) jīngxiǎn xiǎoshuō 惊险小说

thrilling lìngrén máogǔ sǒngrán 令人毛骨悚然

thrive (of plant) zhuózhuàng shēngzhǎng 茁壮生长; (of economy) fánróng 繁荣

throat hóulóng 喉咙

throb n & v/i (of heart etc) tiàodòng 跳动

through 1 prep (across) chuānguò 穿过; (during) zài ... qījiān 在...期间; Monday ~ Friday xīngqī yī

zhì wǔ xīngqī yī zhì wǔ **2** *adj*
be ~ (of couple) wánle
完了; **I'm ~ with X** (with
person) wǒ yǔ X juéjiāo
我与 X 绝交; (with task)
wǒ wánchéng le X 我完
成了 X

throw 1 *v/t* rēng 扔;
(disconcert) shǐ ... cāng-
huáng shīcuò 使 ... 仓皇
失措 **2** *n* tóuzhì 投掷

◆**throw out** rēngdiào 扔掉;
husband, drunk niǎnzǒu
撵走

thumb *n* mǔzhǐ 拇指

thumbtack túdīng 图钉

thump 1 (blow) zhòngjī 重
击; (noise) pēng 砰

thunder *n* dǎléi 打雷

thunderstorm léiyǔ 雷雨

Thursday xīngqī sì 星期四

thwart héngxiàng 横向

Tiananmen (incident) liùsì
shìjiàn 六四事件; (square)
Tiān'ānmén 天安门

Tibet Xīzàng 西藏

Tibetan 1 *adj* Xīzàng 西藏
2 *n* Xīzàngrén 西藏人;
(language) Xīzàng yǔ 西
藏语

ticket piào 票

ticket machine shòupiàojī
售票机

ticket office shòupiàochù
售票处

tickle *v/t* gézhi 胳肢

tidy person zhěngjié 整洁;
room zhěngqí 整齐

◆**tidy up** *v/t* shōushi 收拾

tie 1 *n* (necktie) lǐngdài 领
带; (sp: even result) píngjú
平局 **2** *v/t* knot dǎjié 打结;
hands jì 系

tight 1 *adj* clothes, (hard
to move) jǐn 紧; security,
windows yán 严; (not
leaving time) jǐncòu 紧凑

tighten screw shǐ ... biànjǐn
使 ... 变紧; control shǐ ...
yángé 使 ... 严格; security
shǐ ... yánjǐn 使 ... 严谨

time shíjiān 时间; (occasion)
cì 次; **have a good ~!** wánr
kāixīn diǎn! 玩儿开心
点儿！; **what's the ~?**
jǐdiǎnle? 几点了？; **all
the ~** yìzhí 一直; **in ~** jíshí
及时; **on ~** ànshí 按时; **in
no ~** lìkè 立刻

time limit qīxiàn 期限

timetable shíjiān biǎo 时
间表

time zone shíqū 时区

timid miǎntiǎn 腼腆

timing shíjiān xuǎnzé 时间
选择; (of actor, dancer)
shíjiān fēncùn 时间分寸

tinted eyeglasses fǎnguāng 反
光; paper zháosè 着色

tiny jíxiǎo 极小

tip¹ n (of stick, finger) jiān
尖; (of cigarette) yānzuǐ
烟嘴

tip² n (piece of advice)
quàngào 劝告; (money)
xiǎofèi 小费

tippy-toe: on ~ yòng jiǎojiān
用脚尖

tire¹ (on wheel) chētāi 车胎

tire² v/i láolèi 劳累

tired lèi 累; be ~ of X duì X
yànjuàn 对X厌倦

tissue ANAT zǔzhī 组织;
(handkerchief) zhǐjīn 纸巾

title piānmíng 篇名; (of
person) tóuxiánr 头衔儿

to 1 prep ANAT dào 到; ~ China
dào Zhōngguó 到中国;
give X ~ Y jiāng X gěi Y 将
X 给 Y; from Monday ~
Wednesday cóng xīngqīyī
dào xīngqīsān 从星期一
到星期三 **2** with verbs:

learn ~ drive xuéxí jiàshǐ 学
习驾驶; nice ~ eat hǎochī
好吃 **3** adv: ~ and fro
láihuí 来回

toast 1 n kǎo miànbāo 烤面
包; (drinking) gānbēi 干杯
2 v/t (when drinking) wèi...
gānbēi 为...干杯

tobacco yāncǎo 烟草

today jīntiān 今天

toe n jiǎozhǐ 脚指

together yìqǐ 一起; (at the
same time) tóngshí 同时

toilet cèsuǒ 厕所

toilet paper wèishēngzhǐ
卫生纸

toiletries wèishēngjiān
yòngpǐn 卫生间用品

token (sign) xiàngzhēng
象征

tolerant kuānróng 宽容

tolerate noise róngxǔ 容许;
person róngrěn 容忍

toll (for bridge, road)
tōngxíng fèi 通行费;
TELEC diànhuà fèi 电话费

toll-free TELEC miǎnfèi
diànhuà 免费电话

tomato (in northern China)
xīhóngshì 西红柿; (in
southern China) fānqié

蕃茄
tomato ketchup fānqiéjiàng
蕃茄酱

tomorrow míngtiān 明天;
the day after ~ hòutiān 后
天; **~ morning** míngchén
明晨

ton dūn 吨

tone (of color) fēnggé 风
格; MUS yuèyīn 乐音; **~ of
voice** shēngdiào 声调

tongue n shétou 舌头

tonic (water) tānglìshuǐ 汤
力水

tonight jīnwǎn 今晚

tonsillitis biǎntáoxiàn yán 扁
桃腺炎

too (also) yě 也; (excessively)
tài 太; **me ~** wǒ yě 我也; **~
much** tàiduō 太多

tool gōngjù 工具

tooth yáchǐ 牙齿

toothache yáténg 牙疼

toothbrush yáshuā 牙刷

toothpaste yágāo 牙膏

top 1 n (of mountain, tree)
dǐng 顶; (upper part)
shàngbù 上部; (lid: of
bottle etc) gài 盖; (of class,
league) zuì yōuxiù 最优
秀; (clothing) shàngyī 上

衣; (MOT: gear) zuì gāodǎng
最高档; **on ~ of** zài ... zhī
shàng 在 ... 之上; **at the ~
of** zài ... zuìshàng 在 ... 最
上 2 adj branches zuìdǐng
最顶; floor zuìgāo yīcéng
最高一层; management
gāojí 高级; speed, note
zuìgāo 最高

topic tímù 题目

torment n & v/t zhémo 折磨

torture n & v/t zhémo 折磨

toss v/t ball zhì 掷; **~ a coin**
zhìbì 掷币

total 1 n zǒngshù 总数 2 adj
amount zǒng 总; disaster
juéduì 绝对; stranger
wánquán 完全 3 v/t F car
zálàn 砸烂

totally wánquán 完全

touch 1 n chùmō 触摸;
(sense) chùjué 触觉; SP
biānxiàn wài 边线外; **lose
~ with X** yǔ X shīqù liánxì
与 X 失去联系; **keep in
~ with X** yǔ X bǎochí liánxì
与 X 保持联系 2 v/t
chùmō 触摸; (emotionally)
shǐ gǎndòng 使感动 3 v/i
mō 摸

touching adj gǎnrén 感人

touchy *person* mǐngǎn 敏感

tough *person* jiānqiáng 坚强; *meat* bùyì jǔjué 不易咀嚼; *question* nán 难; *material* jiānrèn 坚韧; *punishment* wúqíng 无情

tour 1 *n* lǚyóu 旅游 2 *v/t* *area* cānguān 参观

tourism lǚyóu yè 旅游业

tourist lǚyóuzhě 旅游者

tourist information office lǚyóu zīliàochù 旅游资料处

tour operator lǚyóu gōngsī 旅游公司

tow *v/t* zhuài 拽

toward *prep* xiàng 向

towel máojīn 毛巾

town zhèn 镇

town hall zhèn zhèngfǔ dàlóu 镇政府大楼

toxic yǒudú 有毒

toy wánjù 玩具

trace 1 *n* (*of substance*) wēiliàng 微量 2 *v/t* (*find*) xúnzhǎo 寻找

track *n* (*path*) xiǎojìng 小径; (*for racing*) pǎodào 跑道; RAIL guǐdào 轨道

tractor tuōlājī 拖拉机

trade 1 *n* màoyì 贸易

(*profession*) hángyè 行业 2 *v/i* (*do business*) jīngyíng 经营 3 *v/t*: **~ X for Y** yòng X huàn Y 用X换Y

trade fair màoyìhuì 贸易会

trademark shāngbiāo 商标

tradition chuántǒng 传统

traditional chuántǒng 传统

traditional characters fántǐzì 繁体字

traffic *n* jiāotōng 交通; (*in drugs*) fànmài 贩卖

traffic circle huánxíng jiāochā 环形交叉

traffic cop F jiāotōng jǐng 交通警

traffic jam jiāotōng dǔsè 交通堵塞

traffic light hónglǜdēng 红绿灯

tragedy bēijù 悲剧

tragic búxìng 不幸

trail 1 *n* (*path*) xiǎojìng 小径 2 *v/t* (*follow*) gēnzōng 跟踪; (*tow*) tuōlā 拖拉

trailer tuōchē 拖车; (*mobile home*) péngchē 篷车

train[1] *n* huǒchē 火车

train[2] *v/t* & *v/i* SP xùnliàn 训练; (*of teacher etc*) péixùn 培训

trainee shíxí shēng 实习生

trainer SP jiàoliànyuán 教
练员

training SP xùnliàn 训练; (of
new staff) péixùn 培训

train station huǒchēzhàn
火车站

traitor pàntú 叛徒

tranquilizer zhènjìngjì 镇
静剂

transaction jiāoyì 交易

transfer 1 v/t diàodòng 调
动; passengers zhuǎnjī 转
机 2 v/i (when traveling)
qiānyí 迁移 3 n (move, of
money) diàodòng 调动; (in
travel) diàohuàn 调换

transform v/t gǎibiàn 改变

transformer ELEC biànyāqì
变压器

transfusion shūxuè 输血

transition guòdù 过渡

transitional guòdù 过渡

translate fānyì 翻译

translation fānyì 翻译

translator fānyì 翻译

transmission (of program)
bōfàng 播放; (of disease)
chuánrǎn 传染; MOT
biànsùqì 变速器

transmit program bōfàng 播

放; disease chuánrǎn 传染

transpacific kuàyuè
Tàipíngyáng kuàyuè 太平洋

transparent tòumíng 透明

transplant v/t & n MED yízhí
移植

transport v/t & n yùnshū
运输

trap 1 n (for animal) xiànjǐng
陷井; (question etc) quān-
tào 圈套 2 v/t: be ~ped
xiànrù quāntào 陷入圈套

trash (garbage) lājī 垃圾;
(poor product) fèipǐn 废品

trashy lièzhì 劣质

traumatic chuāngshāngxìng
创伤性

travel 1 n lǚxíng 旅行; ~s
lǚtú 旅途 2 v/i & v/t lǚxíng
旅行

travel agency lǚxíng shè
旅行社

traveler lǚxíngzhě 旅行者

traveler's check lǚxíng
zhīpiào 旅行支票

travel expenses jiāotōng
fèiyòng 交通费用

travel insurance lǚxíng
bǎoxiǎn 旅行保险

tray tuōpán 托盘

treacherous bùzhōng 不忠

tread 1 n zúyīn 足音; (of tire) tāimiàn 胎面 2 v/i zǒuguò 走过

treason pànguó zuì 叛国罪

treasure n cáifù 财富

Treasury Department Cáizhèng Bù 财政部

treat 1 n kuǎndài 款待 2 v/t materials zhìlǐ 处理; illness zhìliáo 治疗; (behave toward) duìdài 对待

treaty tiáoyuē 条约

tree shù 树

tremble fādǒu 发抖

tremendously (very) hěn 很; (a lot) hěnduō 很多

tremor (of earth) zhèndòng 震动

trend qūxiàng 趋向; (fashion) cháoliú 潮流

trendy xīncháo 新潮

trial LAW shěnpàn 审判; (of equipment) shìyàn 试验; on ~ LAW shòushěn 受审

triangle sānjiǎo xíng 三角形

trick 1 n jìmóu 计谋; (knack) jìqiǎo 技巧 2 v/t qīpiàn 欺骗

trigger n bānjī 扳机
♦ trigger off chùfā 触发

trim v/t hair, hedge xiāo 削; costs xuējiǎn 削减

trip 1 n (journey) lǚxíng 旅行 2 v/t & v/i (~ up) bàndǎo 绊倒

triumph n shènglì de xǐyuè 胜利的喜悦

trivial suǒsuì 琐碎

troops jūndui 军队

trophy jiǎngbēi 奖杯

tropical rèdài 热带

trouble 1 n (difficulty) kùnnan 困难; (inconvenience) máfan 麻烦; (disturbance) sāoluàn 骚乱; no ~ méi wèntí 没问题 2 v/t (worry) dānyōu 担忧; (bother, disturb) máfan 麻烦; (of back, liver etc) shǐ bù shūfu 使不舒服

troublemaker dǎoluànzhě 捣乱者

trousers Br kùzi 裤子

truce xiūzhàn 休战

truck kǎchē 卡车

truck driver kǎchē sījī 卡车司机

true zhēn 真; friend gòu 够; come ~ shíxiàn 实现

truly zhēnde 真地; Yours ~

cízhì 此 致

trunk (of tree) shùgàn 树干;
(of elephant) xiàngbí 象鼻;
(large case) dà píxiāng 大
皮箱; (of car) xínglǐ xiāng
行李箱

trust n & v/t xìnrèn 信任

trustworthy zhídé xìnrèn 值
得信任

truth shìshí 事实

truthful chéngshí 诚实

try 1 v/t chángshì 尝试; LAW
shěnpàn 审判 2 v/i shìshì
试试

T-shirt yuánlǐng shān 圆
领衫

tub (bath) yùgāng 浴缸; (for
yoghurt, ice cream) hé hé
盒

tube (pipe) guǎndào 管道;
(of toothpaste, ointment)
guǎn 管

Tuesday xīngqī èr 星期二

tug 1 n NAUT tuōchuán 拖船
2 v/t (pull) lā 拉

tuition fǔdǎo 辅导

tummy dùzi 肚子

tumor zhǒngliú 肿瘤

tune n qǔdiào 曲调

tunnel n suìdào 隧道

turbulence (in air travel)
tuānliú 湍流

turkey huǒjī 火鸡

turn 1 n (rotation)
zhuǎndòng 转动; (in road)
zhuàn 转; it's my ~ gāi wǒ
le 该我了; do X a good ~
wèi X zuò hǎoshì 为 X 做
好事 2 v/t wheel zhuàn 转;
corner guǎiwānr 拐弯儿
3 v/i zhuàn 转

◆ turn down v/t offer
jùjué 拒绝; volume, heat
guānxiǎo 关小

◆ turn off 1 v/t TV, engine
guān 关 2 v/i (of driver)
xià 下

◆ turn on 1 v/t TV, engine kāi
开; F (sexually) cìjī 刺激

◆ turn up 1 v/t collar fānqǐ
翻起; volume, heat kāidà
开大 2 v/i (arrive) lòumiàn
露面

turnover FIN chéngjiāo liàng
成交量

turnpike gāosù gōnglù 高
速公路

turnstile ràogǎn 绕杆

tuxedo lǐfú 礼服

tweezers nièzi 镊子

twice liǎngcì 两次

twin shuāng bāo tāi 双胞胎

twin beds liǎng zhāng

chuáng 两张床
twinge (of pain) cìtòng 刺痛
twist 1 v/t cuō 搓; **~ one's**
ankle niǔle jiǎohuái 扭了
脚踝 **2** v/i (of road, river)
pánxuán 盘旋
two èr 二; (with measure

words) liǎng 俩
tycoon jùtóu 巨头
type 1 n (sort) zhǒnglèi
种类 **2** v/t & v/i (with
keyboard) dǎzì 打字
typical diǎnxíng 典型
tyrant bàojūn 暴君

U

ugly chǒulòu 丑陋
ulcer kuìyáng 溃疡
ultimate (definitive) zuìhǎo
最好; (final) zuìhòu 最后
ultimatum zuìhòu tōngdié 最
后通牒
umbrella sǎn 伞
umpire n cáipànyuán 裁
判员
UN (= United Nations)
Liánhéguó 联合国
unanimous yízhì tóngyì 一
致同意
unassuming qiānxùn 谦逊
unavoidable bùkě bìmiǎn 不
可避免
unaware: be ~ of méiyǒu
chájuédào 没有察觉到
unbalanced bù pínghéng
不平衡, PSYCH shīcháng

失常
unbearable nányǐ rěnshòu
难以忍受
unbelievable nányǐzhìxìn
难以置信; F heat, value
jíduān 极端
uncertain future kěnéng
gǎibiàn 可能改变; origins
bú quèdìng 不确定
uncle (mother's brother)
jiùjiu 舅舅; (father's
elder brother) bóbo 伯伯;
(father's younger brother)
shūshu 叔叔; (mother's
sister's husband) yífu 姨父;
(father's sister's husband)
gūfu 姑父; (to older non-
related men) shūshu 叔叔
uncomfortable bù shūshì
不舒适

unconditional wú tiáojiàn
无条件

unconscious MED shīqù
zhījué 失去知觉；PSYCH
xiàyìshí 下意识

uncontrollable kòngzhì
bùliǎo 控制不了

uncover jiēkāi 揭开；plot
jiēlù 揭露

undeniable bùkě fǒurèn 不
可否认

under prep zài ... xiàmian
在 ... 下面；(less than) bú
dào 不到

underage: be ~ wèi dào
fǎdìng niánlíng 未到法
定年龄

undercarriage qǐluòjià 起
落架

undercut v/t COM xuējià
qiǎng ... shēngyì 削价抢
... 生意

underdog chǔyú lièshì de
yìfāng 处于劣势的一方

underdone bù shútòu 不
熟透

underestimate v/t guòfèn
dīgū 过分估计

undergo treatment jiēshòu
接受；experience jīngshòu
经受

underground adj also POL
dìxià 地下

undergrowth guànmùcóng
灌木丛

underline v/t text xià huàxiàn
下划线

underlying problems gēnběn
根本

underneath 1 prep zài ...
dǐxià 在 ... 底下 2 adv
xiàngxià 向下

underpants nèikù 内裤

underskirt chènqún 衬裙

understaffed rényuán bùzú
人员不足

understand 1 v/t lǐjiě 理解；
language dǒng 懂 2 v/i (see
the reason) míngbai 明白

understandably kě lǐjiě 可
理解

understanding 1 adj person
tōngqíng dálǐ 通情达理
2 n (of situation) lǐjiě 理
解；(agreement) xiéyì 协议

understatement zhòngshì
qīngshuō 重事轻说

undertaking (enterprise)
shìyè 事业；(promise)
xǔnuò 许诺

underwear nèiyī 内衣

underworld (criminal) hēi

shèhuì 黑社会

undisputed wúkě zhēngbiàn 无可争辩

undress v/i tuō yīfu 脱衣服

unearth *remains* fājué 发掘

unemployed shìyè 失业

(*from state enterprise*) xiàgǎng 下岗

unemployment shìyè 失业

uneven *quality* bù yízhì 不一致; *surface* bù píng 不平

unexpected chūhū yìliào 出乎意料

unfair bù gōngpíng 不公平

unfaithful bù zhōng 不忠

unfavorable *report* fùmiàn 负面; *conditions* búlì 不利

unfit (*physically*) bú jiànkāng 不健康; (*morally*) bú shìhé 不适合

unforeseen wèi yùjiàn dào 未预见到

unforgettable nánwàng 难忘

unforgivable bù kě ráoshù 不可饶恕

unfortunately búxìng de shì 不幸的是

unfriendly lěngmò 冷漠

ungrateful bù lǐngqíng 不

领情

unhappiness bù yúkuài 不愉快

unhappy bù yúkuài 不愉快; *customers* bù mǎnyì 不满意

unharmed píng'ān wúyàng 平安无恙

uniform 1 *n* zhìfú 制服 2 *adj* yízhì 一致

unify tǒngyī 统一

uninhabited huāng wú rényān 荒无人烟

unintentional fēi gùyì 非故意

union POL liánméng 联盟; (*labor* ~) gōnghuì 工会

unique dúyīwú'èr 独一无二

unite 1 v/t tǒngyī 统一; *family members* tuánjù 团聚 2 v/i tuánjié 团结

United States (of America) Měiguó 美国

unity tǒngyī 统一

universal pǔbiàn 普遍

university *n* dàxué 大学

unkind kèbó 刻薄

unleaded *adj* wúqiān 无铅

unless chúfēi 除非

unlikely bú dà kěnéng 不大可能

大可能

unload xiè 卸

unlucky dǎoméi 倒霉;
person búxìng 不幸

unmistakable juéwú jǐnyǒu
绝无仅有

unnatural fǎncháng 反常

unnecessary bú bìyào 不
必要

unofficial fēi zhèngshì 非
正式

unpack *v/t* dǎkāi 打开

unpaid *work* wúcháng 无偿

unpleasant shǐ rén bù
yúkuài 使人不愉快

unpopular *person* bú shòu
huānyíng 不受欢迎; *step*
bùdé rénxīn 不得人心

unpredictable fǎnfù
wúcháng 反复无常

unproductive *meeting*
méiyǒu jiéguǒ 没有结果;
soil bù féiwò 不肥沃

unprofessional bú jìngyè
不敬业; *workman* zāogāo
糟糕

unrealistic bú xiànshí 不
现实

unreasonable bù hélǐ 不
合理

unreliable bù kěkào 不

可靠

unrest dòngluàn 动乱

unruly bù guījù 不规矩

unsatisfactory bùnéng
lìngrén mǎnyì 不能令
人满意

unscrew xuánsōng 旋松;
top níngkāi 拧开

unsettled *weather, stock
market* yìbiàn 易变;
lifestyle bù wěndìng 不
稳定

unskilled wú tèshū jìnéng 无
特殊技能

unsuccessful bù chénggōng
不成功; *candidate, attempt*
shībài 失败

unsuitable bù héshì 不合适

untidy língluàn 凌乱

until *prep* zhídào 直到; *not
~ Friday* zhídào xīngqī wǔ
cái 直到星期五才

untiring *efforts* bújuàn 不倦

untrue bù zhēnshí 不真实

unusual bùtóng xúncháng 不
寻常

unusually yìcháng 异常

unwell bù shūfu 不舒服

unwilling: *be ~ to do X*
búyuàn zuò X 不愿做 X

up 1 *adv* xiàngshàng 向上;

~ on the roof zài wūdǐng shang 在屋顶上; **be ~** (out of bed) qǐchuáng 起床; (of sun) shēngqǐ 升起; (of prices, temperature) shàngshēng 上升; **what's ~?** zěnmele? 怎么了?; **be ~ to something (bad)** méi zuò shénme hǎoshì 没做什么好事; **it's ~ to you** nǐ lái juédìng 你来决定 **2** prep: **further ~ the mountain** zài wǎng shānshàng yìxiē 再往山上一些 **3** n: **~s and downs** gānkǔ 甘苦

upbringing jiàoyǎng 教养

update v/t file, records xiūdìng 修订

upheaval (emotional) jùbiàn 剧变; (physical) biàndòng 变动; (political, social) dòngluàn 动乱

uphold rights wéihù 维护; (vindicate) zhèngshí 证实

upkeep n bǎoyǎng 保养

upmarket adj restaurant, hotel gāojí 高级

upper part shàngbù 上部; stretches of a river shàngyóu 上游; deck shàngcéng 上层

uprising qǐyì 起义

uproar (loud noise) xuānxiāo 喧嚣; (protest) kàngyì 抗议

upset 1 v/t glass nòngfān 弄翻; (emotionally) shǐrén nánguò 使人难过 **2** adj (emotionally) nánguò 难过; **have an ~ stomach** gǎndào chángwèi bùshì 感到肠胃不适

upstairs 1 adv zài lóushàng 在楼上 **2** adj room lóushàng 楼上

up-to-date data zuìxīn 最新; fashions xīnshì 新式

upturn (in economy) hǎozhuǎn 好转

uranium yóu 铀

urban dūshì 都市

urge 1 n yùwàng 欲望 **2** v/t: **~ X to do Y** jiélì cuīcù X zuò Y 竭力催促 X 做 Y

urgency jǐnjí 紧急

urgent job jí 急; letter jǐnjí 紧急

us wǒmen 我们

US(A) (= **United States** (of **America**)) Měiguó 美国

use 1 v/t shǐyòng 使用;

skills, knowledge yùnyòng 运用; *car* yòng 用; *pej: person* lìyòng 利用 **2** *n* shǐyòng 使用; **be of no ~ to X** duì X méiyǒuyòng 对 X 没有用; **it's no ~** méiyòng 没用

used¹ *car etc* yòngguò 用过

used²: **be ~ to X** duì X xíguàn 对 X 习惯; **get ~ to X** duì X zhújiàn shìyìng 对 X 逐渐适应

useful yǒuyòng 有用

useless *information* méiyòng 没用; F *person* chàjìn 差劲; *machine* bùnéng yòng 不能用

user yònghù 用户

user-friendly yònghù yǒuhǎo 用户友好

usual tōngcháng 通常; **as ~** xiàng wǎngcháng yíyàng 像往常一样

usually tōngcháng 通常

U-turn U xíngwān X 形弯; *fig* zhuǎnxiàng 转向

V

vacant *building* kōng 空; *look* mángrán 茫然

vacate téngchū 腾出

vacation *n* xiūjià 休假; **be on ~** dùjià 度假

vacationer dùjiàzhě 度假者

vaccinate jiēzhòng yìmiáo 接种疫苗

vaccine yìmiáo 疫苗

vacuum 1 *n* PHYS zhēnkōng 真空 **2** *v/t floor* xīchén 吸尘

vacuum cleaner xīchénqì 吸尘器

vague bù mínglǎng 不明朗; *feeling* móhu 模糊

vain 1 *adj person* zìfù 自负 **2** *n*: **in ~** báifèilì 白费力

valid *passport* yǒuxiào 有效; *reason* yǒu gēnjù 有根据

valuable 1 *adj* yǒu jiàzhí 有价值 **2** *n*: **~s** guìzhòng wùpǐn 贵重物品

value 1 *n* jiàzhí 价值 **2** *v/t* zhēnshì 珍视

van huòchē 货车

vanilla xiāngcǎo 香草

vanish xiāoshī 消失

vapor qì 汽

variable *adj* kěbiàn 可变; *moods* duōbiàn 多变

variation biànhuà 变化

varied *quality* bùtóng 不同; *range* gèzhǒng gèyàng 各种各样; *diet* fēngfù 丰富

variety duōyànghuà 多样化; *(type)* zhǒnglèi 种类

various *(several)* jǐge 几个; *(different)* bùtóng 不同

varnish 1 *n* qīngqī 清漆; *(for nails)* zhǐjiǎ yóu 指甲油 2 *v/t* tú 涂

vary *v/i* biànhuà 变化; *it varies* bù yīyàng 不一样

vase huāpíng 花瓶

vast jùdà 巨大; *knowledge* yuānbó 渊博

VCR (= *video cassette recorder*) lùxiàngjī 录像机

veal xiǎo niúròu 小牛肉

vegetable shūcài 蔬菜

vegetarian *n* sùshízhě 素食者

vehicle chēliàng 车辆

vending machine zìdòng shòuhuòjī 自动售货机

venereal disease xìngbìng 性病

ventilation tōngfēng 通风

venture *n (undertaking)* màoxiǎn 冒险; COM tóujī huódòng 投机活动

venue dìdiǎn 地点

verb dòngcí 动词

verdict LAW cáijué 裁决; *fig* dìnglùn 定论

♦ **verge on** héshí 核近

verify *(check out)* héshí 核实; *(confirm)* zhèngmíng 证明

vermin hàichóng 害虫

versatile *person* duōcái duōyì 多才多艺; *gadget* duō gōngnéng 多功能

verse *(poetry)* shī 诗; *(part of poem, song)* jié 节

versus SP, LAW duì 对

very *adv* hěn 很; *was it cold? – not ~* lěngbùlěng? – bù zěnme lěng 冷不冷? – 不怎么冷; *the ~ best* zuìhǎo 最好

vessel NAUT chuán 船

veteran 1 *n* tuìwǔ jūnrén 退伍军人 2 *adj (old)* lǎoshì 老式; *(experienced)* lǎoliàn 老练

veterinarian shòuyī 兽医

via jīngguò 经过; *(by means*

of) tōngguò 通过

viable *plan* qièshí kěxíng 切实可行

vibrate *v/i* zhèndòng 振动

vice èxí 恶习

vice president fù zǒngtǒng 副总统

vice versa fǎnzhī yìrán 反之亦然

vicinity dìdiǎn 地点

vicious *dog* xiōnghěn 凶狠; *attack, temper* èdú 恶毒

victim shòuhàizhě 受害者

victory shènglì 胜利

video *n & v/t* lùxiàng 录像

video camera shèxiàngjī 摄像机

video cassette lùxiàng dài 录像带

video recorder lùxiàngjī 录像机

Vietnam Yuènán 越南

Vietnamese 1 *adj* Yuènán 越南 **2** *n* Yuènánrén 越南人; *(language)* Yuènán yǔ 越南语

view 1 *n* fēngjǐng 风景; *(of situation)* guāndiǎn 观点; *in ~ of* jiànyú 鉴于 **2** *v/i* *(watch TV)* kàn 看

viewer *TV* guānzhòng 观众

viewpoint guāndiǎn 观点

vigor huólì 活力

village cūnzhuāng 村庄

villager cūnlǐrén 村里人

vindictive yǒu bàofù xīn 有报复心

vine pútao 葡萄

vintage 1 *n* *(of wine)* shēngchǎn niánfèn 生产年份 **2** *adj* *(classic)* jīngdiǎn 经典

violate *rules, sanctity* wéifǎn 违犯; *treaty* wéibèi 违背

violation: traffic ~ wéifǎn jiāotōng fǎguī 违反交通法规

violence bàolì 暴力

violent bàolì 暴力; *gale* měngliè 猛烈

VIP (= *very important person*) yàorén 要人

viral *infection* bìngdú 病毒

virtual shízhì 实质

virtually *(almost)* jīhū 几乎

virus MED, COMPUT bìngdú 病毒

visa qiānzhèng 签证

visibility néngjiàn dù 能见度

visible *object* yìjiàn 易见; *difference* míngxiǎn 明显

anger yì chájué 易察觉

vision shìlì 视力；REL *etc*
yōulíng 幽灵

visit *n* & *v/t* bàifǎng 拜访；
(*to place, country*) yóulǎn
游览

visitor kèrén 客人；(*to
museum etc*) cānguānzhě
参观者；(*tourist*) yóukè
游客

visual shìjué 视觉；*arts*
zhíguān 直观

visualize xiǎngxiàng 想象；
(*foresee*) shèxiǎng 设想

vital (*essential*) bìbù kěshǎo
必不可少

vitamin wéitāmìng 维他命

vitamin pill wéitāmìng
yàopiàn 维他命药片

vivid *color* xiānyàn 鲜艳；
imagination etc huóyuè
活跃

vocabulary cíhuì 词汇

voice 1 *n* shēngyīn 声音
2 *v/t opinions* biǎodá 表达

voicemail diànhuà dálùjī 电
话答录机

volcano huǒshān 火山

voltage diànyā 电压

volume (*of container*)
róngliàng 容量；(*of
work, liquid*) liàng liàng；(*of
business*) é 额；(*of book*) cè
册；(*of radio etc*) yīnliàng
音量

voluntary *adj helper* zhìyuàn
志愿；*work* yìwù 义务

volunteer 1 *n* yìgōng 义工
2 *v/i* zhìyuàn 志愿

vomit *v/i* ǒutù 呕吐

voracious *appetite* lángtūn
hǔyàn 狼吞虎咽

vote 1 *n* xuǎnpiào 选票
2 *v/i* POL tóupiào 投票；~
for / **against** tóu zànchéng
piào / fǎnduì piào 投赞成
票 / 反对票

voucher piàoquàn 票券

voyage hánghǎi 航海

vulgar cūsú 粗俗

vulnerable (*to attack*) bóruò
薄弱

W

wad n (of absorbent cotton etc) tuán 团; (of bills) dá 沓

wade báshè 跋涉

wag v/t tail, finger yáodòng 摇动

wage n gōngzī 工资

wagon RAIL chǎngpéng huòchē 敞篷货车

wail v/i (of person, baby) tòngkū 恸哭

waist yāobù 腰部

waistline yāowéi 腰围

wait 1 v/i děngdài 等待 **2** v/i děng 等

waiter nán fúwùyuán 男服务员

waiting list děnghòuzhě míngdān 等候者名单

waiting room děnghòushì 等候室

waitress nǚ fúwùyuán 女服务员

wake v/i: ~ (**up**) xǐnglái 醒来 **2** v/t huànxǐng 唤醒

wake-up call huànxǐng diànhuà 唤醒电话

walk 1 n bùxíng 步行; **go**

for a ~ qù sànbù 去散步 **2** v/i zǒu 走; (as opposed to taking the bus etc) zǒulù 走路; (hike) chángtú túbù lǚxíng 长途徒步旅行

wall qiáng 墙

wallet qiánbāo 钱包

wallpaper n bìzhǐ 壁纸

Wall Street Huá'ěrjiē 华尔街

wander v/i (roam) mànbù 漫步; (of attention) zǒushén 走神

want 1 n (need) xūyào 需要 **2** v/t yào 要; (need) xūyào 需要; ~ **to do** X xiǎngzuò X 想做 X; **he** ~**s a haircut** tā děi jiǎn tóufa 他得剪头发

want ad suǒqiú guǎnggào 索求广告

wanted (by police) bèi tōngjí 被通缉

war n zhànzhēng 战争

warden (of prison) jiānguǎnrén 监管人

warehouse cāngkù 仓库

warfare zhànzhēng 战争
warhead dàntóu 弹头
warm 1 adj nuǎnhuo 暖和; welcome rèqíng 热情 2 v/t shǐ nuǎnrè 使暖热
warmhearted rèxīncháng 热心肠
warmth wēnnuǎn 温暖; (of welcome) rèqíng 热情
warn jǐnggào 警告
warning n jǐnggào 警告
warped fig fǎncháng 反常
warrant n xǔkězhèng 许可证
warranty bǎodān 保单
warship jūnjiàn 军舰
wartime zhànshí 战时
wary: be ~ of jǐnfáng 谨防
wash 1 n xǐdí 洗涤 2 v/t & v/i xǐ 洗
♦ wash up xǐyīxǐ 洗一洗
washbasin liǎnpén 脸盆
washer (for faucet etc) diànquān 垫圈
washing machine xǐyījī 洗衣机
Washington Huáshèngdùn 华盛顿
washroom guànxǐshì 盥洗室
waste 1 n làngfèi 浪费;

(industrial) fèiwù 废物 2 adj fèiqì 废弃 3 v/t làngfèi 浪费
waste basket fèizhǐlǒu 废纸篓
watch 1 n (timepiece) shǒubiǎo 手表 2 v/t movie, TV kàn 看; (spy on) jiānshì 监视; (look after) zhàokàn 照看 3 v/i kàn 看
water 1 n shuǐ 水; ~s NAUT línghǎi 领海 2 v/t plant jiāo 浇 3 v/i (of eyes) liúlèi 流泪
water chestnut gāncǎo lìzi 甘草栗子
watermelon xīguā 西瓜
waterproof adj fángshuǐ 防水
wave¹ n (in sea) bōlàng 波浪
wave² 1 n (of hand) zhìyì 致意 2 v/i (with hand) huīshǒu 挥手 3 v/t flag huīwǔ 挥舞
way 1 n (method) fāngfǎ 方法; (of behaving etc) fāngshì 方式; (route) lùxiàn 路线; this ~ (like this) zhèyàng 这样; (in this direction) zhètiáolù 这条路; by the ~ shùnbiàn

407

wènyīxià 顺便问一下; **lead the ~** yǐnlù 引路; **lose one's ~** mílù 迷路; **be in the ~** (obstruct) dǎnglù 挡路; **no ~!** juéduì bù! 绝对不! **2** adv F (much) yuǎnyuǎn 远远

way in rùkǒu 入口

way of life shēnghuó fāngshì 生活方式

way out n chūkǒu 出口; fig (from situation) chūlù 出路

we wǒmen 我们

weak coffee dàn dàn 淡; government, currency bóruò 薄弱; (physically) xūruò 虚弱; (morally) ruǎnruò 软弱

weaken 1 v/t xuēruò 削弱 **2** v/i biànruò 变弱

wealth cáifù 财富

wealthy fùyǒu 富有

weapon wǔqì 武器

wear 1 n: **~ (and tear)** sǔnhào 损耗 **2** v/t (have on) chuān 穿

♦ **wear out 1** v/t shǐ pífá 使疲乏; shoes yònghuài 用坏 **2** v/i (of shoes, carpet) yòngjiù 用旧

weary kùnfá 困乏

weather n tiānqì 天气

weather forecast tiānqì yùbào 天气预报

web (COMPUT, of spider) wǎng 网

web site wǎngzhǐ 网址

wedding hūnlǐ 婚礼

wedding ring jiéhūn jièzhǐ 结婚戒指

Wednesday xīngqīsān 星期三

weed n zácǎo 杂草

week xīngqī 星期; **a ~ tomorrow** xiàyīzhōude míngtiān 下一周的明天

weekday xīngqī yī dào wǔ 星期一到五

weekend zhōumò 周末; **on the ~** zhōumò 周末

weekly adj & adv měizhōu yícì 每周一次

weep kūqì 哭泣

weigh 1 v/t chēng … de zhòngliàng 称 … 的重量 **2** v/i cèchū zhòngliàng 测出重量

weight zhòngliàng 重量

weird guàiyì 怪异

welcome 1 adj shòu huānyíng 受欢迎; **you're ~!** biékèqì! 别客气! **2** n *(for guests etc)* huānyíng 欢迎 **3** *v/t guests* yíngjiē 迎接; *decision etc* duì ... gǎndào yúkuài 对 ... 感到愉快

welfare jiànkāng 健康; *(financial assistance)* fúlì jiùjì 福利救济

well¹ *n* jǐng 井

well² **1** *adv* hǎo 好; *as ~ (too)* yě 也; *as ~ as (in addition to)* hái 还; *very ~ (acknowledging)* shì 是; *(reluctance)* hǎoba 好吧; *~, ~ ! (surprise)* yōu, yōu! 呦, 呦! ; *~ ... (uncertainty, thinking)* āi ... 哎 ... **2** *adj*: *be ~* jiànkāng 健康

well-behaved xíngwéi guījù 行为规矩

well-dressed yīzhuó zhěngjié 衣着整洁

well-known zhòngsuǒ zhōuzhī 众所周知

west **1** *n* xīmiàn 西面; *the West* Xīfāng Guójiā 西方国家 **2** *adj* xī 西 **3** *adv* xiàngxī 向西

West Coast *(of USA)* Xī Hǎi'àn 西海岸

western **1** *adj* zài xībù 在西部; *Western* Xīfāng guójiā 西方国家 **2** *n (movie)* xībùpiàn 西部片

Westerner Xīfāngrén 西方人

wet *adj* shī 湿; *(rainy)* duōyǔ 多雨

what **1** *pron* shénme 什么; *~ is it? (what do you want?)* zěnmele? 怎么了？; *~ about ...?* ... zěnmeyàng? ... 怎么样？ **2** *adj* shénme 什么; *~ color?* shénme yánsè? 什么颜色？

whatever **1** *pron* búlùn shénme 不论什么; *(regardless of)* bùguǎn shénme 不管什么 **2** *adj* rènhé 任何

wheat xiǎomài 小麦

wheel **1** *n* lúnzi 轮子 **2** *v/t bicycle* tuī 推

wheelchair lúnyǐ 轮椅

when **1** *adv* shénme shíhou 什么时候 **2** *conj* dāng ... de shíhou 当 ... 的时候; *~ I was a child* dāng wǒ shì ge háizi de shíhou 当我是个孩子的时候

whenever wúlùn shénme

shíhòu 无论什么时候

where 1 *adv* nǎr 哪儿; **~ should I put this?** wǒ bǎ zhège fàng nǎr? 我把这个放哪儿? **2** *conj*: **this is ~ I used to live** zhè shì wǒ céngjīng zhùguò de dìfang 这是我曾经住过的地方

wherever 1 *conj* wúlùn nǎlǐ 无论哪里 **2** *adv* dàodǐ zài nǎlǐ 到底在哪里

whether shìfǒu 是否

which 1 *adj* nǎyīge 哪一个 **2** *pron* (interrogative) nǎge 哪个; (relative): **the book ~ I bought** wǒ mǎide nèiběn shū 我买的那本书

whichever 1 *adj* rènhé 任何 **2** *pron* wúlùn nǎge 无论哪个

while *conj*: **~ … zài … shíqī** 在 … 时期

whip 1 *n* biānzi 鞭子 **2** *v/t* (beat) biāndǎ 鞭打; cream jiǎodǎ 搅打

whirlpool xuánwō 旋涡; (for relaxation) ànmó yùgāng 按摩浴缸

whiskey wēishìjìjiǔ 威士忌酒

whisper 1 *n* ěryǔ 耳语 **2** *v/i* qièqièsīyǔ 窃窃私语 **3** *v/t* dīshēng shuō 低声说

whistle 1 *n* (sound) kǒushàoshēng 口哨声; (device) shàozi 哨子 **2** *v/i* fā xūxūshēng 发嘘嘘声

white 1 *n* báisè 白色; (person) báirén 白人 **2** *adj* cāngbái 苍白; person báirén 白人

White House Bái Gōng 白宫

who ◊ (interrogative) shéi 谁; **~'s that?** nà shì shéi? 那是谁? ◊ (relative): **the man taught me** jiāoguò wǒ de nèige rén 教过我的那个人

whoever wúlùn shì shéi 无论是谁

whole 1 *adj* zhěngge 整个 **2** *n* zhěngtǐ 整体

wholesale 1 *adj* pīfā 批发 **2** *adv* yǐ pīfājià 以批发价

wholesome cùjìn jiànkāng 促进健康

whose *pron & adj* shéide 谁的; **~ is this?** zhè shì shéide? 这是谁的?

why wèishénme 为什么

wicked xié'è 邪恶

wicket (in station, bank etc) guìtái 柜台

wide adj kuānkuò 宽阔; experience fēngfù 丰富; range guǎngfàn 广泛

widely used, known guǎngfàn 广泛

wide-open dàkāi 大开

widespread biànbù 遍布

widow guǎfù 寡妇

widower guānfū 鳏夫

width kuāndù 宽度

wife qīzi 妻子

wild adj animal, flowers yě shēng 野生; applause rèliè 热烈

wildlife yěshēng niǎoshòu 野生鸟兽

will¹ n LAW yízhǔ 遗嘱

will² n (willpower) yìzhì 意志

will³ (future) huì 会 ◊: the car won't start chē qǐdòng bù liǎo 车启动不了 ◊:~ you tell her that ...? nǐ kě yǐ gàosù tā ... ma? 你可以告诉她 ... 吗?

willing lèyú 乐于

willingly gānxīn qíngyuàn 甘心情愿

win 1 n shènglì 胜利

2 v/t huòshèng 获胜 3 v/i yíngdé 赢得

wind¹ n fēng 风

wind² 1 v/i (of path etc) wānyán 蜿蜒 2 v/t cloth etc chánráo 缠绕

window chuānghu 窗户; COMPUT shìchuāng 视窗

windowsill chuāngtái 窗台

windshield dǎngfēng bōlí 挡风玻璃

wine pútáojiǔ 葡萄酒

wing n chìbǎng 翅膀; SP biāncè 边侧

wink 1 n zhǎyǎn 眨眼 2 v/i (of person) shǐ yǎnsè 使眼色

winner huòshèngzhě 获胜者

winnings yíngdéde qián 赢得的钱

winter n dōngtiān 冬天

winter sports dōngjì yùndòng 冬季运动

wipe v/t cā 擦; tape mǒdiào 抹掉

wire jīnshǔsī 金属丝; ELEC diànxiàn 电线

wiring ELEC xiànlù 线路

wisdom zhìhuì 智慧

wise yīngmíng 英明

wish 1 n yuànwàng 愿望;
best ~es zhùhǎo 祝好
2 v/t: **I ~ that ...** yàoshì ...
jiù hǎo le yào shì ... 就好了
3 v/i: **~ for** qídǎo 祈祷

wit (humor) jīzhì yōumò 机
智幽默

with ◊ (accompanied by,
proximity) hé ... yìqǐ 和
... 一起; **she came ~ her
sister** tā hé tāde mèimei
yìqǐ láide 她和她的妹妹
一起来的; **a meeting ~
the President** yǔ zǒngtǒng
huìmiàn 与总统会面;
~ no money méiyǒu qián
没有钱 ◊ (agency) yòng
用; **write ~ a brush** yòng
máobǐ xiězì 用毛笔写
字 ◊ (cause) yóuyú 由于;
shivering ~ fear yóuyú
kǒngjù ér chàndǒu 由于恐
惧而颤抖 ◊ (possession)
yǒu yǒu; **the house ~ the
red door** yǒu hóng mén de
nèige fángzi 有红门的那
个房子

withdraw v/t complaint
chèxiāo 撤消; money tíqǔ
提取; troops chèhuí 撤回

withdrawn adj person gūpì 孤僻

wither v/i diāoxiè 凋谢

within prep (distance) bù
chāoguò 不超过; (inside)
zài ... lǐmiàn 在 ... 里面;
(in time) zài ... zhīnèi 在
... 之内

without méiyǒu 没有; **~
looking** méi kàn 没看

withstand jīndezhù 禁得住

witness n (at trial) zhèngrén
证人; (of accident, crime)
mùjīzhě 目击者

witty adj jīzhì 机智

wok guō 锅

woman nǚrén 女人

women's lib fùnǚ jiěfàng 妇
女解放

wonder 1 n (amazement)
jīngqí 惊奇 **2** v/i gǎndào
jīngyà 感到惊讶

wonderful jíhǎo 极好

wood mù 木; (forest) shùlín
树林

wooden mùzhì 木制

wool yángmáo 羊毛

woolen adj yángmáozhì 羊
毛制

word n cí 词; (promise)
nuòyán 诺言

wording cuòcí 措辞

word processing wénzì chǔlǐ
文字处理

work 1 n gōngzuò 工作
2 v/i gōngzuò 工作; *(of machine)* yùnzhuǎn 运转;
(succeed) zòuxiào 奏效

◆ **work out 1** v/t *solution* zhǎochū 找出 **2** v/i *(at gym)* dàliàng yùndòng 大量运动; *(of relationship etc)* qǔdé chénggōng 取得成功

workaholic n F gōngzuò-kuáng 工作狂

worker gōngrén 工人

work day gōngzuòrì 工作日; *(not a holiday)* fēi xiūxiri 非休息日

workmanship jìyì 技艺

work of art jīngzhide wùpǐn 精致的物品

work permit gōngzuò xǔkě 工作许可

world shìjiè 世界

worldwide adj biànjí shìjiè 遍及世界

worn-out pòjiù 破旧; *person* jīnpílìjìn 筋疲力尽

worried dānyōu 担忧

worry 1 n dānyōu 担忧
2 v/t dānxīn 担心; *(upset)*

shǐrén yōuchóu 使人忧愁
3 v/i dānyōu 担忧

worse 1 adj gènghuài 更坏
2 adv gèng bùhǎo 更不好

worsen v/i biànde gènghuài 变得更坏

worst 1 adj zuìhuài 最坏
2 adv zuìzāo 最糟

worth adj: **be ~ ...** FIN zhí ... 值...; **be ~ seeing** zhídé kàn 值得看

worthless wú jiàzhí 无价值; *person* méiyòng 没用

worthwhile *cause* zhídé zuò 值得做

would: ~ you like to ...? nǐ xiǎng ... ma? 你想...吗？;
~ you tell her that ...? qǐng nǐ gàosù tā ... hǎoma? 请你告诉她...好吗？

wound n shāng 伤

wrap v/t *gift* bāo 包; *(wind)* chánrào 缠绕

wrapping paper bāozhuāng-zhǐ 包装纸

wreck 1 n cánhái 残骸 **2** v/t huǐhuài 毁坏; *plans* huǐmiè 毁灭

wreckage cánhái 残骸

wrecker tuōchē 拖车

wrench n *(tool)* bānzi 扳子

wriggle v/i niǔdòng 扭动

wrinkle n zhòuwén 皱纹

wrist shǒuwàn 手腕

wristwatch shǒubiǎo 手表

write 1 v/t xiě 写; (check kāi 开 **2** v/i xiě 写; (of author) xiězuò 写作; (send a letter) xiěxìn 写信

writer zuòzhě 作者

writing (as career) xiězuò 写作; (hand-writing) zìjì 字迹; (words) wénzì 文字; (script) shūxiě tǐxì 书写体系

writing paper xìnzhǐ 信纸

wrong 1 adj cuòwù 错误; **be ~** (of person) cuòle 错了; (morally) bú duì 不对; **what's ~?** zěnme le? 怎么了？; **there's something ~ with the car** chē yǒu diǎn máobìng 车有点毛病 **2** adv cuòwù 错误; **go ~** (of person) fàn cuòwù 犯错误; (of plan etc) chūxiàn wèntí 出现问题 **3** n bù gōngzhèng de shì 不公正的事

wrong number bōcuòle hàomǎ 拨错了号码

XY

X-ray n X guāng zhàopiān X 光照片

yacht yóutǐng 游艇

Yangtze River Chángjiāng 长江

Yank F Měiguó Lǎo 美国佬

yard¹ (of institution) fāngchǎng 放风场; (behind house) yuànzi 院子; (for storage) duīchǎng 堆场

yard² (measurement) mǎ 码

yawn 1 n hēqian 呵欠 **2** v/i dǎ hēqian 打呵欠

year nián 年

yearly adj & adv měinián 每年

yell 1 n jiàohǎn 叫喊 **2** v/i rāngrang 嚷嚷

yellow 1 n huángsè 黄色 **2** adj huáng 黄

yellow pages huángyè 黄页

yes shìde 是的 ◊ (repetition of verb etc): **are you cold?** ~ nǐ lěng bu lěng?

– lěng 你冷不冷？– 冷
◊ (agreeing) duì 对；*he
should go* – ~ tā yīnggāi
qù – duì 他应该去 – 对
◊ (accepting suggestion)
xíng 行

yesterday zuótiān 昨天；
the day before ~ qiántián
前天

yet *adv: as* ~ dàocǐ wéizhǐ
到此为止；*is he here* ~?
– *not* – tā láile ma? – hái
méine 他来了吗？– 还
没呢

yield 1 *v/t harvest* chūchǎn 出
产；*interest* shēngxī 生息
2 *v/t* (to enemy) tóuxiáng 投
降；(of traffic) rànglù 让路

yogurt suānnǎi 酸奶

you (singular) nǐ 你；(plural)
nǐmen 你们；(polite) nín

您；(polite plural, rare)
nínmen 您们

young *person* niánqīng 年
青

your, yours (singular) nǐde
你的；(plural) nǐmende
你们的；(polite singular)
nínde 您的；(polite plural)
nínmende 您们的

yourself nǐ zìjǐ 你自己

yourselves nǐmen zìjǐ 你
们自己

youth qīngchūn niándài 青
春年代；(young man) xiǎo
huǒzi 小伙子；(young
people) qīngshàonián 青
少年

youth hostel qīngnián zhā
odàisuǒ 青年招待所

yuan (Chinese money)
yuán 元

Z

zap *v/t* COMPUT (delete)
xiāochú 消除

Zen Buddhism Chánzōng
Fójiào 禅宗佛教

zero líng 零

zip code yóuzhèng biānmǎ
邮政编码

zipper lāliàn 拉链

zone qū 区

zoo dòngwù yuán 动物园

Numbers

0	○ líng		20	二 十 èrshì
1	一 yī		30	三 十 sānshí
2	二 èr *or* liǎng*		40	四 十 sìshí *etc*
3	三 sān			
4	四 sì		21	二 十 一 èrshíyī
5	五 wǔ		35	三 十 五 sānshíwǔ
6	六 liù		99	九 十 九 jiǔshíjiǔ
7	七 qī			
8	八 bā		100	百 bǎi
9	九 jiǔ		105	一 百 零 五 yìbǎi líng wǔ
10	十 shí			
11	十 一 shíyī		300	三 百 sānbǎi
12	十 二 shí'èr		350	三 百 五 十 sānbǎi wǔshí
13	十 三 shísān *etc*		356	三 百 五 十 六 sānbǎi wǔshíliù

1,000	千 qiān
1,005	一 千 零 五 yìqiān líng wǔ
1,050	一 千 零 五 十 yìqiān líng wǔshí
5,300	五 千 三 百 wǔqiān sānbǎi
10,000	万 wàn
65,300	六 万 五 千 三 百 liùwàn wǔqiān sānbǎi
100,000	十 万 shíwàn
1,000,000	百 万 bǎiwàn
10,000,000	千 万 qiānwàn
100,000,000	万 万 wànwàn
100,000,000	亿 yì

The following more complex characters are also used on bills, checks etc.

0	零 líng		7	柒 qī
1	壹 yī		8	捌 bā
2	貳 èr		9	玖 jiǔ
3	叁 sān		10	拾 shí
4	肆 sì		100	佰 bǎi
5	伍 wǔ		1,000	仟 qiān
6	陆 liù			

Ordinal numbers

Ordinal numbers are formed by putting **dì** in front of the cardinal numbers:

1	一 yī		3	三 sān
1st	第一 dìyī		3rd	第三 dìsān
				etc
2	二 èr			
2nd	第二 dì'èr			

* **liǎng** is used when the number two is used in combination with a measure word.